Romance of the Rails

RANDAL O'TOOLE

Romance of the Rails

Why the Passenger Trains We Love Are Not the Transportation We Need

CATO INSTITUTE
WASHINGTON, D.C.

ISBN: 978-1-944424-94-7
eISBN: 978-1-944424-95-4

Jacket design: Jon Meyers.
Printed in Canada.

Library of Congress Cataloging-in-Publication Data available.

This book is for
Vickie
who I met on the
San Francisco Zephyr
December 28, 1978
proving there is still
Romance on the Rails

CONTENTS

INTRODUCTION

In June 1938, Baldwin Locomotive Works of Eddystone, Pennsylvania, delivered three steam locomotives, numbered 700, 701, and 702, to the Spokane, Portland & Seattle (SP&S) Railway. Built to pull passenger trains between Portland and Spokane, these grand machines were the culmination of more than a century of improvements to steam technology, as Baldwin had constructed more than 62,000 locomotives since founder Matthias Baldwin built his first in 1831.

The 68-foot-long boilers of the 700-class series rested on one-piece, cast-steel frames that ingeniously included hollow spaces to hold compressed air for a train's air brakes. Fitted with roller bearings on every wheel to minimize resistance, superheaters in the boiler so that every drop of water was converted to steam before entering the cylinders, and some of the largest fireboxes ever used for oil-burning locomotives, the 700-class engines were considered "exceptional" by rail historian Robert Le Massena.[1]

I was fortunate enough to help restore the SP&S 700 to fully operational status in 1989 and 1990. The railroad had donated the locomotive to the city of Portland in 1958, and it sat in a city park for more than two decades before it was removed for restoration in the early 1980s. The all-volunteer crew doing the work included welders, boiler makers, machinists, woodworkers, and other skilled craftsmen. I possessed none of those skills, so I did grunt work and wrote and edited the group's newsletter.

More than 110 feet long including the tender, standing 17 feet tall, and weighing 440 tons when loaded with fuel and water, the locomotive was an awesome sight at any time, but especially when steamed up and in motion. Even standing still, the breathing of the air compressors, the whir of the steam turbine powering the locomotive lights, and various other sounds made it seem alive. At mainline speeds, the chuff of the cylinders combined with the intermittent, multitoned whistle made it abundantly clear this was no Disneyland toy. As of this writing, it is the third-most-powerful operating steam locomotive in the world.

With four pilot wheels to help the locomotive navigate curves at high speeds, eight 77-inch-tall driving wheels, and four trailing wheels to hold the weight of a firebox as big as a moderate-sized bedroom, the locomotive was known as a 4-8-4. This made it a Northern, named after one of the SP&S's parent railways, the Northern Pacific, the first railroad to order a locomotive with this wheel arrangement in 1926. Locomotive refinements between 1926 and 1938 included roller bearings, higher-pressure boilers, and more efficient methods of injecting water into the boiler.

"The year 1937 represents the high-water mark of steam locomotive development and construction," wrote Le Masenna three decades later.[2] Locomotives were not only bigger, they were twice as powerful per ton as locomotives from just two decades earlier. Advances such as roller bearings and large fireboxes increased locomotive efficiencies in ways not revealed by ordinary measurements of power. The 700-class fireboxes, for example, were large because the locomotives were based on a Northern Pacific design that burned low-grade coal. The SP&S modified them to burn oil, which was far more efficient. Thanks to its huge firebox, the 700 could pull a 12-car train at 100 miles per hour, turning the wheels just 440 revolutions per minute, and the locomotive crew didn't have to worry about running out of steam as long as there was water in the tank because the boiler could turn five gallons of water into steam every second.

The first diesel locomotives—then called "oil electrics" to avoid the stigma of a German name so soon after World War I—went into use in 1924, but Baldwin was convinced steam would remain preeminent for decades. In 1930, Samuel Vauclain, the company's chairman and a notable locomotive designer in his own right, predicted steam would remain the dominant form of railroad power for at least another 50 years. Despite the appearance of lightweight diesel-powered passenger trains in 1934, another Baldwin executive argued in 1937 that diesel locomotives could never handle the job of pulling heavy freight, and "sometime in the future, when all this is reviewed, it will be found that our railroads are no more dieselized than they are electrified."[3]

In March 1939, however, just nine months after Baldwin delivered the 700s, General Motors (GM) produced the first-class FT diesel locomotive and sent it on an 83,764-mile tour of 20 major railroads, pulling trains in 35 states. The FT—which stood for 1,400 horsepower (even though it was really just 1,350) but was also an abbreviation for freight—was actually four different units, each powered by a 16-cylinder engine, which powered electric motors for each wheel. Skeptical railroaders knew steam locomotives with two to four cylinders were complicated enough to maintain, and they shuddered at the thought of maintaining a locomotive with 64 cylinders.

Yet on the tour, the 5,400-horsepower FT easily outperformed the best steam locomotives in existence. The SP&S Railway, for example, had the engine pull a 6,000-ton freight train up a continuous grade for nearly 100 miles. The FT was able to sustain an average speed of 26 miles per hour, while the SP&S's most powerful steam locomotive, a 4-6-6-4 rated to produce about 50 percent more power than one of the 700s, could manage only 10 miles per hour. SP&S's parent company, Northern Pacific, required three steam locomotives to pull its premiere *North Coast Limited* passenger train over the Rocky Mountains if the train had more than 12 cars. Without assistance, the FT pulled a 17-car train over the passes and easily stayed on schedule.[4]

As a result of this demonstration tour, that first FT became known as "the diesel that did it" because it persuaded most in the railroad industry that diesel-electric locomotives were superior to steam. It "must be ranked as perhaps the most influential piece of motive power since Stephenson's Rocket," said *Trains* magazine editor David P. Morgan, "for in one stroke it broke steam's historic monopoly of freight traffic and thereby forecast total dieselization, here and abroad."[5]

Diesels didn't have to stop for water every hundred miles or so, and they could be in service 98 percent of the time, while steam locomotives were down for maintenance as much as half the time. A diesel locomotive cost more than a similarly powered steam locomotive, but because of their service records, two diesels could work as many hours per week as three or four steamers, and with lower fuel and maintenance costs. Running two or more steam locomotives on a single train required separate crews for each locomotive, while a half dozen or more diesels could be operated together by a single crew. Any one of these advantages made diesels a threat to steam; all of them together were fatal to the future of steam locomotion.

General Motors ended up selling more than 7,600 FTs and successor F-unit locomotives to the railroads, as well as thousands of other engine styles. By the end of 1956, most major American railroads had completely converted their steam-powered locomotives to diesels, and they would have done so several years earlier had not World War II intervened. Baldwin attempted to convert to diesel production, but it eventually went out of business after making its last locomotive, a diesel switch engine, in 1956. Its failure to fully adapt to the needs of the new diesel technology was one reason why it went out of business. Single-piece, cast-steel frames worked for steam, for example, but they tended to crack due to the vibrations of diesels with their high number of revolutions per minute.[6]

TECHNOLOGY REPLACEMENT

Historians consider the rapid conversion of steam to diesel to be a classic example of *technology replacement*. Transportation history is full of such replacements, from sailing ships to steamships, canals to railroads, and horsecars to electric streetcars. This book is about the replacement of urban railcars and intercity passenger trains with other forms of transportation and the curious efforts by American governments to prevent or reverse that replacement. Since 1970, federal, state, and local governments have spent hundreds of billions of dollars building new passenger rail lines and restoring old ones despite knowing not a single penny of that cost would ever be recovered out of passenger fares.

I write this book as a love letter to a dying friend, as I've been thrilled by passenger trains since I was five years old. I rode my first train from Grand Forks, North Dakota, to Portland, Oregon, in 1958. That summer, we drove in my parent's first new car from Oregon to Ohio, where my father's family lived, and then to North Dakota, where my mother's family lived. With no vacation time left, my father drove home alone, leaving my mother and me to enjoy a few weeks in Grand Forks before taking the train back to Oregon.

I don't remember much of the train ride, but I do remember asking my mother before we left what the fastest train in the world was. "The *Western Star!*" she proudly but incorrectly answered. Great Northern Railway's premiere train, the *Empire Builder*, bypassed Grand Forks, and the secondary *Western Star* was the only direct connection between Grand Forks and the West Coast, so it was natural for us to take it. Since then, the Great Northern has always been my favorite. Considering my later economic and political beliefs, I couldn't have picked a better railroad to love, for the Great Northern was the first transcontinental to be built without government subsidies.

For Christmas that year, my parents gave me my first model train, a silver passenger train lettered for the Burlington, the Great Northern's connecting railroad that really did operate the world's fastest train. The following Christmas was even more special, as my father had secretly painted all of those silver cars with Great Northern's orange-and-green color scheme. I still treasure those cars.

Two years after that first train ride, my mother, infant brother, and I returned to North Dakota on Northern Pacific's *North Coast Limited*. The *Western Star* no longer went to Grand Forks, so my grandfather had to drive 80 miles to Fargo to pick us up, regardless of what train we took. Instead of a Great Northern train, my mother was probably attracted to the *North Coast Limited* by Northern Pacific's Slumbercoach, which offered sleeping car rooms at coach fares. I remember the narrow beds in the rooms, walking with another little boy to the train's observation car, and most of all riding in the dome cars, which offered 360-degree views of the countryside.

When I was 16, I volunteered to work for the Oregon Electric Railway Historical Society, helping society founder Paul Class restore and operate the group's collection of streetcars. Soon thereafter, my first paying job was helping Paul cosmetically restore an old Portland streetcar to be the centerpiece in a new restaurant, the first in a chain called the Old Spaghetti Factory.

Since then, I've traveled hundreds of thousands of miles by train in 10 countries on four continents. On one cross-country trip, I met Vickie, the woman I eventually married, proving there is still romance on the rails.

While we were helping to restore the SP&S 700, I purchased and briefly owned five railroad passenger cars that we hoped to restore to operate with the locomotive. I've performed living-history portrayals of James J. Hill, the builder of the Great Northern and SP&S railways, in educational programs aimed at helping people understand the importance of railways to American life today and in the past. At night, I dream of riding in a dome car, and my nightmares, such as they are, are of enjoying train rides so much that I fail to get off at my scheduled stops.

Though few people can say they love passenger trains more than I do, I am but one of millions of Americans who have a nostalgic view of intercity passenger trains, streetcars, and other forms of rail passenger transportation. In an era of congested highways, the streetcars that once could be found in every American city of more than 15,000 people seem like a carefree way to travel. Compared with today's sardine-can-like airliners, the idea of a luxury passenger train with room to wander, gourmet meals in the dining car, and beautiful scenery in full view out the windows, has a lot of appeal. The sleek, streamlined passenger trains of the 1930s through the 1950s made an especially indelible impression on most Americans, and I still think riding in a dome car is the most elegant form of travel imaginable.

Early in my career, I joined the National Association of Railroad Passengers (NARP) and supported more funding for Amtrak. Later, I realized Amtrak was poorly managed and supported Amtrak reform. More recently, along with NARP founder Anthony Haswell—who is sometimes called the Father of Amtrak—I became completely disillusioned with the idea of government-run trains and have argued for abolishing the heavily subsidized federal passenger rail corporation.

My attitudes toward urban transit have also undergone a transition. In 1972, as an undergraduate student, I wrote a paper for the Oregon Student Public Interest Research Group (OSPIRG) advocating low-cost transit improvements in Portland aimed at attracting people out of their auto-mobiles and reducing air pollution. When the director of OSPIRG later became general manager of TriMet, Portland's transit agency, he imple-mented some of those improvements, and transit ridership surged. To be honest, I didn't propose rail transit reform in 1972 simply because I didn't think there was much chance of that happening. However, I later became more skeptical of rail transit when Portland built an expensive light-rail line, followed by more lines that were even more expensive.

That skepticism has led some people to call me "anti-transit" and "anti-passenger train." But I'm not. If someone could design a rail sys-tem that attracted riders and efficiently moved them from place to place, I'd be the first to endorse it. As this book will show, however, this is no more likely to happen than the freight railroads converting back to steam power. The next technology replacement will not be people trading in their cars for high-speed trains and light rail. Rather, it will be people trading in their human-driven cars for increasingly autonomous cars that drive themselves.

The short answer to the question of why passenger trains and streetcars have been replaced by planes, cars, and buses is that rails are more expen-sive and less flexible than the alternatives. To understand why, the first 10 chapters of this book will delve deep into the history of rail to show how passenger rail transportation once worked, who it worked for, and what has changed so that it no longer works today. This history demon-strates why statements such as, "High-speed trains have faster downtown-to-downtown times than flying" or "Light rail provides an alternative to congested roads going to work" are not relevant. Chapter 11 discusses the question of why passenger rail seems to work in Europe and Asia but not in North America.

Chapters 12 through 17 will each focus on a different kind of passen-ger rail, from streetcars to high-speed rail. Finally, Chapter 18 will demon-strate why we love trains, but also why we can't expect them to do for us what they did in the 19th century.

Passenger rail was once an important part of our history, but today it represents a drag on our economy. I still love passenger trains, but I don't think other people should have to subsidize my hobby.

1. THE TRANSCONTINENTAL RAILROADS

I see over my own continent the Pacific Railroad, surmounting every barrier;
I see continual trains of cars winding along the Platte, carrying freight and passengers;
I hear the locomotives rushing and roaring, and the shrill steam-whistle,
I hear the echoes reverberate through the grandest scenery in the world.

—Walt Whitman

For Walt Whitman, a trip on the first transcontinental railroad was as much spiritual as physical. But for the builders, the real journey was financial. The same would be true for rail lines built or proposed in the 21st century.

In 2009, newly inaugurated President Barack Obama let members of the U.S. Senate know he wanted Congress to begin funding the construction of a high-speed rail network. Congress responded by dedicating $8 billion of "stimulus funds" in the American Recovery and Reinvestment Act to high-speed rail. In promoting high-speed trains, Obama frequently referred to the nation's first transcontinental railroad, which was completed in 1869.

"In the midst of civil war, we laid railroad tracks from one coast to another that spurred commerce and industry," Obama stated incorrectly (the tracks were nearly all laid after the Civil War) in his 2009 State of the Union address. "America is the nation that built the transcontinental railroad," he added in his 2011 address. "The jobs created by [the railroad] didn't just come from laying down tracks. . . . They came from businesses that opened near a town's new train station." He clearly expected the same benefits from high-speed rail.

In a television interview shortly after the 2011 State of the Union address, Obama mistakenly stated, "Abraham Lincoln helped to build the intercontinental railroad," a gaffe he repeated in a speech a few months later.[1] These may have been just slips of the tongue, but if Obama knew the real history of the first transcontinental railroad, he might have been more hesitant to cite it as a precedent for a government-built high-speed rail program. Far from being an economic boon, the heavy government subsidies to the first transcontinental railroad resulted in the biggest political corruption scandal of the 19th century.

Before the Railroads

The transcontinental railways were not the first American transportation projects to receive government subsidies. In 1816, it cost less to ship goods 3,000 miles from Europe to America than it did to haul them another 35 miles inland from the Atlantic coast.[2] As a result, about 85 percent of Americans lived within a few miles of the eastern coastline. Yet after the Louisiana Purchase in 1803, the nation claimed land extending as far west as 2,000 miles. New forms of transportation would be needed if that land was ever to be settled, and many people encouraged government support for that transportation. While a few of those projects were successful, most of them illustrate government's inability to distinguish economic winners from losers.

The first effort to overcome the nation's overland transportation problems was to build toll roads, which were called turnpikes. More than 1,500 turnpike companies, a quarter of all new start-ups, were chartered between 1792 and 1845.[3] The roads they built reduced transportation costs and tended to be well maintained, paid for out of toll revenues.

In contrast, the National Road, which the federal government began building in 1811, was poorly maintained because Congress provided money for repairs only intermittently, and what little maintenance work was done was poorly supervised. Economist Daniel Klein describes the road as "America's first great and glorious boondoggle" because it cost far more to build, per mile, than private roads and was "often in poor condition." In places where the National Road competed directly with the private Pittsburgh Turnpike, travelers preferred the latter because it offered a smoother ride.[4]

Even with the turnpikes, shipping by land remained far more expensive than water-based transportation. Rivers helped, but until the perfection of steamboats, they mainly provided one-way transportation, and even steamboats could operate only in deep rivers. One solution to this conundrum was to build canals, extending the benefits of water-based shipping inland. But canals cost far more to build than roads, and little private capital was available for such projects in early 19th-century America. By 1816, private investors had built a few canals, but these tended to be short—the longest was about 27 miles—and combined added up to only about 100 miles in length.

In 1817, the New York legislature agreed to fund construction of the 364-mile-long Erie Canal, connecting Buffalo and the Great Lakes with Albany and the Hudson River. The first 75 miles of the canal opened just two years later, and it was completed in 1825. Revenues easily covered construction and operating costs and were sufficient to stimulate expansion of the canal's capacity.[5] Moreover, by giving New York City the best access to lands west of the Appalachians, the canal insured that city's status as America's number one shipping, financial, and urban center.

The Erie Canal's success led to a huge boom in government-subsidized canal construction, much of which was promoted by Philadelphia, Baltimore, Norfolk, and other eastern cities eager to capture some of the growth enjoyed by New York. Few of these projects were successful, however, due to both geographic differences and poor timing.

Pennsylvania attempted to emulate New York with a canal from Philadelphia to Pittsburgh, but the mountains of Pennsylvania were much higher and more rugged than those of upstate New York. While the Erie Canal reached as high as 650 feet above sea level, the route selected for the Pennsylvania canal reached to over 2,200 feet. At its highest point, a portage railroad was built instead of a canal, which meant freight had to be transferred from boat to rail, then back to boat again, greatly increasing costs. Despite the marginal success of this canal, Pennsylvania continued to subsidize additional canals as late as 1842, by which time railroads were providing serious competition to canals. Most if not all of these later canals lost money, putting the state deeply in debt.[6]

Although the federal government did not assist in the construction of the Erie Canal, after the success of that venture, Congress was persuaded to help build several other canals. It granted four million acres of land to canal builders in five states and purchased $3 million ($75 million in today's money) worth of stock in canal companies, including the Chesapeake and Ohio Canal. The states themselves borrowed more than $60 million (some $1.5 billion today) to fund canal construction. The failure of numerous canals, however, left Indiana, Ohio, and Pennsylvania in virtual bankruptcy and strained the credit of other states as well.[7]

By 1850, the United States had more than twice as many miles of railroads as canals, and it should have been clear to anyone that railroads were the superior technology due to their higher speeds, lower maintenance costs, and ability to operate year round, while reaching many places canals could not. Yet political pressures resulting from the creation of a subsidized canal industry led states to continue subsidizing new canals. The state of New York, for example, completed the Genesee Canal in 1856. Although only about a third of the length of the Erie Canal, the Genesee cost far more to build, and total revenues before it was closed some two decades later were no more than one-seventh of its construction costs.[8]

Steamboats were another way of extending water-based transportation inland. The first commercial steamboats in America began operating in 1815 and were the dominant form of inland travel from about 1825 to 1850. Aside from a few million dollars spent on clearing waterways to make them navigable, neither the federal government nor the states spent much money subsidizing the steamboat industry. However, New York and Louisiana granted monopolies to steamboat operators on the unlikely premise that no one would invest in the new technologies needed to build and operate steamboats without monopoly power. These monopolies increased costs to shippers and travelers, and historian George Taylor notes that an 1824 Supreme Court decision against the monopolies led to "a tremendous expansion of steam navigation on eastern rivers, harbors, and bays."[9]

By 1830, the same type of boilers that powered steamboats, combined with improved metallurgies that made iron rails possible, enabled the construction of the first few miles of railroads in the United States. Rail miles outnumbered canal miles by 1840, and by the beginning of the Civil War, there were about eight times as many miles of rail as of canals. The lack of settlements in most of the nation's interior actually stimulated construction, as it made rights of way far less expensive than in Europe, and American rail miles outnumbered European miles by 1840, a situation that continues to this day.

Ironically, some of the obstacles faced by early American railroads came from states that had invested heavily in canals, especially New York, Ohio, and Pennsylvania. New York went so far as to forbid freight shipments on railroads paralleling the Erie Canal except in winter months, when the canal did not operate, and the state further required railroads to pay tolls equal to those paid by canal users.[10] Thus, far from encouraging innovation, the states created barriers when they backed outdated technology.

RAILROAD LAND GRANTS

Before 1850, government subsidies to the railroads came mainly from the states, which borrowed tens of millions of dollars, usually to buy railroad stock, but sometimes to build railroads outright. Federal support up to that year consisted of providing assistance to railroad surveys and in reducing import tariffs on iron used for railroad construction. Such tariff reductions ended in 1843 in order to promote the American iron industry at the expense of imports.[11]

Naturally, railroad promoters lobbied to have the federal government support construction, especially west of the Appalachians, where the government owned much of the land. Congress succumbed to them in 1850, granting more than 3.7 million acres of land to the states of Illinois, Mississippi, and Alabama to support construction of a railroad from Chicago to Mobile, Alabama.[12] By 1856, the Illinois Central had been built from Galena to Cairo, Illinois, receiving 2.6 million acres of land from the state. Most of the cost of construction was paid for with loans using the land grants as collateral. Another railroad, the Mobile and Ohio, built the portion from Mobile to Columbus, Kentucky, a few miles south of Cairo. Construction halted there with the outbreak of the Civil War in 1861.

The Illinois Central land grant set a precedent, opening the floodgates for further land grants. During the 1850s, Congress gave some 18 million acres of land to 10 states to support 45 railroads.[13] But the big grants came in the 1860s, when the construction of the transcontinental railroads began.

In 1862, Congress passed the Pacific Railroad Act, granting five square miles of land for every mile of railroad built between Council Bluffs, Iowa, and San Francisco, California. The act also provided that the federal government would loan the Union Pacific (building from the east) and Central Pacific (building from the west) railroads funds to pay for construction: $16,000 per mile for lands east of the Rocky Mountains and west of the Sierras; $48,000 per mile in the two mountain ranges; and $32,000 per mile between the two mountain ranges.

The justification for these subsidies seems weak today. As historian Richard White observes, "There was no commercial necessity for a transcontinental railroad and no set of investors willing to fund" one. Much of the route dictated by Congress, particularly through Wyoming and Nevada, was not only uninhabited but practically uninhabitable. Noting that investor John Murray Forbes, who controlled the Chicago, Burlington & Quincy, was uninterested in turning that railroad into a transcontinental, White adds, "The more men knew about running railroads for profit, the less likely they were to become involved in the Pacific Railroad."[14]

In 1871, Canada had strong geopolitical reasons to subsidize its transcontinental railroad. The Red River Colony in what is now Manitoba had engaged in an armed rebellion in 1869 and 1870, and the railroad allowed the government to have a larger presence in the area. Meanwhile, businesses in British Columbia had closer economic ties to Seattle, Portland, and San Francisco than to Toronto or Montreal, and many wanted to join the United States rather than Canada. The promise to build the Canadian Pacific Railway persuaded British Columbians to join the Canadian confederation.

By comparison, there was no political necessity to build a transcontinental railroad in the United States. The South already had its network of railroads in 1860, and no one thought that building another one would help prevent or win the Civil War. California and Oregon were already states, and Washington had been a territory since 1853; while they were eager for transcontinental railroads, no one feared they would secede and join Mexico or Canada if they were not built.

The Pacific Railroad Act's supporters in Congress, particularly those from California, claimed the subsidies were somehow a "military necessity" resulting from the war. But by the beginning of 1864, neither railroad had managed to build even the initial 40 miles the law required to be eligible for subsidies, mainly because five square miles of land plus loans were an insufficient inducement to investors to fund even that minimal amount of construction.

To spur construction, Collis Huntington of the Central Pacific and Thomas Durant of the Union Pacific lobbied Congress for more generous subsidies in 1864. With the help of a liberal distribution of stocks and bonds to key legislators, they convinced Congress to pass a revised bill, doubling the land grant to 10 square miles per mile of track; allowing the railroads to issue their own bonds whose repayment, including interest, would be guaranteed by the federal government; and reducing the minimum construction requirement to 20 miles per railroad. Even the 20-mile requirement proved so onerous that in 1865, the railroads convinced Congress to allow them to issue 100 miles' worth of bonds in advance of construction.

THE CREDIT MOBILIER SCANDAL

These revised terms, combined with the end of the Civil War, allowed construction to begin in earnest. The leaders of both companies soon realized that under the terms of the law, the real money was to be made in construction, not the operation of the railroads. Durant understood this first, and he created a company called Credit Mobilier that became the sole bidder on Union Pacific construction contracts. Credit Mobilier built the rail line as cheaply as possible but billed the Union Pacific the full amount provided for by the law, pocketing the difference. This left Union Pacific shippers on the hook for eventually repaying the inflated

15

construction costs. At the same time, Durant and his associates collected millions of dollars in excess construction payments.

Huntington and his partners, Charles Crocker, Mark Hopkins, and Leland Stanford—known as the "Big Four"—soon grasped the benefits of this arrangement and contracted most Central Pacific construction first to Charles Crocker and Company, then to the Contract and Finance Company, both of which they controlled. Although Central Pacific had a variety of stockholders and directors, Crocker, Hopkins, Huntington, and Stanford were the sole directors and stockholders in the Contract and Finance Company. To obtain even greater returns, the Central Pacific persuaded California's state geologist to testify that the mountains—and therefore the $48,000-per-mile loans—began just seven miles outside of Sacramento, even though the next 22 miles or so were fairly flat.

In 1870, after the two railroads had been joined, minority holders of stock in the Central Pacific sued the Big Four for violating their fiduciary trusts as directors of the railroad by giving such lucrative contracts to the Contract and Finance Company. They settled the suits by paying the stockholders $400 to $1,000 per share for their stock.[15]

In 1872, the *New York Sun* published a series of letters revealing that Massachusetts Congressman Oakes Ames, who was also on the Union Pacific and Credit Mobilier boards of directors, had given stock in Credit Mobilier at discounted prices to those members of Congress "where they will do the most good to us." Ultimately, at least 14 members of Congress were implicated in the Credit Mobilier scandal, but only Oakes Ames and one other member (who just happened to be the only Democrat who received stock) were punished for it, and then only by censure.

It was not until 1887, when most of those members of Congress who had received shares of stock were no longer in office, that President Cleveland convened the Pacific Railway Commission to formally investigate the scandals. The investigation was hampered by the fact that Charles Crocker had managed to lose the 15 volumes of accounting books for the Charles Crocker and Contract and Finance Companies: he testified that Mark Hopkins, who was by then conveniently deceased, might have accidentally thrown them out.[16] The commission nevertheless estimated that Central Pacific paid the construction companies roughly twice the actual construction costs, earning the partners profits of at least $16.5 million ($275 million in today's dollars). The owners of Credit Mobilier are estimated to have enjoyed a similar windfall.[17]

Central Pacific received 7.9 million acres of land and $27.9 million worth of bonds. Union Pacific received 11.4 million acres and $27.2 million worth of bonds. Although the federal government made semiannual payments on the 30-year bonds at 6 percent simple interest, the railroads convinced the courts they should not be obligated to repay the government until the full 30 years had expired. At that time, they agreed to pay the bonds plus the interest the government had actually paid, not the interest they would have had to pay if they had been charged for the entire 30 years that they refused to pay. That saved them roughly $56 million in interest charges.[18]

When the railroads finally repaid the loans in 1899, economist Hugo Meyer claimed that "for the government the whole outcome has been financially not less than brilliant."[19] But the repayment represented just a 3.2 percent rate of return on the government's investment, which was low for the times considering that the railroad builders were eager to borrow money at 6 percent and many railroads regularly paid 8 percent dividends to stockholders. Meyer may have meant the government was fortunate the railroads paid it anything at all, as one had gone into receivership in 1893 and the other one nearly did so as well.

Congress had also approved land grants, but no loans, for several other transcontinental railroads. The Southern Pacific—controlled by the same Big Four who controlled the Central Pacific—received 6.8 million acres for building a line from Los Angeles to New Orleans. The Santa Fe and the Atlantic & Pacific, which the Santa Fe would eventually take over, received 15.3 million acres for building from Kansas City to Los Angeles. The biggest grant of all was to the Northern Pacific, which received 38.6 million acres for building from Duluth, Minnesota, to the Puget Sound.

The Central Pacific thrived due to its access to silver mines in western Nevada. All of the other subsidized transcontinental railroads except the Southern Pacific eventually went bankrupt, and the Southern Pacific avoided bankruptcy only because Huntington (once again violating his fiduciary responsibilities to Central Pacific's stockholders) cross-subsidized it with earnings from the Central Pacific.

Nineteenth-century government transportation policies illustrated all of the dangers that would eventually be repeated when government took over urban transit and intercity rail transportation in the 20th century. First, as illustrated by the National Road, politicians love to fund new projects but have little interest in maintaining them. Second, as illustrated by the canal debacles, once one successful line is built, political pressures force governments to extend lines into many unsuitable and financially questionable areas. Third, once government spends money helping to develop a particular technology, it will continue to do so long after it becomes obsolete.

THE FIRST UNSUBSIDIZED TRANSCONTINENTAL

In 1893, the year in which all of the above-mentioned bankruptcies took place, a Minnesota railroader named James J. Hill showed the world how to build a transcontinental railroad without government subsidies. Hill and four other investors had purchased the bankrupt St. Paul and Pacific Railroad in 1878. The St. Paul and Pacific came with a land grant, which still didn't prevent it from going bankrupt. While Hill raised some money by selling the land, his goal was to put farmers on the land who would raise crops that would then be shipped on his railroad. In any case, because Hill and his associates paid the previous owners fair-market value for the railroad and its land, it cannot be said that they were subsidized by the land grant.

Hill had not originally intended to build his railway going west, instead planning a north-south route. Extending north to Winnipeg in 1879, Hill renamed the line the St. Paul, Minneapolis, and Manitoba Railway. Hill and his coinvestors planned to make it part of the Canadian Pacific's route to British Columbia. When the Canadian government insisted on an all-Canada route, Hill dropped out of the Canadian Pacific consortium and concentrated on expanding his own railroad.

Fortunately, the Manitoba line accessed some of the most productive wheat lands in the world, making it highly profitable. In some years, Hill's railroad hauled nearly a quarter of the nation's spring wheat harvest.[20] On top of paying 8 percent dividends on its stock, the Manitoba was profitable enough to fund rapid expansion. By 1886, the railway had reached what is now Minot, North Dakota, a town named for Manitoba executive and Hill protégé Henry Minot.

The stretch from Minot to the Rocky Mountains had little to attract a railroad, partly because much of the land was on Indian reservations. However, the Rockies were the site of valuable gold and copper mines in Helena and Butte. The Northern Pacific served Helena and the Union Pacific served Butte, and both railroads had a quiet agreement not to challenge each other's monopolies. Hill, however, had no such compunctions. After getting Congressional approval to build across the reservations and paying the Indians for the rights of way, Hill carefully planned his next step.

In 1887, Hill hired 8,000 men and 3,300 teams of horses to extend his railroad west. He could have built from both Minot and Helena, but the Northern Pacific naturally quoted high prices to ship rails and equipment to Helena. Between April and November, therefore, Hill built more than 640 miles of track from Minot to Helena, the most any railroad has ever built from one end of track in one season. "I have been up at the front, and I find it pays to be where the money is being spent," Hill wrote one of his associates.[21] Reaching Butte in early 1888, Hill immediately began shipping mineral ores for half the price charged by the Northern Pacific and Union Pacific.

Hill was one of the first railroaders to understand that railroads had transitioned from a lightweight, high-margin service to a heavy-weight, high-volume service, and he built his railroad to provide such service with low grades and minimum curvature. "What we want over our grades is a heavy tonnage," he wrote Montana copper king Marcus Daly, "and the heavier it is the lower we can make the rates."[22] Hill's line regularly carried more tons per train and more ton-miles per route mile than any western railroad.

In 1889, his sights clearly set on the Pacific Coast, Hill decided his railroad needed a more evocative name. Having visited and been impressed by the railways in England, he named his after one of them: the Great Northern Railway.

After two profitable years serving midwestern farms and Montana mines, Hill was ready for the next step: building across the Rocky and Cascade Mountains to the Puget Sound. Construction crews finished the line to Seattle in January 1893, just a few weeks before the failure of the Philadelphia and Reading Railroad set off a depression that bankrupted nearly 200 other railroads, including the Northern Pacific, Union Pacific, and Santa Fe, along with 500 banks and 15,000 other businesses.

Bankrupt railroads continued to operate but were temporarily shielded from paying interest on their bonds. Wall Street bankers assumed that, because Great Northern's competitors wouldn't have to pay interest, they could cut their rates and force the Great Northern into bankruptcy as well. But Hill had built his railroad to transport people and freight, not to get land grants, so its costs were low enough, says Hill biographer Albro Martin, that "the Great Northern could make money at a rate that would—and frequently did—land its competitors in the poorhouse."[23]

Hill became known as the "empire builder" because his steamships and railroads eventually reached from Yokohama to Buffalo and from Winnipeg to Galveston. In the process, Hill showed that the western transcontinental railroads would have been eventually built even without federal subsidies. Thanks to the subsidies, however, most of them were both poorly built and built too soon, leaving them in a financially shaky position for many years. Nor is it clear that their construction greatly stimulated development of the West. After all, until 1900, freight could move from California to the East Coast less expensively, and almost as quickly, by sea as by the transcontinental railroad.[24] Southern Wyoming and northern Nevada, which were crossed by the Union Pacific and Central Pacific railroads, remain to this day some of the least-densely populated lands in the nation.

Much of the growth that did take place in the West before 1900 was unrelated to the transcontinental railroads. After the opening of the Central Pacific, Nevada's population fluctuated primarily in response to changes in the mining industry, which was adequately served by Central Pacific shipping its ore to California without using a transcontinental line. After the opening of the Union Pacific, Wyoming's population grew, but not as fast as Colorado's, which was not initially served by the Union Pacific but whose mines were reached by the Denver and Rio Grande, Colorado Midland, and several other railroads that received no federal subsidies.

Historian Richard White argues that federal subsidies to transcontinental railroads actually did more harm than good for western economies.

"Without the extensive subsidization of a transcontinental railroad net-work, there might very well have been less waste, less suffering, less environmental degradation, and less catastrophic economic busts in mining, agriculture, and cattle raising," he says. If the country had built the railroads when they were needed instead of when the government subsidized them, he concludes, "it could have built them more cheaply, more efficiently, and with fewer social and political costs."[25]

In 1862, steam trains were the latest technology, and railroad stocks were comparable to internet stocks today, so the idea of building a transcontinental railroad seemed to make sense. Today, however, few people want to crisscross the country with 50- to 130-year-old technologies that most Americans stopped using decades ago.

2. THE GROWTH OF URBAN TRANSIT

Others will see the shipping of Manhattan north and west,
and the heights of Brooklyn to the south and east,
Others will see the islands large and small;
Fifty years hence, others will see them as they cross, the sun half an hour high;
A hundred years hence, or ever so many hundred years hence, others will see them,
Will enjoy the sunset, the pouring in of the flood-tide, the falling back to the
sea of the ebb-tide.

—Walt Whitman, *Crossing Brooklyn Ferry*

Ferry boats were the first form of urban mass transit in America, and also the first to stimulate suburban growth. Other forms of mass transit such as streetcars had also appeared by 1856, when Walt Whitman's 146-line poem, *Crossing Brooklyn Ferry*, from which the above lines are taken, was first published. Whitmam was enthralled by this new service, so it never occurred to him that ferry boats themselves might soon be replaced by other technologies. Contrary to his belief that people would be riding the same ferry and seeing the same sights long after he wrote the poem, the Brooklyn Bridge replaced the ferry less than 30 years after the poem was published.

That bridge included streetcar tracks connecting Manhattan to Brooklyn. The first streetcar line in Manhattan opened in 1832, more than 50 years before the great bridge opened. John Mason, president of

Chemical Bank and founder of the New York and Harlaem (later Harlem) Railroad, planned to build a steam railroad from New York City to Albany, but until that could be achieved, he was willing to earn a little revenue with horse-drawn rail cars running in city streets. Over the next 70 years, steel, steam, and electricity shaped both our cities and our transportation systems.

America's First Cities

To understand this story, we have to go back a couple of decades to 1810, before American cities had any mass transit other than a few ferry boats. American cities in 1810 weren't anything like the cities of today. New York, America's largest city, had just 96,000 people, about the same as Brockton, Massachusetts, Dearborn, Michigan, or Beaverton, Oregon, have today. Today, these are suburbs, but New York in 1810 looked much like a suburb today, mostly made up of two-story buildings and an occasional three- or four-story building.

The main difference between cities of 1810 and the suburbs of today is that many of the houses and other buildings in 1810 were physically adjacent to one another—row houses—rather than separate homes with side yards, and each residence in 1810 housed more people than the homes of today. New York City's population density in 1810 was about 25,000 people per square mile, or 10 times greater than the average density of modern urban areas in the United States. New York City achieves a similar density today because of mid-rise and high-rise developments. Because family sizes in 1810 were much larger than today, and single houses were more likely to be the home of multiple families, New York City reached that same density in 1810 without tall buildings.

Only the wealthiest city dwellers in 1810 owned horses, so transportation for most people was limited to foot travel. This led people to pack themselves into dense housing not only because land was expensive but also to minimize the amount of walking needed to reach jobs and markets. Nor were jobs particularly concentrated in one part of the city, as America's few factories were mainly located near sources of waterpower, not in port cities such as New York, Philadelphia, or Boston. As a result, population and job densities were roughly the same throughout a city.

Over the next century, new technologies enabled both denser development and faster transportation. The result was a concentration of jobs in city centers, while residents who could afford newer forms of transportation lived farther out. In the 1840s, residents began calling the business district in New York *downtown*, a reference to the fact that it was at the southern end of Manhattan, and south is "down" on most maps. By the 1870s, Americans in other cities were calling their business districts downtown as well, even if they weren't at the southern end of those cities.[1] This formed the basis of the *monocentric city*, in which most jobs and the densest housing were at the center, surrounded by lower-density residential areas farther out. In the following century, newer technologies led to the decentralization of both population and jobs, rendering the monocentric city obsolete.

The Ferry Boat

New Jersey inventor John Stevens was responsible for the first decentralizing technology: the steam-powered ferry boat. Stevens' father, also a John Stevens, had owned merchant ships and became a wealthy landowner in New Jersey. In 1784, the state elected him to the Continental Congress, and he presided over the state convention in which New Jersey became the third state to ratify the new Constitution. The family was wealthy enough that, even at age 35, the younger Stevens was able to pay $90,000 (more than $2 million in today's money) for a large farm on the Hudson River in New Jersey that he called Hoboken.

In 1804, Stevens designed the first modern propeller and built the world's first screw-propelled, steam-powered boat. In 1809, he built a larger steamboat, the *Phoenix*. The New York legislature had granted Robert Fulton a monopoly to operate steamboats on the Hudson River, so Stevens sailed the Phoenix to Philadelphia, making the first steam-powered voyage on the open ocean. Starting in 1811, he operated it as a steam-powered ferry on the Delaware River. In 1811, he also started using a third steamboat, the *Juliana*, in ferry service between Manhattan and Hoboken. Fulton ignored this violation of his monopoly for a time, but he forced Stevens to shut it down in 1813.[2]

In 1824, another New York–New Jersey ferry operator, Thomas Gibbons, successfully challenged the monopoly in a Supreme Court case that ruled states could not grant monopolies in interstate commerce.[3] Stevens soon reinstated his ferry service to Hoboken, where he built a "pleasure resort" for New Yorkers to visit and where, he hoped, they would buy lots for first or second homes.[4] Eventually, the Stevens family made Hoboken into one of the first New Jersey suburbs of New York City.

Despite his fondness for steamboats, Stevens was skeptical of canals and therefore opposed construction of the Erie Canal. In 1812, he wrote a 46-page pamphlet arguing "the superior advantages of rail-ways and steam carriages over canal navigation." "I can see nothing to hinder a steam carriage moving on its ways with a velocity of 100 miles an hour," he predicted.[5] People at the time must have thought him a lunatic, as no one had ever built a steam locomotive to run on rails, and most people had never even seen one of the few primitive railroads that then existed, mainly to serve mines. To demonstrate their viability, in 1825, Stevens built America's first steam locomotive and a circular track on his property, inviting visitors to see the locomotive pulling passenger cars around the track as fast as 12 miles per hour.

In 1830, John Stevens helped start the Camden and Amboy Railroad, one of America's first intercity railroads, and his son Robert became president. Robert designed the t-shaped rail that was the forerunner of most rails in use today as well as the first railroad spikes to fix that rail to the ground.[6]

The Omnibus

In the meantime, New York City itself had grown so large that many people found it difficult to walk from one end of the city to the other. Abraham Brower, who owned a livery stable in the city and operated stagecoach lines to Harlem and other nearby towns, saw this as an opportunity. In 1827, he ordered a special, 12-passenger, horse-drawn coach with four rows of three seats, two facing forward and two backwards. The seats were accessed by two entryways on either side of the open-sided coach. He called this coach the *Accommodation* and ran it up and down

Broadway for 1.5 miles between Wall Street and Bleecker Street, charging a shilling (12.5 cents) for a ride of any length. The service was so successful that he quickly ordered a second 12-passenger coach, but this one had a single door at the rear with inward-facing seats running the length of the coach. This coach, which Brower called the *Sociable*, had closed sides more suitable for inclement weather.[7]

Brower's service was similar to one started in 1826 by a French industrialist named Stanislas Baudry, who built a 16-passenger, horse-drawn coach to move people from the center of Nantes to some bathhouses he had built on the edge of the city. He called the coach an *omnibus*, a Latin word that means "for all." Baudry's original coach was so successful that he expanded the service to several other French cities, including Bordeaux, Lyon, and Paris.[8] While the word omnibus has since grown to have other meanings, the first known use of the word in English was an 1829 reference to an omnibus vehicle.[9]

No one knows whether Brower had heard of Baudry's omnibus when he started his operation in 1827, but he had certainly heard of it by 1831. That year, he hired 21-year-old John Stephenson, who had recently finished his apprenticeship as a coach builder, to build an even larger vehicle capable of seating 20 people. Like the *Sociable*, the new coach had a rear door with seats the length of the car. Brower called this coach the *Omnibus*. Stephenson was soon the nation's leading builder of omnibuses, constructing hundreds of them for operations in New York, Philadelphia, Washington, and other cities.[10]

When John Mason decided to run a horse-drawn car on the New York and Harlaem Railroad's tracks in New York City, he hired John Stephenson to build the coach. The first horsecar line ran for just under a mile from Prince Street to 14th Street on the Bowery, which at the time was a prestigious address and home to the city's largest theater. When the service was inaugurated, then mayor Walter Bowne claimed, "This event will go down in history as the greatest achievement of man."[11]

As it turned out, Mason's horsecar was ahead of its time. Instead of the tall, t-shaped rails designed by Robert Stevens, the horsecar ran on iron straps bolted directly to the pavement. These didn't entirely obstruct traffic, but they were high enough to annoy the drivers of omnibuses and other wheeled vehicles, who strongly protested their use. Although New Orleans built a similar line in 1835, the omnibus rather than the horsecar remained the dominant form of urban street transit for the next two decades.

In 1833, the year after Mason's horsecar began operating, there were 80 omnibuses in New York City. Over the following two decades, the number grew to nearly 700, run by 22 different companies. In 1853, the peak of omnibus service, New York City omnibuses averaged more than 13,000 trips per day carrying 120,000 people. Omnibus service also appeared in Baltimore, Boston, Chicago, Cincinnati, Philadelphia, and Pittsburgh, as well as smaller cities such as Albany, Louisville, Milwaukee, Providence, and Rochester.[12]

THE COMMUTER TRAIN

While horsecars were not yet successful in the city, by the mid-1830s, the United States was at the beginning of a boom of intercity railroad construction. John Mason's New York & Harlaem and Robert Stevens' Camden & Amboy were just two of many railroads being built from various seaports to inland destinations. Three different railroads radiated from Boston by 1835, and seven by 1845. In 1839, the Eastern Rail-Road connecting Boston and Salem began offering season tickets to commuters at discounted prices, and most of the other railroads in the region followed suit. Initially, the lower prices were aimed at filling seats on trains that were already operating, but in 1843, the Boston & Worcester began operating special trains just for commuters. By 1849, Boston railroads operated 208 daily passenger trains, of which 118 went no further than 15 miles, suggesting that many of their patrons were commuters.[13]

Even with the discounts, says historian Charles Kennedy, the fares were "too costly to attract daily commuters from the artisan or labor class." Instead, the season ticket holders were "businessmen," that is, middle-class workers. In 1855, the railroads sold about 6,500 annual passes to suburbanites commuting into the city.[14] This is not a huge number considering that the greater Boston area had about 200,000 people, indicating that most people couldn't afford to take the train to work.[15]

Despite being limited to the well off, steam-powered commuter trains soon became an important generator of suburbs in New York, Chicago, Philadelphia, and San Francisco, among other cities. Between 1847 and 1861, 11 different rail lines were built from downtown Chicago, leading to rapid suburban development. Evanston and Lake Forest on the Milwaukee Road, Hyde Park on the Illinois Central, and most famously Riverside on the Chicago, Burlington & Quincy were all laid out as suburban developments after being connected to Chicago by railroads. By 1873, Chicago railroads offered at least 100 commuter trains to the suburbs each day. As in the case of Boston, fares were too high to be affordable to working-class commuters. Making them even more elitist, some suburbs such as Riverside required residents to build homes costing at least $3,000, compared with under $1,000 for a working-class home in Chicago itself.[16]

While ferryboats, horsecars, and steam-powered commuter trains allowed the upper classes to escape to the suburbs, the rise of urban factories centralized jobs. With steam engines providing the power, factories no longer had to locate near flowing streams, so many located in New York, Philadelphia, and other cities that were the nexus of flows of raw materials from the hinterlands and the markets for the finished products. Steam was used to power New York printing presses as early as 1823. By 1825, New York City was the furniture-making, book-printing, and ship-building capital of the nation.[17]

A single furniture factory could employ 100 people yet occupy only a fraction of a city block. While competition reduced some omnibus fares from a shilling to half a shilling (6.25 cents), typical nonfarm wages averaged only a dollar a day, so even a half shilling put omnibuses out of the reach of many people.[18] Steam-powered commuter trains to the suburbs were even more expensive. Thus, factory workers had to commute on foot, so both population and job densities grew. By 1840, much of New York City and Philadelphia was made up of four- and five-story buildings. The average population density of lower Manhattan exceeded 70,000 people per square mile. Those few who could afford their own horses or to ride omnibuses commuted from lower-density areas in upper Manhattan or rode ferries to New Jersey or Brooklyn.

In 1838, John Stephenson built a six-story coachworks on East 27th Street near what is now Madison Avenue. One floor was probably used to warehouse parts. Other floors included woodworking mills, metalworking and blacksmith shops, and paint and varnish shops. A central boiler powered wheels that turned belts and pulleys throughout the building to serve machine tools and a freight elevator. After several expansions, he was producing more than five omnibuses or horsecars a day, yet his factory occupied little more than two acres of land, and most of his 300 employees probably walked to work from nearby apartments.

THE RISE OF THE HORSECAR

Despite John Mason's 1832 horsecar line in New York City, horsecars did not become popular until a French-American inventor named Alphonse Loubat figured out how to overcome the problem of rails impeding traffic. Loubat had helped build Mason's original street railway, but it was not until 1852 that he hit upon the idea of running cars on grooved rails recessed into the pavement instead of rails rising above the pavement. After he installed the first such grooved street railway in New York City, horse-drawn railcars quickly replaced omnibuses.

"Railways could not make any progress in our streets, so long as their economy and advantages were overbalanced by the evil of their projection above the surface of the pavement," said one writer in the *New York Times* in 1852, "but now with the introduction of the groove rail, they are going ahead, and must continue to go ahead."[19] Go ahead they did: By 1860, there were 60 miles of horsecar lines in Manhattan and another 72 miles in Brooklyn, both increasing by 150 percent by 1870.[20] Horsecars quickly replaced omnibuses in other cities as well. By 1888, horsecars could be found on more than 5,800 miles of track in 300 American cities.[21]

Having built the first horsecar for the New York and Harlaem line, John Stephenson was easily able to segue his business of building omnibus coaches into building horsecars. For many years, his company was the largest streetcar builder in the nation. Between 1876 and his death in 1891, his company built more than 25,000 horsecars, on top of thousands of horsecars and omnibuses in the previous 45 years. In 1904, rival streetcar builder John A. Brill called Stephenson a "genius" and the "father of the industry" who "so completely developed the art of car building . . . that practically nothing since has been added to it."[22]

After the Civil War, Stephenson himself became a suburban commuter when he built a large home fronting on Long Island Sound in New Rochelle. Originally a summer home, he eventually lived in it year round. To get to his factory, he would take a horsecar to the New Haven train station in New Rochelle. There, he'd catch a 40-minute steam-train trip to Grand Central Depot, which opened in 1871. From Grand Central, he would take another horsecar to his factory. The horsecars would have charged a nickel each, while the standard fare on the steam train would have been about 40 cents. Even with a commuter discount, his roundtrip fares probably totaled at least 70 cents, far too much for any of his workers, many of whom were paid little more than a dollar a day.

Rail lines cost more to install than an omnibus that rolled on existing streets. In 1875, the Minneapolis Street Railway Company spent $6,000 per mile (about $125,000 in today's dollars) on its first rail line.[23] An 1889 trade journal article estimated the average cost of rail lines was $7,000 per mile.[24] Against that initial cost, however, rails offered smoother rides and less rolling resistance, so two horses could pull a railcar at higher speeds than six to eight horses could move a similar-sized omnibus. This meant fewer horses were needed to serve any particular route, greatly reducing operating costs. However, the transition to horsecars changed the nature of the business from one in which many omnibuses were owned by driver-entrepreneurs to one in which horsecar lines were owned by investors who hired drivers as employees.

The horsecar's faster speeds expanded the range of territory that commuters and other travelers could reach in a reasonable time. This allowed the development of lower-density residential areas outside of crowded city centers. After the first horsecar line opened in Philadelphia in 1856, residents "grasped not only the transit significance of the invention but its real estate implications as well," says historian John Stilgoe.[25] "A beneficial effect" of the horsecars, wrote a Philadelphia attorney in 1859, "will be to enable everyone to have a suburban villa or country home, to spread the city over a vast space."[26]

While that was a nice dream, the reality was that most workers could still not afford horsecar fares. Lower operating costs allowed most horsecar operators to reduce fares to a nickel, a rate that would remain a street-car standard for decades.[27] Even a nickel, however, was more than some could afford for daily commutes. "Streetcar fares, while inexpensive, were still beyond the means of many unskilled workers," says historian Roger Simon. "It was the growing middle class, the clerks, professionals, shop-keepers, and highly skilled craftsmen, who could best afford to use the streetcar for daily commutation."[28]

Horses were far from a perfect form of power, of course. They were slow, expensive to maintain, had difficulties pulling railcars up steep hills and in ice and snow, and produced copious amounts of urine and excrement, the latter of which was a source of tetanus. In 1882, street railways required about 100,000 horses to pull 18,000 cars. The horses ate 150,000 tons of hay and 11 million bushels (176,000 tons) of grain annu-ally, which naturally produced corresponding amounts of manure, much of which landed in city streets.[29] Since horses produce about one-and-a-half pounds of manure for each pound of food they eat, and car horses were on the streets about four hours a day, they would deposit well over 100,000 tons of manure on city streets each year.

"All forms of economic activity yield external benefits and involve social costs," says economist George Hilton, "but the social costs of horse traction were the most offensive in the history of transportation."[30] "Almost from the day it collected its first fare the street railway industry searched for a way to replace the horse," agrees transportation historian John White. "Every conceivable power source was tried: steam, compressed air, clock springs, ammonia, cable. Most failed."[31]

After the Civil War, for example, many street railways purchased small steam locomotives that were covered with a wooden shell shaped like a horsecar that supposedly would be less likely to frighten horses. Called *steam dummies*, they could pull more people than horses, but despite the best efforts of their designers, people complained "the engines caused great noise, emitted large quantities of smoke and cinders, and frightened horses."[32]

Compressed air and batteries could not handle long distances, while early internal combustion engines were not powerful enough to move loaded streetcars. Early experiments with electric power fared poorly as well.

THE CABLE CAR

In 1869, an engineer named Andrew Hallidie saw a horsecar driver whipping five horses to get them to pull a car up a steep hill in San Francisco. Hallidie manufactured wire rope for bridge cables and similar purposes. In 1867, he developed an aerial cable system for moving mineral ores. The 19th century was the age of steam power, and if the noise and pollution coming from steam locomotives prevented railway companies from using them in city streets, then one alternative, Hallidie realized, was to power the cars with stationary steam engines. In 1873, Hallidie opened the first of several San Francisco cable-car lines. By 1880, the city had five such lines totaling 11.2 miles.[33]

Cable cars could go twice as fast as horsecars and cost only about half as much to operate. However, their initial costs were much higher—$200,000 a mile compared with less than $10,000 for horsecar lines.[34] In addition, many in the street railway industry feared the cable slots would become jammed with ice and snow in the winter. Those fears were dispelled when the Chicago City Railway Company opened the first successful cable-car line outside of San Francisco in 1882. By 1884, the company had 43 miles of cable-car routes.[35] A single steam engine replaced 1,000 horses and 200 stablemen. Soon, 469 cable cars carried 27 million Windy City riders per year.[36]

The Chicago line demonstrated that cable cars were economically viable outside of San Francisco as long as there were enough customers to repay the capital costs. Within six years, 11 other cities had built cable-car lines. These included some of America's largest cities: New York (then consisting solely of Manhattan); Philadelphia; Brooklyn; St. Louis; Cincinnati; Omaha; and Kansas City. These cities had 130,000 people or more, as did San Francisco and Chicago. During the next four years, five more cities—Baltimore, Cleveland, Pittsburgh, Providence, and Washington, D.C.—would build cable-car lines, and these cities also had 130,000 people or more, suggesting that cities of that size or larger could generate enough passengers to pay off the high initial cost of cable cars.

In a small but rapidly growing town in California, developers devised a different way of paying for cable cars. Los Angeles only had 11,000 people in 1880, but it grew to more than 50,000 by 1890. In 1885, developers of the Bunker Hill neighborhood hoped they could sell their real estate for higher prices if potential residents were served by a rail line, but the grades were too steep for horsecars. So they built a cable-car line with the expectation that real estate sales would cover capital costs, while passenger fares would cover operating costs. Soon, real estate developments in Oakland, Sioux City, Spokane, West Seattle, San Diego, and Portland—all cities that might otherwise be considered too small to support a cable-car line—incorporated such a line to promote land sales. Apparently, cable cars were viable in cities with fewer than 130,000 people only if someone other than the riders paid the capital costs.

THE TROLLEY CAR

Even in big cities, George Hilton observed, cable-car lines made economic sense for just six years and five days, which was the time between the opening of Chicago's first cable-car line on January 28, 1882, and the opening of the first successful electric streetcar line in Richmond, Virginia, on February 2, 1888. Between 1888 and 1891, about 15 more cities would build cable-car lines, either because developers didn't trust the new electric technology or because city governments objected to overhead electric wires. By 1913, however, cable-car lines had either shut down or converted to electric power in all but three cities: Tacoma (which converted in 1938), Seattle (whose cable cars lasted until 1940), and, of course, San Francisco.

Prior to 1888, various inventors had attempted to build electric streetcar lines in such cities as Montgomery, Alabama, and South Bend, Indiana. None of these systems were reliable, and some were converted to cable cars, while others simply failed. It took an electrical genius named Frank Sprague to solve the basic problems of streetcar design. Sprague, who ought to be as famous as Nicola Tesla, went on to play an important role in many other transportation systems.

Sprague graduated from the United States Naval Academy in 1878, after which he served as a midshipman on, coincidentally, the U.S.S. *Richmond*. In 1883, he left the Navy and went to work for Thomas Edison. While Edison was interested in lighting up America, Sprague was more interested in using electrical motors to power railcars. After a year with Edison, he left to form his own company, the Sprague Electric Railway and Motor Company.

Sprague contributed several inventions that made electric streetcars feasible. First, he developed innovative electric motors that Edison himself endorsed. Second, Sprague invented a regenerative braking system that helped slow the railcars as it helped conserve energy. Third, he improved the poles used to transfer electricity from overhead wires to the cars. Finally, perhaps most important, he developed a suspension system that insulated the electrical motors from rough rides but allowed a direct connection between the motors and the wheels.

In late 1887 in Richmond, Virginia, Sprague agreed to install a power plant and 12 miles of track and overhead wires, as well as convert 40 horsecars to electric streetcars in Richmond. He and his company managed to do this in just 90 days. Officials with streetcar companies in other cities were particularly impressed that Sprague's cars were able to climb a 10 percent grade and that more than 20 streetcars could start simultaneously without overloading the system. Though he lost money on the Richmond contract, his system worked so well that he soon had contracts for electric streetcar lines in more than 100 other cities, and competing companies used Sprague's inventions to build lines in many other cities.[37]

Electric streetcars overcame several problems inherent with cable cars. First, the weight of the cable limited the length of cable-car lines. A four-mile cable weighed around 60,000 pounds and could support just a two-mile cable-car route because the cable had to make a roundtrip. The weight was so great that most of the energy produced by the steam engine running a cable-car line was consumed just moving the cable. Second, if a cable became frayed, it could get stuck in a car's grip, making it impossible to stop, with sometimes deadly results. Third, cable cars had a difficult time going around corners, partly because frequent bending tended to fray cables, so most cable-car lines travelled in straight lines or made just one or two turns.

Sprague's trolley cars—so called because the trolley arm trolled for electricity the way an angler trolls for fish—not only solved these problems, they cost half as much to build as cable-car lines and cost less to operate than either horsecars or cable cars.[38] They were much faster than any horsecar and most cable cars, and electric streetcars could also be larger, enabling them to move more people. As a result, says Hilton, the electric streetcar "was one of the most rapidly accepted innovations in the history of technology." By 1902, 97 percent of street railways were electric.[39]

As shown in Figure 2.1, streetcar ridership grew by 450 percent in the first two decades after Sprague perfected the electric trolley. By 1902, every single American city of 15,000 or more people, and nearly two-thirds of all cities with 5,000 to 15,000 people (including 40 percent of cities with just 5,000 to 6,000 people), had a street railway system.[40] By 1920, more than 1,000 American cities (including suburbs of other, larger cities) had electric streetcars.[41] Streetcar ridership, however, peaked in 1920, then began a slow decline.

Figure 2.1
Transit Ridership, 1890–1920

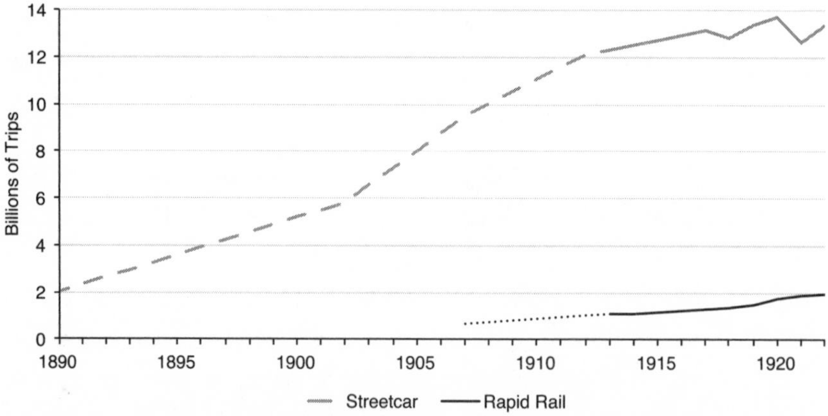

Source: *Public Transportation Fact Book 2016*, American Public Transportation Association.
Note: Dotted and dashed lines indicate data are available only for 1890, 1902, 1907, 1912, and annually thereafter.

Real Estate Developers

The higher speeds and lower costs of the streetcar opened up land that was formerly inaccessible to city residents. This led to the first full-time real estate developers, who would typically purchase tracts of land outside of a city, build a streetcar line from the city center to that land, and then sell subdivided lots. "Streetcar companies and land speculators were often one and the same," says architectural historian Sean Craft. The first such development, naturally, was in Richmond, where developers formed the Brookland Railway and Improvement Company to build a streetcar line and sell land north of the city's center.[42]

These and other developments that followed the streetcar lines became known as *streetcar suburbs*, and they can be found all over the United States. Streetcar suburbs were intermediate in density between the pedestrian-oriented cities of the mid-19th century and the automobile suburbs of the late 20th century. Single-family homes or duplexes were typically built on 50-by-100-foot lots, equivalent to about eight homes per acre, so no one had to walk far to get from their home to a streetcar stop.

Like the cable-car developments in the 1880s and early 1890s, many electric-streetcar developers in the 1890s and early 1900s relied on land sales to pay the capital cost of the streetcar lines, while collecting only enough in fares to pay the operating costs. In many cases, landowners themselves would build streetcar lines in order to promote the sale and development of their lands.

- In 1889, developers in Lexington, Kentucky, organized the Belt Land Company to sell land on the city's periphery and the Belt Railway Company to access that land.[43]
- Led by Nevada Senator Francis Newlands, the Chevy Chase Land Company owned 1,713 acres northwest of Washington, D.C., and opened the Rock Creek Railway in 1892 to give potential residents of Chevy Chase access to the town.[44]
- In 1907, the Van Sweringen brothers built a streetcar line to 1,300 acres of land they owned known as Shaker Heights, outside of Cleveland.[45]

- In San Francisco in 1908, developers of an area called Parkside (now part of the Sunset District) created the Parkside Transit Company to build a 1.5-mile-long streetcar line from the southern edge of Golden Gate Park so that the Parkside Realty Company could sell lots on several hundred acres of land.[46]
- In Los Angeles, Henry Huntington—nephew of the Southern Pacific's Collis Huntington—built much of the Pacific Electric system to access his real estate projects in Redondo Beach, Pasadena, and the San Fernando Valley.[47]

Streetcar developers in other cities used different business models. Moses Sherman built streetcar lines throughout Los Angeles and Phoenix, sometimes to access his own land, but more often other people's land. In the latter cases, he would always demand that the other landowners front the capital costs of the streetcars. "We might build five, or six, or even 7 miles of road, and we might build less, according to the amount of money [the landowners] raise," he wrote in a 1907 letter. "But the understanding is that the Railway Company does not put in anything."[48] In Chicago, streetcar builder Charles Yerkes worked with land developer Samuel Gross, who probably built more homes in Chicago than anyone else. "Yerkes would buy land, run a streetcar line through it, hire Gross to build the streets, sewers and homes and watch the real estate appreciate," says historian Greg Borzo.[49]

THE ELECTRIC INTERURBAN

Within cities, most electric streetcars averaged between 10 and 15 miles per hour, which seems slow today but was at least double the speed of a horsecar. But it wasn't long before someone realized Sprague's technology could be applied to railcars running between cities at higher speeds. One of the first successful electric interurban railways opened in 1893 over the 14 miles between Portland and Oregon City. Electric interurbans cost far less to operate than steam trains. The biggest interurban networks were in the Midwest; by 1908, every town in Ohio of 10,000 people or more was connected with its neighbors by electric lines.[50]

In most cases, interurban lines were built to compete against existing steam railroads. There were exceptions, however. In 1910 through 1912, when James J. Hill was expanding his empire in Oregon, he had his favorite railway engineer, John F. Stevens, construct an electrified line between Portland and Eugene. To compete with him, Southern Pacific electrified one of its two routes between Portland and Eugene. Both companies operated large interurban vehicles over these lines.[51]

Elevated Rapid Transit

Within cities, one more rail transit technology was perfected at about the same time: rapid transit, known today as *heavy rail*. Running on their own exclusive rights of way with no grade crossings, rapid-transit trains didn't have to worry about colliding with pedestrians or other vehicles. This usually meant running on platforms elevated above the streets or in underground tunnels. Because elevated platforms were unsightly and tunnels expensive, only a few major cities built true rapid-transit lines.

New York experimented with an elevated cable-powered line in 1868, but it was short lived and soon converted to steam power. More successful steam-powered lines were installed in New York in the 1870s and Chicago in the 1880s.[52] In 1891, Sioux City, Iowa, real estate developer Arthur Garretson spent $586,000 (about $15 million in today's dollars) to build a three-mile elevated line to access his properties in the Morningside neighborhood. This line originally used steam trains but was converted to electric streetcars in 1892. The company operating the line went bankrupt after the panic of 1893 and removed the elevated portion of the route in 1899, suggesting that elevated trains were financially feasible only in big cities.

In large cities, demand for rapid transit was too great to be served by individual railcars; platforms for New York's first elevated were initially long enough to serve trains of at least five cars at a time. Steam remained unpopular due to noise, cinders, and pollution, but electrification of rapid-transit lines posed a problem because early electric motors weren't powerful enough to pull such long trains.

In 1897, General Electric and other companies were trying to build electric locomotives big enough to power Chicago's rapid-transit trains while light enough to not overload the pillars that supported the elevated lines. One evening at dinner, GE's project manager was told by an assistant that the person who had installed dumbwaiters in the Chicago hotel in which he was staying was submitting a competing plan, and "we both had a good laugh over it." When he found out that person was Frank Sprague, suddenly "it wasn't so funny." Sprague came to Chicago, and "the story was he had no shop; no organization; no installers—just a toothbrush and an idea, but Ye Gods, what an idea!" the GE engineer related many years later.[53]

Sprague's idea was to include small motors in each car, effectively making them all lightweight locomotives, something that seems self-evident today but which no one else had previously conceived. Steam trains requiring more than one locomotive needed separate crews for each locomotive. Sprague realized, however, that individually electrified cars could be wired together so that just one driver could control all of the cars. To prove the concept, Sprague wired two cars together but left them uncoupled. "During acceleration and up to the time the air brakes were applied, there was but a small variation in the space" between the cars, an observer reported. By early 1898, Sprague had installed electric motors in 120 cars, and Chicago's South Side Elevated Railroad completely converted from steam to electric cars. The new system greatly reduced costs, and the line's profits doubled.[54] The remaining elevated lines in Chicago soon followed, as did those in Boston and New York.

The Subway

Even electrified elevated lines were a nuisance because they were noisy and blocked sunlight to the street. The only alternative was to build rapid-transit lines underground. London built steam-powered underground rapid-transit lines as early as the 1860s. They used locomotives designed to minimize smoke and steam emissions, partly by burning high-quality "smokeless" coal, but the results were only partially successful.[55] American cities didn't build subways until Sprague perfected the electrical power and control systems. Boston opened an underground line in 1897, but it was for streetcars rather than multiple-car, rapid-transit trains. New York City began building the nation's first rapid-transit sub-way line in 1900, and it began operating in 1904.

With top speeds of 45 miles per hour and average speeds better than 20 miles per hour, New York's subway was true rapid transit. By compar-ison, at 12 to 15 miles per hour, the elevated lines were not much faster than electric streetcars. The subway, more than anything else, brought the newly created boroughs of New York City together.

Boston, Chicago, and Philadelphia all followed with their own sub-ways. Rochester, New York, built a short subway that streetcars and inter-urban lines used in the downtown area, but it would be more accurate to call it an underpass than a true subway, as it was built at ground level with a highway built above it. A few other cities, including Cincinnati, attempted to build subways, but they were unsuccessful. Like elevated trains, the high cost of subways meant they made economic sense only in the largest, densest cities. As shown in Figure 2.1, rapid-transit ridership (elevated trains and subways together) tripled between 1907 and 1920, but because rapid-transit lines were found in only a few cities, it did not impact the lives of most Americans the way streetcars did.

By 1910, electric streetcars, interurbans, steam and electric commuter trains, and rapid-transit lines had all reduced the real cost of travel, mea-sured both in time and dollars, by enough to allow not just middle-class workers but also highly skilled working-class employees to move to the suburbs. At the same time, new building technologies encouraged central-ization of urban jobs. Chicago's 16-story Monadnock Building was con-structed in 1891 without the use of steel for structural support. To support the load, the walls had to be six feet thick at their base.

Taller buildings without steel would have required such thick walls that the space gained through height would be lost to the walls. The same Bessemer steel that provided rails for trains and streetcars to roll on solved this problem by providing structural support for taller buildings. The first steel-framed skyscraper, Chicago's 10-story Rand McNally Building, was built in 1889, and soon steel buildings were much taller.

Accessing the higher floors, however, required fast elevators. Elisha Otis didn't invent the elevator, but he developed the first safety brake that would automatically stop an elevator from falling if the cables holding it failed. The elevators he made in the 1850s were powered by steam. The first passenger elevator he built traveled at the stately speed of one foot every one-and-a-half seconds, which might have been acceptable in the five-story hotel it was installed in but was too slow for much taller buildings. In 1880, the German company Siemens demonstrated the first electric-powered elevator, but it wasn't much faster.[56]

In 1892, fresh from installing streetcar lines in scores of cities, Frank Sprague decided to get into the elevator business. His elevators were the first to have push-button controls. More important, they were fast—the first one he installed in a high-rise building went 10 feet per second—and carried larger loads than any of their predecessors. He installed nearly 600 such elevators (plus the dumbwaiter in the Chicago hotel mentioned above) before selling his company to Otis in 1895.[57]

The skyscrapers built with steel frames and electric elevators provided room for factories and offices filled with thousands of workers. As many as 4,000 jobs might be located in a single city block. Before 1900, most factory workers could still not afford nickel streetcar fares, so this led to high-density housing projects, or tenements. These tenements tended to be four- and five-story buildings because elevators were still too expensive to serve working-class housing.

Thus, the 20th century began with a radical new vision of a city, one that no one could have imagined a century earlier. In this vision, most jobs were concentrated in increasingly tall skyscrapers. Lower-income workers lived in mid-rise developments within walking distance of those skyscrapers. Higher-income workers enjoyed single-family homes or duplexes with yards in compact neighborhoods connected with the urban core by streetcars or, in the biggest cities, rapid-transit lines. Those with the highest incomes lived in large suburban estates connected with the core by steam-powered commuter trains or electric interurban lines.

To this day, this vision of a monocentric city haunts Americans, many of whom think a city isn't a "real city" unless it has a dense downtown job center. Yet the reality is that the forces that created the monocentric city in the early 19th century began to disappear less than a decade after New York City opened its first subway line. As a result, urban plans, including transit plans, based on this vision or one derived from it are doomed to fail.

3. THE GOLDEN AGE OF PASSENGER TRAINS

My heart is warm with the friends I make,
And better friends I'll not be knowing,
Yet there isn't a train I wouldn't take,
No matter where it's going.

—Edna St. Vincent Millay, *"Travel"*

Historian Albro Martin has called the period from 1897 (the end of the recession after the Panic of 1893) to 1920 "the Golden Age of train travel" in America, as the rapid growth in passengers was paralleled by a growth in the number and quality of passenger trains (Figure 3.1). The Great Northern Railway benefitted as much as any railroad from that growth: between 1890 and 1920, Great Northern passenger revenues grew by 9 percent per year.

James Hill's son and successor as president and chairman of Great Northern's board, Louis Hill, was especially enthusiastic about passenger trains. The Northern Pacific and Union Pacific railroads both heavily advertised Yellowstone Park as a tourist destination, and Louis wanted a similar national park on the Great Northern line. With the help of conservationists such as George Bird Grinnell, he persuaded Congress to create Glacier National Park, whose southern border was outlined by the Great Northern Railway.

Figure 3.1
Millions of Passenger Rail Trips

Source: *Historical Statistics of the United States, Millennial Edition, series Df949.*
Note: Passenger train ridership rose rapidly between 1897 and 1920, but then declined just as rapidly after 1920. Even the heavy military traffic during World War II did not return ridership to its 1920 levels.

Louis proceeded to spend more than a million dollars of the railroad's money building and buying a fabulous chain of hotels in and around the park, including one just outside Glacier's northern border in Canada's Waterton National Park. He justified this expense by saying his goal was to increase passenger traffic on Great Northern trains.[1] Hotels offered by Great Northern's Glacier Park Company included the Glacier Park (opened 1913), Many Glacier (1915), and Prince of Wales (1927) hotels. Other lodgings included the Belton (1910), Sperry (1914, sadly burned in 2017), and Granite Park (1914) chalets, all of which Great Northern built, as well as the Lake MacDonald Hotel, which Great Northern purchased in 1930, and several more that no longer exist. With the possible exception of Yellowstone, no other American national park has such an extensive chain of hotels, and certainly none built by a single railroad.

By 1914, more than 13,000 people per year were riding Great Northern trains to visit Glacier National Park. While this was a small share of Great Northern's total number of passengers, the average passenger on all Great Northern trains rode just 64 miles in 1915, while travelers from the east would ride 1,100 miles on the *Glacier Park Express* or another

Great Northern train to get to Glacier. Thus, the park added substantially to the railroad's revenues.

Bolstered by vacationers and business travelers, the *Official Railway Guide* of passenger timetables had grown by 1920 to more than 1,500 pages long and listed more than one thousand different railroads (though not all carried passengers). The index of stations alone filled well over 250 pages, each listing about 350 stations, for a total of more than 90,000 different cities and towns that could be reached by train. Some of those stations were in Canada or Mexico, but the vast majority were in the United States. The timetables in the guide showed more than 9,000 trains per day connecting those cities.

By this time, passenger trains appeared to be an indelible part of American culture. Edna St. Vincent Millay's famous poem, *Travel*, was written during this Golden Age and published in 1921.

The "chuff-chuff" of steam locomotives and "clickity-clack" of wheels crossing joints between the 39-foot-long rails provided a rhythm that musicians found irresistible, in part because the slow acceleration when leaving stations and deceleration when arriving, punctuated by bells and whistles along the way, offered a euphemism for sex. The first song about a train was "The Carrollton March," written in honor of the Baltimore & Ohio Railroad in 1828. Since then, hundreds of composers of both classical and popular music would emulate the sound of trains in their works.

One of the things that made those rhythms possible was slow speeds, as "clickity-clacks" blurred together when trains were fast. The average speed of trains in 1936, the earliest year for which the Interstate Commerce Commission (ICC) kept records, was 34 miles per hour.[2] It was significantly less than that in 1920. One of the fastest trains in the 1920 *Official Guide of the Railways*, New York Central's *Twentieth-Century Limited*, averaged 49 miles per hour between New York and Chicago. The Burlington Route's fastest train in the hotly competitive Chicago–Minneapolis corridor averaged 34 miles per hour. More typical was Great Northern's premiere train, the *Oriental Limited*, which averaged less than 30 miles per hour between St. Paul and Seattle. Many local trains poked along at an average of just 16 miles per hour. Of course, top speeds were somewhat faster than average speeds, but few 1920 trains other than the *Twentieth-Century Limited* and its competitor, the *Broadway Limited,* ever exceeded 50 miles per hour in regular service.

Especially on longer journeys, observed historian Martin, passengers seemed to value comfort, luxury, and safety. "Speed was the enemy of all of these," he noted, "and it is the enemy of track maintenance as well." As a result, "until the commercial airliner began to be taken seriously and the modern highway speeded up vehicular travel, the railroads did not go in heavily for added speed."[3] The fastest trains were ones that had stiff competition: the *Twentieth-Century Limited*, for example, competed against Pennsylvania's *Broadway Limited*, whose line was 50 miles shorter. On the Chicago–Minneapolis route, Burlington's line was about 20 miles longer than those of competitors Milwaukee Road and North Western. Because railroads on these competitive routes tended to schedule their top trains for the same times, the railroad with the longer route had to have the fastest average speeds.

After 30 years of more-or-less steady growth, Great Northern passenger revenue peaked in 1920. In fact, the number of rail passengers, passenger miles, and passenger revenue nationwide all peaked in 1920. Per capita passenger miles peaked at 466 in 1919, remaining at 465 in 1920 (Figure 3.2). Some of these numbers temporarily improved during World War II, but only because of large-scale movements of military personnel.

RALPH BUDD USES HISTORY TO PROMOTE RIDERSHIP

After enjoying a steady increase in passenger travel for more than two decades, railroaders were stunned when rail trips declined 16 percent and passenger miles fell by 20 percent in 1921. The United States was suffering from the postwar depression of 1920–1921, but passenger miles had actually grown slightly from 1919 to 1920, so the huge drop in 1921 was unexpected. Even worse, ridership failed to recover during the Roaring 20s. From 1921 to 1923, passenger miles grew by just 2 percent, and that was the high point of the 1921–1930 decade. By 1929, passenger miles had fallen by 33 percent from 1920, and would fall nearly 50 percent more by 1933.

With James Hill dead and his son Louis losing interest in running the railroad, the person who had to deal with the declining number of passengers on the Great Northern was Ralph Budd. Born on an Iowa farm in 1878, Budd was just 19 when he graduated from college with a degree in civil engineering. He was soon working for the Rock Island Railroad,

Figure 3.2

Per Capita Passenger Train Ridership and Miles

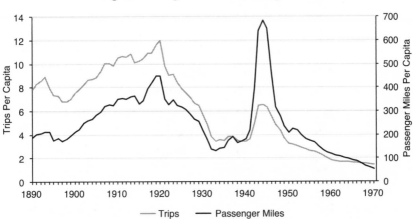

Source: *Historical Statistics of the United States, Millennial Edition*, passenger miles in series Df950, Df951 divided by population in series Aa7.

Notes: The average American rode passenger trains 12 times in 1920, the most of any year in history. Except for a brief surge in World War II military traffic, passenger miles peaked at just under 450 per person in 1919 and 1920. These numbers include commuter trains, which accounted for about 58 passenger miles per capita in the 1920s, declining to about 22 passenger miles per capita in the 1960s.

where he caught the eye of the railroad's chief engineer, John F. Stevens. Stevens had worked for Hill locating the Great Northern's widely envied crossing of the Rocky Mountains in Montana and its not-so-enviable crossing of the Cascades in Washington state.

John Frank Stevens was a distant relative of John Stevens, the ferry boat operator and founder of Hoboken, as all Stevenses trace their ancestry to Airard Fitz-Stephens, a Norman nobleman who commanded the flagship used in William the Conqueror's invasion of England in 1066. An American Stevens genealogy mentions both families, but they do not share a common ancestor in the United States, as both had forebears who emigrated separately from England to the United States in the 17th century.[4]

In 1905, Theodore Roosevelt made John F. Stevens the chief engineer of the Panama Canal, and Stevens brought Budd with him. While Stevens solved problems relating to construction of the canal itself, Budd rebuilt the railroad paralleling the canal. In 1910, Hill tapped Stevens to finish construction of a rail line from Spokane to Portland. Stevens put Budd to work building a branch line to Bend, Oregon, and locating a line from there into California.

When the Union Pacific–Central Pacific, Canadian Pacific, Northern Pacific, and other transcontinental lines were completed, the companies held elaborate ceremonies to commemorate the pounding of the last spike. James J. Hill, however, attended only one last-spike ceremony, and that was for the branch line to Bend built by Ralph Budd. Hill was so impressed with Budd's work that he brought him back to St. Paul. Initially, he named Budd the chief engineer for the Great Northern, but then Hill made him "assistant to the president" and a member of Great Northern's board of directors. By 1916, when Hill died, Louis held the titles of chairman of the board and president, but—according to Albro Martin—Budd was really the de facto president. James Hill had let members of Great Northern's board of directors know that when Louis was ready to step down as president, they should put Budd in his place. In 1919, at the age of 40, Budd became the youngest railroad president in America, just in time to deal with the decline of the passenger train.

James Hill was known for his analytical skills, and his protégé Budd was no different. The average length of Great Northern passenger trips grew from 68 miles in 1915 to 80 miles in 1920, and they continued to grow through the next decade, exceeding 200 miles in 1931. Budd therefore took a two-pronged approach to what everyone in the industry called "the passenger problem": promoting long-distance travel while reducing the costs of short-distance travel.

To encourage long-distance travel, he completely re-equipped the railroad's premiere transcontinental train, the *Oriental Limited*. Debuting in 1924, the new train featured a barber shop, breads and pies baked in the dining car's own kitchen, and a 4 o'clock tea service in the observation car. The barber also served as a valet, pressing men's suits so they could get off the train in fresh clothing. A ladies' maid offered manicures and hair dressing services.

To provide daily service, seven complete trains were needed to operate continuously between Chicago and the Pacific Northwest, and the railroad bought enough equipment for an eighth train to use as a spare.

To publicize the new train, Louis Hill and Budd invited newspaper editors and correspondents from major papers in New York, Chicago, Boston, Philadelphia, St. Louis, and other eastern cities to accompany them on a "chairman's special" using the spare set of equipment. The group spent a day in Glacier Park and time in Great Falls, Wenatchee, and other scenic cities on their way to Seattle. Once in Seattle, they took regular trains to Portland and Seaside on the Oregon coast.

During this trip, Budd realized the emphasis on Glacier Park and other scenic areas gave people the impression that there was "nothing worthwhile looking at" between Minneapolis and the Rocky Mountains. In fact, he knew "the country distinctly has a past and a great many stirring things happened many years before what we call our present civilization came here at all." He thought "it would be quite an accomplishment if we would let the transcontinental traveler know that almost every inch of the way there is something that keeps the country from being dreary and uninteresting."[5]

To reach that goal, Budd sponsored two "historical expeditions" in 1925 and 1926. For each expedition, he invited a dozen or more professional historians and other experts to give lectures along the way, many of which were later printed in various journals. He commissioned the design and construction of six monuments, all of which survive to this day, that would be dedicated during the expeditions. One of them, the Astoria Column in Oregon, receives around 400,000 visitors a year. To give people a greater sense of history, he persuaded the U.S. Post Office to change the names of several towns along the way to commemorate early explorers and pioneers.

He commissioned the publication of more than a dozen booklets providing in-depth information about historic sites, making them available to passengers on the *Oriental Limited* for many years after the expeditions. Most of the booklets were written by Grace Flandrau, a novelist who grew up in the same St. Paul neighborhood and who wrote the same genre of books as F. Scott Fitzgerald. Her 1923 novel, *Being Respectable*, was a national bestseller that Fitzgerald said was "better than [Sinclair Lewis'] *Babbitt*." Yet, after it was published, Flandrau fretted that she had "shot my wad."[6]

Budd and Louis Hill came to her rescue, offering a free pass on Great Northern trains to visit historic sites, use of the caretaker's cabin on Hill's ranch near Glacier Park for writing, and $100 a month (more than $1,100 in today's dollars) if she would write about the region. Intrigued by the opportunity to work "with the delectable and so fabulously intelligent Mr. Budd," Flandrau ended up writing 11 booklets for the railway, most of which related to the historical expeditions, and went on to a new career of writing nonfiction books and magazine articles.[7]

The 1925 Upper Missouri Historical Expedition went from St. Paul to Glacier Park, stopping to dedicate monuments and take historic tours along the way. Paying participants included corporate executives, wealthy investors, writers, and schoolteachers. The first monument was in the tiny town of Falsen, North Dakota, near a spot where the French explorer Pierre Gaultier de la Varennes (known as Verendrye), the English explorer David Thompson, and the Lewis & Clark Expedition all stopped to camp several decades apart. Budd persuaded the Post Office to change the name of the town to Verendrye, and the group dedicated a monument to David Thompson.

A town called Mondak on the Montana–North Dakota border stood near the site of an early Astor trading post named Fort Union. Budd contemplated trying to rebuild a portion of the trading post (which was later done by the National Park Service) but rejected it as too expensive. Instead, he invited 400 Native Americans from 11 different tribes to participate in an "Indian Congress" near the town, which the Post Office obligingly renamed Fort Union.

This congress played a key role in the modern American Indian movement. Since 1899, plains Indians had been confined to reservations, most of which were run by various missionaries intent on converting the Indians to Christianity. When Budd proposed to bring Indians off the reservations to Fort Union, the superintendents of the reservations objected, saying that encouraging Native Americans "to show off their old-time dances and customs in their old-time finery" would interfere with the missionaries' "five-year program" to turn the Indians into farmers and was "absolutely inimical to the religious welfare of the Indian." In other words, allowing the Indians to engage in "old-time customs" would counter the official efforts to suppress their religion and culture.[8] Budd ignored the letter, and although he brought the Indians to Fort Union solely for entertainment, they used the congress as an opportunity to renew intertribal friendships and promote their political goals.[9]

In Glacier Park, Budd wanted to commemorate the discovery of the pass that gave the Great Northern the lowest-elevation crossing of the Rocky Mountains in the United States. Electus Litchfield, the architect who Budd hired to design the six monuments, had proposed a simple sandstone slab, but in this case, Budd overruled him and hired a young artist, Gaetano Cecere, to sculpt a statue of his mentor, John F. Stevens. This was, as far as Great Northern publicists could find, the first time in America that a statue had been erected to a still-living person. Cecere later sculpted statues in the American capitol, the Smithsonian, and the 1939 New York World's Fair.

After the statue's unveiling by his grandson, Stevens gave a speech, saying, "It is a common truism that corporations have no souls," Stevens said. "But I think that you will all agree with me that one corporation has a soul, and that it is wonderfully shown here today, and besides soul, this one has lasting memory."[10]

Although Budd had persuaded several state governors and state historical societies to cosponsor the tour, everyone understood that one of the underlying goals was to promote the railroad. In this regard, it was highly successful, as the tour generated more than 1,200 stories and dozens of laudatory newspaper editorials around the country.

Budd was so excited that he was already planning the next tour as he rode from Glacier Park to the railroad's St. Paul headquarters. This 1926 trip was even more ambitious, beginning in Chicago and extending to Seaside, Oregon. Called the Columbia River Historical Expedition, the group dedicated monuments in Bonners Ferry, Idaho; Wishram, Washington (renamed from Falls Bridge); and Astoria, Oregon. It also presented various tours and pageants in Grand Forks, Spokane, and several other cities along the way. The Fort Union Indian Congress was repeated, and the mayor of Spokane had been so impressed by the 1925 congress that he had the city hold an Indian congress of its own that was timed to coincide with the tour's return from Seaside.

From Wishram, Budd could look across the Columbia River to the Deschutes River canyon, where he had built the rail line to Bend, Oregon. He no doubt pointed this out to his son, John, who had joined the tour while on summer break from studying engineering at Yale University. John wasn't the only student on the tour: Budd had persuaded a nonprofit group called the American Goodwill Society to sponsor 40 American and five French high school students to join the tour. The students were selected based on speeches they gave about the role of French pioneers in America, and a few of the students were invited to repeat their speeches at various tour stops.

On Coxcomb Hill outside of Astoria, the railway built a 125-foot-tall tower modeled after Trajan's Column in Rome. An interior staircase allowed people to reach a viewing platform from which they could see the Columbia River and Pacific Ocean. A painting by Italian artist Attilio Pusterla spiraled around the outside of the column portraying historic scenes of the Columbia River. Pusterla later did frescoes in both the U.S. and Canadian capitol buildings.

The Astoria Column cost $27,000 to construct, or about $300,000 in today's dollars, which was more than Budd was willing to spend. It so happened, however, that Great Northern's largest individual stockholder at the time was John Jacob Astor's great-grandson, Vincent Astor, and Budd persuaded him to contribute most of the cost. The town of Astoria had 10,000 residents, nearly 8,000 of whom turned out for the monument's dedication.

For historians, the tours were certainly a great success. Decades later, Pulitzer Prize–winning historian Michael Kammen wrote that the expeditions were "an exemplary instance of business leadership's playing a major role in history education."[11] But it is difficult to tell whether the expeditions helped boost the railway's passenger business.

In 1925, Great Northern officials suggested that a third expedition might take place in 1927, but it never happened. After the second expedition, Budd wrote Flandrau, saying that "it appears that crops through the Northwest may be poorer than the average," and that no third expedition would take place. In fact, Great Northern freight revenues grew every year from 1924 to 1929, so it is more likely that Budd concluded that the tours weren't boosting the passenger business as much as he hoped.

Great Northern's advertising continued to emphasize the history of the Northwest, at least until Budd left the company in 1931. Budd's selection of historic sites was later vindicated when Congress turned Fort Union, Verendrye, and several of the other sites visited by the tours into national historic sites or other parts of the National Park System. It is quite possible that the expeditions generated some passenger business, but certainly not enough to reduce the decline in passenger miles.

Nor did Great Northern's Glacier Park hotels live up to Louis Hill's hopes and expectations. When he started planning the hotels in 1910, fewer than 5 percent of American families owned an automobile, and Louis could not possibly have foreseen that the moving assembly line pioneered by Henry Ford in 1913 would put cars in the hands of more than half of all American families by 1926.

During much of the 1920s, the hotels covered their operating costs, but they never earned enough money to recover their capital costs.[12] Park attendance grew rapidly, but most tourists arrived by automobile, while the 13,000 who took the train to the park in 1914 grew to just 15,000 in 1929.[13] The good news was that, unlike other rail travel, the numbers of people taking the train to the park didn't significantly decline, at least not until the Depression. Even in the 1920s, most automobile tourists probably could not afford to stay in elegant hotels. The Great Northern built tourist camps for them, but they didn't bring in much revenue and certainly didn't promote passenger train ridership.

Whether or not the historic expeditions or Glacier Park hotels made a difference, the Great Northern did experience an increase in long-distance passenger traffic during the 1920s. Between 1923 and 1929, day coach revenues declined by nearly a third, while sleeping car and parlor car revenues grew by 16 percent. Because fares did not change during this period, the decline in short-distance ridership was partly offset by the growth in long-distance riders.

RALPH BUDD PROMOTES THE BUS

To deal with the loss of short-distance riders, Budd looked for alternative, low-cost means of moving passengers on Great Northern's branch lines. The railway operated trains that terminated at such minor towns as Plentywood, Montana (population 888 in 1920, 1,900 today); Antler, North Dakota (population 265 in 1920, 27 today); and Tintah, Minnesota (population 249 in 1920, 60 today). One solution that many railroads tried was motorcars, individual railcars powered with an internal combustion engine that usually had separate compartments for baggage and passengers. But Budd had a different idea: buses.

Budd recognized the superiority of cars over trains for short-distance travel. "The radius of travel of an individual multiplies many times when he becomes the owner of an automobile," admitted Budd. "His sense of independence and freedom, and his ability to give himself and family enjoyment not otherwise obtainable are sufficient reasons for sacrifices, if necessary, in other directions in order to have a car. For short distance travel the most ideal way yet devised is by private automobile," which accounts for "most of the railways' loss of passenger traffic." While automobiles might be costing the railroads short-distance passengers, Budd pointed out they also gave the railroads business shipping parts to auto makers and finished cars to markets. [14]

For short-distance travel once provided by trains, Budd realized, people who don't have cars or prefer not to drive would find that "the motor bus affords a substitute." Rail motorcars could "take the place of the steam train on light traffic runs" at about a third of the cost of a steam train, noted Budd. But they "are subject to the inherent limitations of any vehicle operating on railroad right of way." While motorcars could only stop at designated stations, buses could pick people up on any highway or street, in front of any office, hotel, or home. [15] Because they were even less expensive to operate than rail motorcars, buses could operate more frequently: for the same cost as one trip per day by steam train or three by motorcar, buses could make at least five trips per day.

In 1925, more than 6,500 bus companies served 7,800 different routes in the United States. Most bus companies were small, owning an average of just two buses. While other railroad executives grumbled that these buses weren't taxed and regulated as much as the railroads, Budd embraced the bus in 1925 by buying Northland Transportation, a midsized bus company in Minnesota. He encouraged Eric Wickman, the company's founder, to remain as its president. With financial backing from Great Northern, Wickman started buying other bus companies, at one point purchasing 160 companies in a few weeks. By the end of 1926, Northland owned about half the buses and bus routes in Minnesota.[16]

Whereas the railroad's logo consisted of a mountain goat encircled by the words "Great Northern," Northland's logo was a moose encircled by "Northland Transportation." The bus company discretely cooperated with the railroad by providing service that ran parallel to Great Northern branch lines that didn't attract enough passengers to support passenger trains, while at the same time not competing with the railroad over its main lines. In a few cases where state regulators required the railroad to provide passenger service that couldn't pay its way, Budd subsidized the bus company to maintain service. Budd was pleased to observe that, when buses replaced branch line passenger trains, ridership increased by 25 percent, showing buses could compete against the automobile better than trains, at least over short distances.[17]

"Under Ralph Budd's leadership the Great Northern became the first railroad to create a comprehensive bus system as an adjunct to its rail service," says historian Douglas Shaw. Other railroads, including the New Haven, Pennsylvania, and Southern Pacific lines, soon followed Budd's example. In 1928, Wickman started a new company called Motor Transit Corporation headquartered in Chicago, eventually renaming it after the logo of one of the companies it purchased, a running greyhound. Great Northern, Pennsylvania, and Southern Pacific were quick to invest in the new company, with Great Northern selling Northland to Greyhound at a healthy profit and then buying back a portion of Motor Transport.[18]

While Budd was finding a low-cost alternative for passengers on short routes, he further upgraded services on long-distance routes. In 1929, he finished a major project left to him by Great Northern Railway founder James J. Hill by building a 7.9-mile-long tunnel under the Cascade Mountains, turning the weakest part of the Great Northern's transcontinental route into one of the railway's strengths. Budd's mentor, John F. Stevens, had located the best route across the Rocky Mountains of any railway in the United States, but the route he located in the Cascades left much to be desired. It was higher in elevation, had steeper grades, more curvature, and received more snow than the Northern Pacific and Milwaukee Road routes to the south.

These problems were only partially solved by a 2.6-mile-long tunnel opened in 1900, seven years after the railway's completion to the Puget Sound. Even with the tunnel, the elevation at the summit was 3,400 feet, compared with 2,852 feet on the Milwaukee Road and 2,564 feet on the Northern Pacific. Heavy snowfalls forced the Great Northern to build miles of snowsheds, yet these failed to protect trains from a serious avalanche that killed 96 railroad employees and passengers in 1910. During his last trip over this route in 1915, Hill told Budd he should build a new, longer tunnel.[19]

Opened in 1929, the new Cascade Tunnel had a maximum elevation of 2,883 feet. Though this was still slightly higher than the Milwaukee or Northern Pacific, the tunnel's length meant most of the heavy snowfalls took place on the mountain above it, not on the tracks. With an interior grade of 1.6 percent, the single-track tunnel wasn't perfect, but it greatly reduced the railroad's operating costs in the Cascade Mountains.

To commemorate the opening of the tunnel, Budd inaugurated a new train called the *Empire Builder*, after the legendary founder of the railroad. The train was not only more luxurious than the five-year-old *Oriental Limited*, it was 10 hours faster between Chicago and Seattle or Portland, thus saving passengers a full business day.

Always eager to use the latest technology, Budd decided to promote the new train with one of the first nationally broadcast radio shows in history. Called *The Empire Builders*, the weekly show hit the airwaves on January 12, 1929, just three weeks after NBC had put together the nation's first coast-to-coast radio broadcast system. The show continued for two-and-half years, with most episodes presenting a story about Northwest history with a regular cast, including a young Italian-American actor named Don Ameche. Of course, many of the shows mentioned Glacier Park and encouraged people to take Great Northern trains to see sights described in the show. Broadcast live from NBC studios, the show pioneered the use of special sound effects to imitate trains and other noises, and many of the devices for creating these effects were developed by Great Northern workers in the company's St. Paul shops.

Budd also finished another of Hill's desired projects, the construction of the line from Bend, Oregon, into California that he had personally surveyed in 1910. Completed in September 1931, this line connected with the Western Pacific and Santa Fe to provide an "Inside Gateway" to compete with Southern Pacific between the Pacific Northwest and southern California. When construction began on this route, Budd had planned to run a section of the *Empire Builder* to San Francisco, but that plan, as so many others, was foiled by the Depression.

Budd was a visionary, but he was also a realist, recognizing that the automobile was the "most ideal way yet devised" for short-distance travel. Rather than bemoan the loss of short-distance rail travelers, he provided them with an economical alternative in the form of buses while concentrating rail services on long-distance travel. This strategy worked in the 1920s, but a new strategy would be needed in the 1930s.

4. THE GOLDEN AGE OF RAIL TRANSIT

You must take the "A" train
To go to Sugar Hill way up in Harlem
If you miss the "A" train
You'll find you missed the quickest way to Harlem
Hurry, get on, now it's coming
Listen to those rails a-thrumming
All aboard, get on the "A" train
Soon you will be on Sugar Hill in Harlem.

—Billy Strayhorn

Downtown job concentration linked with compact suburban neighborhoods by various forms of rail transit led to a golden age of urban transit that coincided almost exactly with the golden age of intercity passenger trains. American cities had 38 times as many miles of electric streetcar lines in 1920 as in 1890. Streetcar (including horsecar and cable-car) ridership grew from about two billion trips in 1890 to nearly 14 billion in 1900. Rapid-transit ridership grew from nearly none in 1890 to two billion trips in 1920. Ridership on steam-powered commuter trains from the suburbs was much smaller but reached about 200 million trips in 1920. In every year from 1905 to 1930, the average urban resident rode transit between 200 and 300 times, compared with 38 trips per urban resident in 2017.[1]

The conditions creating this golden age started to disappear as early as 1913 when Henry Ford began his first moving assembly line to produce his cars. More than anything else, these moving assembly lines would be the downfall of urban rail transit. But even before 1913, the rail transit industry operated in the shadow of several economic problems.

OVERCROWDED RAILCARS

One of the first problems was a complaint later heard about urban freeways: public transit was *too popular.* "The better the service of street railways, the faster does the city population grow, the more do the people ride, and the greater is the congestion of traffic, and the louder the complaints of the public," a writer observed in 1892. The result was that "the demand for rapid-transit facilities increases faster than the supply." Because of overcrowding, "everybody thinks that their own city is in the worst plight, and the managers of their street railways are the meanest men on the face of the earth."[2]

Such overcrowding resulted from the simple fact that transit lines were profitable only when filled to capacity during rush hours. "The profits are in the straps," said transit managers, referring to "straphangers" standing after every seat was filled. "Crowding during rush hour is inevitable," argued August Belmont, the operator of the New York City's first subway. "If a day ever comes when transportation during rush hours is done without crowding, the companies doing it will fail financially."[3]

Railroad-owned commuter trains tended to operate only during rush hours, when it was most profitable for them to do so. But to get the franchises to build their rails in public rights-of-way, the owners and operators of street railways generally had to agree to provide certain levels of service throughout the day. The New York City subway wasn't in a public right-of-way, but the city financed its construction and awarded Belmont the right to operate it, again with the expectation that it would operate throughout the day and not just during the most profitable times.

Belmont was wrong, however, that crowding was inevitable. There are two solutions to periodic high demand: one is queuing (crowding) and the other is pricing. If transit companies had charged, say, 10 cents a ride during rush hours and 5 cents the rest of the day, some of the people traveling during rush hour would have chosen to travel at other times of the day, thereby alleviating the crowding. The companies didn't do so for one simple reason: It wasn't allowed. As public utilities, their fares were strictly regulated by city councils or state public utility commissions. This leads to the second economic shadow over urban transit: the nickel fare.

Transit Regulation

As discussed in Chapter 2, the evolution of transit from omnibuses to horsecars to electric streetcars resulted in a steady reduction in fares from 12.5 cents for the omnibuses to 6.25 cents for horsecars to 5 cents for streetcars. This was partly because electric streetcars cost less to operate than horsecars and omnibuses, but it was also because the 19th century was generally a time of deflation. From the end of the Civil War to 1900, average consumer prices declined by nearly 50 percent. By the end of the century, the nickel fare had become so engrained into the public consciousness that people believed it was some sort of entitlement.

Deflation ended, however, at the end of the 19th century. Prices rose by more than 20 percent between 1899 and 1915, and by 1919, they had increased to more than in 1865. Yet few transit companies were allowed to respond by increasing fares. Most New York City transit services, for example, were required to provide rides for a nickel until 1948, by which time other consumer prices were three times greater than they had been in 1900.

Fare regulation imposed a particular hardship on transit operations because they were labor-intensive, and labor costs grew even faster than consumer prices. Compared with 1900, hourly wages of skilled laborers nearly quadrupled by 1920, and by 1948, they were 10 times as much, while New York City transit fares were still fixed at 5 cents.[4]

Declining Infrastructure

A third shadow threatening the rail transit industry was aging infrastructure. Rails, railcars, and electrical facilities all had expected lifespans of 30 years or less. More than 100 electric streetcar lines had opened in 1890 or before and were due for replacement in 1920. This posed a particular problem for lines built to support real estate developments. If the land sales paid the capital costs and fares only covered the operating costs, there was no money to pay for replacement costs. Some lines not associated with real estate developments had gone bankrupt because of their inability to repay loans for the original construction costs; most were taken over by other companies for pennies on the dollar, earning profits from operations but not enough to rehabilitate lines as they wore out. Even many highly profitable lines would find it difficult to pay for capital replacement, since inflation had greatly increased costs by 1920.

Dual Subways

New York City responded to complaints of overcrowding by proposing to finance more subway lines. Belmont vehemently opposed such plans, fearing that competing lines would take away some of his customers and all of his profits. Belmont's Interborough-Metropolitan controlled the rapid-transit lines in Manhattan and the Bronx, while another company, Brooklyn Rapid Transit, controlled most of the lines in Brooklyn. The city proposed to greatly expand the subway system at a cost of about $289 million, of which the city would pay $152 million, Belmont's company would pay $77 million, and the Brooklyn company would pay $60 million. The city's share was to be recovered by payments made to it by the two companies out of their profits. After several years of negotiations, the two companies agreed to the plan in 1913 on the condition they would be guaranteed profits equal to the profits they earned the last year before the agreement before having to pay anything to the city.[5]

Belmont's company had already been paying the city a share of its profits to recover the costs paid by the city to construct the first subway lines. In 1913, the rapid-transit companies were so profitable, says historian Clifton Hood, that "no one even imagined a situation in which subway revenues might prove inadequate to cover costs." But by the time the new plan went into effect in 1919, the situation was changed: rising automobile ownership combined with rising operating costs meant the companies would return almost nothing to the city. Over the following two decades, the two companies collected more than half a billion dollars in fare revenues yet paid the city only $2.1 million. Instead of recovering its costs, the city ended up losing more than $460 million.[6]

As it turned out, construction of the new subway lines, most of which opened by 1920, didn't hurt Belmont's system. Overall ridership on New York City subways grew by 50 percent between 1920 and 1930, while ridership on Belmont's subways grew by 60 percent.[7]

THE MUNICIPALIZATION DEBATE

Even as New York City was using taxpayer dollars to expand its subway system, a fierce debate raged among politicians and scholars over municipalization—that is, city ownership and operation of urban transit systems. "Your cities in America keep your sewers, which lose money; you keep your streets, which cost money; you keep your parks and other activities which cost money; but you give away your street railways, your gas companies, your electric lighting and your telephone companies which make money," the mayor of Berlin told a conference of American business leaders and city officials. "We in Germany think that is bad business. If any one of you gentlemen as a banker gave away his good loans and only kept his bad loans, very soon he would be bankrupt."[8]

The progressives made the municipalization of street railways one of their major goals at the turn of the 20th century.[9] They believed that, because government wouldn't need to pay dividends to stockholders, it could provide equal or better service to customers at lower cost. After Glasgow, Scotland, took over its private streetcar system in 1894, they bragged it reduced fares by a third even as it improved employee conditions. Progressives also claimed that Glasgow and other municipally built streetcar lines in Britain were better constructed than those in America. However, their main evidence for that was that British cities spent 50 percent more per mile constructing rail lines; it never occurred to municipalization advocates that the higher costs might be due to government inefficiency.[10]

Skeptics of municipalization pointed out that American city dwellers had access to far more streetcar service than British urbanites.

Every American city of 15,000 people or more had a streetcar line in 1902, yet nearly half of British cities between 15,000 and 70,000 people had no streetcars, including at least one city of more than 60,000 residents. Both countries had about 25 million urban residents in 1900, yet the United States had almost 10 times as many miles of streetcar lines. Britain's shortfall was due, critics said, to laws discouraging private construction and the failure of cities to fill the gap.[11]

In 1902, West Seattle was the first American city to buy and operate a private streetcar line.[12] The city of Seattle annexed West Seattle in 1907, and then spent $400,000 (about $7.5 million today) building two other lines that began operation in 1914. This quickly proved to be a disaster because revenues were less than operating expenses.[13] Not discouraged, Seattle voters agreed to buy the city's profitable private streetcar system for $15 million (about $170 million today) in 1918. This was an even bigger disaster, as revenues from the system were insufficient to repay the bonds; there was no money to expand the system; and state courts decided Seattle did not have the authority to subsidize a system that everyone thought would earn a profit.[14] Seattle's cable-car line lasted until 1940 largely because the city did not have the funds to replace it with an electric trolley.

The first American city to build and operate its own transit line was Monroe, Louisiana. The town had fewer than 10,000 residents when its city council decided to build an electric streetcar system in 1904. Two years later, it opened four different lines totaling 8.5 miles.[15]

San Francisco took over a cable-car line in 1912 and converted it to an electric trolley. The San Francisco Municipal Railway built several more lines in the 1910s and 1920s, mainly on routes requiring tunnels that would have been too expensive for a private operator to build. Yet most of the city's streetcar lines remained in private hands until 1944. Southern Pacific ran commuter trains from San Francisco south into San Mateo and Santa Clara counties, but none of the transit lines built by the city ever crossed the county line.

Despite the best efforts of the progressives, municipalization did not make many inroads into the transit industry before 1940. Less than a quarter of one percent of American streetcar miles were municipally owned in 1917. In addition to Monroe, San Francisco, and Seattle, municipalized lines were located in seven other cities and towns: Alexandria, Louisiana; Bismarck, North Dakota; Lincoln, Illinois; Pekin, Illinois; St. Louis, Missouri; Tacoma, Washington; and Yazoo City, Mississippi.[16] Over the next two decades, only two more major cities municipalized transit: Detroit in 1922 and Phoenix in 1925.

DISPERSION

Social reformers supported municipalization because they hoped extension of rapid-transit lines would help disperse working class families then trapped in high-density tenements within walking distance of downtown jobs. Edward Bassett, known as the "father of zoning" because he wrote New York City's first comprehensive zoning ordinance in 1916, also supported the extension of rapid-transit lines to the outer limits of Brooklyn, the Bronx, and Queens.

Bassett was one of many people disturbed by Jacob Riis' 1890 book, *How the Other Half Lives*, which was filled with photographs of immigrant families jammed into four- to six-story tenement buildings at densities as high as 1,000 people per acre.[17] Due to high rents and the cost of living in Manhattan, a "man cannot bring up a family; thus the city becomes a devourer of families." On the other hand, without rapid transit, "If a man wanted to escape to the outland where he could bring up a family of five children and live in the sun [meaning in a one- to two-story home], he has had to travel an hour out and an hour back, sometimes an hour and a half and an hour and a half back—too much to take out of a working man's time."[18]

Rapid transit would solve this dilemma, Bassett argued, allowing even unskilled workers to leave the horrific tenements. Bassett's idea depended on keeping cross-town fares to a nickel (meaning riders would be allowed to transfer from one company's lines to another at no extra cost). Since wages earned by unskilled workers had grown by 50 percent since 1890, many of them could afford nickel fares but not, Bassett feared, dime fares. Considering August Belmont's opposition to the construction of new subway lines, Bassett assumed private developers wouldn't build enough subways or keep the fares low enough to be affordable to unskilled workers, which is why he advocated for government ownership.

Bassett's argument may have fit New York City, where Brooklyn, the Bronx, and Queens served as suburbs of Manhattan. In other cities whose suburbs were separate political entities, city ownership wouldn't be enough, as the city would probably not have the legal authority and certainly would not have the political interest in building to the suburbs. In most such cases, some sort of regional authority would be needed, and such regional transit agencies would not be conceived of for another 50 years.

New York City residents traveled the expanded subway system in heated subway cars at speeds unheard of just a few decades before when travel was by unheated horsecar. They did so at fares that, considering inflation, were less than half of the rates charged by the horsecars. Yet, far from being grateful for this progress, they remained upset about over-crowding. In 1918, they elected as mayor a man who vowed to keep transit fares at 5 cents and to expand the subway system still further.

Mayor Hylan Gets His Revenge

John Hylan had worked as a locomotive engineer for the Brooklyn Union Elevated Railroad (later part of the Brooklyn-Manhattan Transit, or BMT) while studying law in his spare time. In 1897, just before taking the bar exam, Hylan was driving a train at what he said was the prescribed speed around a sharp corner when an official stepped out of a switch tower to cross the tracks and was nearly killed. The official, who Hylan said "was a very old man," was "angered by his narrow escape" and fired Hylan.[19] He soon built up a law practice that paid much better than the railroad, but some people think his grudge against the railroad may have contributed to his future political views towards the rapid-transit companies.

Hylan became mayor of New York in 1918. Three years later, a state body known as the Transit Commission proposed to expand the IRT and BMT subway systems. Whether due to his grudge or because he was influenced by proponents of municipalization, Hylan came out against that plan and proposed instead for the city to build a third subway system that it would both own and operate. In 1924, the state legislature approved a plan allowing the city to build such a system. Although the first lines did not open until 1930, the new system, known as the Independent system, or IND, eventually included seven lines extending 190 miles.[20]

Subway historian Clifton Hood notes that the IND represented more than just municipalization of an activity that was formerly private. The IRT and BMT lines had extended into the outer boroughs of the city, opening them up for real estate development and helping to disperse a population that was once packed into lower Manhattan. But Hylan's goal of competing with the IRT and BMT systems that he hated meant the IND lines did not open up new territory, and instead mainly replaced elevated lines owned by the IRT and BMT. Though it may have been unintentional, Hylan had effectively rejected the policy of dispersal urged by Edward Bassett and other social reformers.

Most early 20th-century transit companies were profitable and opposed to municipalization, but they still had to deal with the twin problems of rising labor costs and aging infrastructure, problems exacerbated by the political obstacles to raising fares. One answer was consolidation of all streetcar lines in each city under one owner. "Neither horsecar lines nor cable lines had any apparent economies of scale," observe economists Ross Eckert and George Hilton, so there was little incentive for one company to control all the lines in a city. However, they add, "the ability to generate electric power in any section of a city, and to use it at central business districts, stadia, fairgrounds, or wherever it might be required, was an economy of scale so great that virtually all major cities experienced a rapid unification of their street railway systems in the late 1890's and the first decade of the [twentieth] century."[21]

INDUSTRY CONSOLIDATION

The development of electric streetcars transformed the transit industry. Where many omnibuses were owned by their drivers, horsecar lines required a large enough investment that entire lines were owned by one company and drivers became employees. At the same time, cities were often served by several different horsecar companies, each running separate lines, as there were no real economies of scale encouraging consolidation.

The electric streetcar introduced such economies of scale because one large power plant cost less than several small ones. Thus, while individual streetcar lines might be built by different companies, often as a part of real estate developments, they were quickly consolidated into one company in each city. For example, Seattle was served by 25 different streetcar companies in 1900; by 1907, they had all merged into one. Often, that company was also the local electrical utility, which saw the streetcars as a captive customer.

Further economies of scale led to the creation of public utility holding companies that owned large numbers of electric utilities and streetcar companies. One of the most famous holding companies was actually a consortium of such companies controlled by Samuel Insull, a business manager who helped Thomas Edison found the Edison General Electric Company, the forerunner of General Electric. In 1892, he moved to Chicago to take over the Chicago Edison Company.

At the time, Chicago Edison was one of nearly 30 electric companies in Chicago. Insull soon realized that he could take over many of these companies and reduce rates by having them pool their power. In 1907, he combined these separate companies into Commonwealth Edison. Over the next two decades, he bought hundreds of other electric companies in dozens of states, building larger power plants to support them. Among the companies he purchased were the Chicago, South Shore & South Bend Railroad; the Chicago, North Shore & Milwaukee; and several other interurban electric railways, plus the Chicago Rapid Transit elevated lines.[22]

By 1929, Insull controlled more than 4,400 different operating companies serving 6.3 million people in 39 states.[23] Insull realized his monopoly control of formerly competitive companies in Chicago would be controversial, but he believed the economies of scale would offset the benefits of competition for consumers, and for many years he proved it by lowering electric rates. To minimize controversy, in 1897 he became the first in the electric industry to support state regulation of his companies, which Illinois began to do in 1914.[24] He was pictured on the cover of *Time* magazine in 1926, and again in 1929, as a hero who helped bring electricity to the masses.

Insull wasn't the first to create holding companies to control electric utilities and streetcars. In 1890, Henry Villard, who had once been president of the Northern Pacific Railroad, formed the North American Company, initially to control the power company and street railways of Milwaukee. Eventually, North American acquired utilities and street railways in other parts of Wisconsin, Kansas, Illinois, Iowa, Missouri, and even Washington, D.C. In 1905, General Electric created a holding company called Electric Bond and Shares that bought electric utilities and streetcar companies across the country, from Florida to Washington.

Many other holding companies soon followed these examples. In 1906, Associated Gas and Electric Company was formed to own electric companies, streetcar companies, and interurban lines in New Jersey, New York, Pennsylvania, and other Atlantic states. In 1910, the Cities Service Company was incorporated and would eventually own electric utilities and streetcar companies in Arizona, Arkansas, Colorado, Maryland, Mississippi, Missouri, New Mexico, North Carolina, Ohio, and Oklahoma. In 1914, the American Water Works and Electric Company was formed to control utilities and interurban rail lines in Maryland, Pennsylvania, and West Virginia. In 1917, the Wateree Electric Company was formed to control electric and streetcar companies in North and South Carolina; in 1924, it changed its name to Duke Power. In 1925, the Central Public Service Company was formed to purchase electric companies and streetcar lines in a number of states, including Michigan, Ohio, Oregon, Virginia, and West Virginia. In 1929, Commonwealth & Southern Corporation was formed to buy companies in many Southern states.

One of the more interesting holding companies was Stone & Webster, an engineering firm formed in 1889. Though it initially provided engineering and construction services to electric companies, the partners soon realized they could take over and run some of those companies. In the wake of the Panic of 1893, it acquired the Nashville Electric Light and Power Company. Soon thereafter, it owned electric companies, streetcar companies, and interurban electric railways in Florida, Georgia, Iowa, Kentucky, Louisiana, Massachusetts, Michigan, Texas, Virginia, and Washington.

Stone & Webster didn't just manage the companies; it helped build the infrastructure they needed, including power plants and power lines. The company often accepted as payment for its services stock in the client companies, which is how it came to control so many. In 1915, a company engineer named Charles Birney helped design a small streetcar he called the safety car, because it would move only when the doors were fully closed, and the driver held down a pedal called a deadman control. Soon known as Birney cars, they used a pay-as-you-board system, saving the cost of a separate fare collector. The cars could be used on lightly traveled lines or to provide increased frequencies on more heavily used routes.

While many previous streetcars were custom built in small numbers to the specifications of streetcar companies, the Birney cars were mass produced by several manufacturers, and so were sometimes called the Ford of the streetcar industry. Production began in 1917, peaked at nearly 1,700 cars in 1920, and continued until 1930.

In addition to controlling streetcar companies, holding companies such as Insull's helped shape urban areas. Although Insull was a disciple of Thomas Edison, who favored the use of direct current (DC) power, he quickly realized the advantages of Nicholas Tesla's alternating current (AC) power, which, unlike DC, could be transmitted for hundreds of miles. This allowed Insull to string lines from his power plants to many relatively remote communities, which, in turn, allowed people to spread out further from the central cities. As historian David Nye observed, electricity and the automobile enabled millions of Americans to fulfill "a centuries-old preference for single-family dwellings."[25]

THE MOTOR BUS

Another answer to the transit industry's economic problems came in the form of a new technology: the motorized bus. Americans still used the term "omnibus" when motorized buses were first introduced in the early 20th century. Whatever they were called, most streetcar companies were reluctant to adopt them, partly because many were controlled by electric companies and partly because the operating costs of early buses were higher than those of electric streetcars.

The first motor bus operation was a unique case: due to the opposition of local residents—including, ironically, several railroad executives—New York's Fifth Avenue was the only avenue in Manhattan lacking horsecar service along at least some portion of its length. Instead, the Fifth Avenue Coach Company ran omnibuses on the street. In 1900, the company tested a battery-powered omnibus (which the *New York Times* called a *'bus*, with the apostrophe indicating an abbreviated form of omnibus) to the avenue.[26]

The experiment was apparently not successful, and in 1905, the company tried a gasoline-electric hybrid bus designed by General Electric, in which a 45-horsepower gasoline motor turned a generator supplying power to electric motors. This worked better, and by 1907, the company had replaced all of its horses and horse-drawn omnibuses with gasoline-electrics. The fare of 10 cents was supposed to be high enough to allow the company to earn a profit even as it supposedly provided frequent enough service for all passengers to have seats. By 1908, its standard bus was an open-topped double-decker, with 16 seats downstairs and 18 seats on the upper deck, and it ran them up and down the avenue every three minutes.[27]

As mentioned, Fifth Avenue Coach was an unusual case because rails weren't allowed on that avenue. It took two more decades of technological improvements, but—as will be described in Chapter 6—by 1927, buses were an effective alternative to streetcars.

5. THE SILVER AGE OF PASSENGER TRAINS

I am riding on a limited express, one of the crack trains of the nation.
Hurtling across the prairie into blue haze and dark air go fifteen
all-steel coaches holding a thousand people.
(All the coaches shall be scrap and rust and all the men and women
laughing in the diners and sleepers shall pass to ashes.)
I ask a man in the smoker where he is going and he answers: "Omaha."

—Carl Sandburg, *"Limited"*

On May 26, 1934, a gleaming silver train made a nonstop journey of more
than a thousand miles from Denver to Chicago in just over 13 hours.
Thousands of Americans turned out along the Chicago, Burlington &
Quincy right of way to see a train unlike any they had ever seen before.
At a time when most passenger trains were painted dark green or brown
to hide the dirt from coal smoke, this one's mirror-like finish reflecting
the sun was made of stainless steel, a material still unfamiliar to most
people in 1934, and it was powered by a relatively clean diesel engine.
At a time when passenger trains averaged less than 34 miles per hour, this
one made its trip at twice that speed and reached top speeds of well over
110 miles per hour. At a time when people had to open the windows of
train cars crossing the prairie on warm spring days, this one was fully air
conditioned.

Everything about this train, from its power plant to its very name, was the brainchild of Ralph Budd. In the early 1930s, it was Budd alone who realized that several new technologies could revolutionize the railroad industry, particularly the passenger train. He combined these technologies into a single package that would help the rail passenger business recover from the doldrums caused by the rise of the automobile and the Great Depression.

Having completed the projects left to him by James J. Hill, Budd departed Great Northern at the end of 1931 and on January 1, 1932, became president of the Chicago, Burlington & Quincy Railroad. Though Great Northern and Northern Pacific each owned 48.6 percent of the Burlington Route, the Burlington was actually larger than either of its parent companies, operating more miles of track and earning more revenues and profits. It also ran many more passenger trains, including trains on the Chicago–Omaha–Denver, Chicago–Twin Cities, Chicago–Kansas City, Kansas City–St. Louis, Denver–Dallas, and Dallas–Houston routes, among many others. Like other railroads, its passenger revenue had been declining since 1920, falling by 82 percent by 1932.

In taking the job, Budd moved from St. Paul to Chicago, a city that would celebrate its 100th birthday in 1933 with the Century of Progress Exposition. This fair gave railroads and manufacturers an opportunity to show off their latest technologies.

One of those technologies was metallurgy. Railroad passenger cars built in the 1920s were made of ordinary carbon steel, which rail historian John White notes was a "relatively weak, highly corrosive material."[1] Coaches weighed 65 to 80 tons, and sleeping cars and diners weighed 80 to 90 tons. Lighter-weight materials would allow for faster accelerations, higher speeds, and lower fuel costs. Less-corrosive materials would reduce maintenance costs and give cars longer lifespans. So when Pullman came to the Chicago fair with an all-aluminum car weighing only 37 tons, many in the rail industry took note.

Budd, however, was more intrigued by a different material. Stainless steel had been developed in 1912 by Germany's Krupp Steel Works but not publicly revealed until 1920. The 18-8 stainless steel—18 percent chromium, 8 percent nickel, and 74 percent low-carbon steel—that is used in modern-day pots and pans was developed in England in the 1920s. Stainless steel was not only rustproof, it was two to three times stronger than ordinary steel or aluminum. Stainless steel was more expensive, but its only other disadvantage was that ordinary welding broke down its crystalline structure, reducing its strength and making it vulnerable to corrosion. As a result, Europeans used it mainly for small items such as kitchen utensils, surgical and dental instruments, and mirrors.

To insure a place in the record books as the world's tallest building, Walter Chrysler and architect William Van Alen topped the Chrysler Building in New York City with a stainless-steel cap in 1929.[2] However, this was purely decorative, and did not make use of the alloy's tremendous strength. It did, however, inspire Edward Budd, whose company built auto bodies for Dodge and other car makers, to think about the structural uses of the metal. First, his company developed a way to weld two sheets of stainless steel together without weakening the metal by passing a high electric current through the sheets for a fraction of a second. Budd called this process *shot welding*, apparently a portmanteau of *spot* welding and electric *shock*.

Because the Depression had greatly reduced orders for his automobile bodies, he next turned to aircraft and railroads. His company designed and built an airplane out of stainless steel but couldn't find a buyer. He also built some experimental railcars. Being used to automobiles, he used pneumatic rubber tires to improve comfort and minimize the impact on rail joints. While the Pennsylvania, Reading, and Texas & Pacific railroads tried them, the rubber tires were unsuccessful, and some of the cars were scrapped within a year, while the others saw their rubber tires replaced with steel wheels.

In September 1932, just nine months after taking the reins at the Burlington, Ralph Budd visited Edward Budd's factory in Philadelphia. The two had never met, and it would take a later biographer to uncover the fact that they were distant relatives.[3] After examining one of the gasoline-powered railcars, the railroad executive was impressed with the metal, though less so with the engine and rubber tires.

The Chicago fair introduced Budd to the latest example of another new technology: diesel engines. The General Motors exhibit at the fair featured an entire moving assembly line making Chevrolets. Fairgoers could order a car at the beginning of their visit, watch it being made, and drive it away when they left the fair. The assembly line was powered by electricity generated by two 600-horsepower diesel engines displayed in the GM exhibit.

The Great Northern under Ralph Budd had purchased an early "oil-electric" locomotive in 1925. Although advertising showed the locomotive pulling a train like the *Oriental Limited*, the two 300-horsepower engines in the locomotive weren't powerful enough to pull multiple cars at passenger train speeds, and Great Northern used the locomotive exclusively as a switch engine. Budd also knew about a large diesel engine the railway had purchased to pump fresh air into the new Cascade Tunnel during construction, but it weighed far too much to be used in a railroad locomotive. The trade-off between power and compact size was a result of the weak steel alloys of the day that couldn't contain internal combustion without being thick and heavy.

Those older diesels operated on a four-stroke cycle in which each cylinder fired only every other revolution of the crankshaft. GM's new diesel used a two-stroke cycle in which each cylinder fired every revolution, nearly doubling the engine's horsepower but also increasing the heat generated by the engine. The engine used a new steel alloy called Cromansil that was much stronger and could handle heat better than ordinary steel, resulting in a lighter motor. Whereas the diesel engines of the 1920s weighed at least 80 pounds for each unit of horsepower they produced, GM's new diesel weighed just 22 pounds per horsepower.[4]

Much of the work on that diesel had been done by Richard Dilworth, a completely self-taught engineer who claimed to have gone to school for only a half day in his life. Born in Seattle in 1885, he left home at the age of 12 and took a series of jobs that taught him to be a machinist, electrician, and engine builder. In 1926, he was made chief engineer of the Electro Motive Corporation, which manufactured railcars powered by its own electric motors that in turn were powered by gasoline engines manufactured by the Winton Engine Company.[5] In 1930, GM bought both Electro Motive and Winton, and put Dilworth and his associates to work designing a better diesel engine.

When Budd saw this engine at the fair, he said he was "immediately . . . set afire," because he realized the new diesels were small and light enough to fit in a locomotive and powerful enough to pull a train. Within two months of the fair's opening, he had ordered a diesel from GM and a stainless-steel, three-car train—with steel, not rubber, tires—from Edward Budd. Like the diesels at the fair, but unlike a diesel-powered automobile, the engines wouldn't directly drive the wheels when installed in a locomotive but instead turned a generator that powered electric motors. For this reason, they were called oil electrics in the 1920s and diesel electrics in the 1930s after the German stigma had faded.

A third technology displayed at the fair also became a vital part of Budd's new train: air conditioning. Although Pullman had experimented with mechanical air conditioning of a few sleeping cars as early as 1927, the Baltimore & Ohio was the first railroad to install air conditioning in a passenger car in 1930. The system was so successful that the railroad completely air-conditioned one of its trains between New York and Washington by 1931 and its New York–St. Louis and New York–Chicago overnight trains in 1932. In 1933, the railroad displayed an entire air-conditioned train at the fair.

Even more than metallurgy or diesels, air conditioning was the technology most essential for Budd's vision for passenger trains. In non-air-conditioned trains, people opened the windows for fresh air in hot weather. That was fine for trains going 30 miles per hour, but a train with open windows going 80 or 90 miles per hour would create uncomfortable and possibly dangerous conditions for passengers. Budd understood this: Instead of the traditional open platform used on the *Oriental Limited* and other early 20th-century luxury trains, the faster 1929 *Empire Builder* put a completely enclosed solarium at the rear of its last car.

The final factor in Budd's new train was less a technology than a style: streamlining. Many of the buildings in the Century of Progress Exposition were in the streamline moderne style. The aluminum car Pullman exhibited at the fair, known as the Railplane, was billed as the first streamlined passenger car. Designed by aircraft engineer William Stout, who also designed the Ford Trimotor and several highly aerodynamic concept cars, the Railplane was essentially the fuselage of an airplane on rails.

The stainless-steel railcars Edward Budd had previously built weren't streamlined and were rather ugly. Fortunately, the Budd Company hired architect Paul Cret to help design the Burlington train. Cret's previous design of the Folger Shakespeare Library in Washington, D.C., combined neoclassical and art deco styles. With the help of Cret and his firm, Budd's new train was carefully streamlined both for eye-catching appeal and to reduce wind resistance.

John Harbeson, a young architect working for Cret, designed the exterior of the train, including the distinctive shovel-nose power car. The Cret firm also designed the fluting of the exterior stainless steel, which was not only visually striking but added to the car's strength. In addition to the visible portions of the train, the Budd Company streamlined the undercarriage as well. Wind tunnel tests at the Massachusetts Institute of Technology found the streamlining reduced drag by up to 47 percent at high speeds. Instead of the dark tones found in non-air-conditioned cars likely to be made dirty by coal smoke, Paul Cret's interior featured pastel colors and indirect lighting.

Ordinary steel passenger cars had grown to be 80 feet long held up by a large metal beam or sill that ran the length of the car. But stainless steel was strong enough to provide its own structural support. The stainless steel in the train's corrugated roof was only about one-fiftieth of an inch thick—about the same as a business card—yet it served the same structural purpose of a sill, thus saving that much more weight.

To save even more weight, the train had a smaller profile than standard passenger cars. Where a typical heavyweight coach was about 14 feet tall, Budd's train was just 12 feet, 7 inches tall. The entire train, including engine, baggage compartment, and passenger compartments, weighed about 82 tons, or roughly the same as a single Pullman car or heavyweight coach. With 72 seats, the weight per seat was less than 2,300 pounds, vs. well over 6,000 pounds per seat, including the weight of the locomotive, in a typical local steam train.

COMPETING STREAMLINERS

Both Budds were under pressure because the Union Pacific, inspired by the Pullman Railplane, announced it had ordered its own streamlined train from

Pullman. Union Pacific and Burlington competed directly with one another between Omaha and Denver and between Kansas City and Denver. Pullman would deliver its train a few weeks before Budd did, thus earning Union Pacific the distinction of having the nation's first modern streamliner. However, Union Pacific's train was inferior to Burlington's in several key ways.

First, its aluminum body was far more prone to corrosion than stainless steel. The body was painted, but Union Pacific ended up retiring its first streamliner after just six years, and it scrapped its first seven aluminum streamlined trains by 1953. Burlington's first diesel-powered train was still going strong after more than three million miles and 25 years of nearly continuous service, and it, along with many other trains and cars built by Budd in the 1930s, still exists.

Second, unwilling to trust GM's untested diesel, Union Pacific used a less efficient distillate engine (also built by GM) in its train, in which the fuel was ignited by spark plugs. Third, the exterior design was far less appealing, and the yellow-and-brown paint far less striking than Budd's stainless steel. Similarly, the Pullman-designed interiors were an evolutionary improvement on the Pullman cars preceding it, but not the revolutionary change Paul Cret designed into the Burlington train. To cap it off, someone at Pullman or Union Pacific elected to put a tiny kitchen in the tail of the train, obstructing the view of everyone who enjoyed watching the scenery roll by from a rear-facing window or platform. Budd, meanwhile, wrapped windows around a distinctive parabolic rear end, setting the pattern for scores of observation cars built over the next two decades.

Burlington needed to make one more decision before presenting its new train to the public: what to call it. Union Pacific had cornered the market on the term "streamliner," and Ralph Budd wanted something different. Another Burlington executive suggested using the last word in the dictionary to indicate it was the last word in passenger trains. The last word wasn't very interesting, but Budd recalled from Chaucer's *Canterbury Tales* that Zephyrus was the god of the West Wind and a symbol of Spring renewal. Because Burlington's slogan was "Everywhere West" and the goal of the train was to renew passenger service, he suggested the name *Zephyr*. The *New York Times* goggled at the thought of a railroad president reading Chaucer, but that was typical of Budd.

When introduced to the public in February 1934, Union Pacific's streamliner excited national interest because it was so different from steam trains. Still, many previous passenger trains had been painted yellow, while few people had ever seen stainless steel before except perhaps for decorative use. So when the *Zephyr* appeared two months later, it nearly eclipsed the Union Pacific train. Budd delivered the train to the Burlington in Philadelphia on April 18, after which the train took a five-week tour of nearly 50 cities, where it was inspected by more than 500,000 people. On May 24, the train arrived in Denver, just in time for Ralph Budd's greatest publicity stunt ever.

Chicago's 1933 Century of Progress fair was so successful that the city decided to repeat it in 1934. At 7:04 on the morning of May 26, the fair's opening day, the *Zephyr* left Denver on a daring, 1,015-mile trip to Chicago. Both Budds were on board, along with other Burlington, GM, and Budd Company officials and members of the press. The silver streak was given priority over all other trains, and Burlington put guards at every one of the nearly 1,700 grade crossings along the route. At the time, the Burlington's fastest train on the route took 26 hours, but Ralph Budd went so far as to promise officials at the Century of Progress fair that the *Zephyr* would arrive within 14 hours to be part of a transportation pageant.

The train easily sustained speeds of 100 miles an hour or more for one 19-mile stretch, and 112.5 miles per hour for three miles. To prove how smoothly the train ran, Ralph Budd pulled out a straight-edge razor and gave himself a shave. The train arrived in Chicago in just 13 hours and 5 minutes, easily breaking records for the longest nonstop train trip. Because of the train's economy and the low cost of diesel oil, fuel for the entire trip cost less than $15.[6] The *Zephyr*'s triumphant on-time entry into the Century of Progress pageant earned front-page headlines in the *New York Times*, *Chicago Tribune*, *Denver Post*, and many other papers.

After the exposition, Budd put the *Zephyr* to work between Kansas City and Lincoln, Nebraska. The steam train it replaced took nearly seven hours and carried an average of 25 people, but on a five-hour schedule, the *Zephyr* carried an average of 45 paying passengers. Not only did it often fill all 72 seats, people sometimes stood in the aisles to ride the new train, leading Burlington to order another car. People were clearly attracted to the train by more than just the five-hour timetable, because when the *Zephyr* was temporarily replaced by a steam train running on the same schedule, ridership dropped by 30 percent. While increasing revenues, the train also saved money, as it cost just 34 cents a mile to operate, compared with 64 cents for the steam train it replaced.

Budd's vision of passenger trains took the rail industry by storm. Between 1934 and the beginning of World War II, railroads ordered 90 new streamlined passenger trains from manufacturers. Half of them were built by Budd of stainless steel, and three-fourths of them were powered by diesels. None were powered by a distillate engine as used in Union Pacific's first streamliner. By 1941, Burlington itself had a dozen streamlined zephyrs covering such routes as Chicago–Twin Cities, Chicago–Denver, and Denver–Dallas.

Stainless steel was more expensive than ordinary steel, but many railroads wanted the look of stainless steel even if they weren't willing to pay Budd's higher prices. Pullman was too proud to license Budd's shot-welding process, so it made most of its new streamliners from Corten steel, which was strong but still rust prone, and bolted fluted stainless-steel panels on the outside to imitate Budd's fluted cars. These "ersatz stainless steel" cars, as historian John White called them, cost about $50,000 each compared with $65,000 for a Budd stainless-steel car. This eventually proved not to be a successful economy measure because rainwater seeped in behind the panels and rusted the Corten steel, forcing railroads to remove the panels and do major repairs. Meanwhile, Union Pacific's bet on aluminum proved wrong, as just 13 of the new trains were made of it, and most were scrapped by 1955.

Nor were diesels absolutely essential, as 22 of the new trains were powered by steam locomotives, which cost less to buy but more to operate than diesels. The Chicago & North Western, Milwaukee Road, New Haven, New York Central, Norfolk & Western, Pennsylvania, Santa Fe, and Southern Pacific railroads ordered new steam locomotives covered with streamlined or semi-streamlined shrouds. Other railroads added shrouds to existing steam locomotives. Out of the more than 100,000 steam locomotives built for American railroads, fewer than 215 were streamlined in some way, but these provided highly attractive images that remain etched in people's memories today.

In some cases, the streamlined steam locomotives were just for show, and the trains were not significantly faster. But the Milwaukee Road's steam-powered *Hiawatha* often exceeded 100 miles per hour on its route between Chicago and the Twin Cities. The railroad, which was in receivership, saved money by building its own fleet of streamlined passenger cars and purchasing streamlined steam locomotives built especially for that train. Partly because it served a more heavily populated corridor, the *Hiawatha* carried more passengers and earned more profits than the *Twin Zephyrs* it competed with. However, the Milwaukee and other railroads quickly shifted to diesel after the war.

Milwaukee Road probably chose steam to power the *Hiawatha* in 1935 because the little diesel engine used in the *Zephyr* was not powerful enough to pull the full-sized train the rail line wanted to run. Although steam locomotives could go as fast as diesels, they had to stop frequently for water. This was an issue for railroads such as the Santa Fe that crossed hundreds of miles of desert on their way to California.

Another problem with steam locomotives was that they caused significant wear and tear on the tracks at high speed. "When a steam locomotive heavy enough to pull a long train went 70, it did one of two things," writes Richard Dilworth's biographer. "Either the wheels pounded the track, often leaping clear of the track for a fraction of an inch, or the nose of the monster began swaying back and forth. If you corrected for one weakness, you enhanced the other. Until the high drivers and connecting rods were eliminated, it would never be any different."[7]

To compete with steam, Dilworth increased the number of cylinders in GM's diesel engine from six to eight, boosting it to 900 horsepower. He then put two of these in one locomotive, with each engine turning a generator powering one of the sets of wheels. Such an 1,800-horsepower locomotive was used to power the six-car *Twin Zephyrs* in December 1936. Another 1,800-horsepower unit with the help of a 16-cylinder, 1,200-horsepower booster unit powered the 10-car *Denver Zephyr* that began operating in November 1936.

Putting two of these units back-to-back created a 3,600-horsepower locomotive, which was enough to pull almost any passenger train. Two GM demonstrators of this configuration were tested by the Baltimore & Ohio and Santa Fe railroads in 1935. Santa Fe was impressed enough that it ordered 11 1,800-horsepower units, clad in stainless steel, from GM. At the same time, it ordered enough stainless-steel passenger cars from Budd to provide three trains between Chicago and Los Angeles, along with trains from Los Angeles to San Diego and Bakersfield to Oakland.

The Union Pacific streamliners *City of Portland, City of Los Angeles,* and *City of San Francisco* already operated from Chicago to the coast. Like the original streamliner, these had a smaller profile than standard trains. The Santa Fe trains, however, were the first full-profile streamliners, allowing plenty of room for luggage racks, upper and lower berths, and other fixtures common in older cars.

On October 14, 1935, during a press run, the *Mark Twain Zephyr*—the fourth train built by Budd for the Burlington—set a world record by sustaining a speed of 122 miles per hour for 3 miles. Just over a year later, on October 23, Burlington took the new 10-car *Denver Zephyr* on another record-setting run from Chicago to Denver. The train covered the 1,017 miles in 12 hours and 12 minutes, for an average speed of 83 miles per hour. As Ralph Budd pointed out, Denver was 4,700 feet higher in elevation than Chicago, so the 1934 run to Chicago went downhill, but the 1936 run back to Denver was faster even though it had to go uphill.

These were publicity stunts, but many of the zephyrs were fast in actual service as well. The *Denver Zephyr* took 16 hours to travel between Chicago and Denver, 10 hours less than its steam predecessor, for an average speed of nearly 65 miles per hour. In 1940, Burlington reduced the scheduled time for the *Twin Zephyrs* from Chicago to St. Paul to just six hours, for an average speed of 71 miles per hour.[8] For many years, the *Twin Zephyrs,* which frequently hit top speeds of over 100 miles per hour, were the fastest scheduled trains in the world over parts of their route. Milwaukee's *Hiawatha* and Chicago & North Western's *400* matched the *Zephyr's* time but not its average speed, as their routes were a few miles shorter.

MAKING PASSENGER TRAINS PROFITABLE AGAIN

Despite their initial high cost and the economic doldrums of the 1930s, the new streamlined trains proved to be highly profitable. "It would appear that the solution of the problem" of declining passenger traffic "has been found in the streamline train," concluded a 1938 report by Coverdale and Colpitts, an engineering consulting firm.[9] The report reviewed dozens of the new trains and found that they not only attracted new riders but also earned more than twice their operating costs. The report didn't speculate on whether the operating profits were sufficient to cover the capital and fixed costs, but the fact that the Burlington, Union Pacific, Milwaukee, and other railroads kept buying new streamlined trains suggested they did.

The original *Zephyr* certainly did, as its operating profits in its first year were 37 percent of its capital costs. It continued to serve Burlington through 1960, and during most of those years it earned similar profits, thus easily covering its capital costs and its share of fixed costs.

Between 1933 and 1937, the number of passengers riding Burlington trains grew by 22 percent, while passenger miles grew by 52 percent, indicating people were using trains for longer trips. Burlington's passenger revenues grew by 45 percent. "While better business conditions were largely responsible for this improved showing," commented Burlington's 1936 annual report, "the inauguration of *Zephyr* service contributed substantially."[10] Because rail passenger revenues for the nation as a whole grew by just 34 percent in the same time period, the zephyrs probably did boost Burlington's business.

The stainless-steel streamliners had other repercussions as well. Because the *Denver Zephyr* and Santa Fe's *Super Chief* were both overnight trains, they included sleeping cars. Pullman, which had a virtual monopoly on sleeping car operations in the United States, objected to operating sleeping cars built by another manufacturer. It reluctantly agreed to operate the cars on these two trains provided that the Burlington and Santa Fe railroads promised to place all future sleeping car orders with Pullman. Santa Fe gave in and ordered sleeping cars with stainless-steel panels from Pullman, but Burlington refused, and instead added heavyweight sleeping cars painted silver with shading to imitate fluting to its overnight zephyrs.

Together, Budd, Burlington, and Santa Fe complained to the federal government about Pullman's heavy-handed tactics, and in 1940, the Justice Department filed an antitrust lawsuit against Pullman. Three years later, a federal district court judge in Philadelphia ordered Pullman to sell either the manufacturing company or the operating company. In 1947, Pullman sold the operating company to a consortium of 57 different railroads. The company also decided to sell more than 600 streamlined passenger cars and several thousand heavyweight cars to the railroads, so the operating company dealt only with operations, not car ownership.

The breakup of the Pullman monopoly on sleeping cars was a mixed blessing for the railroads. On one hand, it led to more innovative passenger car construction. On the other hand, when the sleeping cars were all owned by Pullman, it could send the cars to wherever they were needed most, such as the Northwest during the summer and Florida during the winter. This became more difficult after railroads owned the cars, forcing railroads to keep more cars than they needed on a year-round basis.

In 1941, the American Association of Engineering Societies awarded Ralph Budd the John Fritz Medal, considered the highest award given to an engineer. Previous recipients of the medal had included George Westinghouse, Alexander Graham Bell, Thomas Edison, Alfred Nobel, Orville Wright, and Guglielmo Marconi. In 1925, Budd himself had presented the award to his mentor, John Stevens. The 1941 award specifically mentioned Budd's "vision and courageous leadership in advancing the technological frontiers of high speed railroad transportation."

Budd's insight about the ability of diesels to power railroad trains proved particularly prescient. In 1933, not even many GM officials thought diesels would make serious inroads into the steam locomotive's dominance over the railroads any time soon. The success of the *Zephyr* led GM to accelerate its research program, and by 1938, Richard Dilworth had produced a new engine called the 567, so-named because each cylinder displaced 567 cubic inches.

In 1939, Dilworth put a 1,350-horsepower, 16-cylinder version of this engine in a unit it called the FT. It sent four of these units coupled together as one locomotive on a tour of the nation, demonstrating to the railroads that a diesel could easily be superior to steam. Nearly two dozen railroads, including Burlington and Great Northern (but, curiously, not Union Pacific), almost immediately ordered more than one thousand FTs. Counting improved versions F2 through F9, GM eventually made more than 7,600 F units. In less than two decades after the first FT, diesels had almost completely replaced steam on American railroads in one of the most remarkable technological transitions in history.

A few railroads briefly resisted the diesel revolution, mostly because they were located in coal country and could purchase it more cheaply than diesel oil. To overcome the problem of reciprocating steam locomotives pounding the track, the Pennsylvania, Norfolk & Western, and Chesapeake & Ohio lines—all coal-hauling railroads—experimented with steam turbines after World War II. But it was too late: Dilworth's FT and later locomotives had so many advantages over steam that they took over everywhere, and the few coal-hauling railroads that tried to stick with steam were unable to compete with the benefits of GM's mass production methods.

Budd's tenure at Burlington was notable in other fields as well. In 1929, Burlington emulated its parent railroad, Great Northern, in starting its own bus company. By 1935, the Burlington Transportation Company had extended bus service to Los Angeles and San Francisco, well beyond Burlington's rail operations. In 1936, Burlington and Santa Fe bus subsidiaries agreed to form the National Trailways Bus System. Where Greyhound consisted of separate operating companies, most of which were majority owned by Greyhound, Trailways was a consortium of independent companies that coordinated schedules and marketing. Budd therefore participated in the creation of both national bus systems.

THE FIRST DOME CAR

Rail passenger ridership boomed during World War II, but wartime restrictions prevented railroads from adding to their streamliner fleets. Near the end of the war, however, many began ordering new equipment. Great Northern inaugurated the streamlined *Empire Builder*, the first postwar overnight streamliner, in February 1947. Even before then, Budd had one more innovation to add to his growing fleet of zephyrs.

In July 1944, Cyrus Osborn, the general manager of GM's Electro-Motive Division, rode in a diesel locomotive cab and later the cupola of a caboose on the Denver & Rio Grande Western's scenic route through the Rocky Mountains, and he realized these seats had a much better view of the scenery than from inside a passenger car. When he returned to his office in Lagrange, Illinois, he asked his engineers if they could put a dome on top of a passenger car to give travelers a 360-degree view. They not only decided they could, they spent $25,000 building a model of such a car.

Osborn showed the model to his friend, Ralph Budd, and told him GM would not patent the idea so that the railroads and railcar manufacturers could freely use it. Budd immediately ordered his shops to convert a stainless-steel coach into a dome car. Introduced in July 1945, the car proved extremely popular, leading Budd to quickly order two dozen dome cars from the Budd Company. The company eventually owned 45 such cars, more than any other railroad. Over the next decade, Budd and other manufacturers built a total of 227 dome cars, and railroads rebuilt nine others from existing flat-topped cars. These cars were built for about 30 American and Canadian streamliners and would end up serving another dozen or so trains as some railroads downsized their dome fleets. When first introduced, the domes proved so popular that when one railroad added them on a particular route, railroads competing in that corridor were often forced to quickly add them to their trains.

While speed was meant to attract business travelers, domes were designed to attract tourists. The first Burlington train to be equipped with domes was the *Twin Zephyr*, noted at the time for being the fastest train in the world but also a train whose route up the Mississippi River inspired the Burlington slogan, "Where nature smiles 300 miles." On less scenic routes, or overnight routes, Burlington did not add domes quickly, if ever.

When Burlington began planning a new train for the Chicago–Oakland route that it shared with the Denver & Rio Grande Western and Western Pacific railroads, the railroads realized speed was less important than sightseeing. As a result, they made no attempt to match the schedule of the *City of San Francisco*, which went over Chicago & North Western, Union Pacific, and Southern Pacific rails in less than 40 hours. Instead, the *California Zephyr* was timed to see the best scenery in daylight even though this meant the journey would take more than 10 hours longer than the *City* train.

After cruising overnight from Chicago to Denver on the Burlington, passengers would fill all 120 dome seats to see the Rocky Mountains on the Rio Grande. Then the train would pass through Nevada's bleak land-scape at night, and passengers would return to the domes the next morn-ing to see the crossing of the Sierra Nevada through the Feather River Canyon. Despite the longer schedule, the *California Zephyr* consistently outsold the *City of San Francisco*.

Burlington and its partners inaugurated the *California Zephyr* in March 1949. When Ralph Budd retired from the Burlington six months later, having reached the mandatory retirement age of 70, *Railway Age* magazine called him the "dean of railroad presidents." "The Burlington, with Budd in command," noted railroad historian Richard Overton, "was virtually a training school for railway executives. Men like [Santa Fe president] Fred Gurley, [Rock Island president] John Farrington, [Western Pacific president] Fred Whitman, [Budd's Burlington successor] Harry Murphy, and [New York Central president] A. E. Perlman, all of whom went on to head great railways, served varying terms on the C.B.&Q. while Budd was at its head."[11] Budd also infected most of these future presidents with his enthusiasm for passenger trains.

Budd influenced the transportation industry in more personal ways as well. His older son, Robert, became a top executive at Greyhound. His younger son, John, went to work for the Great Northern Railway. In 1947, he left Great Northern to become president of the Chicago & Eastern Illinois Railroad. At 39, he was younger than his father when the latter became president of Great Northern. Great Northern hired him back in 1949 and made him president in 1951, a position he held until Great Northern merged with Northern Pacific in 1970 to form the Burlington Northern company. He remained CEO or chairman of that company until 1972. The two Budds presided over the Great Northern Railway for 32 years of its 80-year existence, while James and Louis Hill presided over it for just 29 years.

At the time of Ralph Budd's retirement, railroad officials across the country were still optimistic about postwar passenger train ridership. With close to 300 streamlined trains operating each day, and more ordered every year, Budd's zephyrs had created a silver beacon of hope for the rail pas-senger industry. That optimism would fade rapidly over the next decade.

6. THE DECLINE OF URBAN RAIL TRANSIT

The People who live back in Cincinnati
They rode the trolley streetcars everywhere
They sent some trolley streetcars to old Hong Kong
They wanted brand-new buses for their fare.

—Art Lund

URBAN EVOLUTION

As streetcar companies evolved, cities evolved as well, and a primary cause of that evolution was the moving assembly line Henry Ford first created in October 1913 for producing the Model T. This new manufacturing system, which some called "Fordism," would have profound effects on urban transit, intercity passenger trains, and cities themselves. Rising automobile ownership was only one, but not necessarily the most important, of those effects.

Ford's impact on urban transit was first seen soon after the opening of the moving assembly line, when a Los Angeles owner of a Model T touring car named L. P. Draper gave a passenger a short ride for a nickel in July 1914. Draper had discovered that all he needed was a chauffer's license and he could use his car to earn money. By the end of the year, more than one thousand people in Los Angeles had emulated Draper's example. *Jitney* is a word of unknown origin that was often used to mean a nickel, so their cars—most of which were Model T touring cars—came to be called by that name, while the drivers were sometimes called *jitneurs*.[1]

In 1914, a Model T touring car cost $490, or $50 more than a runabout. But the runabout had just one row of seats while the touring car had two. It also had running boards where extra passengers could stand, and as jitneys, they sometimes carried as many as 14 passengers. This made the touring car the ideal jitney. Thanks to the moving assembly line and other improved manufacturing techniques, Ford reduced the price of the touring car from $950 in 1910 to as low as $360 in 1916.[2] Jitneurs were therefore able to easily buy these cars in 1914 and 1915.

Jitneys were faster, more reliable, and more flexible than streetcars. During less busy times of the day, jitneurs were often willing to go out of their way to drop people off at their door. As a result, they quickly had a noticeable effect on streetcar revenues. By the end of 1914, Los Angeles Railways claimed the jitneys were costing it $600 a day in lost revenue. Fanned by a recession that began in 1914, the jitney idea quickly spread to other cities. During just four weeks in early 1915, for example, the number of Kansas City jitneys grew from zero to four hundred, carrying 45,000 to 50,000 trips per day.[3] By spring 1915, the editors of a new trade journal called *The Jitney Bus* estimated there were 62,000 jitneys in the country.

Streetcar companies reacted strongly against the "jitney menace." In exchange for franchises to use certain streets, the street railways paid taxes and helped maintain the streets, including, in some cases, paving them and plowing snow in the winter. The jitneys paid no taxes yet drove ahead of streetcars picking up passengers at streetcar stops, which the companies saw as a violation of their franchise.

At first, they hoped jitneurs would realize the jitneys didn't really cover the cost of overhead, depreciation, insurance, and so forth. But as one driver said, he already "had the car. And having stuck my $500 into it, it might just as well keep running."[4] This difference between charging high enough fares to cover all costs, which railroads had to do, versus covering just variable costs, which was what all car owners needed to do to justify each additional trip, would plague the railroads as long as they tried to compete with the automobile.

Transit companies responded by asking cities to regulate the jitneys in order to level the playing field. The cities were eager to do so, as they were no more interested in losing the tax revenues coming from the streetcar companies than the companies themselves were interested in losing customers. Within an incredibly short time, considering how many different cities were involved, cities across the nation enacted ordinances requiring jitney operators to obtain licenses, purchase liability bonds, and meet various safety rules. Some cities required jitney operators to work at least 6 to 12 hours per day, which is more than many wanted to work. Others required the jitneurs to follow certain routes or banned them from the most lucrative routes.[5]

In 1915 alone, 125 cities passed anti-jitney regulations, reducing the number of jitneys in those cities by as much as 100 percent. When Los Angeles passed jitney regulations in 1916, the number of jitneys fell from 1,000 to just 32. By the end of 1918, the number of jitneys operating in the country had fallen by more than 90 percent.[6]

But eliminating the jitney menace didn't stop the transit industry's troubles. Ford's moving assembly line allowed him to not only reduce the price of his cars but also to double worker pay from $2.50 to $5.00 per day. Some people thought this was an altruistic gesture on Ford's part.[7] Others thought he did it so his employees "could afford the products they worked on all day."[8] But the real reason he increased pay was because assembly line work was boring and his factory was suffering from a high turnover rate. Raising the pay made his employees want to stay, which improved both productivity and quality.[9] As other companies adopted moving assembly lines and similarly increased pay, cars like Ford's Model T became affordable to far more people. Less than five percent of American families had a car in 1913; by 1926, it was more than 50 percent.

The conventional story that transit ridership declined because increasing automobile ownership allowed people to move to lower-density areas where transit didn't work as well is at least partly true. Between 1910 and 1917, the number of automobiles registered in the United States grew faster than 40 percent per year. The rate slowed after that, but over the next decade, more than 1.5 million cars per year were added to the nation's fleet. In 1910, there was one private automobile for every 44 families. By 1920, there was one for every three families; by 1930, one for every 1.3 families.[10] This growth in automobile ownership certainly correlates with the decline in streetcar ridership after 1920. On the other hand, between 1915 and 1927, the number of automobiles in New York City grew by 26 percent per year, yet subway ridership during that time more than doubled.[11]

Although increasing car ownership and use was an important factor, Ford's moving assembly line had an even greater effect because it changed manufacturing. Before the moving assembly line, products such as John Stephenson's streetcars were made in multistory buildings, with each floor dedicated to one or more parts in the process. Moving assembly lines, however, were horizontal, so they required a lot of land. Ford's Highland Park Plant, which built Model Ts, covered 130 acres. His Rouge River Factory, which built Model As, covered 900 acres. Such large factories couldn't fit into city centers, where land was expensive, so they moved to the suburbs. Working-class jobs moved to the suburbs first, then the working class followed.

The moving assembly line turned the monocentric city into a poly-centric city, with concentrations of jobs in many different locations. Because more people had cars, they didn't have to live close to the factories and other job centers that employed them. While it is easy for a hub-and-spoke mass-transit system to serve one major job center, it is more difficult to design a mass-transit system to serve multiple job centers.

Retail soon followed manufacturing away from downtown into the suburbs. In 1909, Kansas City housing developer J. C. Nichols relied on the opening of new streetcar lines to make his subdivisions valuable. By 1913, enough of his homebuyers owned automobiles that he opened his first subdivision with no streetcar line and advertised the fact that people could drive to downtown faster than they could get there by street-car.[12] Nine years later, he opened Country Club Plaza five miles south of downtown Kansas City, the nation's first suburban shopping mall designed to accommodate auto drivers.[13]

In the late 1920s, a downtown Portland grocer named Fred G. Meyer noticed the police ticketing many of his customers' cars for illegal parking. He gathered the tickets from their cars and went to the police station and paid them, taking down the addresses of each of the car's owners. Mapping the addresses, he realized many of his customers were coming from northeast Portland, so in 1931, he opened a new store that soon filled an entire city block. In addition to groceries, the store sold variety goods, drugs, hardware, gasoline, and automobile services. In 1933, it expanded into clothing. By 1938, he turned the entire roof of the store into a parking lot, thus saving his customers from the worry of receiving parking tickets.

Meyer called his store a "one-stop shopping center," and he opened dozens of such stores throughout the Northwest. In about 1960, the homonymously named Frederick G. Meijer toured Meyer's stores and was inspired to open similar stores in Michigan and other midwestern states, calling them "Thrifty Acres." In the early 1970s, an Arkansas retailer named Sam Walton, whose stores sold a variety of goods but not groceries, toured Fred Meyer's stores. Walton had been reluctant to sell groceries due to their lower profit margins, but Meyer convinced him that they brought people into the stores more frequently and increased sales in other departments. Beginning in the 1980s, with help from Fred Meyer executives, Walton began offering groceries in his variety stores, which he called "supercenters." Many people credit the first supercenter to Frederick G. Meijer, but the credit should go to Fred G. Meyer.[14] Whereas downtown department stores were located on streetcar or rapid-transit lines, shopping malls, supermarkets, supercenters, warehouse stores, and other 20th-century retail improvements all depended on automobiles to bring their customers to the stores.

Many city officials and downtown property owners considered decentralization of manufacturing and retailing a "virulent disease."[15] Decentralization was a particular threat to cities that lacked the power to easily annex their suburbs because they relied heavily on taxes collected from downtown property owners. Typically, the 1 percent of land located in a city's downtown produced 20 to 30 percent of the city's property tax revenues. When businesses moved to the suburbs, downtown property values fell. This not only reduced city revenues, it also reduced the city's legal ability to borrow money because debt limits were based on assessed property values. A 1941 study found that if New York City used accurate assessments for Manhattan real estate, its bonded debt would have exceeded the debt limit and the city would have been legally bankrupt.[16]

With the help of urban planners, officials wrote endless downtown revitalization plans, urban renewal plans, and rapid-transit plans, all attempting to restore the monocentric city. All were doomed to fail because the forces of decentralization—transportation, telecommunications, and assembly-line manufacturing—were simply too strong. Rather than rebuilding cities to fit transit systems, as urban planners seemed to be attempting, transit companies needed to adapt their systems to the evolving cities.

MOTOR BUSES

In 1921, a family of four brothers named Fageol, who manufactured trucks, tractors, and other motor vehicles in California, were the first to build a motor bus from the ground up rather than simply putting a passenger compartment on a truck chassis. Fageol buses had a lower center of gravity and were easier to board than truck-based buses.[17] These and similar buses had several natural advantages over streetcars for transit systems trying to adapt to a polycentric urban area.

First, streetcars required dedicated infrastructure that was expensive to build and expensive to maintain. Buses, through fuel and other taxes, shared their infrastructure costs with cars and trucks. Second, with the extension of paved streets, bus routes could change overnight to serve new job centers without the time and expense of building new rail lines. Third, the flexibility of buses meant that, unlike a streetcar, a disruption in service would not affect other vehicles down the line.

Buses also had regulatory advantages over streetcars. Most city franchises required streetcar companies to maintain and sometimes pave the streets they used, while buses were able to use streets paved by others at little cost. Between 1911 and 1920, New York City streetcar companies spent nearly a quarter of their total revenues paving streets.[18] Streetcar franchises also often fixed fares at 5 cents or gave the city more regulatory powers over the streetcars than buses. New York's Fifth Avenue Bus Company, for example, charged riders a dime even though Manhattan streetcars were forbidden from charging more than a nickel. Streetcar franchise holders were also generally required to pay the cities an annual fee or tax to use the streets, while most buses paid only the fuel and other taxes paid by any road user.

Buses had shorter lifespans than railcars, but they also cost less, so the average cost per seat mile tended to balance out or favor buses. The streetcars' longer lifespans actually worked against them, because bus riders enjoyed new vehicles more frequently.

The main disadvantage of early buses was their high operating costs. The primitive gasoline engines of the day needed to be very large to power heavy vehicles such as trucks or buses, and so were put under a long hood that extended in front of the passenger compartment. This limited the passenger capacity to, typically, around 20 to 30 people, whereas streetcars typically had 60 seats and standing room for more.

As of 1922, according to Walter Jackson, a transit analyst who had done extensive comparisons of buses with streetcars, "not more than a score or so of our 800 to 900 operating railway companies have undertaken bus operation." Though buses had lower capital costs, Jackson indicated their operating costs were higher than streetcars. While buses could compete with streetcar companies that charged 10 cents per ride, they would have a hard time competing with a nickel fare, Jackson concluded.[19] Still, buses had enough advantages over streetcars that new streetcar construction ground almost to a halt, and transit companies provided new services using buses.

Bus technology rapidly improved in the 1920s. Superior metallurgy allowed for smaller, lighter engines. Multispeed transmissions replaced electric motors. In 1927, the Fageol brothers introduced a new bus called the Twin Coach because they replaced the gasoline engine under the long hood with two smaller engines over the rear axles. Because almost the entire length of a bus was now able to carry passengers, a 35-foot bus could earn 50 to 100 percent more revenue. The Twin Coach Model 40, meaning 40 seats, revolutionized bus manufacturing and made buses faster and less expensive than streetcars in all three categories of costs: capital, maintenance, and operation.[20]

Most streetcars still had more seats than buses, but that wasn't necessarily an advantage because the buses could make up for their smaller capacity by operating more frequently, which benefitted passengers. Because

60-seat streetcars required two on-board workers—a driver and a conductor to collect fares—while 40-seat buses with pay-as-you-board systems only required a driver, the labor costs of three buses were less than two streetcars. Some streetcar companies adopted pay-as-you-board systems with just one on-board worker, but they tended to use smaller vehicles with about the same capacity as buses.

The Twin Coach 40's innovative design transformed the economics of the transit industry. Suddenly, it made sense to use buses not just to supplement but actually replace streetcar lines. By the time of the 1929 stock market crash, at least 200 cities and towns, including Albuquerque; Ann Arbor; Boise; Burlington, Vermont; and Danbury, Connecticut, completely replaced their streetcars with buses. While most larger cities still had street railways at the beginning of the Great Depression, the golden age of streetcars was clearly over.

TROLLEY BUSES

As previously noted, some streetcar companies may have been slow to adopt motor buses because the companies were owned by electric power companies that viewed transit as an electricity consumer. But they could replace streetcars with rubber-tired transit powered by electricity using trolley buses that captured their power from overhead wires like the streetcars. The Eastern Trackless Trolley Company built demonstrator models of such buses as early as 1887 but was unable to sell any.[21]

The first actual use of a trolley bus was in Laurel Canyon, then a suburb of Los Angeles, where a real estate developer named Charles Mann converted two Oldsmobile trucks into electric-powered vehicles fed by an overhead wire. Starting in 1911, the Laurel Canyon Utilities Company operated these vehicles on a regular schedule to give buyers of Mann's real estate easy access to their properties. The company replaced the trolley buses with steam-powered vehicles in 1915.[22]

One of the first large-scale uses of trolley buses was on Staten Island, where a municipally owned streetcar agency wanted to expand service but didn't have the resources to build more rails. Instead, it installed trolley wires and operated trolley buses from 1921 to 1927. The trolley buses served as feeders to electric streetcars, but an analysis showed the 30-seat trolley buses cost less to operate than motor buses or electric streetcars of comparable size.[23] Eventually, more than 50 American cities used trolley buses, but their use was never as widespread as electric streetcars had been or motor buses would soon become.[24]

THE DECLINE OF THE STREETCAR

Streetcar route-miles peaked in 1919 at 47,941.[25] Miami was the last major city to see private construction of a new electric trolley system, with a line opening in 1922 and interurban extensions to Coral Gables and Miami Beach in 1926.[26] Despite that construction, the closure of other lines meant streetcar mileage declined through the 1920s. Like intercity rail, streetcar ridership peaked in 1920. However, trips per urban resident peaked a few years before, indicating that the automobile and other forms of urban transit were having an impact even before 1920.

During the Roaring 20s, the growth in bus ridership alone was enough to account for the decline in streetcar ridership (Figure 6.1). From 1922—the

Figure 6.1

Billions of Transit Trips Per Year

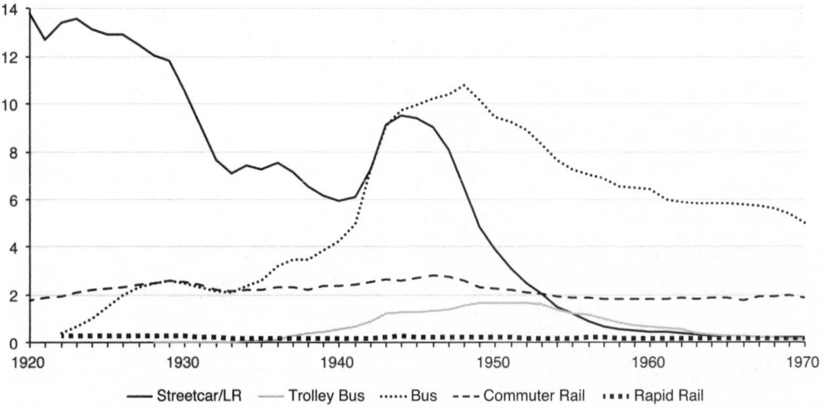

Source: *Public Transportation Fact Book, 2016,* American Public Transportation Association.
Note: During the 1920s, the decline in streetcar trips was made up for by the increase in bus trips. Bus ridership grew in the 1930s but not fast enough to make up for the decline in streetcars. After 1948, all forms of transit declined.

earliest year for which bus numbers are available—to 1929, annual streetcar ridership declined by 1.6 billion trips, while buses gained 2.2 billion trips per year, capturing all of the streetcar riders and then some.

In some cities, such as Detroit, private bus companies began to operate in competition with the streetcars. In other cities, such as Cleveland, the streetcar companies themselves began operating buses, especially when opening up new routes. In New York City, the threat to streetcars wasn't from buses but subways. Even as subway ridership grew by 50 percent in the 1920s, New York City streetcar ridership fell by 25 percent.[27]

Interurban rail lines declined as well. Ridership data are not available, but the number of miles of electric interurban rail lines peaked in 1916 at 15,580. They remained above 15,000 until 1922, then fell to 10,400 by 1930. The Depression put the electric interurban industry into the red, and it received only a slight reprieve during World War II. By 1950, only about 1,500 miles of interurban lines still carried passengers.[28] "Few industries have arisen so rapidly or declined so quickly," say George Hilton and John Due, "and no industry of its size has had a worse financial record."[29]

If the 1920s were painful for the streetcar industry, the 1930s were agonizing. Between 1929 and 1933, total transit ridership fell by more than a third. Although bus and rapid-transit ridership each declined by only about 20 percent, streetcars lost 40 percent of their riders.

One of the victims of the Depression was Illinois electricity magnate Samuel Insull, whose heavily leveraged empire collapsed in 1932. Insull had encouraged his workers and customers to buy shares in the power companies he controlled. When a corporate raider started buying up shares in the late 1920s, Insull borrowed heavily to buy back shares to maintain control, using shares he owned as collateral for the loans. When stock prices declined after 1930, the banks demanded more shares as collateral. Eventually, Insull had no more to give, and both he and other investors in the holding companies lost everything.

Although Insull's holding companies went bankrupt, his operating companies remained in business, his power plants continued to generate electricity, and his railcars continued to roll. Yet investors lost close to a billion dollars, at least $150 million of which came out of Insull's pockets. Insull claimed to be broke and dependent on his son for food and shelter, but he had enough money to go to Europe, and when the federal government threatened to prosecute him for fraud, he spent two years there avoiding extradition. After he finally surrendered in 1934, he was tried three times for fraud and embezzlement but acquitted each time.[30]

Not satisfied, Congress passed the Public Utility Holding Companies Act in 1935. It required that holding companies limit utility investments to one state so they couldn't avoid state regulation by claiming interstate operations. The law also required regulated electric companies to sell off subsidiaries in nonregulated industries, which included streetcar companies, in order to protect ratepayers from overcharges. For example, if an electric company owned a construction company, the latter could charge the electric company an exorbitant price for building a power plant. That cost would then be factored into the regulated rates paid by electricity customers.

This logic didn't seem to apply to streetcar companies, which were customers of, not suppliers to, the electric companies. Nevertheless, power companies were directed to sell off streetcar systems, leading rail transit advocates to call this the "Death Sentence Act" because "streetcars lost a major source of monetary support."[31] According to them, the forced sale of the streetcar companies had "disastrous consequences" for the streetcar industry because electric companies were supposedly happy to absorb streetcar losses in order to sell them electricity and get deductions from their federal, state, and local taxes.[32] They failed to explain, however, why electric companies would tolerate long-term losses merely for the sake of some tax deductions.

The notion that electric companies were happy to cross-subsidize streetcars is contradicted by the San Antonio Public Service Company, an electric utility that owned the local streetcar company and in turn was itself owned by a holding company named American Light and Traction. The company's franchise to operate its 90 miles of streetcar lines in city streets was scheduled to expire in 1940. In 1923, it began running buses to suburbs beyond the end of the streetcar lines.

By 1928, the company realized buses were faster, cheaper, and more comfortable than the streetcars. Whatever profits the Public Service Company made selling electricity to the streetcars weren't enough to cover the streetcars' higher costs. In fact, those costs were so much higher that the company offered to pay the city of San Antonio $250,000—nearly $4 million in today's dollars—to let it out of its streetcar franchise seven years early and to replace all of its streetcars with buses. The city agreed, so in April 1933, San Antonio became the largest city in the country to completely convert its streetcar lines to buses.

By then, streetcars had already disappeared from more than 350 smaller cities and towns, including Albuquerque, Boulder, Colorado Springs, Great Falls, Olympia, and Tucson. Between 1933 and the onset of World War II, streetcars would disappear from more than 230 other cities, including Austin, Fresno, Ft. Worth, Honolulu, Miami-Miami Beach, San Jose, Seattle, and Trenton. Thanks to these and many other closures, streetcar ridership fell by nearly half between 1920 and 1940, with buses picking up about half of those former streetcar riders.

Transit boomed during World War II, with streetcar ridership growing by 60 percent between 1940 and 1944. That boom, combined with wartime rationing, delayed streetcar conversions, with only about 10 systems closing in 1942 through 1945. After the war, conversions accelerated, with cities such as Atlanta, Buffalo, Denver, Oakland, Portland, Providence, and San Diego losing streetcars by 1950. As a result, streetcar ridership declined by nearly 60 percent between 1944 and 1950. This time, other transit modes didn't pick up the slack, as ridership on both buses and rapid transit both fell.

Not every streetcar company was eager to convert to buses. In 1929, some of the larger companies formed a group called the President's Conference Committee to design a standardized railcar that could be mass produced like the Birney cars, but with higher capacities. As completed in 1935, the design included a streamlined body, insulation to reduce noise, and various safety features. Between 1936 and 1951, multiple manufacturers built 5,000 PCC cars, as they were known, and sold them to transit systems in 33 American cities. Baltimore, Philadelphia, and Pittsburgh each had several hundred cars, while Detroit, Los Angeles, and Minneapolis had well over one hundred. Newark continued to operate them in regular service until 2001, and San Francisco still operates them as vintage trolleys, but with a significant local customer base.

Another streetcar improvement emerged in 1936, when the double-decked San Francisco–Oakland Bay Bridge opened. Originally, its upper deck was reserved for cars, while its lower deck had two sections: one for trucks and one for railcars. To carry large numbers of people over the bridge, Oakland's transit company, the Key System, ordered special cars it called "bridge units." They were much longer than streetcars and rode on three sets of wheels, with the front half of the car swiveling independently from the rear. Multiple cars could be coupled together to carry large numbers of people across the bay. On a portion of their routes, they operated in streets like streetcars, but over the rest of their routes, they had an exclusive right of way like interurbans. All these features would be later used in what we now call light rail.

Yet mass-produced streamlined railcars and light rail weren't enough to stop streetcars from disappearing from American cities. In 1974, El Paso converted its last streetcar line to buses. That left just seven American cities—Boston, Cleveland, New Orleans, Newark, Philadelphia, Pittsburgh, and San Francisco—with streetcar lines, and two more—Chicago and New York—with rapid-transit and commuter-rail lines. Boston and Philadelphia also had rapid transit, and Boston, Philadelphia, and San Francisco still had commuter-rail lines as well. Because Newark and New York City are in the same urbanized area, just eight out of the nation's hundreds of urban areas still had some form of rail transit.

The Imaginary Streetcar Conspiracy

Godwin's law asserts that any internet debate, if it lasts long enough, will eventually result in one side associating the other with Nazism or Hitler. A transportation corollary to Godwin's law would hold that any debate over highways and transit will eventually lead transit advocates to raise the Great Streetcar Conspiracy. According to this conspiracy theory, a consortium of GM, Firestone Tire, Chevron, and Phillips Petroleum deliberately destroyed America's streetcar industry by buying streetcar systems and replacing them with inferior buses, thereby forcing commuters to buy cars to get to work.[33]

This myth came from a misrepresentation of a federal antitrust action against General Motors' efforts to sell its buses. In the early 1930s, a GM subsidiary, Yellow Coach, had about 30 percent of the market for transit buses. Recognizing that many smaller streetcar companies were losing money and couldn't afford to rehabilitate their worn-out rail systems, GM offered to finance a conversion to buses in the same way it finances the sale of automobiles. Transit companies in Kalamazoo and Saginaw, Michigan, as well as Springfield, Ohio, gratefully accepted the offer.

Then, in 1935, the franchise for Portland, Oregon's transit company, Portland Traction, was about to expire, and the company's streetcar system was fairly worn out. Rather than approach the company with an offer to finance new buses, GM created a new company, the Portland Motor Coach Company, and submitted its own bid for a franchise.[34] Portland Traction convinced the city to extend its franchise, and instead of buying buses from Yellow Coach, it purchased trolley buses from Mack Trucks.[35] It also persuaded the American Transit Association to publicly condemn GM for threatening its business.[36] Realizing that alienating its potential customers was a bad strategy, GM backed off.

The antitrust action had to do with GM's association with National City Lines, a transit holding company. Though some accounts claim GM created this company, in fact it was founded independently in 1920. By 1938, it owned 29 transit companies and wanted to buy more. It approached GM, Firestone, and the two oil companies seeking financing to buy more companies in exchange for which it would buy Yellow buses and the other companies' products when it needed them. The companies agreed, and, flush with cash, National City bought another 30 or so companies. To later deflect charges it was trying to monopolize the market for buses, GM agreed to allow National City to add Mack Trucks to the consortium, and some of the buses purchased by National City companies were manufactured by Mack.

The addition of Mack failed to placate federal regulators, and in 1947, they brought a suit against National City and the investing companies, charging violations of the Sherman Antitrust Act. In 1949, they were acquitted of some charges and convicted of others. GM was fined $5,000, its treasurer was personally fined $1, and it and the other companies were ordered to sell their interest in National City, which they soon did.

During the period when GM and the other companies were invested in National City, 23 of the transit companies owned by National

City converted their streetcar systems to buses. A few cities, including Kalamazoo and Saginaw, had already made the conversion before National City bought them in 1936 or GM invested in National City in 1939. Others, including Los Angeles Transit Lines, the Oakland Key System, and St. Louis Public Service Company, still operated some of their streetcar lines when GM and the other companies divested themselves of National City. In fact, Los Angeles Transit purchased new PCC cars while it was owned by National City, and other companies may have done so as well.[37]

In short, transit companies were buying buses, and the investors wanted to make sure they bought GM buses, Firestone tires, and fuels and lubricants from Chevron and Phillips. But they didn't hasten the process of converting streetcars to buses.

In 1974, however, an antitrust attorney named Bradford Snell argued in testimony before Congress that GM's real goal was to destroy the transit industry. Electric streetcars were superior to automobiles, Snell maintained, and GM "realized that as long as people had adequate mass transportation they wouldn't buy" cars. "The only way to bring about a situation where it sold more cars," Snell insisted, "was to eliminate rail alternatives and to supplant them with buses which were unattractive."[38]

Snell went well beyond the facts, claiming GM was responsible for "the destruction of more than 100 electric surface rail systems," including systems in New York, Philadelphia, Baltimore, St. Louis, Oakland, and Los Angeles, when in fact National City never had an interest in New York, Philadelphia, and Baltimore, while St. Louis, Oakland, and Los Angeles companies converted to buses only after GM sold its interest in National City. Snell also claimed the 1947 antitrust suit charged GM with trying to destroy transit systems, when in fact it was only charged with trying to monopolize the sale of its buses.

Snell further charged that GM became a major investor in Greyhound in order to destroy the intercity rail industry.[39] Tell that to Ralph Budd or the management of the Pennsylvania, Southern Pacific, and other major railroads that also owned shares of Greyhound. Snell claimed GM used its power as the nation's leading shipper to force railroads to buy its diesel locomotives, when in fact many railroads that exclusively or predominantly used locomotives from other builders still enjoyed business carrying GM shipments. Snell specifically alleged that the New Haven Railroad earned a profit in all the years that it used electric locomotives but went bankrupt after GM persuaded it to convert to diesel.[40] In fact, New Haven was already in receivership when it converted its steam locomotives to diesel, and, contrary to Snell's claim, it never did convert its electrified lines to diesel.

Snell's wild claims were immediately refuted by transportation economist George Hilton. Testifying before the same Senate subcommittee, Hilton said Snell "couldn't possibly be correct, because major conversions in society of this character—from rail to free wheel urban transportation, and from steam to diesel railroad propulsion—are the sort of conversions which could come about only as a result of public preferences, technological change, the relative abundance of natural resources, and other impersonal phenomena or influences, rather than the machinations of a monopolist."[41] Hilton specifically addressed each of Snell's claims, noting that, in converting some streetcar lines to buses, National City "did not act markedly differently from the industry as a whole."[42]

When GM and the other companies first invested in National City, said Hilton, the "conventional wisdom of the industry" was that "streetcars were preferable for heavily traveled lines, trolley buses for intermediate, and internal combustion buses for more lightly traveled lines." By 1952, however, diesel buses had become so efficient that they were considered the most suitable in almost all circumstances, the main exception being in tunnels, where diesel fumes would have been obnoxious if not deadly. Such tunnels explained why streetcars survived in Boston, Newark, Philadelphia, Pittsburgh, and San Francisco. Streetcars in Cleveland and New Orleans, the only other two cities that still had them in 1974, used private rights of way the transit companies did not want to give up.[43] Except in these special cases, Hilton argued, streetcars would have disappeared with or without GM.

Van Wilkins was a senior editor for the strongly pro–rail transit *New Electric Journal*, yet he admitted in 1995 that "a great deal" of what Snell said in the 1974 hearings "was inaccurate." "The idea of a conspiracy provides a simple and comfortable explanation for what was the result of a very complex set of circumstances," he noted. For example, National

City Lines bought Salt Lake City's transit company in 1944, when it was still running one streetcar line it had "abandoned in 1941 but restored to service as the result of a wartime edict." The transit company had in fact decided to convert all its streetcars to buses in the early 1930s, well before National City involvement, yet Snell blamed that conversion on the General Motors conspiracy.[44]

University of California at Berkeley transportation economist David Jones proposed an alternative explanation of GM's behavior. Rather than trying to monopolize the bus market, he, said, it was trying to demonstrate its latest models. In 1936, the company—following the accelerated research spurred by the Burlington *Zephyr*—introduced its first diesel bus. Although it was far superior to gasoline-powered buses, it didn't sell well at first. By providing capital to National City Lines, Jones argued, GM provided seed money for more diesel bus sales in order to demonstrate to the rest of the industry that diesels were a viable technology.[45]

Another of Snell's misrepresentations was that National City Lines' subsidiary, Pacific City Lines, "undertook the dismantlement of the $100 million Pacific Electric system."[46] That claim inspired the movie *Who Framed Roger Rabbit*, in which a land developer tries to shut down the Pacific Electric system in order to make money from land sales along a freeway that would replace the "Red Car." In fact, neither National City nor Pacific City ever owned the Pacific Electric system. As Sy Adler, an associate professor of urban studies at Portland State University, concluded, "everything Bradford Snell wrote . . . about transit in Los Angeles was wrong."[47]

"Snell's study was, at best, sloppy and poorly researched," says historian Scott Bottles. "The entire diatribe is riddled with factual errors and poorly drawn conclusions." For instance, Snell mistook the Pacific Electric for the Los Angeles Railway Corporation throughout his essay. Snell's most egregious error was in asserting that the antitrust violations committed by GM and National City Lines ruined a healthy transit industry. Nothing could be further from the truth, because the industry was already dying long before GM's involvement.[48] If there was a conspiracy to destroy streetcar companies, say Minnesota transit historians John Diers and Aaron Isaacs, then "indict everyone who bought an automobile" between 1920 and 1950.[49]

Despite repeated debunking, the streetcar conspiracy myth remains alive and well, having been breathlessly retold in such recent books as Stephen Goddard's 1994 *Getting There*[50] and Jane Holtz Kay's 1997 *Asphalt Nation*.[51] Portland State University planning professor Martha Bianco argues that the myth is a "strategic tool" used by rail advocates.[52] Bianco points out that in 1987 *60 Minutes* had a segment that repeated many of Snell's errors.[53] A few months later, Walt Disney released *Who Framed Roger Rabbit?* She suspects that these two events helped persuade Congress to pass two key pieces of legislation, the Clean Air Act of 1990 and the Intermodal Surface Transportation Efficiency Act of 1991, that penalized the automobile and began large subsidies to rail transit.[54]

One of Snell's key arguments was that the inferiority of buses compared to streetcars played a crucial role in GM's nefarious scheme to force people to buy cars instead of ride transit. In fact, as Hawaiian transportation expert Cliff Slater observes, transit riders welcomed buses because they were faster, safer, more comfortable, and could go places the rails didn't go. Snell called a decision by New York City to replace most of its streetcars with buses in the mid-1930s "the turning point in the electric railway industry." Yet, Slater notes, the buses boosted ridership by 62 percent.

As previously mentioned, between 1922 and 1929, declines in streetcar ridership were more than matched by increases in bus ridership. "Thus," says Slater, "it was the bus rather than the family automobile that caused the initial decline in streetcar ridership."[55] When Cincinnati replaced streetcars with buses, it supposedly sold some of its railcars to Hong Kong, which led Art Lund to record the song that begins this chapter. Whether those cars ended up in China or not, it was true that people appreciated "brand-new buses" in place of worn-out streetcars. "Buses were clearly a better way to go and would have taken over with or without GM," agrees University of Arizona transportation researcher Sandra Rosenbloom.[56]

More evidence for Slater's thesis can be seen from rapid transit, whose ridership grew steadily until 1930. Between 1920 and 1930, New York City subway ridership grew by 54 percent, and rapid-transit ridership in Boston, Chicago, and Philadelphia grew by 11 percent. Buses are an excellent substitute for streetcars but not as good a substitute for rapid transit, so the growth in rapid transit as streetcars declined showed that buses, not cars, were primarily responsible for the decline in streetcar ridership in the 1920s.

Although the Depression reduced rapid-transit ridership, the economy's effect on streetcars was far more severe. New York subways carried just 9 percent fewer riders in 1940 as in 1930, while Boston, Chicago, and Philadelphia rapid-transit lines gained 3 percent more riders. Considering population growth, however, that represents a 26 percent decline in per capita trips in New York City and an 11 percent decline in the other three cities.

Between buses, streetcars, and rapid transit—the three forms of transit for which we have numbers dating back to the 1920s—transit ridership continued to grow until 1926, when it reached 17.3 billion trips. By 1929, total ridership was still 98.5 percent of the 1926 peak. Per capita ridership peaked at 296 trips per urban resident in 1912 but remained above 270 trips through 1926. By 1929, it had declined to 251 trips, then plummeted to 171 trips in 1933. The war temporarily pushed total ridership above 23 billion trips per year, but per capita ridership never again reached 280 trips per urban resident, the level it had been during most of the 1910s.

This suggests that although increasing auto ownership and job decentralization may have slowed the growth of transit ridership, and particularly affected per capita ridership, the biggest effects of these changes would not be seen until after World War II. If there was a turning point, perhaps it was 1926, the year ridership peaked but also the year that a majority of American families acquired an automobile. While the downward trend from 1926 to 1929 was short, it is not likely the industry could have rebounded to the 1926 levels if the Depression hadn't intervened, because there were too many factors promoting decentralization and making personal transportation far superior to any form of mass transit.

7. THE DECLINE OF INTERCITY PASSENGER TRAINS

The world judges the railways by their passenger services.
If this is the window through which we are viewed,
we must wash it and shine it, or else cover it with a dark shade.

—John M. Budd

The worst train crash in Burlington history took place on April 25, 1946, and the aftermath of that crash would have negative repercussions for passenger trains throughout the nation. On that day, two trains left Chicago's Union Station at 12:35 p.m. They were actually one train operated in two sections: The first section, known as the *Advanced Flyer*, consisted of eight baggage and express cars as well as four coaches for short-distance travelers and a dining car (typically called a diner). The second section, called the *Exposition Flyer* because it handled the transcontinental traffic to the West Coast, had three coaches for long-distance travelers, five sleeping cars, and a diner.[1] When the train reached Denver, the two would be combined into one for the journey to Oakland.

The trains departed Chicago at the same time on two different tracks. After five miles, they both converged onto the same track, with the second train about three minutes behind the first. Despite being so close, they zipped along on Burlington's "race track" at about 80 to 85 miles per hour.

About 25 miles outside of Chicago, a brakeman on the first train thought he saw something fall off one of the cars on the train. He informed the conductor, who decided to stop the train for an inspection. The train stopped in Naperville, Illinois, then a town of about 5,000 residents.[2]

Normally, when a train slows for a stop, a flagman in the last car on the train drops flares and other signals to warn any trains behind it that a train is stopped. But the flagman on the *Advanced Flyer* happened to be in another car, where he said he was better able to inspect the train as it went around a curve before Naperville, and he wasn't able to perform the emergency duty. Unfortunately, the train happened to stop a little beyond this curve, making it invisible to the following train until it also rounded that curve.[3] When the *Advanced Flyer* stopped, there were two signals between it and the *Exposition Flyer:* the first one turned yellow and the second one, also hidden by the curve, turned red.

William Blaine, the engineer on the diesel-powered *Exposition Flyer*, was 68 years old, highly experienced but nearing retirement. When he saw a yellow signal before rounding the curve, he knew the signal meant he should reduce his train to "medium speed" (about half his previous speed) so he could safely stop if the next signal was red. But he also knew the signals would turn yellow any time his train approached to less than three minutes behind the *Advanced Flyer*. Normally, if that happened, he could ease off on the throttle and let his train slow down so it would fall to more than three minutes behind, and the next light would be green. This was called "riding the yellow," and although it did not comply with the rules, it usually wasn't a problem. But a train usually did not make a full, unscheduled stop around a blind corner.[4]

After rounding the curve, he could see that the next signal was red and the *Advanced Flyer* was stopped on the track in front of him. He applied the brakes, but his train failed to slow to less than 45 miles per hour before it hit the first train. His locomotive tore through the rear coach of the *Advanced Flyer*, killing most of the occupants.

The eight heavyweight baggage cars on the *Advanced Flyer* were followed by two Budd-built stainless-steel coaches built in 1940, a Budd-built stainless-steel diner built in 1938, and two heavyweight coaches. Budd built the original *Zephyr* without sills, relying on the strength of the stainless-steel body to support the low-profile train. When the company started building full-profile passenger cars, it included small sills made of stainless steel, and the sill on the 1938 diner was a little more than eight inches across. In 1939, the Association of American Railroads set a new standard requiring passenger cars to be able to withstand an impact with 800,000 pounds of force. This led the Budd Company to increase sills to as much as 18 inches across,[5] but it was too late for the *Advanced Flyer*.

When its heavyweight coach weighing 139,700 pounds was forced into the lightweight diner, which weighed only 110,700 pounds, the diner's sill collapsed, and the car was bent into a U shape, smashing most of it to pieces. Many of the people in this car were also killed.[6] A total of 45 people died, most of them in the last coach or the diner.[7]

The fireman aboard the *Exposition Flyer* was one of the few people killed who were not in one of those two cars, but engineer Blaine managed to survive. His behavior after the accident, however, was peculiar. Someone bandaged his head wound, and he then hitched a ride back to Aurora, saying he had to catch a train. At Aurora, he was recognized and hospitalized. His injuries were apparently permanently debilitating, as he never returned to work after the accident. Although four different accident investigations took place—by Burlington itself, the DuPage County Coroner, a grand jury, and the Interstate Commerce Commission (ICC)—none of them formally interviewed Blaine, so all that is known about what he did during the accident came from a hospital interview.

In that interview, he claimed that he used emergency braking as soon as he saw the red signal and stopped train. Trains have two sets of brake controls, one for the locomotives and one for the cars: in an emergency, both are applied. However, when his locomotive was examined after the crash, only the brakes for the cars had been applied. In tests conducted by the Burlington after the accident, a train of similar size that applied both sets of brakes stopped in time to prevent a crash.

The coroner's report recommended that Blaine be charged with manslaughter, and the ICC report blamed the accident on "failure to operate the following train in accordance with signal indications." After these reports were issued, however, a Burlington shop discovered a defective brake hose on one of the *Exposition Flyer*'s cars, although they could not tell if this defect caused, or was caused by, the accident. Perhaps because of this finding, the grand jury concluded there wasn't enough evidence to indict Blaine.[8]

The Naperville crash led to several changes in safety policies on the Burlington and other railroads. First, the Burlington announced it would no longer allow high-speed trains to operate just three minutes apart, instead requiring 15 minutes of separation. This new policy would have completely prevented the Naperville crash. Second, Burlington also added a new signal—a flashing yellow—that would designate a more serious situation than an ordinary yellow.[9] Third, the grand jury and ICC both urged railroads not to combine cars and locomotives that did not meet the 1939 collision standards on the same train with those that did.[10] That change would have saved the lives of passengers in the *Advance Flyer's* dining car.

The ICC Kills High-Speed Trains

The biggest change, however, came in 1947 when the ICC issued an order setting speed limits for trains throughout America. Under the order, passenger trains would be limited to 79 miles per hour unless the railroads installed equipment that displayed signals inside the locomotive cabs. The ICC began contemplating this rule on May 20, 1946, less than a month after the Naperville crash, and it used the Naperville accident to justify the new speed limits.[11]

Years later, in 2008, Congress required that railroads operating either passenger trains or freight trains carrying hazardous materials to install "positive train control" systems that would bring trains to a halt if the signals required it but the engineer failed to do so. Although this would have satisfied the 1947 ICC regulation, the ICC at the time required only that locomotive cabs be equipped with a signal inside the cab reflecting the outside signal. Because all the evidence indicates Blaine was aware of the signals, the new ICC rule would not have prevented the Naperville crash. Moreover, even if his train had been moving at the new 79 mile-per-hour speed limit instead of 80 to 85, it wouldn't have made much difference to the final crash.

The technology required by the ICC order had been perfected in the 1910s by none other than Frank Sprague, the streetcar, rapid-transit, and elevator wizard. Sprague developed this system to insure safe operations of the scores of tracks serving New York City's Grand Central Terminal. To eliminate air pollution, the locomotives serving Grand Central were electric powered, and Sprague's system could automatically stop these locomotives even if the drivers failed to do so. Today this is called *positive train control*. Positive train control could not be easily installed on steam locomotives, which were entirely mechanical, so Sprague's system settled for putting signal lights in the cabs of the locomotives.

Large railroads are organized in *divisions* of several hundred miles each. The ICC was so impressed with Sprague's system that, in 1922, it ordered all major passenger railroads to install the system on one division, In 1924, they expanded this order to require many of the larger railroads to install it on two divisions. The railroads grumbled about the requirement, but the Great Northern, Northern Pacific, and Burlington railroads all hired Sprague to install his system on the divisions needed to comply with the ICC order.[12]

Few railroads installed it on any lines except those required divisions, however, and by 1950, only about 13,000 miles, or 7 percent, of the nation's mainline rails had such equipment. This included much of Chicago & North Western's route from Chicago to Omaha, part of Milwaukee Road's route from Chicago to the Twin Cities, and most of New York Central's and Pennsylvania's routes from New York to Chicago.

To comply with the new rule without slowing existing trains, railroads would have to install the equipment on another 27,000 miles of track and in thousands of locomotives.[13] The Pennsylvania Railroad estimated the cost to be around $4,000 per track mile, plus $2,260 per locomotive (multiply by 10 to get today's dollars). Other railroads had even higher estimates.[14] This meant the total cost would have been well over $100 million, or more than $1 billion in today's dollars. Freight cars spent most of their time in classification yards, so freight trains wouldn't particularly benefit from higher speeds. Because passenger service in 1950 produced only about 10 percent of the railroads' revenues, in most cases, the cost of the signals wouldn't be worth it for passenger trains alone.

The railroads argued in vain that there was no evidence that high-speed trains suffered more accidents than low-speed trains. In fact, the commission's own data showed there were actually more accidents where speed limits were below 60 miles per hour than above. The commission ignored such protests.[15]

"There is no question but that the introduction of cab signals or automatic train control adds somewhat to the safety of operation," Southern Pacific General Manager J. W. Corbett told the ICC in a hearing. "Of course, there are many other refinements which add to the safety of operations, and there is a very practical problem as to which or how the available funds for such improvements will be expended."

"That is right," responded ICC Commissioner William Patterson, "and when you get to the final analysis here, it is a question of whether you should determine how these funds should be used or whether the government should, isn't that right?" Patterson was the commissioner who wrote the investigation report for the Naperville crash, and he obviously made this into his personal crusade. Patterson had worked for several railroads as a brakeman and conductor for 16 years before he took a job with the ICC as safety inspector in 1914. Franklin Roosevelt appointed him to be one of five ICC commissioners in 1935.[16]

"I will certainly say the decision should be left with the management," Corbett replied, "because I think we have demonstrated our desire to surround our operations with every possible safeguard." But Commissioner Patterson insisted Congress had "given the Commission the responsibility," so it was going to exercise it.[17]

Corbett had an excellent point, however. Since Frank Sprague had invented the automatic train control system, the number of deaths due to train collisions had declined by about 90 percent, but this decline was mainly due to other factors such as a decline in the number of passenger trains. The Naperville crash was both tragic and horrific, yet it wasn't clear the ICC rule would have prevented it. On the other hand, other kinds of railroad accidents killed thousands of people a year. In 1946, the year of the Naperville crash, 128 passengers were killed in train crashes, and more than 2,000 were killed in grade-crossing accidents. Another 1,600 pedestrians were killed while trespassing on railroad rights of way. Money spent installing signals that might or might not prevent collisions between two trains could otherwise have been spent making grade crossings safer or fencing in rights of way.

Despite railroad protests, the rule went into effect on December 31, 1951, with a deadline of the end of 1952 to install the equipment or slow the trains. To compete with the Milwaukee Road and Chicago & North Western lines, which already had the signals installed on parts of their Twin Cities routes, Burlington installed cab signals on 145 miles of track from Chicago to Savanna, Illinois. Rather than install the signals on their Chicago–Denver routes, however, Burlington and Union Pacific added 30 minutes to their scheduled times for the *Denver Zephyr* and *City of Denver*.

To continue running trains between Chicago and Los Angeles in 39¾ hours, Santa Fe installed the equipment on much of its route from Chicago to Kansas City. Union Pacific also managed to keep the same schedule on this route. Southern Pacific and Rock Island, however, had planned to introduce a 39¾-hour train on their Chicago–Los Angeles route, and had even ordered passenger cars and locomotives for the train. But the new rule would have required Southern Pacific to install new signals on much of its portion of the route: Instead, it cancelled its order for the new trains, and the Chicago–Los Angeles train they ran instead required 43¾ hours. Four hours doesn't seem like a big difference, but a sub-40-hour train from Chicago to the West Coast could leave after 5 p.m. and arrive before 9 a.m., taking only one business day. A 43¾-hour train, however, took 1½ business days, making it less attractive to business travelers.

In 1950, the engineering firm of Coverdale & Colpitts published the sixth (and, as it would turn out, last) in a series of reports on "streamline, light-weight, high-speed passenger trains." The report observed that overall passenger ridership had declined by nearly two-thirds from the war years through 1949. But it optimistically speculated about a time "when traffic again builds up to that of 1947."[18] In fact, between just 1947 and 1949, passenger miles had declined by about 25 percent, and they never returned to 1947 levels.

Instead of commenting on the decline, the report took the positive view that ridership in 1949 was still about 50 percent greater than it had been just before the war. Yet the rapid postwar decline was critical to the future of passenger trains. Even if, as the report maintained (without more than anecdotal evidence), "the streamline train has been instrumental in holding to the rails traffic that otherwise would have been lost to" competing modes, a railroad's decision to invest in new trains required more than a one-time boost in ridership.[19] If that boost could not be sustained for the 15- to 20-year life of the equipment, the revenues from the trains might never pay back the investment.

Despite the upbeat tone, any railroad executive reviewing this report would have to be disturbed by the fact that, for most trains for which data were presented, 1949 ridership (measured in passenger miles per train mile) was typically 10 to 20 percent lower than 1948. Most of the Rock Island *Rockets* had lost 10 percent; the Missouri Pacific *Eagles* lost 15 percent; the Southern Pacific *Coast Daylights* lost 12 percent, and the *Sunbeam, Lark,* and *San Joaquin Daylight* lines even more. Only the Milwaukee *Hiawathas* seemed to be holding their own.[20]

In 1950, the nation's railroads were rapidly converting from steam to diesel, a transition most of them would complete well before 1960. A conversion of heavyweight passenger cars to lightweight, streamlined cars seemed to parallel the steam-to-diesel conversion, as both effectively began in 1934. Yet 90 percent of the passenger trains in 1950 were still heavyweights, and even as late as 1970, lightweights still made up a minority of passenger cars in revenue service. The continuing decline in ridership explains why the railroads didn't convert heavyweights to lightweights as swiftly as they converted from steam to diesel.

CRUISE TRAINS MAKE GETTING THERE HALF THE FUN

Having lost most local travelers during the 1920s and 1930s, railroads were now poised to lose most business travelers, partly because of the ICC rule and partly because of improving intercity highways and air service. That left tourists, who were more sensitive to price and less sensitive to the loss of business days than business travelers. In 1960, the earliest year for which data are available, air fares were more than twice as much, per passenger mile, as rail fares, so railroads could advertise that they could save passengers money.

Saving money wasn't enough, however, especially when a family could save even more by driving a car on their summer vacation. Facing competition with trans-Atlantic air service in the early 1950s, the Cunard Lines adopted the slogan, "Getting there is half the fun." To compete with the automobile for tourist travelers, therefore, railroads had to make long-distance trains fun as well. Some installed movie theaters in their trains; others included playrooms for children. But the most popular addition to long-distance trains was the dome car.

Just as Chicago–Twin Cities was one of the most competitive day-train markets in the nation, Chicago–Seattle/Portland was one of the most competitive two-night markets in the nation. Great Northern and Northern Pacific ran trains to both Seattle and Portland. Milwaukee Road also had trains to Seattle, while the Union Pacific had trains to Portland. Union Pacific's *City of Portland* was the fastest train in the corridor, but passengers to Seattle had to change trains in Portland, and the extra time of taking a train to Seattle allowed the other three railroads to be competitive in that market.

As previously noted, Great Northern introduced the first postwar overnight streamliner, the Chicago–Seattle/Portland *Empire Builder*, in February 1947. Milwaukee Road followed with the *Olympian Hiawatha* in June. Both trains took 45 hours to go from Chicago to the Northwest, a great improvement over their predecessors, which required 58½ hours. In 1948, Northern Pacific streamlined its *North Coast Limited*, but— apparently concerned its war-worn tracks couldn't support faster trains— kept it on the old 58½-hour timetable.

In June 1951, Great Northern demonstrated it was still optimistic about the passenger train business when it introduced an entirely new *Empire Builder* just four years after streamlining the train in 1947. The railroad put the 1947 train to work as a secondary Twin Cities–Seattle train, making more stops and taking a slightly longer route to serve cities not on the *Empire Builder* route. A name-the-train contest generated thousands of entries, and John Budd personally selected *Western Star* from the list. Great Northern thus had two completely streamlined transcontinental trains, each of which were arguably better than the *North Coast Limited* and at least equal to the *Olympian Hiawatha*. Northern Pacific finally reduced the

North Coast Limited's time to 45 hours in 1952, but the train's lounge and dining spaces remained inferior to its competitors for several more years.

In January 1953, Milwaukee Road upped the ante by introducing the first full-length dome cars ever built for the *Olympian Hiawatha*. These "super domes" had 68 dome seats and a lounge beneath the dome. The short domes used on Burlington and other trains typically had just 24 seats, but many also had 46 or more revenue seats on the main level. By sacrificing revenue seats, the Milwaukee was able to give more travelers scenic views in just one car. The windows in the dome were five feet high and three feet wide, so passengers enjoyed spectacular views as the train wound through the Rocky and Cascade mountains. Each of the Milwaukee domes cost about twice as much as an ordinary streamlined passenger car and, despite being streamlined, were among the heaviest passenger cars ever built.

To compete, Northern Pacific added four dome cars to each of its *North Coast Limited*s between Chicago and Seattle in 1954. Two of the domes on each train had 46 coach seats beneath the dome, while the other two had rooms for 16 sleeping car passengers. Although they were manufactured by Budd of stainless steel, the domes were painted in Northern Pacific's soothing two-tone green colors, chosen by Raymond Loewy in 1952. Loewy also helped design new lounge cars. Together with the domes, these cars brought the train up to and surpassed the standard set by the *Empire Builder*.

At first, Great Northern was reluctant to buy dome cars to compete in the Chicago–Seattle market. But after Milwaukee Road and Northern Pacific had both ordered them, it was forced to do the same. "In 1951," when it introduced the new *Empire Builder* and *Western Star*, "we were cited as the outstanding railroad in the United States for progress in passenger equipment," a Great Northern executive wrote John Budd in 1952, "and if we do not furnish dome cars we are falling behind in the race."[21]

Budd was persuaded not just to buy dome cars but to spectacularly outdo either of the railway's competitors. In 1955, each *Empire Builder* train was enhanced with three short domes like the Northern Pacific dome coaches and one full-length dome like the Milwaukee super domes. Like Northern Pacific's, Great Northern's domes were built by Budd of stainless steel but painted orange and green. Between the four domes,

Great Northern was able to advertise that the *Empire Builder* had "more dome seats" than any other train in the nation.[22]

Like passengers on a plane, most people riding an Amtrak train from Washington, D.C., to New York today typically find a seat and, other than short trips to the rest room and possibly one to the food service car, stay in that seat for the entire trip. A ride on the *Empire Builder* or *North Coast Limited* in the late 1950s and 1960s was an entirely different experience. The first coach on the *Empire Builder* had 60 seats for short-distance passengers, and these passengers probably did stay in their seats for most of their journeys. In the early 1960s, the first car on the *North Coast Limited* was a Slumbercoach, Budd's low-cost, 40-bed sleeping car.

The next three coaches on the *Empire Builder* all had domes, so many of the passengers in the 46 reserved seats downstairs would often go upstairs to sit in one of the 24 seats that were open to anyone. The coach portions of each of the dome cars were decorated with a variety of stunning linoleum decorations inspired by Haida Indian art but carved and painted by French-American artist Pierre Bourdelle. The coach sections of the *North Coast Limited*'s domes were decorated with paintings of the railroad's 1883 Last Spike ceremony.

Riding in the first dome gave passengers a good view of the locomotives. Riding in the second or third dome gave passengers a better view of other passenger cars in the train. Northern Pacific had a policy of inserting a flat-topped car between each dome so that one dome would not obstruct the view of passengers in the dome behind. Great Northern didn't do this, and it probably didn't make much difference.

Behind the *Empire Builder*'s dome cars was Great Northern's Ranch car, decorated to look like the interior of a dude ranch dining hall. Chairs were upholstered in tan-and-white faux leather designed to look like the coat of a pinto pony. Western red cedar posts and beams separated the bar portion of the car from dining tables and lounge chairs. Decorations included genuine Montana ranch brands, including the G-bar-N brand the railroad had duly registered with the Montana Livestock Commission. The *North Coast Limited* had a similar car called Traveller's Rest, named for a camp on the Lewis & Clark Expedition, whose walls were lined with faux leather hand painted with scenes from the expedition. The Ranch and Traveller's Rest cars offered coach passengers sandwiches, meals featuring two or three low-cost entrees such as veal cutlets or chicken fricassee, and various beverages.

The formal dining car was open to coach passengers, but the railways assumed most coach riders would eat in the Ranch or Lewis & Clark cars. Great Northern therefore put the dining car in the middle of the train's complement of sleeping cars to minimize the walk the average sleeping car passenger would have to take to get to the diner. The train usually had three sleeping cars between the Ranch car and the diner. The *North Coast Limited*'s diner was right behind the Traveller's Rest car.

The *Empire Builder* diner was divided into sections by thick sheets of plate glass on which were etched representations of materials carried by Great Northern freight trains: Minnesota ore docks, North Dakota wheat farms, Washington apple trees, and Cascade Mountain forests. Northern Pacific's diner had similar glass panels etched with an abstract pattern.

At one end of the *Empire Builder* diner, a portrait of James J. Hill glowered at the dining car steward, as if to make sure passengers were given first-class service. The cooks mashed fresh potatoes and baked pies in the train's kitchen, whereas passengers in the Ranch car and on the *Western Star* ate instant potatoes and pastries made in Great Northern's kitchens in St. Paul or Seattle. The dining car menus offered much more variety than in the Ranch or Traveller's Rest cars, typically featuring five or six full meals including fish, chicken, ham, or steak entrees, plus an extensive a la carte section, with such items as lamb chops, chicken pot pie, omelets, and a variety of salads and sandwiches.

On the *Empire Builder*, the full-length dome car was next to the diner. Coach passengers were allowed to walk through the diner to buy drinks in the lower lounge, but the dome itself was reserved exclusively for sleeping car passengers. The front of the bar in the lower lounge had a large Indian-style mural by Pierre Bourdelle, and the lounge was separated into sections by plexiglass panels inlaid with Indian-inspired paintings by Pearson Berlinghof. Bourdelle and Berlinghof had been hired by the Paul Cret firm to provide art for the *Empire Builder* and other Budd-built trains. The windows in the full-length dome itself were as big as those of Milwaukee's super dome. Dome aficionados, however, preferred the short domes because sightseers had more of a 360-degree view of the passing landscape.

Following the *North Coast Limited*'s diner were four or five sleepers, two of which had domes above the sleeping rooms. Following the sleeping cars, the last car on each train was a sleeper-observation car with a parabolic-shaped tail as pioneered by Budd's original zephyr. Before the addition of the full-length dome car, the lounge portion of the *Empire Builder*'s observation car had oversized windows that ran most of the length of the car. The lounge included a small buffet offering drinks and light snacks. After the full-length dome car was added with its lower-level lounge, those lounge-observation cars were bumped to the *Western Star,* while Great Northern rebuilt some sleeping cars to include a small observation room in the parabolic tail. Because there was no beverage service and better views could be obtained from the domes, this room was not heavily used, but it was sometimes occupied by business people for small meetings. The *North Coast Limited*'s observation car had five bedrooms and a large lounge with a small buffet serving drinks and snacks.

All these amenities made the *Empire Builder* and *North Coast Limited* into cruise trains, providing entertaining places to sit in during both the scenic portions and the more boring portions of the journey. In the summer season, the *Empire Builder* had 331 revenue seats and 270 nonrevenue seats, which meant four out of five passengers on board could be some place other than in their assigned seat or bedroom. Other trains, such as the *North Coast Limited, Olympian Hiawatha, California Zephyr,* and Union Pacific's *City* trains, didn't reach the *Empire Builder*'s ratio of nonrevenue to revenue seats but still had many interesting places to sit, including lounges, diners, and observation areas.

Such cruise train features were an important part of attracting passengers to overnight trains, particularly the two-night trains between Chicago and the West Coast. But the vast majority of trains never had domes, and some routes in the east didn't even have enough overhead clearances to permit domes.

THE ULTRALIGHTS OF 1956: THE LAST HOPE FOR PASSENGER TRAINS

In response to the continuing decline in ridership, the railroads and railcar manufacturers introduced five radical new trains in 1956. Indeed, were it not for the fact that most of the trains proved to be abject failures, 1956 would have been the most important year for passenger trains since 1934, the year of the *Zephyr* and Union Pacific streamliner.

The story of the 1956 trains began in 1949, when American Car & Foundry (ACF), the nation's third-largest passenger car builder, built three Talgo trains for the Spanish government-owned railroad. Talgo stands for "Tren Articulado Ligero Goicoechea Oriol," which means "lightweight, articulated train by Goicoechea and Oriol," the latter two words being the last names of the founders of the company that designed the trains. The first Talgo trains were even smaller in profile than the original *Zephyr*. Like the *Zephyr*, the cars were articulated, meaning each pair of cars rested on a common set of wheels. Unlike the *Zephyr*, which used four wheels to support the ends of each pair of cars, the Talgos used only two wheels. Only the locomotive and last car on the train had two sets of two wheels.

Talgo train cars were to the lightweight cars of the 1930s what the lightweights were to heavyweights: much lighter, with a lower center of gravity (which allowed them to go faster around curves), less expensive to build, and less expensive to operate. Today, Amtrak owns Talgo trains that tilt, pendulum-style, when they go around curves to increase passenger comfort. Such tilting was invented by the Pacific Railway Equipment Company, an American firm partly owned by Cortlandt Hill, a grandson of James J. Hill and son of Louis Hill. The company built three cars in 1941; one each for the Great Northern, Burlington, and Santa Fe railways. Talgo didn't adopt tilting until the 1970s, however, so the 1949 trains built by ACF didn't tilt.

Spain proved to be very happy with the ACF-built Talgo trains, using them until 1972. Before shipping all of the trains to Spain, ACF displayed one of them at the Chicago Railroad Fair in the summer of 1949, hoping it could inspire American railroads to try the concept. It took a few years, but by 1956, ACF, Pullman, and General Motors had each convinced two or more railroads to try their own versions of ultralight trains.

In contrast to the 1930s streamliners, whose major goal was to attract new passengers, the main impetus behind the ultralights was cutting costs. By the mid-1950s, many railroads had given up trying to increase passenger ridership. Instead, their goal was to make passenger trains more profitable by reducing expenses. The ultralights promised to do that.

The first to be introduced was GM's Aerotrain, which combined a diesel locomotive styled to look like a jet fighter, with passenger cars made from the same bodies GM used to make Greyhound buses. The locomotive was designed by Charles Jordan, who later created the 1958 Corvette and eventually became chief of design for Cadillac.

GM believed it could use its styling and mass production expertise to improve on the Talgo train's concept of lightweight cars on two-wheel trucks. Unlike the Talgo trains, however, its cars were not articulated, meaning each car had its own four wheels (still fewer than the eight wheels on most lightweight passenger cars). But they were definitely light in weight, and GM bragged that two of its cars weighed half as much as an ordinary coach but carried as many passengers. Moreover, the company claimed the train cars cost only about $1,000 per seat, compared with costs closer to $3,000 per seat for ordinary trains.

The company also said that its cars would be easy to refurbish. While the undercarriage was expected to last many years, passenger car interiors in general wore out quickly. When that happened, GM proposed to simply remove the entire body of the car from the undercarriage and replace it with a new one fresh from the factory. This would cost a lot less, the company claimed, than tearing out and replacing seats, carpet, and other interior fixtures.

GM built two Aerotrains and persuaded the New York Central and Pennsylvania railroads to each try one. In late 1955, New York Central ran an advertisement in national magazines promising, "This Train Will Save an Industry." The ad predicted that the "fast, lightweight new train can revolutionize rail travel, increase employment, and strengthen our national defense." The new train "is 50% lighter than standard trains. It is 60% less expensive to build and 60% less expensive to operate," the ad continued. This would allow the railroad to keep fares low, and "by revitalizing the railroad business, it can lead to more employment." The ad didn't say how the train would strengthen national defense. The Pennsylvania Railroad was similarly enthused about the Aerotrain, and its 1956 calendar featured a painting by artist Grif Teller of an Aerotrain zipping along the Susquehanna River near Harrisburg.

On January 5, 1956, one of the Aerotrains did a press run from Chicago to Detroit on New York Central tracks in four hours, while the other did a press run on Pennsylvania tracks between Washington and Newark. After more demonstration runs on a variety of railroads, including Chicago & North Western, Great Northern, Illinois Central, Santa Fe, Southern Pacific, and Union Pacific, the two trains were put into regular service.

The Pennsylvania train was scheduled to go between New York and Pittsburgh in 7½ hours, the fastest time ever on that route. The New York Central train connected Chicago and Detroit, taking 4⅓ hours. While that was nearly an hour faster than the fastest train on that route, the difference was partly because the Aerotrain stopped only once, while the other trains made at least seven stops.

In February, Rock Island introduced the redundantly named *Jet Rocket* to serve on the 161-mile route between Chicago and Peoria. The *Jet Rocket* combined an Aerotrain-styled locomotive built by GM with cars built by ACF. Like the Talgos, they were articulated but in three-car sets, so one three-car set could be added to or removed from a train at any time.

Pullman called its entry into the ultralight sweepstakes Train X. Built as an obvious imitation of the 1949 Talgo train, Train X had just one axle, or two wheels, under most of the cars. Only the center car had two axles, so the end cars on the train could each have an axle. Train X cars also used a pendulum-tilt system to improve stability when going around curves. Thanks to the tilt system, Pullman promised passengers on Train X would experience a "smoother, more comfortable" ride.

The train was designed to be pulled by a 1,000-horsepower locomotive built by Baldwin-Lima-Hamilton, the company that resulted from the merger of what had once been two of the largest steam locomotive builders in the world. These were among the last locomotives Baldwin built; the company continued to make parts but went out of business about a decade later.

New York Central agreed to try Train X, which it called the *Xplorer*, on its route between Cleveland and Cincinnati. The railroad was excited enough to portray both the Aerotrain and *Xplorer* on the covers of its 1956 timetables. Service began on June 3, 1956, on a 5½-hour schedule, with an average speed of just 45 miles per hour. Although Pullman advertised the train could go 120 miles per hour, New York Central's Cleveland–Cincinnati route didn't have the signaling required by the ICC to go faster than 79 miles per hour, so the train's speed was no faster than other trains on that route.

New York Central's initial enthusiasm for the Aerotrain and *Xplorer* was infectious enough that the New Haven Railroad, which shared Grand Central Terminal with New York Central, bought both a Train X from Pullman and a Talgo train from ACF to operate between New York and Boston. New Haven called its Train X the *Daniel Webster*, and it named the Talgo train the *John Quincy Adams*. Like the *Xplorer*, the *Daniel Webster* was powered by Baldwin-Lima-Hamilton locomotives, one at each end of the train so it wouldn't have to be turned around at the terminuses. Unlike the *Jet Rocket*, the ACF train was powered by Fairbanks Morse diesels, one at each end. Both trains went into service in early 1957.

Meanwhile, Budd introduced two new trains in 1956. Like the Talgo trains, both attempted to reduce costs and weight per passenger, but neither of Budd's trains could be called ultralights. The Pennsylvania Railroad began running the first train, the *Keystone*, between New York and Washington, D.C., in June 1956. In keeping with the Talgo philosophy of having a low center of gravity, the center of the cars was lowered, supposedly allowing higher speeds. But it also meant anyone walking through the cars had to take an annoying three steps down and then three steps up in the middle of each car.

Unlike the Talgo trains, the *Keystones* weren't articulated and didn't rely on just one axle per car. Instead, each car used normal four-wheel trucks. Nevertheless, the cars weighed nearly 25 percent less per seat than an ordinary car used in the New York–Washington, D.C., corridor and, with 82 seats, weighed just 1,130 pounds per seat. Budd said the train cost about $2,000 per seat, compared with $3,000 for a conventional train but only $1,000 for the Aerotrain.

All the Keystone cars built by Budd were coaches, but the Pennsylvania Railroad typically added a conventional parlor car and sometimes a diner or sleeping cars to the *Keystone*. This negated any speed advantage of having a low center of gravity. Though the Pennsylvania Railroad claimed the lower center of gravity would allow it to reduce running times by 15 percent, in fact, the trains were scheduled to go between New York and Washington, D.C., in 3¾ hours, just five minutes faster than the next-fastest train.

In July 1956, Santa Fe introduced what would turn out to be the most important new train of 1956: the bilevel (or, in Santa Fe parlance, hi-level) *El Capitan*. Built by Budd, these double-decked trains included coaches, a diner, and a lounge. All had a lower deck between the wheel-sets with restrooms and baggage racks in the coaches, a coffee shop in the lounge car, and a kitchen in the diner. The upper decks of most of the coaches had 72 seats, well above the 44 seats found in Santa Fe's single-level long-distance coaches. The upper deck of the diner could seat 80 people, while the lounge had 60 seats and a bar serving beverages and light snacks upstairs and 20 seats downstairs. The windows in the lounge car wrapped around the ceiling, providing better views than a coach but not as good as a dome car.

These cars were inspired by bilevel commuter coaches Budd designed and built for Burlington in 1950. The Milwaukee Road and Rock Island railroads also bought bilevel commuter cars from Budd, while the Chicago & North Western and Southern Pacific lines bought similar cars from Pullman and St. Louis Car Company, all for commuter traffic in and out of Chicago or San Francisco. In 1952, Budd proposed to build a bilevel long-distance train, including sleeping cars.

Santa Fe was run by Fred Gurley from 1944 through 1959, and his instincts proved to be as good as his mentor's, Ralph Budd. He ordered two hi-level coaches for test purposes, and Budd delivered them in 1954. After 10 months of testing, Santa Fe suggested some design changes and ordered 47 more, enough for five nine-car trains plus a few spares. Santa Fe, however, did not order hi-level sleeping cars.

The hi-level cars were far from light: the coaches weighed 81 tons and the diners 93 tons. But because each car carried more people, the train weighed nearly 100 tons less than the single-level *El Capitan* it replaced. Santa Fe officials pointed out that, as a long-distance train, the *El Capitan* offered passengers enough legroom to recline their seats nearly flat at night, while the ultralights crammed in seats far more tightly because they were for short-distance travel. As a Santa Fe official told *Popular Science* magazine, "If one of those track-skimming lightweight cars on a Talgo or a Train X were fitted out with comparably wide-spaced seats, it would weigh only seven pounds less, per passenger, than an El Capitan coach."[23] The new cars also reduced operating costs, partly because each coach attendant was able to serve 60 percent more passengers.

The *El Capitan* was by far the most successful of the 1956 trains. It was the only one to generate a repeat order, as Santa Fe bought two dozen more hi-level cars to use on the *San Francisco Chief* and other trains in 1963. The hi-level train was the only one to survive until the creation of Amtrak, and Amtrak still used some *El Capitan* cars as late as 2017. The hi-level cars also inspired Amtrak's current fleet of Superliners.

In contrast, New York Central gave up on its Aerotrain after just six months, returning it to GM. Pennsylvania returned its train after just one year. GM persuaded Union Pacific to try the two trains as the *City of Las Vegas* between Las Vegas and Los Angeles, but that lasted only a few months until October 1957.

All the railroads that tested Aerotrains came to the same conclusion: Whether in short-haul or long-haul service, the Aerotrains were awful. The ride was uncomfortable, particularly at high speeds, and the 1,200-horsepower engines weren't powerful enough to ascend hills such as Cajon Pass east of Los Angeles without helper locomotives. General Motors ended up selling the Aerotrains to Rock Island, which used them as commuter trains on the 40-mile corridor between Chicago and Joliet. For similar reasons, Rock Island withdrew the *Jet Rocket* from the Chicago–Peoria route and turned it into a Chicago–Joliet commuter train. The trains continued in their new roles until 1966.

Pullman's Train X didn't fare any better. The New York Central operated its *Xplorer* for less than 15 months before pulling it from service for the same reason as the Aerotrain: uncomfortable rides. The New Haven also pulled both its Train X and ACF Talgo train after just 15 months of service.

New Haven ordered a third new train from Budd, which had introduced self-propelled rail diesel cars (RDCs) in 1949. The train for the New Haven consisted of six RDCs modified by adding semi-streamlined noses to the end cars and including controls only in those end cars. Called the *Roger Williams*, the train went into service in April 1957. Because it wasn't an ultralight, it was comfortable to ride, and the train continued operating into the Amtrak era and was not retired until 1980.

One more railroad got sucked into the ultralight fiasco. Patrick McGinnis was president of the New Haven railroad when it ordered its ultralight trains, and he promised improved passenger service. Instead, he deferred maintenance: as a result, on-time performance declined to 65 percent, and the board of directors fired him before any of his new trains could be put into service. He then became president of the Boston & Maine Railroad, where he ordered another ultralight Talgo train from ACF. The railroad operated the train for about seven years, initially between Boston and Portland, before scrapping it. McGinnis, meanwhile, was convicted and imprisoned for accepting kickbacks from companies that did business with Boston & Maine, which might explain why he had ordered so many new trains.

Pennsylvania's *Keystone* fared better than the ultralights, operating for a dozen years until 1968. While not considered as successful as the *El Capitan* or *Roger Williams*, there were few complaints about ride comfort, and the railroad might have attracted more riders by operating it at higher speeds if it had ordered lounge, dining, and other cars from Budd that shared the *Keystone*'s low center of gravity.

Of the trains introduced in 1956 and 1957, the ones built by Pullman, ACF, and GM failed, while the trains built by Budd were successful. Budd seemed to recognize that building trains whose sole aim was to reduce costs wouldn't work if they also sacrificed passenger comfort. Building trains that maintained or improved passenger comfort, while reducing weight and cost per passenger, was much more successful. Whatever Budd's secret, it emerged the winner in the 1956 effort to revolutionize passenger trains. Though he never eclipsed Pullman as the leading passenger car builder, Budd's reputation made its cars a passenger favorite from the first *Zephyr* in 1934 through at least the 1980s. Unfortunately, while Budd's innovations could compete against Pullman and other railcar manufacturers, they couldn't enable trains to successfully compete with airlines and automobiles.

8. THE MUNICIPALIZATION OF URBAN TRANSIT

Recent studies of subsidy impacts conclude that direct benefits to transit riders have been small relative to the increase in subsidy, and that the alleged environmental and secondary economic benefits are negligible or non-existent. Some critics—including former transit advocates—complain that subsidies have simply inflated costs instead of providing more, better, or cheaper service for transit riders.

—John Pucher, Anders Markstedt, and Ira Hirschman[1]

POSTWAR URBAN EVOLUTION

Transit ridership boomed during World War II, but the biggest beneficiary of that boom was the bus. In 1938, streetcars still carried half of all transit riders, but by 1942, trips on buses, including trolley buses, outnumbered streetcar trips. Between 1940 and 1945, motor bus ridership more than doubled, and trolley bus ridership grew by 140 percent. Both continued to grow for several years after the war ended. Some of this growth was due to the replacement of streetcar lines. Streetcar ridership grew by 60 percent from 1940 to 1944 but declined slightly in 1945 and fell steadily thereafter. Even at its wartime peak, streetcar ridership was only 70 percent of its prewar peak.

Although rapid transit benefited from the war, at least when compared with Depression numbers, ridership in 1945 was only about 5 percent more than it had been in 1930. New York subway ridership was actually

lower in 1945 than it had been in 1930. In 1947, the city's subway ridership beat the 1930 record by one-tenth of a percent but declined thereafter. Rapid transit in the other three cities with such trains—Boston,
Chicago, and Philadelphia—carried nearly 50 percent more riders in 1945
than in 1940, but their ridership also started declining in 1947.

Like rapid transit, commuter-train ridership grew during the war,
but did not reach its pre-Depression peak. Ridership in 1944 was nearly
60 percent more than in 1940, but it was still 8 percent less than in 1929,
and ridership began declining in 1945, even before the end of the war.

Interurbans benefited little from the war. The industry had been in the
red during the entire Depression and was rapidly being dismantled. The
war put what was left of it in the black—barely—for a few years, but by
1950, almost all the interurbans were gone.

Chicago transit in particular was in trouble by the end of the war. The
companies running Chicago's streetcars and rapid-transit lines had gone
bankrupt during the Depression and were still in receivership at the end
of the war despite the intervening ridership boom. Their rolling stock was
40 to 50 years old and needed replacement, something the companies
couldn't afford to do. Frustrated by regulators who wouldn't allow them
to raise fares, most of the companies' owners were eager to sell their operations to the public. In 1945, the Illinois legislature created the Chicago
Transit Authority with the expectation that once it had taken over the
city's transit systems, it would be able to cover its costs out of fares. The
authority was not allowed to assess taxes of any kind and even had to pay
property, fuel, and other taxes, just like the private companies it replaced.

It took two years to negotiate a price for buying the rail lines, but
the authority finally took control over streetcars and rapid transit on
October 1, 1947. In its first full year of operation, however, revenues fell
short of expenses by nearly a million dollars. Hoping to turn this around,
Mayor Martin Kennelly appointed Ralph Budd to the authority's board
in 1949. Even though he was retired, his fellow transit authority board
members quickly voted him chairman of the board—a position that paid
a full-time salary—and he threw himself into the work.

While banks had been reluctant to loan money to a public agency
that was losing money and had no assured tax support, Budd was able

to use his prestige and connections to sell investment trust certificates for new rapid-transit cars and buses.[2] He quickly realized that changing land-use patterns had rendered obsolete many of the streetcar and a few of the rapid-transit routes. Although the authority had recently taken delivery of 600 PCC streetcars, Budd began replacing streetcars and six of the rapid-transit lines with buses. He sold or scrapped most of the PCC cars well before their time, creatively using some of the parts to make rapid-transit cars.[3]

An acolyte of Bradford Snell claims that Budd's connections with GM make him a part of the great streetcar conspiracy, replacing streetcars with supposedly inferior buses to discourage transit ridership.[4] However, instead of GM's diesel buses, Budd purchased Twin Coach propane-powered coaches made by the Fageol brothers. In 1955, the Fageol brothers sold their company to Flxible, an appropriate name for a bus company because buses were far more flexible than streetcars.[5]

By the time Budd retired as chairman in 1952, the Chicago Transit Authority was collecting enough fare revenue to both cover its operating costs and repay some of its debts. This was partly due to Budd's reduction in operating costs—buses, for example, required only one operator, while streetcars required both a driver and a conductor to collect fares—and partly to fare increases that had been denied to the private companies that preceded the authority.

However, Budd wasn't able to stop the slide in transit ridership. Like almost every other major American city, Chicago's rail transit system was hit by two body blows in the postwar era. First, America's largest cities saw a major exodus of people to the suburbs as working-class families, mobilized by the mass-produced automobile and aided by mass-produced housing in suburban subdivisions, were finally able to achieve the social reformers' dreams of leaving the crowded tenements. While this was good for the workers, it wasn't necessarily good for central cities or their transit systems.

After peaking at 3.6 million people in 1950, Chicago's population declined in every census through 1990. While it recovered slightly in 2000, it fell again in 2010 to less than 75 percent of the 1950 level. This contributed to the Chicago Transit Authority's 31 percent decline in ridership from 1950 to 2010.

Population declines in other cities were even more staggering. After 1950, St. Louis and Detroit lost 63 percent of their residents; Buffalo, Cleveland, and Pittsburgh all lost 55 to 60 percent; Cincinnati 41 percent; Baltimore 35 percent; Boston, Minneapolis, and Providence 30 percent; Philadelphia and Washington, D.C., 25 percent; and New York, Oakland, San Francisco, and St. Paul 10 to 13 percent. New York, Oakland, and San Francisco bottomed out in 1980 and eventually recovered their lost populations, while Boston, Minneapolis, Philadelphia, Providence, St. Paul, and Washington recovered a small portion of their losses after 1980, but the rest were still losing population as of the 2010 census.

Many of these were rust-belt cities, but the decline in manufacturing didn't begin until well after 1960. Except for Buffalo and Pittsburgh, the urban areas around all of these cities grew in every decade after 1950, so the population loss in the cities was more than made up for by growth in the suburbs. The reality was that high-density neighborhoods were thinning out as people's incomes rose and they found their way to low-density suburbs. While population declines may have created financial hardship for some city governments, this was an artifact of state laws restricting the ability of the cities to annex their suburbs. Indianapolis enjoyed strong annexation authority and never saw its population decline, although the center of the city probably lost population.

All of the cities whose populations fell had one thing in common: their cores were built before the development of the electric streetcar, at a time when most working-class employees had to live within walking distance of their work. Many of the high-density buildings they lived in were crowded, dilapidated, and conducive to the spread of both disease and crime. No thanks to the social planners, affordable automobiles liberated many workers by allowing them to move to places where they could find affordable housing.

As if insulted that things hadn't worked according to their plans, planners went on a two-pronged attack to reverse city population declines. First, they demonized the suburbs as vacuous and sterile. A 1956 book titled *The Crack in the Picture Window* argued that the suburbs were "conceived in error, nurtured by greed, corroding everything they touch."[6] No one had criticized the suburbs when the wealthy moved there in the late

19th century, or when the educated middle class moved there after the development of the electric streetcar. But when the working class moved there in the 1950s, the suburbs were suddenly evil. Anti-suburban campaigns were supported by central city governments that resented the loss of tax revenues when people left the cities for their suburbs.

The second approach was to "save downtowns" through urban renewal. Planners declared the left-behind high-density housing to be "blighted," meaning they didn't think rational owners would spend money to gentrify dilapidated buildings because all of the neighboring structures were also in bad shape. To solve this problem, they used tax dollars to take the housing and other buildings by eminent domain, clear them, and build new developments, often in the form of high-rise housing. Planners were clearly still laboring under the monocentric view of the city and the assumption that downtowns should always reign paramount over the rest of the urban area, when in fact downtowns were a relatively new phenomenon and the term itself, as a reference to a central business district, had existed only since the 1840s.[7]

One obstacle they faced was that the former high-density housing they wanted to clear wasn't empty. Much of it was occupied by blacks, immigrants, and others who found it to be more affordable than anything else available to them. The apartments in the 19th-century tenement buildings were too small to entertain guests, so people did their socializing on their porches and sidewalks. These neighborhoods also attracted a few bohemian whites who appreciated the diversity and lively streets created by the immigrant residents who ate unusual foods and entertained outdoors.

One of those bohemians, an architecture critic named Jane Jacobs, was upset to learn New York City had declared her Greenwich Village neighborhood to be a blighted slum and slated it for redevelopment into a series of high rises. To stop this, Jacobs wrote *The Death and Life of Great American Cities*, which had two themes: first, that urban planners didn't understand how cities worked—which was correct—and second, that she *did* understand how cities worked—which was completely wrong. She saw her neighborhood during an instant in time she considered idyllic, when in fact it was in transition from a working-class neighborhood to an immigrant neighborhood to something else. Whatever that something was would not be appreciated by most American families. Her criticism of the postwar high-rise mania, combined with the disastrous failure of those government-built high rises, put a stop to that planning fad. As will be described in Chapter 10, however, *The Death and Life of Great American Cities* would spawn its own equally disastrous planning fad in the 1990s.

One problem suburbanization created for rail transit was that most streetcar and rapid-transit lines were franchised or built by cities and often did not go beyond city boundaries. Other than interurbans, which were pretty much gone by the early 1950s, the main rail transit that crossed city lines was railroad-operated commuter trains. However, the Norman Rockwell image of the suburban housewife meeting her husband at the train station with the family car was a reality in only a few urban areas, mainly New York, Chicago, Philadelphia, Boston, and San Francisco. Even in those areas, most suburban workers commuted by car. The shift of most downtown jobs, other than in the finance industry, to the suburbs wasn't a problem for anyone outside of the transit industry.

The second blow to urban rail transit was a shift in the nature of work. In 1920, nearly 40 percent of all American jobs were in manufacturing, and there were just 1.3 service jobs for every manufacturing job. The number of manufacturing jobs continued to grow through 1980, but that growth was vastly outpaced by the growth in service jobs, so by then, there were three service jobs for every manufacturing job.[8] The service jobs included work in health care, education, wholesale and retail trade, government, and utilities. While manufacturing jobs were concentrated, most service jobs were diffused across urban areas. I call this the *nanocentric* city, because, to the extent that jobs had centers at all, there would be uncountable numbers of such centers in major urban areas. *Nanocentric* also sounds a bit like *noncentric*, meaning there is no one center.

Just as urban planners were beginning to recognize the demise of the monocentric city, the service economy was leaving the polycentric city behind in the dust. Transit did a poor job of serving the polycentric city, with buses working better than rails. Transit is even less suited to serving a nanocentric urban area, especially a growing region whose job locations and patterns shift almost daily.

The Interstate Highway System is often blamed for the demise of urban transit, yet all of these changes were independent of the construction of that system. Curiously, the term *freeway* was coined by Edward Bassett, the father of urban zoning and social reformer who hoped rapid transit would help working-class families escape dense, urban tenements.[9] Highways and automobiles did more to help people escape tenements than rapid transit, but in fact most of that dispersal had already taken place before the interstate highways were built. Congress did not approve that gargantuan project until 1956, by which time annual per capita transit ridership had already fallen to fewer than 100 trips per urban resident. A decade later, fewer than half the miles of the Interstate Highway System had been completed, yet the average urban resident rode transit fewer than 60 times per year.

The original interstate highway proposal from the Bureau of Public Roads was a network of roads bypassing the major cities. The federal planners who designed the system believed that urban roads were a local matter and did not deserve federal funding. However, big-city mayors objected to this plan, believing (probably correctly) that it would hasten their decline. After the Bureau of Public Roads added 4,000 miles of freeways into the hearts of most major cities, Congress approved the revised plan with the support of those mayors. Those freeways became controversial for many reasons, but they didn't kill the transit industry.

A more profound threat to big-city downtowns came when, as will be described more fully in Chapter 9, Congress passed a law in 1958 allowing railroads to discontinue intercity passenger trains upon notification to the ICC. If it didn't object, the railroads could drop the trains in 30 days. It never occurred to Congress to exempt commuter trains from this law, so when railroads proposed to drop such trains, it led to panic among the big cities that depended on them. It is probably true that the job numbers and densities found in Manhattan, and possibly the Chicago loop, can only be served by high-capacity commuter trains and rapid rail. Boston, Philadelphia, and San Francisco downtowns, on the other hand, have far fewer jobs, and buses could have replaced the commuter trains without much problem.

Congress was not likely to respond to the panic over the loss of commuter trains by saying Manhattan should simply die. But it also didn't want to impose on private railroads an obligation to subsidize downtown businesses and property owners. With passage of the Urban Mass Transit Act of 1964, Congress opted for a third alternative, which was to offer federal capital funding to support cities and states that took over the operation of commuter trains. The constitutional justification for such aid was that commuter trains crossed state lines in four of the five urban areas that had them and were, therefore, engaged in interstate commerce. But Congress couldn't pass a spending bill benefitting just four cities, so it offered capital grants to any government transit agency in the country, even though few other transit systems crossed state lines.

MUNICIPALIZATION

By the beginning of 1960, just 12 of the nation's one hundred largest cities had municipalized their transit systems. After Seattle, Detroit, and Phoenix municipalized their transit between 1919 and 1925, it would be 15 more years before another major city would do so. As previously mentioned, New York took over its rapid-transit lines in 1940, and San Francisco purchased its private street railways in 1944. Cleveland municipalized its transit system in 1942, while Boston and Chicago did so in 1947. Chicago also took over its last remaining private bus system in 1952. Sacramento municipalized in 1955, Los Angeles in 1958, and Evansville and San Antonio in 1959.[10]

Municipalization picked up in the 1960s, with Miami, Oakland, Pittsburgh, St. Louis, and eight other large cities taking over their transit systems between 1960 and 1964. Yet when Congress passed the Urban Mass Transit Act, more than three out of four transit systems in the nation's 100 largest cities, and 82 percent of all transit systems in the country, remained in private ownership, including systems in Philadelphia and Washington, D.C. Although a few transit systems lost money, mainly those under public ownership, overall transit revenues were 5 percent greater than operating costs.[11] Ridership was declining, however, and many companies had responded by deferring maintenance and replacement of aging buses.

Led by Albuquerque in 1965, cities and states leapt to take advantage of federal subsidies, often creating county or regional transit districts that could take over transit companies and serve entire counties or urban areas rather than just individual cities. Over the next dozen years, 70 major cities would municipalize transit. By the end of 1980, only two of the nation's largest cities, New Orleans and Greensboro, North Carolina, would still have private transit. New Orleans municipalized its system in 1983, and Greensboro finally followed in 1991.

In some cities, federally funded purchases of new buses and other equipment led to increased ridership. Nationally, however, ridership continued to decline until 1973, when spikes in gasoline prices persuaded some commuters to return to public transit. A more insidious trend was taking place, however. When the industry was mostly private, inflation-adjusted operating costs had declined in parallel with ridership as transit companies reduced service on little-used routes. After 1964, however, operating costs began to grow despite continuing declines in ridership. Between 1964 and 1975, inflation-adjusted fare revenues had fallen 18 percent, yet operating costs had grown by 46 percent.[12]

The reason for the increase in operating costs was simple: transit agencies had the money, so they spent it. State legislatures gave most of the new transit agencies the authority to collect taxes dedicated to their use on transit projects. Sales taxes were a favorite, used as the primary source of operating subsidies in California, Illinois, Massachusetts, and at least 10 other states. Property taxes were the main source of transit funds in Indiana, Maryland, and eight other states. Transit systems in other states, including Connecticut, Rhode Island, Virginia, Wisconsin, and the District of Columbia, relied heavily on a share of state gasoline taxes. Oregon transit agencies collected a payroll tax that was really an income tax invisible to employees because employers paid it.

In 1964, transit fare revenues exceeded operating costs, but some of this revenue was spent on capital replacement. The remaining fares paid for more than 90 percent of transit operating costs. By 1975, however, fares covered just 53 percent of operating costs, and virtually all capital costs came out of taxpayers' pockets.[13] One way transit agencies used this surfeit of funds was to negotiate cushy deals with transit unions. Unions quickly realized that the politicians running transit agencies wanted to avoid strikes. Union members helped elect those politicians, so transit worker pay and benefits quickly grew. After adjusting for inflation, average transit worker pay increased nearly 30 percent from 1964 to 1975.[14]

Until 1975, the federal government offered only capital subsidies to transit agencies. Perhaps spurred by the rise in oil prices, Congress in 1975 began offering operating subsidies as well. While the federal government covered only about 10 percent of operating costs, transit riders' share of operating costs continued to fall, eventually reaching less than a third in 2002, and it has hovered around 32 percent ever since.[15]

The transit systems inherited by municipal transit agencies nearly all followed hub-and-spoke patterns centered in the downtowns. This worked for monocentric cities, but by 1964, few if any urban areas in America were still monocentric. Most transit agencies changed this pattern only by extending bus service deeper into the suburbs, where nearly all residents owned and drove cars. Such service extensions helped children too young to have drivers' licenses and others who didn't have access to cars. But the main benefit for the transit agencies was that they could tax the residents of the communities they served, even if few people in those communities actually rode transit. In addition to union contracts, these service extensions were a major reason for the increase in transit operating costs.

One transit agency, San Jose's Santa Clara County Transit District, attempted to design a transit system that would work in a modern nanocentric urban area. In 1974, the agency began offering a shared, dial-a-ride service that worked something like Uber or Lyft today. People could call the agency's control center and request a ride. They would be picked up at their door by small buses or large vans and dropped off at their destination, with the bus picking up and dropping off other passengers along the way. The agency used computers to identify the best routes for each vehicle.[16]

The first problem the agency encountered was that the call center, which was designed to handle about 10,000 calls a day, was swamped with 80,000 per day. The second problem was that the local taxi companies saw this service as a violation of their franchise and sued, demanding compensation. The third problem was data showing that the dial-a-ride service cost more than three times as much as fixed-route buses yet carried fewer than one-fifth as many people. As a result, the service was shut down after less than six months.[17] Since then, transit agencies have reserved dial-a-ride programs for elderly and disabled passengers.

While sticking with existing hub-and-spoke routes, most managers of newly municipalized transit agencies agreed with private transit operators that buses were superior to streetcars. It was therefore the Los Angeles Metropolitan Transit Authority, not GM or National City Lines, that dismantled the last of the region's Pacific Electric lines in 1961 and the last of city's streetcar lines in 1963.[18] It was likewise the Bi-State Development Authority, not National City, that dismantled the last streetcar lines in St. Louis in 1966.[19] The Chicago Transit Authority abandoned the Windy City's last streetcar lines in 1958.[20] Municipal transit agencies shut down the last streetcar lines in Seattle in 1941, Phoenix in 1948, and Detroit in 1956. The Cleveland Transit System dismantled the city's last street railways in 1954, but kept a grade-separated line and, bucking the trend, opened a new rapid-transit line in 1958. El Paso closed its last streetcar line to Ciudad Juarez in 1974, having kept it that long only because customs officials said it was easier for them to screen travelers on a railcar than on a bus.

After El Paso shut down its international rail route, just eight urban areas had some form of rail transit: rapid transit in New York, Chicago, Philadelphia, Boston, and Cleveland; commuter trains in New York, Chicago, Philadelphia, Boston, and San Francisco; and street railways in Cleveland, New York (Newark), Philadelphia, Boston, San Francisco, Pittsburgh, and New Orleans. That might have been the end of the story. As it turned out, however, the prospect of federal money for rail construction led to a revival of rail transit in the 1970s and 1980s.

After 1970, transit ridership rose and fell mainly in response to population growth and fuel prices, two variables over which transit agencies have little control. As shown in Figure 8.1, annual trips per urban resident peaked at 51 in 1980, thanks largely to the late-1970s energy crisis that sent gasoline prices above $3 per gallon. Ridership bottomed out at 38 trips per urban resident in 1995 as gas prices fell to $1.70 a gallon. Gas prices approached $4 a gallon in 2008, pushing ridership close to 44 trips per urban resident, but prices fell again after 2012, leading to an erosion of both total and per capita transit ridership.

Figure 8.1
Transit Ridership from 1970 to 2017

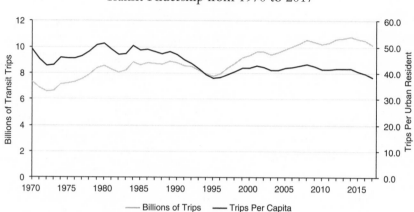

Sources: *Public Transit Fact Book 2016,* American Public Transportation Association, for data through 2014; *National Transit Database,* Federal Transit Administration, for data since 2014. Notes: APTA says that it bases its numbers on the *National Transit Database,* but its ridership is about 2.3 percent higher than the FTA numbers, so for continuity, this chart adds 2.3 percent to the FTA numbers for 2015 through 2017. The 2017 number is based on the calendar year, while previous data are based on transit agency fiscal years.

Municipalization led to a dramatic decline in transit productivity by almost any measure. For example, not counting the war period, the private transit industry carried about 55,000 to 60,000 passengers a year per operating employee. After municipalization, worker productivity rapidly dropped to its current level of about 27,000 trips per operating employee (Figure 8.2), at least a 50 percent decline. This stands out as one of the biggest declines in employee productivity of any industry in history.

Early advocates of municipalization believed government-owned transit systems would collect enough fares to at least cover operating costs, especially since transit agencies would not need to return dividends to stockholders or other owners. Instead, under municipalization, operating costs grew far faster than fares. When adjusting for inflation using the consumer price index, operating costs per transit trip have grown 22 times faster than fares per trip since 1970 (Figure 8.3).

The movement to build new rail transit lines also caused capital productivity to decline. Unfortunately, capital expenditure data are not

Figure 8.2

Transit Trips Per Operating Employee

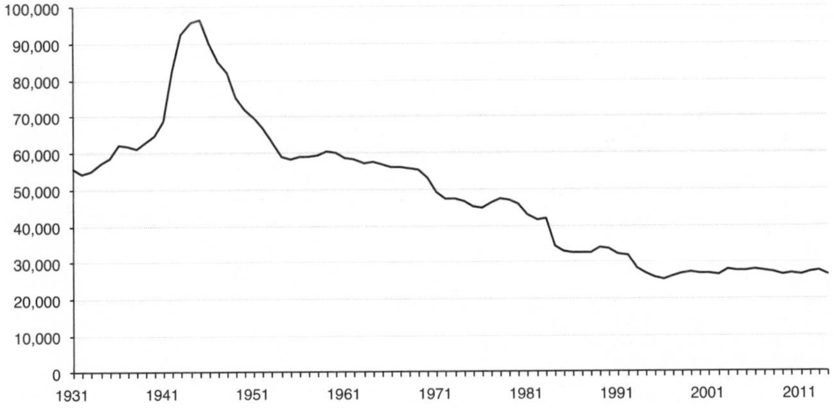

Source: *Public Transit Fact Book 2017,* American Public Transportation Association.

available before 1988, but since then, the inflation-adjusted capital cost per trip has more than doubled (Figure 8.4).

These productivity declines were directly due to the subsidies offered by states and cities as they took over transit systems. "During periods when subsidies have increased most, productivity has declined and costs have

Figure 8.3

Operating Productivity

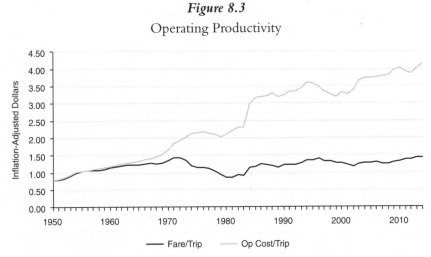

Source: *Public Transit Fact Book 2017,* American Public Transportation Association. Adjusted for inflation using GDP price deflators.

Figure 8.4
Trips Per Capital Dollar

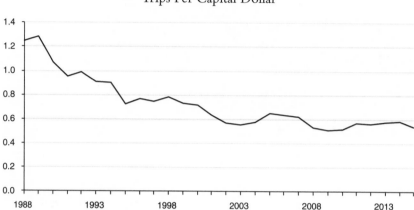

Source: *Public Transit Fact Book 2017,* American Public Transportation Association. Adjusted for inflation using GDP price deflators.

grown most rapidly," one study found. Moreover, when cost differences between bus systems were examined, "it was found that costs were much higher for those systems that relied on large Federal and state subsidies and dedicated state and local transit taxes."[21]

American cities' experiences with municipal transit have provided some important lessons for anyone who looked at them carefully. Progressives believed that with no profit motive forcing them to cut corners or diverting revenues to owners' pockets, enlightened bureaucrats would efficiently manage transit for the public benefit. But as ridership declined, agencies such as the Chicago Transit Authority and San Francisco Muni were forced to turn to politicians for tax support, and when politics replaces profit, the inevitable result is mission creep.

Transit agencies whose original missions were to move people efficiently soon adopted new missions aimed at pleasing politicians: promoting economic development; constructing rail monuments that created jobs for union workers and profits for contractors; and getting people out of their cars and into "green" transportation. In their view, these missions justified continued tax subsidies to transit despite declining per capita ridership and, in many regions, declining total ridership.

9. THE NATIONALIZATION OF INTERCITY PASSENGER TRAINS

To cook up a future for the American passenger train, blackmail 20 railroads into a frying pan, congeal with Woodrow Wilson–era work-rules and Truman-second-term-era diesels and coaches, season with red jackets and a pointless arrow, bring to a boil over Congressional oratory, dilute with one cupful of ICC, add a pinch of NARP, spice with Turbo, employ non-rail cooks, and pour into airline plastic. Serves 43 states and D.C.

—David P. Morgan, November 1971

RAIL RESPONSE TO DECLINING RIDERSHIP

Great Northern Railway builder James J. Hill has often been quoted as saying "the passenger train is like a male teat: neither useful nor ornamental." In fact, there is no record of him actually saying that, and Hill's most thorough biographer, Albro Martin, argues it is "doubtful" that he did.[1] The earliest use of the quote I can find is in a 1951 humor book.[2]

Despite its questionable provenance, writer Peter Lyon was happy to use this quote in his 1968 book, *To Hell in a Day Coach*, to back up his thesis that "America's railway tycoons had decided that it was much more profitable to move freight than people" and therefore did everything they could to discourage rail passengers beginning in the 19th century.[3] This thesis was critical to passenger rail advocates' arguments that the decline of the passenger train was not the fault of passengers but rather the railroads themselves, and that such passenger trains would have been profitable if only the government had operated them.

"When reality is so violently opposed to one's preferences as to be unbearable, the talent of the human mind for finding an alternative explanation in a vast malevolent conspiracy is unbounded," said George Hilton in his review of Lyon's book. Hilton noted that Lyon "relies for analysis on a heavy outpouring of vituperative adjectives and pejorative nouns" and that the book is basically "an argument for perpetuation of a resource allocation.""Since the industry has enormous excess capacity by anybody's standards," Hilton noted (which was true for most of the 20th century but is less true today), "the fact that freight was more profitable than passengers is no explanation" for a supposed executive preference for freight over passengers.

It seems unlikely that James J. Hill, for example, would have truly believed passenger trains were useless, because during his lifetime they regularly generated around 20 percent of Great Northern's revenues. Including mail and express delivery, which were almost always carried on passenger trains, brought the total closer to 25 percent. In the 25 years before Hill's death in 1916, passenger revenues on the Great Northern grew faster than freight. Although passengers also cost more than freight to transport, a large share of railroad expenses was fixed and had to be paid with or without passengers, so Hill would have welcomed any additional revenues that covered their variable costs.

Railroads responded to declining ridership in the 1950s by reducing costs and discontinuing trains with fewer passengers. Other cost reductions included eliminating observation cars, which simplified midroute switching of train cars; simplifying passenger train paint schemes; and reducing the number of dining car services and menu options.

The Pennsylvania Railroad initiated changes to observation cars in 1948 by ordering lounge cars with rear ends that were only slightly rounded, replacing the parabolic rounding pioneered by the *Zephyr*. Such blunt-end cars could be used on the rear of trains but could also be put in the middle. Most of Burlington's and Union Pacific's postwar observation cars also had blunted ends. In the early 1950s, Santa Fe started ordering trains without any observation cars, instead placing lounges midtrain. The *Texas Chief, San Francisco Chief,* and hi-level *El Capitan* never had observation cars, even with blunt ends, and by 1957, the railroad had gone so far as to drop observation cars from its premiere train, the *Super Chief.*

Railroads that ordered unpainted stainless-steel passenger trains didn't have to worry about repainting them. But many streamliners were painted in colorful stripes that were often painstakingly separated by pinstripes. The Southern Pacific *Daylights* were two tones of orange separated by white pinstripes; by 1960, it was painting most of its trains grey or silver or leaving them unpainted except for a single red stripe. Northern Pacific's original streamliner was painted with two tones of green separated by three yellow pinstripes; Raymond Loewy's greens were much prettier, but he also deleted two of the pinstripes. Great Northern painted its passenger cars green with two orange stripes separated by yellow pinstripes, but in 1962, it began painting its locomotives without the pinstripes or one of the orange stripes. In 1967, it went further by replacing the orange-and-green color scheme with blue-and-grey paint with one white stripe and no pinstripes.

Railroads simplified dining car menus by reducing the number of available items. Before the war, some dinner menus offered complete meals featuring eight or more entrees in table d'hôte fashion, along with dozens of a la carte items such as steaks, chops, and fish. By the early 1950s, just six table d'hôte entrees and a handful of a la carte entrees, plus some sandwiches and salads, was more typical. By the late 1960s, many menus offered only three or four table d'hôte entrees as well as three or four a la carte sandwiches and salads.

A more drastic way of reducing expenses was to cancel passenger trains. Railroads discontinued thousands of passenger trains during the 1950s: the 9,000 daily trains operating in 1920 had dwindled to fewer than 3,000 by 1958. Before 1958, railroads wishing to cancel trains needed to apply to state railroad or public utility commissions for permission to do so. If a train served more than one state, the railroad needed the permission of commissions from every state served. Between 1951 and 1956, states had approved 1,274 train discontinuances but denied 197, saying the railroads needed to continue serving communities that had no other options.[4]

Railroads were regulated in other ways as well, particularly regarding fares and rates. Any changes to interstate rail rates required approval from the ICC, and the time-consuming approval process made it difficult for railroads to compete in many markets. One state public utility commission denied a fare increase requested by a railroad because "it has been generally recognized that railroad passenger service, as presently conducted, has not and cannot be operated at a profit."[5] As a result, many railroads were not only losing money on passengers, they were also doing poorly on freight.

The failure of the railroads to share in the postwar prosperity led Congress to pass the Transportation Act of 1958. This law took only token steps to deregulate railroad rate setting and transferred the authority to discontinue passenger trains from the states to the ICC. This meant railroads needed to get permission from only one agency instead of several to cancel interstate trains. The ICC process was also simpler than in some states: the railroad needed to notify only the ICC that it was discontinuing a train, and if it took no action, the railroad could stop running it in as little as 30 days.

In the decade after the 1958 law was passed, the ICC allowed railroads to cancel nearly 750 trains but denied dozens of other proposed discontinuances. In one celebrated case, Northern Pacific petitioned three times to discontinue the *Mainstreeter*, the railroad's secondary transcontinental, and was denied permission each time based on "public convenience and necessity." In the last petition, the railroad stated that the train carried an average of just 34 passengers (calculated by dividing passenger miles by train miles) and lost $3.5 million a year. The commission responded that the *Mainstreeter* stopped in 60 cities not served by the railroad's premiere train, the *North Coast Limited*, and suggested that two of the reasons for declining ridership were that the railroad had downgraded service by removing the train's sleeping car as well as rescheduling it so that it missed connections in various cities.[6]

The issue of "downgrading" became a mantra for passenger train advocates who were convinced trains would do well if only the railroads continued to provide decent service. Many passengers probably never noticed simplified paint schemes or shrinking dining car menus, but they became upset when railroads completely dropped lightly patronized lounge or dining cars from trains. Passenger train advocates accused rail-roads of deliberately downgrading services in order to discourage ridership so they could justify dropping trains from the schedules. Southern Pacific in particular raised public ire in the early 1960s when it replaced some of its dining cars with automat cars containing giant vending machines dispensing sandwiches and other foods and beverages.

In 1966, the ICC refused to allow Southern Pacific to discontinue a train because the railroad appeared to have deliberately discouraged people from riding it. It deleted the train from its published timetables, its agents denied the train existed, and it closed ticket offices hours before the train was scheduled to depart. "Whenever it appears," the ICC said, "that a carrier has deliberately downgraded its service in order to justify discontinuance of a train irrespective of the actual or potential needs of the traveling public, the Commission will order the service to be continued."[7]

Many people not only objected to downgrading; they also wanted railroads to upgrade their passenger trains. In objecting to the discontinuance of the *Mainstreeter*, for example, the Pasco, Washington, city council noted "that there are other trains in the country making substantial profit and, indeed, upgrading their trains to the point where they are appealing to the public (example: trains from Washington, D.C., to the various Eastern cities)." In fact, as will be described later in this chapter, the trains from Washington, D.C., mentioned in the letter were not only not profitable, they were a federally subsidized experiment.

Passenger train supporters tended to classify railroads as either passenger friendly or passenger hostile. The former group included the Santa Fe and Great Northern lines. Great Northern's chief operating officer, Robert Downing, noted that company CEO John "Budd made it clear to his senior management that, while some trains would have to come off, he wanted every officer of the company to see that remaining trains were run well and a credit to the company."[8]

At the other extreme was the supposedly passenger-hostile Southern Pacific (SP) railroad, whose use of automat cars in place of dining cars would never be forgiven. The SP was led by Donald Russell from 1952 to 1972, the same era that John Budd ran the Great Northern. "Beginning about 1955," says longtime rail reporter Fred Frailey, "as soon a train became unprofitable" by failing to cover its direct, separable costs, Russell "immediately sought to remove it from the timetable." On the other hand, Frailey said, in order to keep train revenues above their direct costs, Russell would make "cost-cutting moves others interpreted as direct sabotage of Southern Pacific's passenger trains."[9] This suggests that the distinction between passenger-friendly and passenger-hostile railroads may have been unfair, and apparent downgrades such as the automat car should really have been classed as failed experiments just like the ultralight trains.

Air travelers today complain about cramped seats, inedible (or no) food, and overbooked planes, but air travel continues to grow, and the airlines fill on average 85 percent of their seats. In contrast, even railroads such as the Santa Fe and Great Northern that welcomed passengers couldn't stop the decline in rail ridership.

The last straw for many railroads came in 1967, when the U.S. Post Office cancelled all its mail contracts with the railroads, electing to move first-class mail by air and truck. Despite Morgan's argument that the passenger business should stand on its own, the fact was that most railroads moved mail and passengers on the same trains, thus earning twice the revenue for the same basic cost. Mail revenues actually exceeded passenger revenues on many trains, so cancellation of the mail contracts led to more passenger trains being discontinued. Frailey, for example, counted Kansas City Southern as one of the more passenger-friendly railroads. Yet within three months of the loss of its mail contracts, it notified the ICC that it wanted to discontinue all of its passenger trains.[10]

When Great Northern, Northern Pacific, and Burlington merged into Burlington Northern in 1970, the "passenger-friendly" Great Northern had eight trains left on its timetable, while the "passenger-hostile" Northern Pacific had six. Burlington, which had been passenger friendly until the loss of its mail contracts, had eight, not counting its share of the *Empire Builder* and *North Coast Limited*.

WHO SHOT THE PASSENGER TRAIN?

The failure of the 1956 ultralight trains left the rail industry discouraged about the future of passenger rail service. The number of airline passengers and passenger miles exceeded rail for the first time in 1957; intercity buses pulled ahead of rail in 1962.[11] While Burlington, Great Northern, Santa Fe, and a few other railroads persevered, most rail officials believed it was only a matter of time before railroads would be used solely for freight.

In 1956, growing passenger train deficits led the ICC to ask its staff for a report on the problem. The agency solicited input from the railroads operating passenger trains as well as the state commissions that regulated them. Published in September 1958, the 20,000-word report by Howard Hosmer was pessimistic about the future of passenger trains, predicting that "sleeping-car service will have disappeared by 1965 and the coach service by 1970."[12]

In a complex operation like a railroad, it is always difficult to determine whether an individual project such as a train makes money because so many of the costs are fixed. The ICC had created a formula for the railroads to distribute fixed costs between passenger and freight trains. Many passenger train advocates, however, claimed this formula was biased against passenger trains. Northwestern University transportation professor Stanley Berge argued that passenger train deficits were a "myth" and that a more reasonable accounting would show that most passenger trains were profitable.[13]

The Hosmer report directly addressed this issue, pointing out that under the ICC formula, the rail passenger industry had lost money in every year since 1930 except for the war years. Even when counting only costs solely related to passenger service, however, the industry had been losing money since 1953. Measured this way, nationwide passenger train deficits were $1 million in 1953, growing to $114 million in 1957 and projected to be $140 million in 1958. Although some trains covered their direct operating costs, most did not, so "any effort to determine more or less precisely how many hundreds of millions should be added by way of apportionment of common expenses seems hardly worthwhile."[14]

The report noted that passenger trains had several unjust strikes against them. Federal union work rules required the railroads to pay engine crews a full-day's pay for every 100 miles they worked, and train crews for every 150 miles. These rules were established in 1919, when train speeds averaged about 20 miles per hour; in 1958, average speeds were

40 miles per hour, and some trains averaged 60 miles per hour or more. These rules meant that the Burlington and Union Pacific had to pay the equivalent of 10⅓ days of work for the engine crews for each 16½-hour run of the *Denver Zephyr* and *City of Denver*.[15]

A second problem the passenger trains faced was that federal, state, and local governments were subsidizing the competition. Since 1925, Congress had spent about $1.6 billion building airports at little or no cost to the airlines.[16] Because the federal dollars were given to states and localities as matching funds, local governments must have spent at least $1.6 billion on airports themselves. As public entities, the airports paid no taxes, whereas the railroads paid a huge amount of taxes, some of which were used to subsidize the airports.

For example, in 1950, the city of Toledo, Ohio, pressured New York Central into building a new passenger station at a cost of $4.9 million. The railroad then paid taxes on the station of about $43,000 a year. Meanwhile, Toledo spent $3.9 million in public funds to build an airport in 1955 and subsidized its operations every year. In Montana, the Great Northern Railway paid $2,241 a year in taxes specifically to support the Cut Bank airport, while Western Airlines, which actually used the airport, paid just $23.[17]

The situation wasn't helped by a 1955 report issued by the Commission for Intergovernmental Relations, which Congress had created in 1953 to review the relationship between the federal government and the states. The report admitted that airports were heavily subsidized but argued that such subsidies should be continued. In a statement that infuriated every railroad executive in the country, a staff report to the commission claimed that asking private users to pay for airports "would violently wrench the economics of the industry."[18] The commission agreed, using somewhat milder language, saying that "A switch to private financing would radically affect the economics of civil aviation, as presently constituted, and would hinder its growth," adding that such a shift "can be made only gradually, if at all."[19]

President Eisenhower apparently did not agree. In 1958, he told Congress that "it is increasingly appropriate that [private airport] users pay their fair share of the costs" and that "we should redouble our efforts to find ways and means to reduce and ultimately eliminate all subsidies for airlines."[20] He specifically proposed a tax on aviation fuels similar to the gasoline tax that paid for highways. Congress ignored him and did not set up a system of airport user fees until 1970.

Similar subsidies existed for highways. Although state governments have paid for most state highway costs out of fuel taxes and other user fees since 1930, federal road spending came out of general funds before 1956. Hosmer estimated that since 1921, various governments had spent $111 billion on roads, of which $49 billion came from user fees.[21] Congressional passage of the Federal Aid Highway Act of 1956, which dedicated federal gas and other road user taxes to the Interstate Highway System, eliminated federal subsidies; John Budd called this law "a long step forward in recognizing the validity of the user charge concept."[22] However, cities and counties continued to pay most local road costs out of general funds, and still do so today.

Hosmer stated that "none of the suggested means of reducing the deficit, such as revision of labor agreements, lower taxes, discontinuance of subsidies for motor and air transportation, and more revenue from mail can be considered promising."[23] By that, he meant there was little political support for any of these changes. The report made no attempt to speculate on whether passenger trains would be viable if they did occur.

The report addressed the persistent myth that rail managers either ineptly or maliciously allowed passenger service to deteriorate in order to replace profitable passenger trains with even more profitable freight. "The railroads have never lacked advice from numerous and various quarters to the effect that improvements in their equipment and service would be reflected in better earnings from their passenger service," Hosmer cynically observed. Some railroad commissions had even denied railroad petitions to cancel trains, telling the railroads they should buy new, lower-cost equipment and specifically mentioned Talgo, tubular, and Aerotrains.[24]

Hosmer pointed to early reports that the ultralights were failing. But beyond this, he didn't buy into the claim that railroads weren't investing in passenger trains, noting that in the decade prior to the report, the rail industry had spent more than $1 billion ($10 billion in today's dollars) on new passenger cars and locomotives. Thus, he said, "the railroads cannot be justly charged with undue conservatism in modernizing their passenger facilities. Rather it appears that they did not foresee the enormous loss of passenger traffic which has occurred, depriving them of any return on this investment."[25]

The real problem was simple economics. The New York Central and Pennsylvania railroads charged $65.92 for a first-class ticket to travel from New York to Chicago, Hosmer noted, while first-class airfare for that same trip was just $47.95. Coach fares for the same trip were $35.55 by rail, $31.66 by air, and $23.40 by bus. While the average cost of driving was 10.8 cents a mile, the variable cost was just 3.8 cents, so driving would cost about $30, and "when there are two or more passengers, the cost per person is sharply reduced."[26] Hosmer didn't say so, but even if subsidies to highways and airports had abruptly ended, the costs of flying and driving would still have been less than traveling by train.

"For more than a century the railroad passenger coach has occupied an interesting and useful place in American life," Hosmer concluded, "but at the present time the inescapable fact—and certainly to many people an unpleasant one—seems to be that in a decade or so this time-honored vehicle may take its place in the transportation museum along with the stage-coach, the sidewheeler, and the steam locomotive." Although subsidies for other forms of travel were a problem, Hosmer hinted they were less important than personal preferences. "It is repetitious to add that this outcome will be due to the fact that the American public now is doing about 90 percent of its traveling by private automobile and prefers to do so," he said.[27]

Hosmer didn't directly address why people preferred driving and flying to taking the train. Other economic studies published around the time of the Hosmer report, however, found that people's incomes were positively related to driving and flying but negatively related to train riding. The studies found that every 1 percent increase in income would increase driving by 1.2 percent and flying by 2.5 percent, presumably because the increased income meant more people could afford cars and airfares. Meanwhile, the same 1 percent increase in income would reduce train travel by 0.6 percent, presumably because that travel had shifted to driving and flying.[28]

David P. Morgan, the pithy editor of *Trains* magazine, was more willing to believe that passenger trains could survive if Congress and others corrected the injustices against the railroads. In "Who Shot the Passenger Train?"—a 38-page article that was the longest and possibly most important in the publication's history—Morgan argued that the passenger train was not "technologically obsolete" but "was shot in the back."[29] Like Agatha Christie's *Murder on the Orient Express*, the villain was not a single assailant but several. Drawing heavily on the Hosmer report, Morgan pointed to union work rules, excessive government regulation, unfair subsidies to highways and airports, unfair taxation of the railroads, and railroad managers who found it easier to deal with freight (which Morgan described as a wholesale business) than passenger transport (which Morgan called a retail business).[30]

Morgan admitted that all but the last of these culprits hindered rail freight operations as much as they did passenger trains, yet most railroads were able to earn a profit on their freight business. Still, he argued that fixing these problems would bring many, if not all, passenger trains closer to profitability. Certainly, the resurgence in rail freight after the 1980 deregulation suggested that many passenger routes that were marginal in the 1950s might have been profitable if deregulation had happened sooner.

Morgan believed in particular that the medium-distance travel market—between 100 and 500 miles—was "uniquely subject to rail exploitation" because it was long enough to compete with cars and short enough to compete with air. In the 500- to 1,000-mile market, Morgan thought, rail could provide overnight trips that were competitive with airlines. Above 1,000 miles, rail could only compete "on a cruise basis where 'getting there is half the fun.'"[31]

Both Hosmer and Morgan dismissed charges that the U.S. Post Office was deliberately harming passenger trains by using air carriers to ship non-airmail packages. Hosmer pointed out that although rail revenues from mail were declining, most of that decline wasn't due to increased airmail or even trucks.[32] Morgan was more direct, saying that passengers should pay their way and not expect to be cross-subsidized by railway postal revenue. "Head-end business is not a crutch which the passenger train needs to survive," he argued.[33]

Unfortunately, Morgan concluded his article with a "train of tomorrow" that was actually a failed train from yesterday. Based on a 1957 Chesapeake & Ohio concept, it was simply a slightly refined ultralight train, with articulated cars running on one axle per car—exactly the formula of the failed 1956 Train X and Talgo trains.[34] The New York Central, Pennsylvania, Union Pacific, and other railroads had already rejected the ultralights by the time Morgan's article was published, and because Hosmer had noted this fact in his report, Morgan must have known it as well.

Despite this glaring fault, Morgan's article had many insights and useful recommendations. Of course, none of them were acted on until well after it was too late to revive private passenger trains in the United States. Union work rules remained frozen until years after Amtrak took over in 1971. Most airports started paying their way (though not their taxes) after Congress passed the Airport and Airway Revenue Act of 1970, four months before it passed the Rail Passenger Service Act creating Amtrak. Congressional deregulation of the railroads would wait until 1980.

"Nobody is being asked to bail out the passenger train in the sense of making it a Federal ward," said Morgan. "All that is asked is simple justice."[35] Just eight years later, an attorney named Anthony Haswell, frustrated by the lack of "simple justice," formed the National Association of Railroad Passengers specifically to lobby to make the passenger train a federal ward.

In fact, there were many, even in 1958, who wanted to nationalize the railroads. The United States did just that during World War I, although the railroads argued that the need to do so stemmed from the federal government's overregulation. In 1906, Congress gave the ICC the power to regulate railroad rates, and the rates set were inadequate to keep up with the demand. Although there were plenty of rail lines in the country—some said too many—there weren't enough terminal facilities to handle all of the traffic brought in by those lines. Great Northern Railway founder James J. Hill gave many speeches in the intervening years on the need for more terminal facilities, but he noted that "the railroads can pay money only as they are permitted to earn it."[36]

Due to the inadequate facilities, the railroads were unable to meet wartime demands, so on the advice of the ICC, President Woodrow

Wilson ordered the federal government to nationalize them in December 1917. In March 1918, Congress passed a law affirming this takeover but requiring the government to return the railroads to their former owners within 21 months of a peace treaty in as good a condition as they were when taken over. The war ended less than eight months later, but because the United States Senate refused to affirm the Treaty of Versailles, supporters of federal control argued the government did not have to return the railroads to their previous owners. Nevertheless, it finally did so in 1920, having operated the railroads during a longer period of peace than of war.

During the slightly more than two years the government ran the railroads, it built some new terminal facilities, raised worker pay, and ordered $380 million worth of new railroad cars and locomotives (worth about $4 billion today). At the same time, it lost $714 million (about $7.5 billion today) on operations and deferred maintenance to such a degree that the railroads successfully collected $677 million (about $7 billion) in damages.

One person who thought the government should retain ownership of the railroads was Joseph Eastman, a member of the ICC. In 1919, he admitted private ownership worked when "keen competition" promoted "efficiency." But the railroads, he argued, faced too little competition to benefit from such efficiency. Eastman concluded, therefore, that federal control made a lot more sense because managers could insure freight and passengers travelled on the most efficient and least congested routes.[37]

Having lost that debate, Eastman continued to advocate federal regulation of the railroads for at least two more decades. Between 1933 and 1936, Eastman held the New Deal position of Federal Coordinator of Transportation, giving him even more power to regulate the railroads than the ICC. As economist James Nelson pointed out at the time, it was ironic that the federal government was increasing regulation of a supposedly monopoly industry at the same time that industry was facing increasingly intense competition from trucks, buses, and other modes of travel.[38]

Eastman sought to save railroads money by reducing terminal facilities he thought were duplicative; fortunately for the nation, the railroads successfully resisted this measure, as those facilities turned out to be vital during World War II.[39] In response to railroad complaints that they were overregulated while highway trucks were not, Eastman could have deregulated the railroads; instead, he persuaded Congress to regulate truckers.[40] Eastman used carrots as well as sticks to influence railroad policy, persuading the Public Works Administration to make loans to the New Haven and Baltimore & Ohio railroads to help them buy their first streamliners.[41]

As the Roosevelt Administration was preparing for World War II, Eastman—who by then chaired the ICC—probably would have urged Roosevelt to once again take over the railroads. This was forestalled, however, when Ralph Budd met with Roosevelt and Eastman in September 1939. Budd argued the railroads were offering far better service, with greater safety, than they had before World War I, adding that they had even reduced rates in recent years. Roosevelt was so taken with Budd that when he created the Council of National Defense in 1940, he named him the Commissioner of Transportation.[42] After the United States entered the war, Roosevelt gave Eastman the even more powerful job of director of the Office of Defense Transportation, though Eastman admitted he thought Budd should have gotten the job.[43]

With Eastman and Budd doing little more than exhorting railroad officials to keep their facilities in good condition, private operation of the railroads during World War II far excelled public operation during World War I. As a 1949 Brookings Institution report noted, "The railroads handled 74 per cent more freight and 100 per cent more passenger traffic than during the First World War with one quarter fewer cars, one third fewer locomotives, and one quarter fewer men."[44] Budd was convinced that before Eastman died in 1944, he had been persuaded that private operation of the railroads was preferable to government ownership.[45]

THE HIGH-SPEED GROUND TRANSPORTATION ACT OF 1965

For two decades after the war, federal policy toward the railroads was limited to continued regulation by the ICC, and few advocated government takeover of the railroads. Then in 1964, the government-owned Japanese National Railways introduced the *Shinkansen*, the world's first rail line specifically built for high-speed passenger trains. With a top speed of 130 miles per hour and an average speed between Tokyo and Osaka of 86 miles per hour, the train immediately displaced American trains as the fastest in the world. The *Shinkansen* (which will be discussed in more detail in Chapter 10) had a literal and metaphorical electrifying effect on American politicians and rail advocates.

At the time Japan introduced its high-speed train, the United States had already put several astronauts into orbit around the earth and was just five years away from sending men to the moon. American jet airliners routinely cruised four times faster than the top speed of the *Shinkansen*. Americans owned one private automobile for every 2.7 people and traveled by car an average of 7,000 miles per person per year, both figures far higher than anywhere else in the world. Yet to some people conditioned by the space race and the missile gap, the *Shinkansen* was evidence the United States was falling behind in another technology race.

One of those people was Claiborne Pell, a United States senator from Rhode Island. Pell was also influenced by *Megalopolis*, a book by French geographer Jean Gottmann, whose thesis was that the area from southern New Hampshire to northern Virginia was "an almost continuous stretch of urban and suburban areas" that formed a single economic unit with common problems, including "transportation, land use, water supply, cultural activities, and use and development of resources."[46] Moreover, because it was broken into 11 states and more than 100 counties, the region's residents would be unable to solve those problems themselves. "Local government powers and planning theory in general are not adapted to deal with the entanglements of the new situation," he wrote.

Gottmann's book fed the growing—and totally unrealistic—panic over urban sprawl and the fear that the nation's prime farmlands were being eaten up by urban development. Contrary to Gottmann's claims, in fact, the area he defined as Megalopolis was far from a continuous stretch of urban development. In 2010, 50 years after Gottmann was doing research for his book, 70 percent of the land in the counties Gottmann included in his megalopolis was still rural. It would have been even higher in 1960.

The idea of regional planning was becoming popular in the early 1960s. In 1962, the same year in which Gottmann's book was published, Congress passed a law requiring all local governments in metropolitan

areas of 50,000 people or more to create a metropolitan planning organization that would decide how to spend that region's share of federal transportation dollars. Yet as Jane Jacobs noted, "A region is an area safely larger
than the last one to whose problems we found no solution."[47] In other
words, the failures of city planning would not be fixed by giving planners
authority over even larger, more complicated areas. Because accurately
predicting the future needs of a region is virtually impossible, regional
planners instead typically tried to impose their preconceived notions of
what the region should look like, and those notions were often based on a
nostalgic impression of what cities looked like a generation or two before
the planners.

Pell was no different, as he was convinced the solution to megalopolis' transportation problem lay in a 1930s technology: high-speed passenger trains. He persuaded Congress to pass the High-Speed Ground
Transportation Act of 1965 that authorized the Department of Commerce
(the Department of Transportation did not yet exist) to give out grants
for high-speed train "demonstration" projects. Two major demonstration
projects were funded, one for trains powered by electricity, suitable for
Pennsylvania Railroad's route between New York and Washington, D.C.,
and one for trains to operate in areas that had no electric power, suitable
for the New Haven Railroad's route from New York to Boston.

Funding for the latter type of train was given to United Aircraft, which
built a train based on plans developed by the Chesapeake & Ohio Railroad
in the late 1950s. In fact, it was the same regrettable train endorsed by
David P. Morgan in "Who Shot the Passenger Train?" The train consisted
of cars that would tilt around corners to reduce passenger discomfort.
Each car shared a single pair of wheels with the adjacent cars. The first and
last cars on the train were the power cars, with two pairs of wheels at the
nose end providing the power and a turret above the level of the rest of
the train where the engineer and fireman sat.

United Aircraft's main modification to the design was to replace the
diesel engines with gas-powered turbine engines, essentially the same
engines used in turboprop airplanes. The gas-turbine engines were smaller
than the planned diesels, so United Aircraft used the extra space to extend
the turret in the power cars to create something similar to a dome car

for passengers. United Aircraft contracted the Pullman Company to build two trains, with United Aircraft's subsidiary Pratt & Whitney providing the power.

In a 1967 test on Pennsylvania Railroad tracks in New Jersey, the TurboTrain, as it was called, exceeded 170 miles per hour. In actual service between Boston and New York, the trains' top speeds were 100 miles per hour, and their average speed was 63 miles per hour. The trains operated for about eight years before being replaced by more conventional diesel- and electric-powered trains. The Canadian National Railroad also purchased several TurboTrains and operated them for a little longer but had numerous difficulties. Geoffrey Freeman Allen, the editor of *Jane's World Railways*, concluded the TurboTrains had too much untested technology. "From transmission to suspension to auxiliaries, far too many vital components seemed to have been translated straight from the drawing board to the series production line," he wrote.[48]

The other train funded by Pell's law, the Metroliner, was more successful. Built by Budd and powered by General Electric motors, it was based on a passenger car Budd had built as a demonstrator in 1956 to compete against the ultralights being produced by Pullman and American Car & Foundry. Like the ultralights, the car weighed about half as much as a regular streamlined car. Unlike them, each car rode on two four-wheel trucks, so they offered a better ride than cars riding on single-axle trucks. Each car was also independent of the other cars, so they could be made into trains of any length.

In the same test when the TurboTrain topped 170 miles per hour, the first Metroliner reached 164 miles per hour. When placed in actual service between New York and Washington, the trains operated at top speeds of 120 miles per hour. Metroliners that went nonstop from New York to Washington covered the distance in 2½ hours, or better than 90 miles per hour. Some Metroliners stopped at Newark, Philadelphia, and Baltimore, adding 10 minutes to the trip and reducing the average speed to 85 miles per hour. Other Metroliners also stopped at Trenton and Wilmington, requiring nearly three hours for the entire trip, for an average speed of 76 miles per hour.[49] By comparison, today's fastest *Acela*, which makes five stops, completes the journey six minutes faster, for an average speed of 78 miles per hour. There are no nonstop *Acela*s, so the fastest trains today take 23 minutes longer than the nonstop trains of 1969.

JOURNEY TO AMTRAK

While Pell's law improved service between Boston and Washington, D.C., railroads elsewhere continued to discontinue trains. Yet many rail advocates believed David P. Morgan's contention that passenger trains could be profitable if they were properly marketed and didn't face hostility from railroads that had grown more oriented to freight service. One of those rail advocates was an attorney from the Midwest named Anthony Haswell.

Born in Dayton, Ohio, Haswell earned an economics degree from the University of Wisconsin in 1953 and a law degree from the University of Michigan in 1958. After working briefly for the Illinois Central law department and as a public defender in Chicago, he founded the National Association of Railroad Passengers (NARP) in 1967 and served as its first executive director.[50] NARP lobbied Congress to find a solution, specifically promoting the idea of a single national entity to operate all passenger trains. In 1969, NARP persuaded a Senate committee to hold hearings on nine different bills offering various approaches to the passenger train problem. These ranged from offering modest financial support to having the federal government take over all passenger trains. Although the committee staff issued a report favoring the latter idea, Congress took no action.[51]

The events that led Congress to create Amtrak go back to Claiborne Pell's High-Speed Ground Transportation Act. The Pennsylvania and New Haven railroads agreed to use their tracks between Boston and Washington as test beds for the Metroliners and TurboTrains funded by that act. By the time the trains went into service, the two had merged with the New York Central line into the Penn Central. But in June 1970, just nine months after the Senate hearings instigated by NARP, Penn Central went spectacularly bankrupt, becoming the largest corporate bankruptcy in American history.

There were several reasons for the bankruptcy. The first, and most important, one was that none of the railroads had been financially healthy before the merger. In addition to losing most of their passenger business to automobiles and buses, they had lost most of their short-haul freight business to trucks, and such short-haul traffic made up a larger share of railroad revenues in the East than in the South or West. There was no reason to think the merger would solve these problems.

Second, the two main railroads in the merger, Pennsylvania and New York Central, were unable to overcome significant cultural incompatibilities. For example, one of the railroads was managed on a divisional model, with everyone in each division reporting to a division superintendent, who in turn reported to the headquarters office. The other was managed on a functional model, in which local officials in each function such as operations, maintenance, and marketing, report directly to an appropriate vice president in the company's headquarters. Either model could work, but the merger required one railroad to change its model almost overnight. Union contracts and computer systems were also incompatible.

Finally, the executives of the new railroad had major personality clashes that prevented effective operation. At least one experienced railroader, John Barringer, declared that Penn Central could have been profitable if it had competent management.[52] Barringer was highly respected, having been named Railroader of the Year by *Modern Railroad* magazine in 1969 for successfully returning several marginal railroads to profitability, including the Boston & Maine, Missouri-Kansas-Texas, Monon, and Pittsburgh & Lake Erie lines. His prediction proved true in the long run, as later managers were able to turn the Penn Central, by then known as Conrail, into a profitable operation.

Given incompetent managers and its other problems, however, Penn Central probably would have gone bankrupt even without its money-losing passenger business. Yet many in the rail industry found it convenient to blame the railroad's troubles on passenger trains. This spurred Congress to take action on the bills considered in the 1969 hearing.

Less than four months after Penn Central declared bankruptcy, Congress passed, and President Nixon signed, the Rail Passenger Service Act of 1970. The law created the National Railroad Passenger Corporation, which some shortened to Railpax, specifying that it "shall be a for profit corporation" and "not be an agency or establishment of the United States Government." The Secretary of Transportation would design a national passenger railway network, and Railpax would operate trains on that network. Private railroads still offering passenger service in 1969 were given the choice of continuing to operate their trains at least through the end of 1974 or joining Railpax by paying the corporation a fee over a three-year period based on the amount of money they had declared as losses in 1969. Those that joined could either deduct the fees from their taxes or accept stock in the new corporation. Joining would relieve the railroads of operating any passenger trains after May 1, 1971, when Railpax would take over.

At the time the Railpax bill passed, some members of Congress said that they expected the Railpax system would "include about 80 percent of the trains running in 1970."[53] In fact, the new system unveiled by the railroad near the beginning of April cut the number in half, from about 386 trains per day to 186.[54] The news was even worse outside the Boston-to-Washington corridor because Railpax proposed to increase service in that corridor, which meant the number of trains outside that corridor would fall by well over half. Senator Mike Mansfield of Montana was particularly upset, because of the four trains crossing his state—the *Empire Builder, North Coast Limited, Western Star,* and *Mainstreeter*—only the *Empire Builder,* which had a faster route but served the least populated part of the state, would remain. Other members of Congress were troubled that Arkansas, New Hampshire, Maine, South Dakota, Vermont, and Wyoming were completely left out of the new system.[55]

Several railroads decided not to join Railpax. The Denver & Rio Grande railroad elected to continue operating one train three days a week between Denver and Salt Lake City because it didn't want to deal with the one train each way, seven days a week, that it assumed Railpax would impose upon it. (This put Wyoming back in the system when Railpax used an alternate route over the Rocky Mountains.) The Rock Island Railroad had discontinued a large number of trains in 1970, and the fee for joining Railpax would have been $4.7 million, based on the trains it operated in 1969. Estimating it would cost only $3 million to keep operating its two remaining intercity trains for three more years, however, it stayed out of Railpax. The Southern Railway refused to join because it didn't believe Railpax would provide service that met its standards.[56]

The Santa Fe Railway nearly refused to join for the same reason as Southern, but in the end, the Santa Fe, Burlington Northern, Penn Central, Union Pacific, and 16 other railroads joined Railpax. Most of them elected to deduct the cost of joining from their taxes, but Burlington Northern, Grand Trunk Western, Milwaukee Road, and Penn Central didn't pay enough taxes to make the deduction worthwhile, so they instead accepted stock in the new corporation. They or their successors still own that stock today, although there is continuing debate over what it is worth and what power it gives them over the passenger railroad.

On April 19, 1971, less than two weeks before taking over, the National Railroad Passenger Corporation announced that, on the advice of Lippencott and Margulies, it was going to call itself Amtrak, for "American Tracks," rather than Railpax, which was only an abbreviation for the legislation.

Some saw Comsat, the commercial satellite communications company Congress had created in 1962, as the model for Amtrak. In 1970, Comsat appeared to be well on the road to profitability, and it was eventually privatized. The difference, however, was that satellite communications was a new and developing technology, while passenger trains were an old and fading technology. As George Hilton noted, "never before had Congress directly intervened in the economy to save a service that was being replaced by alternatives."[57]

Secretary of Transportation John Volpe told Congress he thought Amtrak would become profitable within three years. That was when railroad funding of Amtrak would run out, so he probably meant he expected Amtrak could sustain itself after that time. However, some thought Volpe and others claimed Amtrak could be profitable only in order to convince President Nixon to sign the Railpax legislation. Whatever Volpe thought, Anthony Haswell and other rail advocates clearly believed high-quality passenger service could not only cover its costs, it could also restore ridership to 1950 levels.[58]

Others were convinced Amtrak would never make money. Some railroaders hoped Amtrak would quietly shut down most rail service when it ran out of railroad funds in three years. One of the most outspoken was Louis Menk, who as president of Northern Pacific in 1969 made the case for discontinuing the *Mainstreeter* by arguing "the traveling public simply prefers other modes of travel."[59] By 1971, he was CEO of Burlington Northern and, as one of Amtrak's largest stockholders, served on Amtrak's board. Yet even as an Amtrak board member, he remained unenthused about passenger trains, saying they should be allowed to go the way of the stagecoach and the steamboat. After *Fortune* magazine urged Amtrak to improve its services, the author of the article reported that Menk complained to him that "the story was undermining their scheme to kill off the company."[60]

Amtrak's board could have staffed the executive offices of the company with people from the Santa Fe and other railroads known for their high-quality passenger service. Instead, it hired executives from outside the railroad industry. Roger Lewis, Amtrak's first president, had been an executive with Pan American Airways and then CEO of General Dynamics, an aircraft manufacturer and military contractor. Harold Graham, Amtrak's vice president for marketing, was also a former Pan American executive.

Amtrak started operating its truncated rail network on May 1, 1971, using 300 locomotives and 1,190 passenger cars it purchased from the railroads, nearly all of which were near the end of their normal service life. Despite serious reliability problems, the only new pieces of equipment the company ordered during its first two years were six French-made gas-turbine trains, dubbed Turboliners, for use in short-distance corridors such as Chicago–St. Louis and Chicago–Detroit. Anthony Haswell charged that although Congress had offered Amtrak more funds in 1972, Lewis turned it down, saying it was more than Amtrak could "sensibly" spend.[61]

If Lewis agreed with Menk and other railroad executives that Amtrak's purpose was to wind down rail passenger service, their plan was foiled by the oil crisis of 1973. Amtrak ridership surged, and passenger train defenders argued America could save energy if Congress gave Amtrak more money to subsidize increased rail service.

In late 1973, 2½ years after taking over the nation's passenger trains, Amtrak finally placed a large-scale order for new equipment: nearly 500 cars to be built by the Budd Company. Slightly more than half of these cars were 84-seat coaches for short-distance service. Slightly less than

20 percent were 60-seat coaches for longer-distance trains. These cars had leg rests, not just footrests, making them more suitable for overnight service. The remainder included facilities for various food services, but each also had at least 23 coach seats. The cars cost an average of about $541,000 apiece, or about $2.3 million in today's dollars. Budd delivered the cars to Amtrak in 1975.

In 1975, Amtrak placed an order for cars suitable for long-distance, overnight trains. Based on Santa Fe hi-level cars, Amtrak's Superliners, as the company dubbed them, included two styles of coaches, lounge cars, diners, and sleeping cars. Although the Santa Fe cars had been designed and built by Budd, the low bidder for this order was Pullman. This proved unfortunate because Pullman, unlike Budd, had not built any passenger cars for more than a decade. Having to relearn many manufacturing techniques considerably delayed production of the cars, and the first ones were not put into service until four years after Amtrak placed the order, while the last ones took two more years to deliver. The average cost was about $850,000 each, or $3 million in today's dollars. Pullman probably lost money on the order, as it reputedly vowed never to make another passenger car, and it never has.

Responding to the problems it suffered trying to operate the equipment it inherited from a variety of railroads made by a variety of manufacturers, Amtrak attempted to "Amstandardize" everything. The new single-level cars were called Amfleet; diners were called Amcafes; first-class cars were called Amclubs. Employees and railfans made fun of this, calling the thin mattresses offered in the sleeping cars Ampads and the tiny stations built in some cities Amshacks.

In the West, the use of double-decker cars meant an end to dome cars with their 360-degree scenic views. "America can't afford to subsidize sightseers," grumbled Amtrak's president when asked about this, failing to recognize that sightseeing was the primary reason a lot of people would take a long-distance journey by train instead of air. "Apart from the question whether it has any excuse for existence," noted railroad fan and transportation economist George Hilton, "Amtrak seems to me to have all the antique charm of a Travelodge and a Denny's—and to be equally worthy of enthusiasm."[62]

In early 1976, Congress passed the Railroad Revitalization and Regulatory Reform Act, which was a first step towards rate deregulation of the railroads. The law also approved the reorganization of Penn Central into Conrail and authorized Amtrak to buy the Northeast Corridor tracks between Boston and Washington. While some of the Northeast Corridor is owned by local transit agencies, Amtrak was able to purchase a majority of it for a mere $85 million and paid for most of that by giving Conrail trackage rights for its freight trains.

While $85 million seemed like a bargain for 363 route-miles of track, it also committed the federal government to modernize and maintain the corridor. Over the next 25 years, the Department of Transportation spent $2.5 billion improving the corridor, including some track work and installation of new signals. This did not increase speeds, but it did increase the number of trains that could use the corridor. Between 1995 and 1999, Amtrak spent another $1.6 billion electrifying the portion of the corridor between New Haven and Boston. [63] This allowed Amtrak's then-new *Acela* to reach top speeds of 150 miles per hour over a short stretch of track and to cover the distance from Boston to New York in three hours and thirty-five minutes. This saved 40 minutes over regular Amtrak trains, but was only four minutes faster than the United Aircraft TurboTrain in 1969. [64]

10. AMERICAN CITIES REDISCOVER RAIL TRANSIT

Lyle Lanley: I've sold monorails to Brockway, Ogdenville, and North Haverbrook, and, by gum, it put them on the map! Well, sir, there's nothing on earth like a genuine, bona fide electrified, six-car monorail. What'd I say?

Everyone: Monorail

Lanley: What's it called?

Everyone: Monorail

Lanley: That's right!

Everyone: Monorail! Monorail! Monorail!

Lanley: I swear it's Springfield's only choice;

Throw up your hands and raise your voice.

Everyone: Monorail!

Lanley: What's it called?

Everyone: Monorail!

Lanley: Once again!

Everyone: Monorail!

Marge Simpson: But Main Street's still all cracked and broken.

Bart Simpson: Sorry, Mom, the mob has spoken.

Everyone: Monorail! Monorail! Monorail!

—From The Simpsons: Marge vs. the Monorail

The first rapid-transit system and first light-rail line built in the United States after 1970 were both planned without federal funds. However, they inspired federal funding for almost every rail transit line built since then.

Unfortunately, the methods used to distribute federal funds encouraged cities to build the most expensive, rather than the most efficient, transit systems possible, which helps explain why the number of urban areas with rail transit has grown from eight in 1975 to more than 40 today.

Although Cleveland opened a single rapid-transit line in 1958, the pioneer in building an entire postwar rapid-transit system was the San Francisco Bay Area. San Francisco had streetcars, cable cars, and commuter trains, but it didn't have a rapid-transit system like the ones in New York, Chicago, Boston, and Philadelphia. San Francisco's Commonwealth Club, a group organized "for the nonpartisan study of public issues," had proposed such a system in 1920.[1] In 1936, when the San Francisco–Oakland Bay Bridge opened, San Francisco business leaders feared it would lead to a decentralization of the region into Oakland and other East Bay communities. A rapid-transit system with lines radiating from San Francisco would maintain what they believed was the appropriate preeminence of that city.[2] In 1937, however, San Francisco voters rejected the construction of a subway system.[3]

After the war, San Francisco business leaders persuaded the legislature to create and fund a San Francisco Bay Area Rapid Transit Commission. The commission not surprisingly proposed the construction of a rapid-transit system centered on a tube under the bay between San Francisco and Oakland. The system would serve five counties: Marin, San Francisco, and San Mateo on the west side of the bay and Alameda and Contra Costa on the east side. Santa Clara County (San Jose) had excluded itself from inclusion, as it didn't want to see its jobs drain to San Francisco.

The authors of this plan ignored two important trends. First and most obvious was the decline in rail transit systems all across the country. In the Bay Area itself, buses had replaced the Key System trains crossing the San Francisco–Oakland Bay Bridge as growing auto traffic and declining ridership led the state to remove rails from the bridge in 1958 to make room for more highway lanes. The subtler trend was the replacement of the monocentric urban area with the polycentric one. Of course, downtown businesses in San Francisco were motivated to try to maintain their preeminence over the rest of the region, but to the extent that a rapid-transit system paid for by the region's taxpayers could help do so, it represented a subsidy from suburban businesses and residents to central-city property owners.

Marin and San Mateo counties refused to support the plan partly because, like Santa Clara County, they feared the system would move jobs from their counties to San Francisco. In 1962, however, voters in San Francisco, Alameda, and Contra Costa counties agreed to their parts of the plan. As then envisioned, Bay Bridge tolls would pay for a tube under the bay on the theory that the motorists paying the tolls would benefit from reduced congestion on the bridge. To construct the rest of the rail system, the Bay Area Rapid Transit (BART) commission sold $792 million worth of bonds that would be repaid out of property tax revenues. Planners expected fares would cover operating costs with enough left over to pay for the railcars.[4]

It didn't work out that way. First, construction costs were 50 percent greater than projected, forcing BART to ask the state legislature for the authority to collect a sales tax to cover the additional costs. Second, ridership proved to be only half of that projected, while operating costs proved to be 375 percent more than projected. BART obtained federal funding to pay for its railcars and relied on a combination of sales and property taxes to fund operating deficits.[5]

Downtown San Francisco did see more construction of high-rise office buildings. But University of California (Berkeley) planning professor Melvin Webber pointed out that downtown Houston saw even more office construction (measured in square feet per capita) without a rapid-transit system. Without BART, contends Webber, the office space would have been constructed anyway, though some of it might have been built in another part of the Bay Area.[6]

Webber also noted that the taxes paid to construct and support BART are regressive, while BART riders tend to be wealthier than average. "The percentage of income paid to provide tax support for each ride taken is 40 times greater for an individual in the lowest income group than for one in the highest income group," says Webber. "Clearly, the poor are paying and the rich are riding."[7]

BART ridership eventually grew, but for every additional BART rider, the region lost more than one bus rider. This reflected a reduction in bus service as the region's Metropolitan Transportation Commission, which allocates state and federal transportation funds to agencies in the region, diverted funds to BART that would otherwise have gone to bus agencies. A local transit advocate called BART a "vampire" that "sucks the life blood out of every transit agency with which it comes into contact."[8]

Public officials rarely admit they wasted taxpayers' money. Instead, BART emphasized the 80-mile-per-hour top speeds, as opposed to the 35-miles-per-hour average speeds of buses; the questionable economic development benefits; and the unproven claims that its trains reduced congestion, which may have been true for the Bay crossing but were probably not true elsewhere. As a result, Webber accurately predicted BART would "become the first of a series of multi-billion-dollar mistakes scattered from one end of the continent to the other."[9]

Several other cities planned rapid-transit systems in the late 1960s, including Seattle, Atlanta, and Washington, D.C. The Urban Mass Transit Administration, which had been mainly helping local transit agencies buy new buses, offered to pay two-thirds of the cost of a rapid-transit system in Seattle, but in 1968 and again in 1970, voters rejected the local tax increases required to cover the other third of the costs.[10] As a result, UMTA turned its attention to Atlanta.

In 1967, the Metropolitan Atlanta Regional Transit Authority (MARTA) proposed to spend close to half a billion dollars ($2.5 billion in today's dollars) building a 66-mile rapid-transit system. Opponents offered an alternative 32-mile rapid bus system that could move as many people for just $53 million. MARTA rejected this idea without comment and, in 1968, asked voters to agree to a property-tax increase to build a 40-mile starter system. This measure failed due to opposition from suburbanites who felt the system was overly focused on downtown and from blacks who felt the system was overly focused on white neighborhoods.

In 1971, MARTA returned to voters with a 56-mile rapid-transit plan. To gain support from black voters, the agency promised to hold bus fares at 15 cents a ride for seven years. Voters in Atlanta (which sits astride Fulton and DeKalb counties) supported the plan, but suburban voters in both counties opposed it, and voters in suburban Clayton and Gwinnett counties rejected it by more than three to one. The measure passed in Fulton

County by just 400 votes out of more than 100,000 cast, and in DeKalb County by 3,000 votes out of 75,000. As a result, only the segments of the system in those two counties would be built.

Atlanta's experience with rapid transit mirrored San Francisco's. Construction cost nearly 60 percent more than expected, and operating costs were three times the projections.[11] Ridership was about half of that forecast.[12] As in San Francisco, MARTA responded to cost overruns by cutting back on bus service. As a result, from 1985 to 2015, the region's per capita transit ridership fell by two thirds.

Washington, D.C., also built a rapid-transit system using mostly federal dollars. In 1962, planners optimistically estimated that a 103-mile system would cost about $800 million (about $5.0 billion in today's dollars) and that fare revenues would cover all of the operating costs and 80 percent of the capital costs.[13] Planners also predicted the system would carry a third of all of the region's commuters to work.[14] In 1969, Congress agreed to have the federal government cover most of the cost of building the system.[15]

By the time the original 103-mile system was completed in 2001, total costs had reached $8.8 billion in nominal dollars, or close to $20 billion in today's dollars. Operating costs proved to be three times greater than projected, and the system never carried more than about a tenth of the region's commuters.[16] As a result, fares covered only about 60 percent of operating costs and none of the capital costs.

"We didn't lie," one planner explained of the cost overruns. "We just used the most optimistic of forecasts."[17] This pattern of underestimating costs and overestimating ridership is known as "optimism bias," and to Danish planner Bent Flyvbjerg it *is* a form of lying, or, as he more politely calls it, "strategic misrepresentation."[18] As another planner said about the Washington Metro system, "I have no apologies to make for overestimating ridership and revenue" because "it was in the public interest."[19]

San Diego was another city that considered the construction of a rapid-transit system in the 1960s. No action was taken, however, until 1977, when a storm damaged Southern Pacific's tracks to San Diego and the railroad decided to abandon the route. San Diego purchased the line for $18 million (about $56 million in today's dollars) and spent another

$86 million (about $215 million today) improving 13.5 miles for passenger operations and adding overhead wires, for a total average cost of, in today's dollars, about $20 million per mile. This was about a third of the estimated cost of building a new rapid-transit line in the same corridor.

The first modern light-rail line built in America, the San Diego Trolley, opened for business in 1981 between downtown San Diego and San Ysidro on the border with Tijuana, Mexico. Carrying tourists to Mexico and Mexican workers to jobs in San Diego, it proved very popular, and fares covered 90 percent of its operating costs.[20] This inspired many other cities stymied by the high costs of rapid rail transit. "San Diego has shown what can be done with local funding if there is a will," argued a rail transit advocate in Los Angeles.[21]

As a low-cost model for future light-rail projects, however, the San Diego line was highly deceptive. Built under the watchful eye of California Senator James Mills, who introduced the legislation allowing the city to buy the abandoned freight line and convert it to transit, the project cut many corners that later rail planners considered unacceptable.

As built, the trolley operated on a single-track line with sidings. This meant that if a southbound car was delayed coming to a siding, a northbound car would have to wait until it showed up. The line also used as much of the existing infrastructure as possible, replacing less than half the ties and welding existing rails together to smooth the ride. By contrast, later light-rail lines were built from the ground up even if they were using an abandoned rail line. Mills' low-cost methods saved taxpayers' money in the short run but imposed hundreds of millions of dollars of future costs to keep the system running.

Mills was less interested in saving money than in building a region-wide rail transit system. "Freeways build sprawl," he said. "Transit builds cities."[22] This dichotomy is grounded in the old monocentric vision of cities consisting of dense, downtown job centers surrounded by relatively dense housing, a vision that has never applied to San Diego. Mills made no objection when San Diego built more lines that cost far more than the first line yet would carry far fewer riders.

Some of the other cities that considered rail transit were dealing with controversies over the interstate highways that big-city mayors had demanded be included in the Interstate Highway System in 1956. Planners located many of those inner-city highways in formerly high-density neighborhoods that planners considered slums, and the highways were considered a form of urban renewal. However, those neighborhoods were often occupied by blacks, leading to charges of racial discrimination and displacement. "No white mens' roads through black mens' homes" became a rallying cry for freeway opponents.[23] Yet politicians who proposed to cancel freeways would face opposition from the construction companies and union workers who expected to build those freeways.

In 1973, the antifreeway governor of Massachusetts, Francis Sargent, persuaded Congress to allow states to cancel inner-city freeways and spend the federal dollars that would have gone for the freeways on transit capital improvements instead—improvements that could employ the same contractors and workers as the highways. Boston had a rail system that could use federal funds, but this law created a dilemma for politicians in cities that had no rail lines. For example, Portland mayor Neil Goldschmidt wanted to cancel a freeway through east Portland, but if the city spent the hundreds of millions of freeway dollars on new buses for the region's transit agency, the agency wouldn't have enough money to operate all of those buses. In addition, buses, unlike freeways, don't require construction jobs, making it politically hazardous to cancel the freeway without substituting some other construction project.

Goldschmidt's solution was to build a new light-rail line. This would create work for contractors and construction workers while it absorbed the federal dollars without imposing inordinately high operating costs on the transit agency. In other words, he chose light rail because it was expensive, or more specifically, because it had a high capital cost relative to its operating costs. Baltimore, Buffalo, Sacramento, San Jose, and other cities built their first light-rail lines using the same freeway funds. It was Portland's example, however, that caught the eye of President Jimmy Carter, who asked Goldschmidt to become Secretary of Transportation in 1979.

While San Diego's first trolley line took just two years to build, federal red tape meant Portland's light-rail line did not open until 1986, more than a decade after Goldschmidt made the decision to build it. Unlike San Diego's, it proved to be a disaster. Before construction began, one out of ten Portland-area commuters took buses to work. Construction started during a recession, and cost overruns forced Portland's transit agency make heavier cuts to bus service than might otherwise have been necessary. It also increased bus fares by more than the rate of inflation. The result was a drastic decline in overall transit ridership. By 1990, four years after the light rail had opened, the share of Portland-area commuters still taking transit to work had fallen to 6 percent.

Despite their failures, city officials in San Francisco, Atlanta, San Diego, and Portland loudly proclaimed their rail transit lines were great successes. Such endorsements helped spawn many more lines. A few of them proved to be such miserable failures that cities did not extend them. Baltimore opened a subway line in 1987, but because it cost 60 percent more than projected and attracted only about 40 percent of the projected ridership, the city stopped building rapid transit and concentrated on light rail instead. Buffalo's 1989 light-rail line cost 50 percent more than projected and attracted less than a third of the projected passengers, so it built no more rail lines.[24]

Several cities, including Detroit, Jacksonville, Miami, and Tampa, built automated rail systems designed to move people around the downtown areas. Sometimes called "people movers," these invariably fell far short of expectations. Miami's system cost twice the projected amount and attracted just 40 percent of projected riders. Detroit's cost only 50 percent more than projections but attracted just 10 percent of projected riders. None of these systems were expanded, and the cost of operating them became a major burden for the cities or transit agencies.

In most cases, however, shutting down a rail project built with federal funds before the line is fully depreciated—which takes 30 years for most of the fixed assets such as rails, stations, and power facilities—is problematic because the Federal Transit Administration requires a repayment of a pro-rated share of the federal government's costs. Many cities continue to subsidize the operating cost of federally funded lines because operating subsidies cost less than the amount the federal government would demand in repayment. Tampa was able to dismantle its people mover after less than 14 years of operation because it was built without federal funds.

Vermont began operating a commuter-rail line to Burlington in 2000. The federal government provided $17 million for track upgrades but required only that the state operate the line for at least three years. Near the end of the three-year period, a report from the legislative auditor found the train cost twice as much as projected to build, three times as much as projected to operate, carried less than half the projected riders, and collected less than a third of projected fare revenues. The diesel locomotive powering the train produced more air pollution than the automobiles that the line took off the road. As a result, the state cancelled the train at the end of the three-year period.[25] In most cases, transit agencies receiving federal funds don't have that option.

New construction often left contractors hungry enough for more contracts that they were able to persuade political leaders and, when necessary, voters, to build more no matter how poorly the initial lines worked. Due to the poor results from rapid-transit lines in Baltimore and Miami, many cities elected to focus on light rail, which was supposed to be a low-cost alternative to rapid transit. Sacramento opened its first of several light-rail lines in 1987, San Jose opened its first in 1988, Los Angeles in 1990, and Baltimore in 1992. Despite the typical cost overruns and ridership underestimates, these cities would go on to build more light rail.

The New Urbanism

As American cities experimented with different modes of rail transit, architects and urban planners were developing a new theory of how cities work. Having read Jane Jacobs' *The Death and Life of Great American Cities*, these planners conceded the high-rise projects built in the 1950s were not suitable housing for most people. Instead, they turned to Jacobs' Greenwich Village as the model for what they called *the new urbanism*.

In 1991, two of the leading new urbanists, California architect Peter Calthorpe and Florida architect Andrés Duany, met at Yosemite National Park's Ahwahnee Hotel and wrote a set of guidelines that became known as the Ahwahnee Principles. Urban areas, they said, should be "built around transit rather than freeways." Neighborhoods should be compact and "as many activities as possible should be located within easy walking distance of transit stops." To help achieve these goals, they rejected "developer-initiated, piecemeal development" and instead stated that "local governments should take charge of the planning process."[26]

The most important principle of new urbanism was that "All development should be in the form of compact, walkable neighborhoods and/ or districts" with a "diverse mix of activities (residences, shops, schools, workplaces and parks, etc.)"[27] The new urbanists considered low-density suburbs to be "placeless sprawl," and advocated for their "reconfiguration" into more compact, mixed-use communities.[28] In other words, planners replaced the 1950s' one-size-fits-all solution of dense high-rise development with a one-size-fits-all solution of dense mid-rise development.

Light rail became an important part of new urban planning if only because it gave planners an excuse to increase densities to generate transit ridership. Light rail "is not worth the cost if you're just looking at transit," admitted Portland planner John Fregonese. "It's a way to develop your community at higher densities."[29] Fregonese led planning efforts around Portland light-rail stations in the 1990s and later became a partner to Peter Calthorpe.

Light rail was also a key to new urbanists' polycentric view of the city. They saw an urban area as a cluster of communities connected by rail transit. Each community would have a high-density, mixed-use center surrounded by moderately high-density housing. Just as planners of the 1950s clung to the monocentric view well after urban areas had become polycentric, new urban planners adopted the polycentric view after jobs had become so diffused throughout urban areas that the regions were more nanocentric than polycentric.

While new urbanists didn't object to single-family homes, they wanted them on small lots so residents could walk to the community center where they would find stores and a light-rail stop. In essence, they wanted to return to the 1890s, with mid-rise Greenwich Villages and dense, streetcar suburbs of single-family homes and duplexes.

The emphasis on four- to five-story mid-rise developments reveals the new urbanists' lack of any sense of reality. Such developments were common in New York and other older cities in the decades before the electric streetcar and electric elevator were perfected because the lack of affordable transportation other than walking demanded dense communities. When elevators were developed, they were expensive enough that they made economic sense only if buildings were six stories or higher.[30] As a result, after 1900, development was sorted into either low-rise (three stories or less) housing that didn't require an elevator or high-rise (six stories or more) buildings with an elevator. Few mid-rise (four- to five-story) buildings were built anywhere in the United States after 1900 until the advent of the new urbanism in the 1990s.

The new urbanists wanted light-rail stations to be surrounded by "transit-oriented developments" that consisted of four- and five-story buildings with shops on the ground floor and residences above. To overcome the impracticality of putting an elevator in a mid-rise building, cities that built light rail ended up subsidizing most such developments. All of this came about because Jane Jacobs happened to live in a 19th-century mid-rise neighborhood and mistakenly assumed it was somehow the epitome of urban living. "There's no question that [Jacobs'] work is the leaping-off point for our whole movement," admitted Shelley Poticha, the executive director of the Congress for the New Urbanism in 2000.[31]

Many of the cities that built rail transit in the 1980s and 1990s thus became the victims of circular reasoning. They needed to subsidize rail transit to attract dense development, while they needed to subsidize dense development to attract people to rail transit. Even though the vast majority of Americans lived in low-density suburbs, planners had demonized sprawl for so many years that hardly anyone questioned this reasoning.

The inability of rail transit to deal with diffuse urban areas is illustrated by Denver, whose voters approved a $4.7-billion rail transit plan in 2004. The plan called for seven rail lines totaling 155 miles and one 18-mile bus rapid-transit line radiating from downtown Denver to virtually every suburb in the region. At the time of the election, no urban area in America except New York had more miles of rapid-transit and/or light-rail lines. Yet, despite all these routes, planners predicted that, when the system was complete, just 26 percent of the region's jobs would be within a half mile of a rail or bus rapid-transit station.[32]

WOULD YOU LIKE SOME ISTEA WITH YOUR NEW URBANISM?

Congress effectively enshrined new urbanism into law when it passed the Intermodal Surface Transportation Efficiency Act (ISTEA, pronounced ice tea) in 1991. The law created a $2 billion annual fund called "New Starts" to support construction of new "fixed guideway" transit infrastructure, which usually meant rail transit. Prior to ISTEA, Congress distributed most federal transportation funds to states and metropolitan areas using formulas based on factors as population and land area. The New Starts fund, however, was a discretionary fund, meaning the Department of Transportation was supposed to distribute the funds to the most worthwhile projects. In awarding grants from the fund, one of the more important criteria used by the Federal Transit Administration was whether the city in which the rail project was located would provide "transit-supportive development," meaning dense housing or mixed-use developments next to transit stops.

Cities and transit agencies soon realized that because New Starts wasn't a formula fund, the way to get more federal dollars was to plan more expensive transit projects. Although many cities were still committed to light rail, which was supposed to be inexpensive relative to rapid transit, cities planned increasingly expensive rail projects in a race to get "their fair share" of the New Starts fund. For example, in 1996 the executive director of Portland's metropolitan planning agency sent a memo to city officials in the metropolitan area that stated, "the region must take action to bring Oregon's fair share of federal transportation dollars back home or they will be lost to other regions of the country." The action the letter urged them to take was to endorse the construction of light-rail lines that would cost twice as much, per mile, as the most expensive line built in Portland up to that time.[33]

As cities and transit agencies competed for federal dollars, the result was a rapid inflation in light-rail construction costs. In today's dollars, San Diego's first light-rail line, built without federal funds, cost about $20 million a mile. Light-rail lines built with interstate highway turn-back funds in the 1980s typically cost about $30 million a mile. After passage of ISTEA, light-rail lines in the 1990s typically cost about $50 million per mile. In the 2000s, costs rose to about $100 million per mile. The light-rail lines listed in the Federal Transit Administration's 2017 list of recommended projects averaged

$160 million per mile. Seattle recently completed a three-mile light-rail line costing $626 million per mile, and Los Angeles is currently planning to spend $8.5 billion on a nine-mile line, or close to $950 million per mile.[34] And yet, these costly lines will not be capable of moving significantly more people than San Diego's first light-rail line.

WHAT A TRILLION DOLLARS BUYS

Since 1970, when most of the transit industry was municipalized, transit agencies have spent (after adjusting for inflation) more than $1.2 trillion operating transit services. Capital expenditures are not accurately known before 1988, but since then, the industry has spent around $400 billion on capital improvements and maintenance, about two-thirds of which has gone for new rail transit systems that carry a tiny percentage of transit riders. Transit fares since 1970 totaled less than $500 billion, which means subsidies have totaled more than $1.1 trillion.[35]

These subsidies have grown rapidly. Since 1970, operating costs have more than quadrupled even after adjusting for inflation, while fares haven't quite doubled. Capital spending has nearly tripled since 1988 and likely at least quadrupled since 1970. Subsidies in 2016—fares minus capital and operating costs—totaled more than $50 billion, which is comparable to total road subsidies even though roads move 100 times as many passenger miles, and infinitely more freight, than transit.

No other kind of transportation—not even Amtrak—is so heavily subsidized. While highway and airline subsidies are less than 2 cents per passenger mile, and Amtrak subsidies around 30 cents per passenger mile, transit subsidies are close to 90 cents per passenger mile. For each transit fare of $1.52 per trip, taxpayers pay an average of $4.87 (Table 10.1).

The results from this orgy of spending have been dismal. Whereas 8.8 percent of commuters took transit to work in 1970, just 5.4 percent did so in 2016. Whereas the average urban resident rode transit 49 times in 1970, he or she rode it just 38 times in 2017. Some might argue that subsidies slowed the decline of transit, but it isn't clear why taxpayers should spend more than a trillion dollars to postpone the death of a dying industry.

Table 10.1

2016 Subsidies Per Transit Trip and Per Passenger Mile

	Fare/Trip	Cost/Trip	Subsidy/Trip	Fare/PM	Cost/PM	Subsidy/PM
Bus	$1.14	$5.40	$4.26	$0.28	$1.34	$1.06
Commuter Rail	6.21	18.51	12.31	0.26	0.79	0.52
Heavy Rail	1.41	4.32	2.92	0.29	0.81	0.61
Light Rail	1.10	10.41	9.31	0.22	2.07	1.85
Streetcar	0.68	15.07	14.39	0.46	10.12	9.66
Hybrid rail	1.21	16.98	15.78	0.10	1.38	1.29
Total Transit	1.52	6.39	4.87	0.28	1.17	0.89

Source: Calculated from 2016 *National Transit Database*.

Notes: "Bus" includes commuter bus, trolley bus, bus rapid transit, and regular bus. Total Transit includes modes of transit not shown here, including ferries, automated guideways, and paratransit. Data may not add up exactly due to rounding.

Advocates of industrial policy say governments should subsidize young, growing industries that have the potential to make local and national economies wealthier and more competitive. Critics of such policies worry, however, that once government starts subsidizing selected industries, it will be pressured to support declining sectors instead. America's experience with urban transit seems to confirm this view.

Transit advocates claim transit subsidies help low-income people, but numerous studies have shown that providing someone with an affordable automobile will do far more towards helping them obtain and keep a job than providing them with subsidized or even free transit.[36] Advocates claim transit is good for the environment, but most transit systems use more energy and emit more greenhouse gases per passenger mile than driving.[37] Advocates claim transit relieves congestion, but spending $100 million a mile on a light-rail line that will carry one-fifth as many people per day as a freeway lane that costs less than $10 million a mile is not a cost-effective way to reduce congestion, and the evidence shows that increasing transit ridership does not relieve congestion.[38]

New urbanists and other transit advocates argue that transit is somehow vital to cities. Yet Table 10.2 shows transit is all but irrelevant, except as a part of their tax burden, to the vast majority of urban residents outside of New York City. New York is the only urban area in which transit carries more than 10 percent of travel (counting cars and transit but not bikes and pedestrians), and San Francisco-Oakland is the only other urban area in which transit carries more than 5 percent of travel. Transit carries more than 10 percent of commuters to work in just nine major urban areas and 20 central cities (plus a few suburbs of those cities). Outside of New York, rail transit is even less relevant, even in urban areas such as Dallas, Los Angeles, Portland, Salt Lake, and Seattle that have spent billions of dollars building new rail transit lines.

A disproportionate share of transit subsidies has gone into the pockets of rail contractors and railcar manufacturers. Thanks largely to ISTEA, the number of American urban areas that have some form of rail transit grew from eight in 1974 to more than 40 today. In most of these cities, the return to rail transit has been accompanied by a lot of hype but few positive results. Almost every new rail line has cost at least 10 percent

Table 10.2
Transit's and Rail Transit's 2015 Share of Travel and Commuting

	- - - - - - - - - Urban Areas - - - - - - - - -			- - - - Central Cities - - - -	
	Share of Total Travel	Share of Commuting	Rail Share of Commuting	Share of Commuting	Rail Share of Commuting
New York	11.07%	34.6%	25.8%	58.1%	45.1%
Los Angeles	2.02%	5.6%	0.7%	11.8%	0.7%
Chicago	3.73%	13.7%	8.5%	27.7%	13.1%
Miami	1.26%	4.0%	0.5%	10.8%	1.0%
Philadelphia	2.77%	10.9%	4.7%	28.0%	7.5%
Dallas–Ft. Worth	0.60%	1.9%	0.6%	3.8%	0.6%
Houston	0.78%	2.6%	0.1%	4.6%	0.2%
Washington, D.C.	3.84%	17.6%	11.4%	40.3%	21.5%
Atlanta	0.95%	3.8%	1.1%	12.3%	3.6%
Boston	2.86%	15.5%	10.3%	34.2%	21.2%
Detroit	0.39%	1.4%	0.1%	8.7%	0.1%
Phoenix	0.65%	2.5%	0.3%	3.3%	0.3%
San Francisco-Oakland★	5.51%	19.4%	10.2%	36.5%	10.9%
Seattle	3.34%	10.7%	0.8%	19.5%	0.4%
San Diego	1.48%	3.9%	0.6%	4.6%	0.5%
Minneapolis–St. Paul	1.10%	6.1%	0.6%	14.0%	1.0%
Tampa–St. Petersburg	0.40%	1.7%	0.0%	3.8%	0.0%
Denver	1.66%	4.5%	1.0%	6.7%	1.3%
Baltimore	2.42%	8.2%	2.4%	18.1%	3.0%
St. Louis	0.76%	3.3%	0.4%	11.4%	0.9%
Riverside–San Bernardino	0.50%	1.8%	0.7%	3.3%	1.1%
Las Vegas	0.99%	4.4%	0.0%	4.9%	0.0%
Portland	2.39%	8.5%	1.9%	13.0%	2.3%
Cleveland	0.89%	3.9%	0.4%	11.9%	0.7%
San Antonio	0.69%	2.6%	0.0%	3.1%	0.0%
Pittsburgh	1.40%	7.3%	0.7%	18.7%	0.8%
Sacramento	0.72%	2.8%	0.8%	3.5%	0.8%
San Jose	1.07%	4.5%	2.0%	3.2%	0.9%
Cincinnati	0.44%	2.6%	0.0%	8.6%	0.0%
Kansas City	0.25%	1.3%	0.0%	3.6%	0.0%
Orlando	0.64%	2.8%	0.1%	3.3%	0.0%
Indianapolis	0.15%	1.1%	0.0%	1.8%	0.0%
Virginia Beach–Norfolk	0.36%	2.0%	0.1%	0.8%	0.0%

(continued)

The restored Spokane, Portland & Seattle 700 thunders around a curve near Hope, Idaho pulling a train of 16 passenger cars on a 2002 trip from Billings, Montana, to Sand Point, Idaho. Photo by the author.

This 1909 photo shows Great Northern founder and chairman James J. Hill, Northern Pacific president Howard Elliott, and Great Northern president Louis Hill. Though GN and NP were nominal competitors, James Hill and his associates gained control of NP after it went bankrupt in the Panic of 1893. Photo courtesy of the Minnesota Historical Society.

In 1925, Baldwin built this 2-8-8-2 locomotive for the Great Northern Railway that was capable of pulling a 4,000-ton train over GN's Rocky Mountain grades. Great Northern Railway photo.

When General Motors demonstrated a Diesel locomotive more powerful and easier to maintain than steam, Great Northern quickly ordered 96 of them to replace steam locomotives in heavy freight service. Great Northern Railway photo.

Union Pacific's Devil's Gate Bridge, part of the First Transcontinental Railroad. Union Pacific unnecessarily lengthened its route in order to qualify for more federal loans and land grants. Photo by United States Geological Survey.

Great Northern Railways original Gassman Coulee bridge, North Dakota, was 117 feet high and nearly 1,800 feet long. Building without subsidies, Great Northern's founder, James J. Hill, sought the lowest grades and least curvature of any of the western railroads. Great Northern Railway photo.

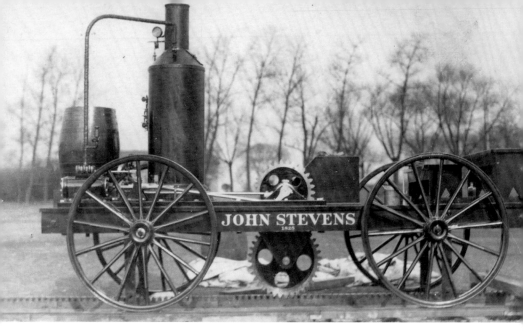

To demonstrate the advantages of railroads over canals, John Stevens built the first steam locomotive in the United States in 1825. This replica was built in 1925 by the Pennsylvania Railroad. Photo courtesy of Archives and Special Collections; S.C. Williams Library, Stevens Institute of Technology, Hoboken, NJ.

This painting shows the 1825 Stevens locomotive in operation, with a few passengers sitting in the back. Image courtesy of Archives and Special Collections; S.C. Williams Library, Stevens Institute of Technology, Hoboken, NJ.

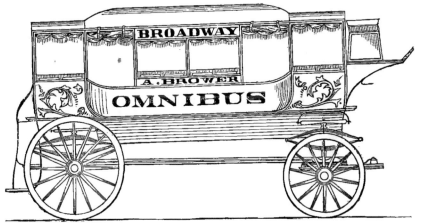

BROWER'S OMNIBUS.

The first vehicle constructed by John Stephenson was this horse-drawn bus called the Omnibus. Stephenson would go on to be the nation's biggest builder of horsecars and streetcars in the 19th century.

One of the Richmond streetcars built for Frank Sprague's electric streetcar project showing the trolley wheel used to pick up electricity from an overhead wire. Image courtesy of the New York Public Library.

After selling his trolley business to General Electric, Frank Sprague (left, New York Public Library photo) developed high-speed electric elevators, the first of which went into New York City's Postal Telegraph Building in 1893 (right, King's Handbook of New York City).

After selling his elevator business to Otis, Frank Sprague developed the first successful electric rapid transit lines for Chicago's South Side Rapid Transit Company. Each car had its own motors, all of which were controllable from the first car on the train. Sprague himself may be at the controls during this early test run of the system. Photo from the collection of John L. Sprague.

Many Glacier Hotel is one of an extraordinary collection of lodges that Louis Hill had built in and around Glacier Park to serve park visitors and, incidentally, attract people to ride Great Northern's passenger trains. Photo by Traveler100.

The lobby of rustic Glacier Park Lodge is lined with giant fir logs that the railroad hauled in from Washington state, yet was incongruously decorated with Chinese lanterns, probably to remind patrons that the Great Northern's premiere train was the *Oriental Limited*. This September 1913 photo was taken on the occasion of James J. Hill's 75th birthday. Photo courtesy of the Minnesota Historical Society.

At the 1925 Fort Union Indian Congress, Ralph Budd (right) examines a peace pipe with Crow Chief White Man Runs Him and Major General Hugh Scott. Photo courtesy of the Minnesota Historical Society.

A few feet away from Great Northern's tracks at Marias Pass, John F. Stevens III unveils a larger-than-life statute of John F. Stevens locating the pass during the winter of 1888. Great Northern Railway photo.

After concluding that buses were superior to trains for short-distance travel, Ralph Budd had the Great Northern become the first railroad to invest in a bus company. With capital provided by the railroad, Northland Bus Company president Carl Wicks bought dozens of other companies and soon offered coast-to-coast service, eventually renaming his company Greyhound.

In addition to being the catalyst behind the formation of Greyhound when he was president of the Great Northern, Ralph Budd played a crucial role in the formation of Trailways when he was president of the Burlington.

New York's original subway tunnels were built by digging trenches in streets and then covering them. This photo showing construction of the 1904 subway line on 42nd Street is courtesy of the New York Public Library.

To avoid disrupting street traffic today, New York uses tunnel boring machines, which are far more expensive, with the East Side Access line (shown) costing as much as $3.5 billion per mile. Photo courtesy of the Metropolitan Transportation Authority of the State of New York.

In 1922, the Fageol brothers built the first buses from the ground up. These buses cost less to buy but more to operate than streetcar lines. After they were introduced, most transit companies stopped building new streetcar lines but didn't convert existing streetcars to buses. Photo from the collection of William A. Luke.

In 1927, the Fageol brothers introduced the Twin Coach bus. Its revolutionary design allowed for 40 seats inside and brought bus operating costs below streetcar costs, leading cities such as San Antonio to scrap their streetcars for buses. Fageol Twin Coach factory photo courtesy of John Fageol.

Ralph Budd peers out of the engineer's side of Burlington's first zephyr during the train's publicity tour. Photo courtesy of the Minnesota Historical Society.

Ralph Budd ordered Burlington shops to create the first modern dome car out of a Budd-built coach. Chicago, Burlington & Quincy photo.

Occupying less than a city block in downtown New York City, John Stephenson's streetcar factory employed 3,000 men. Photo courtesy of the Museum of the City of New York.

To assemble his Model As, Henry Ford built the Rouge River factory. With its moving assembly lines, it covered 900 acres—almost as much as Chicago's Loop. Detroit Publishing Company photograph collection, Library of Congress.

The 1946 crash of two Burlington trains in Naperville, Illinois, led the Interstate Commerce Commission to pass strict speed limits for passenger trains, leading American railroads to stop experimenting with high-speed trains. Photo from the collection of Paul Hinterlong.

Burlington's *Denver Zephyr* and Union Pacific's *City of Denver* (shown) often exceeded 80 miles per hour. But the new ICC speed limits led both Union Pacific and Burlington to slow these trains. Union Pacific publicity photo.

No longer able to compete on speed, railroads attempted to attract travelers with amenities such as sightseeing. The Milwaukee Road added the first full-length "super domes" to its *Hiawatha* trains between Chicago and Seattle in 1953.

Northern Pacific responded in 1954 by adding four dome cars to its *North Coast Limited*. These cars vaulted the train to the lead in Pacific Northwest service.

In 1955, John Budd—Ralph Budd's son—added three dome coaches similar to those on the *North Coast Limited* and one full-length dome similar to the *Hiawatha*, allowing Great Northern to advertise that it had more dome seats than any other train. Great Northern Railway photo.

With four domes, a diner, café car (shown), and two lounges, Great Northern's *Empire Builder* was more of a cruise train than a mode of transportation.

General Motors' Aerotrain and other 1956 ultra-lightweight trains were supposed to reduce costs. But passengers found it so uncomfortable that several railroads rejected it after a few months of testing.

Budd reduced costs by increasing the capacity of train cars without sacrificing passenger comfort. Hi-level *El Capitan* coaches comfortably accommodated 72 people per car compared with 44 in low-level coaches.

To keep streetcars viable, the Electric Railway Presidents' Conference Committee designed a standardized streamlined streetcar. Chicago had 683 of these PCC cars, more than any other city. Photo by H.M. Staug, courtesy of the Krambles-Peterson Archive.

When Ralph Budd was made CEO of Chicago Transit Authority, he quickly realized that buses made more sense than streetcars, so he ordered hundreds of propane-powered Twin Coach buses to replace all of the city's streetcars and even some of its rapid transit lines. Photo from the collection of William A. Luke.

Budd's Metroliner makes its inaugural revenue run from Washington to New York on January 16, 1969 using technology similar to that developed by Frank Sprague in 1898. In non-stop service, the train was faster than any Amtrak train today. Photograph by Roger Puta.

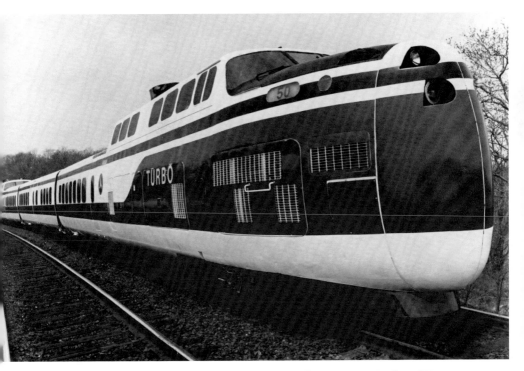

United Aircraft's TurboTrain, which began operating between New York and Boston in 1969, consisted of gas-turbine engines installed in a Pullman-built ultralight train similar to those of the 1950s but with pendulum-tilting for passenger comfort. Sikorsky/United Aircraft photo.

Some Bay Area Rapid Transit control cars have slanted fronts reminiscent of the original Burlington *Zephyr*. The high cost of BART forced cuts to bus service that have significantly depressed the region's total transit ridership. Photo by Maurits90.

In 1981, San Diego built the first modern light-rail line in the United State at a cost of about $20 million per mile in today's money. Light-rail lines planned and under construction today are averaging $160 million a mile and some are well over $500 million a mile. San Diego Metropolitan Transit System photo.

The distinctive shape of the locomotives of the original *shinkansen* (left) led to the "bullet train" nickname, which has stuck even though later trains (right) look very different. Japan's Tokyo-Osaka *shinkansen* line succeeded by capturing most of its passengers from low-speed trains, but it couldn't prevent an 850 percent increase in per capita driving over the next four decades. Photo by Pagemoral.

Spain has nearly bankrupted itself building high-speed rail lines to every provincial capital. Though heavily subsidized, the trains are used mainly by the elites. Photo by David Gubler.

China has the world's most extensive network of high-speed rail lines. Fares are typically 150 percent higher than those of conventional trains, so the high-speed trains are used mainly by the elites. Photo by Colbaltum.

Far from being behind in some technology race, America's railroads are the most productive in the world because they concentrate on moving freight, not passengers. Here, a BNSF train of empty grain cars is outside of Glacier National Park heading toward North Dakota wheat fields. Photo by Matthew Griffin.

A 2009 crash of two Washington Metro trains caused one car to telescope into another, killing nine riders. A National Transportation Safety Board investigation found that the cause was poor maintenance of train signals and the computer systems that controlled the trains. NTSB photo.

Instead of maintaining the existing Metro system in Virginia, the state elected to build a new line to Tysons so that local property owners could use the added transportation capacity to justify higher-density development. Photo by Ryan Stavely.

Seattle's light-rail system is mostly grade-separated from other vehicles and pedestrians, meaning it shares the high-cost disadvantage of rapid transit with the low-capacity disadvantage of light rail. Photo by Atomic Taco.

Honolulu is currently building an elevated rail line whose short platforms mean that it combines the low capacities of light rail with the high cost of heavy rail. Photo by Musashi1600.

Though it takes up no more room than a light-rail line, Istanbul's busway moves far more people per hour than the total capacity of Seattle's high-cost, low-capacity rail system. Photo by Arild Vågen.

The passing lanes that are a part of Bogota's busway mean that it takes more room than a light rail or Istanbul's busway, but it also enables it to move as many people per hour as rapid transit rail lines such as the New York City subway. Photo by Pedro Felipe.

The city of Portland built a streetcar line through downtown, then gave developers at each end of the line hundreds of millions of dollars in subsidies, including city-built parking garages for thousands of cars. The city then credited all of the new development to the streetcar without mentioning the subsidies. Photo by Cacophony.

Though Portland's 66-foot modern streetcars are much longer than a 40-seat city bus, they only contain 30 seats, so most passengers end up having to stand. Photo by Cacophony.

Nashville transit officials claim that the *Music City Star* was cost effective because it didn't cost much to buy used train equipment and run it on existing tracks. But it carries so few riders that it would be less expensive to give every daily round-trip rider a new Toyota Prius every other year for the next 30 years. Photo by the author.

Orlando's SunRail commuter-rail line cost considerably more to start up than the *Music City Star.* After nearly three years of operation, however, embarrassed officials admitted that fare revenues weren't even sufficient to pay to run the ticket machines, much less to operate the trains themselves. In 2016, they collected less than $2 million in fares and spent $39 million on operations and maintenance. Photo by Artystyk386.

Amtrak's Acela reaches a top speed of 150 miles per hour, but the average speed of the fastest schedules is 78 miles per hour. Amtrak claims that it makes money, but this doesn't count the $35 billion or more maintenance backlog needed to keep the Northeast Corridor running. Photo by Ryan Stavely.

California is one of the biggest backers of Amtrak state-supported trains, but Amtrak can't even fill a third of the seats on the average California train. Photo by Jack Snell.

The *Empire Builder* is one of Amtrak's most popular long-distance trains, but it still loses more than $100 per passenger. Photo by the author.

Megabus and Bolt Bus offer competitive services between New York City and Washington, D.C., with fares starting as low as $1.00 (plus 50¢ reservation fee). Photo by the author.

Since California voters approved a high-speed rail line in 2008, projected inflation-adjusted costs have more than doubled from $35 billion to more than $77 billion, most of which the state doesn't have. Artist's conception from California High-Speed Rail Authority.

Washington spent hundreds of millions of dollars to save ten minutes on Amtrak trains between Seattle and Portland. On the inaugural run, the engineer missed a speed limit sign and the train derailed, killing three people. Washington State Patrol photo.

White Pass & Yukon Route trains carry more than 400,000 passengers per year on trips out of Skagway, Alaska. Photo by Daniel Simon.

The *Rocky Mountaineer* is a modern cruise train capitalizing on the incredible scenery in the Canadian mountains. Photo courtesy of ecruising.travel.

Principal Characters and Events in *Romance of the Rails*

John Stevens
1825: Builds first steam locomotive in the United States

Robert Stevens (son of John, C&A president 1830–1845)
1830: John founds and Robert becomes president of the Camden & Amboy RR
1831: Designs first T-shaped rail

John Stephenson (nation's leading streetcar builder, 1830–1893)
1830: Builds Omnibus (horse-drawn bus)
1831: Builds first horse-drawn streetcar

Frank Sprague (the "Tesla of transportation")
1892: Develops first high-speed, pushbutton electric elevator
1888: Develops first workable electric streetcar
1898: Develops first electric multiple-unit rapid-transit system

John F. Stevens (cousin of John & Robert, mentor to Ralph Budd)
1888: Locates Marias Pass for GNRy
1910: Completes SP&S Railway construction

James J. Hill (mentor to John F. Stevens & Ralph Budd, GNRy president 1889–1907)
1893: Completes first unsubsidized transcontinental railway
1910: Starts constructing chain of Glacier Park hotels

Louis Hill (son of James J. Hill, GNRy president 1907–1912)

Courtlandt Hill (grandson of James J. Hill, son of Louis Hill)
1941: Finances company that develops first pendulum cars

Edward Budd (cousin of Ralph Budd)
1934: Builds first of many Burlington zephyrs

Ralph Budd (GNRy president 1919–1931, CB&Q president 1932–1949)
1945: Orders construction of first dome car
1933: Orders first diesel-powered streamline train
1925: Provides capital for what will become Greyhound Lines
1935: Joins Burlington with Santa Fe & other RRs to form Trailways

John Budd (son of Ralph Budd, GNRy president 1951–1970)
1955: Turns *Empire Builder* into cruise train

~1915: Develops automatic train control (ATC)
1925: Installs ATC on GN, NP, & CB&Q Rys

1950: Replaces Chicago PCC cars with buses

1740   1760   1780   1800   1820   1840   1860   1880   1900   1920   1940   1960   1980

This chart shows the connections between Frank Sprague, Ralph Budd, and some of the other major characters and events described in *Romance of the Rails*.

Table 10.2
Transit's and Rail Transit's 2015 Share of Travel and Commuting *(continued)*

	Urban Areas			Central Cities	
	Share of Total Travel	Share of Commuting	Rail Share of Commuting	Share of Commuting	Rail Share of Commuting
Milwaukee	0.83%	4.5%	0.1%	8.1%	0.0%
Columbus	0.38%	2.6%	0.0%	3.0%	0.1%
Austin	0.77%	3.0%	0.3%	4.6%	0.2%
Charlotte	0.53%	3.0%	0.7%	3.9%	0.6%
Providence	0.68%	3.2%	1.0%	8.7%	1.6%
Jacksonville	0.37%	1.7%	0.0%	1.4%	0.0%
Memphis	0.24%	1.3%	0.0%	1.9%	0.1%
Salt Lake City★	1.29%	3.3%	1.5%	5.7%	0.8%
Louisville	0.51%	2.4%	0.0%	3.7%	0.0%
Nashville	0.27%	2.0%	0.2%	2.2%	0.1%
Richmond	0.32%	1.9%	0.0%	5.0%	0.2%
Buffalo	0.71%	4.4%	0.3%	14.0%	0.8%
Hartford	0.72%	3.6%	0.1%	17.9%	0.0%
Bridgeport-Stamford	0.34%	11.2%	8.3%	12.3%	0.0%
New Orleans	0.57%	4.4%	0.4%	7.5%	0.6%
Raleigh	0.18%	1.1%	0.0%	1.7%	0.0%
Oklahoma City	0.09%	0.5%	0.0%	0.6%	0.0%
Tucson	0.75%	3.1%	0.2%	3.0%	0.0%
El Paso	0.81%	1.2%	0.0%	1.9%	0.0%
Honolulu	4.07%	10.5%	0.0%	13.6%	0.0%
Birmingham	0.12%	0.8%	0.0%	2.2%	0.0%
Albuquerque	0.87%	1.4%	0.2%	2.5%	0.3%
McAllen	0.00%	0.6%	0.0%	0.8%	0.0%
Omaha	0.16%	1.2%	0.0%	1.2%	0.0%
Dayton	0.43%	2.0%	0.0%	6.3%	0.0%
Rochester	0.51%	3.6%	0.0%	4.6%	0.0%
Allentown	0.37%	2.0%	0.1%	5.7%	0.2%

Sources: Transit's share of total travel calculated from 2015 *National Transit Database* Service spreadsheet, and *2015 Highway Statistics, table HM-72,* with vehicle miles of travel multiplied by 1.67 to convert to passenger miles of travel; transit's share of commuting from the *2015 American Community Survey, table B08301 for urban areas and places.*

★ Data for the San Francisco-Oakland urban area include the Concord and Livermore urban areas because all residents are served by the same regional transit system. Likewise, data for the Salt Lake City urban area include the Ogden and Provo-Orem urban areas because all residents are served by the same regional transit system.

more than projected, and overruns have averaged 40 percent. Most rail lines carry fewer riders than projected, with actual ridership averaging less than 60 percent of predictions. Few cities have seen transit ridership grow significantly faster than it had been before building rail, and in many if not most cases, growth has actually slowed. That could be for a variety of reasons, but it is at least partly because the high cost of rail transit has led transit agencies to neglect the rest of their transit systems. These issues will be discussed in more detail in later chapters.

11. KEEPING UP WITH THE JONESES

A lack of consideration of what HSR can or cannot offer in reality, or a view based on myths and beliefs that are out of sync with the reality of functioning HSR projects, has been the source of huge financial debacles and the failure of HSR as a transportation strategy.

— Albalate and Germà Bel

On my first visits to most other countries, including Australia, Britain, France, Italy, Japan, Korea, New Zealand, and Switzerland, I've spent much of my time riding trains. Many of my friends who visit these countries return to the United States wondering, "Why can't we have trains like that?" Or, as a writer in the *National Journal* put it, "Why can't America have great trains?"[1] There are many ways to answer this question, but the best way is to see how well the trains in those countries actually work.

JAPAN: HIGH-SPEED TRAINS REPLACE LOW-SPEED TRAINS

During my visit to Japan in 2010, I rode a high-speed *shinkansen* from Tokyo to Kokura, on the island of Kyushu. With one change of trains, I traveled a distance of 688 miles (1,108 kilometers) in less than 5⅔ hours, for an average speed of 122 miles per hour (196 kilometers per hour). Japan has an even faster train called the *Nozomi* that does the same journey in less than five hours, for an average speed of 142 miles per hour.

I decided to return from Kokura on local trains, however, and if I had taken local trains paralleling the *shinkansen*, the trip would have taken more than 25 hours, as the average speed was just 28 miles per hour. Instead, I took trains that followed Japan's northwest coast, a somewhat longer route. Counting the time between transfers, the trains I rode averaged 25 miles per hour. Riding only during daylight hours, I eventually realized I was at risk of missing my plane back to the United States, so I took a train inland to Kyoto and caught a *shinkansen* to Tokyo.

If the primary means of travel were trains that averaged 25 or even 50 miles per hour, a high-speed *shinkansen* would seem revolutionary, and that was pretty much the situation in Japan 70 years ago, when the country was contemplating building the world's first 130-mile-per-hour train. At that time, 80 percent of all passenger travel in Japan was by low-speed trains. Fewer than 3 percent of passenger miles were by car, just 0.2 percent by air, 2 percent by inland waterways, and the remaining 15 percent were by bus.

Japan's trains at the time were run by the Japanese National Railways (JNR). Like Amtrak, JNR was a state-owned corporation that kept its books separate from the national government. Also like Amtrak, JNR was under political pressure to serve as much of the nation as possible, and in fact its rails went to all 46 prefectures that made up the country. Unlike Amtrak, JNR required no subsidies in its early years, as it cross-subsidized service to low-density prefectures with profits from high-density areas. On the other hand, Japan's politicians had greater control over JNR's fares and railroad worker pay than Congress exercises over Amtrak.

Japan, of course, is an island nation whose total area is about the size of Montana. Three-quarters of the country's residents live on the central island of Honshu, whose land area is about the size of Minnesota. Honshu's population in 1960 was 69 million people (over 100 million today), compared with 5.5 million in Minnesota today. Just about half of Honshu's population was concentrated in a narrow corridor between Tokyo and Osaka, where Japan built its first high-speed rail line. This was the route of the 17th-century *Tōkaidō*, or East Sea Road.

Although the Tokyo–Osaka corridor accounted for just 3 percent of JNR's rails, it produced 24 percent of its traffic.[2] In 1956, JNR upgraded the line with electric-powered trains operating at average speeds of slightly more than 50 miles per hour. Yet even with faster trains moving more people per hour, the line was overloaded. So in 1958, JNR and the Japanese government decided to build a high-speed rail line in the corridor. The World Bank provided financial assistance for the project, which cost about $19 billion in today's dollars. Whereas all previous trains in Japan operated on rails that were 3½ feet apart, the rails for the high-speed trains were the U.S. standard gauge of 4 feet, 8½ inches. This meant there would be no conflicts between low-speed and high-speed trains, but it also meant that passengers would have to change trains to go to destinations not served by high-speed routes.

The trains began operating on October 1, 1964, just nine days before the opening of the 1964 Olympics in Tokyo. The line was called the *Tōkaidō Shinkansen*, with *shinkansen* meaning "new trunk line." In English, they were colloquially called *bullet trains* for the shape of the original locomotives used on the route, and the name stuck even though later locomotives didn't have the same shape. Charging premium fares and getting its customers from well-to-do users of low-speed trains, the route was highly successful, and frequencies grew from 60 trains per day in 1964 to nearly 350 today. Not only did fares cover operating costs, in just eight years, it had earned enough to repay the World Bank loans required for construction.

Unfortunately, the Japanese National Railways overall wasn't doing as well. In 1963, the company had enjoyed a string of eight profitable years. But in 1964 and 1965, it lost enough money to wipe out all of the profits it made in the previous eight years. The main reason for the losses was the political demand to serve low-density routes, and the fact that many of the customers on its most profitable conventional trains deserted them for the *shinkansen* didn't help. JNR responded by raising fares. Automobile ownership was growing, however, and passengers responded to those higher fares by finding alternative forms of travel. By 1970, rail's share of passenger travel had fallen to less than half, while the automobile's share had grown to more than a third. The number of passenger miles carried by JNR, which had been growing better than 5 percent per year in the decade before the *shinkansen* opened, effectively stopped growing after 1965, the first full year of *shinkansen* operation.[3]

Miles
309 car
247 crow
Tokyo – Osaka

To add to JNR's financial woes, the government insisted it build more high-speed lines. The second route, known as the *Sanyō* line, was effectively an extension of the *Tōkaidō* line to Fukuoka, the largest city on the island of Kyushu. Opening in 1975 with a tunnel under the water separating the two islands, the line cost about $22 billion in today's dollars; both it and the *Tōkaidō* line cost about $60 million per mile in today's dollars. Although ridership on the *Sanyō* line was lower than on the *Tōkaidō* line, it still earned enough revenues to cover its operating costs.

The same could not be said for the *Tōhoku* and *Jōetsu* lines, both of which were completed in 1985. The *Tōhoku* line went north from Tokyo to Aomori, on the northern tip of Honshu. The *Jōetsu* line crossed the mountains from Tokyo to Niigata, on Japan's northwest coast. Both lines cost more than $125 million per mile in today's dollars, and ridership is much lower than on the *Tōkaidō* line. The *Jōetsu* line is considered particularly scandalous because it was pushed through by Kakuei Tanaka, one of the most powerful—and sinister—members of Japan's House of Representatives in the 1970s, as well as prime minister from 1972 to 1974. Tanaka represented Niigata in the Diet, but he was probably just as motivated by his ties with the construction industry, as he had headed a construction company prior to entering the Diet. Although it was unrelated to the *shinkansen*, Tanaka was twice convicted of accepting bribes, first in 1949 and again in 1983.

These new high-speed lines added little to JNR's total ridership. In fact, the number of passenger kilometers had peaked in 1974, before the completion of the *Sanyō* line, and declined every year after that through 1982. By 1986, it was still 8 percent below the 1974 level, while per capita passenger kilometers were nearly 16 percent below 1974.

On the other hand, the construction of the *Tōhoku* and *Jōetsu* lines added significantly to JNR's debt. JNR was able to borrow money to fund both construction costs and its growing operating deficits because it was one of the nation's largest landowners at a time when Japan was undergoing a property bubble. By 1987, using its land as collateral, JNR had borrowed more than ¥25 trillion ($350 billion in today's dollars), more than 7 percent of the nation's gross domestic product.[4] By comparison, General Motors' debt when it went bankrupt in 2009 was just $35 billion.

In 1986, the Japanese government decided to break up JNR into six major passenger companies and a seventh company dealing exclusively with freight. The smaller companies, the government believed, could operate more efficiently. The new companies would also have more freedom to set their own rates, negotiate labor wage rates, and reduce a bloated labor force. The government initially leased the *shinkansen* tracks to the new companies, but in 1991, it sold the *shinkansen* lines for less than half of what it had cost to build them.

Total revenues from selling JNR covered only a small share of the company's debt. The government expected to cover the rest of JNR's debt by selling the land that had been used as collateral for the debt. Initially, however, the government delayed selling the land because, it claimed, "the government feared it would fuel skyrocketing land prices."[5] In fact, it is more likely the opposite is true: the government feared that putting that much land on the market would rapidly deflate the property bubble on which much of Japan's economy depended in the 1980s. That is exactly what happened, as the bubble burst in 1991 and the government was only able to recover a small portion of the debt from property sales. The bubble would have eventually deflated in any case, but it is likely that government plans to sell JNR land were what caused the bubble to burst at that time.

The three companies that run trains on the main island of Honshu—JR Central, JR East, and JR West—all operated at a profit and were largely privatized. However, the three companies that run trains on the outer islands—JR Hokkaido, JR Kyushu, and JR Shikoku—as well as the freight company, all required continued subsidies from the government and remain under government ownership.

Under the new regime of private ownership, passenger ridership began to grow again, reaching the 1974 peak in 1988, the first full year of post-JNR operation, and it continued to grow by about 1 percent per year over the next decade. In spite of that, trains continued to lose market share to automobiles and planes. In 1990, rail carried less than 30 percent of the nation's passenger miles, while cars carried more than 60 percent (the rest split between buses and planes). The decline continued through 2005, the latest year for which numbers are available, when rail carried just 25 percent of passenger miles and 5 percent of freight ton-miles.[6]

The Japanese government responded to the collapse of the property bubble by trying to stimulate the economy through construction of more high-speed rail lines. The failure of this policy can be seen by looking at Japan's gross domestic product, which since 1991 has been one of the slowest growing in the developed world. New *shinkansen* lines didn't lead to overall economic growth; at best, they merely shuffled it around. While cities with new *shinkansen* service have enjoyed above-average population growth, that growth was balanced by below-average growth and even population declines in cities bypassed by *shinkansen* lines.[7] This means the subsidies required to build the high-speed rail lines can't be justified by the net economic growth that results.

Japanese rail officials have bragged that some *shinkansen* lines have led airlines to stop serving those corridors.[8] There is little reason for joy, however, when a heavily subsidized program displaces a profitable one. Moreover, building high-speed trains in a few corridors failed to prevent airlines from doubling their share of overall domestic passenger travel since 1975, the year the *Sanyō* line opened.

The lesson other nations should have learned from Japan's experience was that high-speed rail is a sensible program in an extremely high-density corridor where almost all travel was previously by conventional rail, but it is likely to lose money in lower-density corridors or where automobile ownership is high. Unfortunately, the lesson they learned instead was that "Japan has fast trains; we need fast trains too to keep up." This has led to a succession of countries claiming record rail speeds or record miles of rail construction without seriously asking whether the transportation benefits of the projects are worth the costs.

ITALY: USING PUBLIC-PRIVATE PARTNERSHIPS TO HIDE DEBT

The first nation to take this lesson to heart was Italy, whose government isn't exactly known for its sound economic policies. In 1977, it opened a *treno ad alta velocita* (TAV, meaning high-speed train) line between Rome and Florence whose top speed was 160 miles per hour, with an average speed of 120 miles per hour. Since then, the country has built a total of 575 miles of high-speed routes, and more are under construction or planned.

Travelers on the 340 miles between Milan and Rome have a choice of 37 high-speed trains a day, the fastest of which takes just under three hours, for an average speed of 120 miles per hour. Fares start (as of this writing) around $54. Travelers can also choose to fly nonstop on Alitalia or EasyJet, which between them offer 28 flights a day. They take 70 to 80 minutes and cost as little as $34. For shorter trips, such as the 160 miles between Florence and Rome, the train is more price competitive—with fares starting at $34 vs. $70—but still slower—80 minutes by train vs. 50 minutes by air.

Like every other country with high-speed rail, Italy's projects were marred by cost overruns and ridership overestimates. In 1992, Italy estimated the seven high-speed rail lines it was then planning would cost $13.6 billion ($21.2 billion in 2015 dollars). By 2006, the cost had more than doubled to $48.3 billion in 2015 dollars.[9] In 2011, engineer Ivan Cicconi calculated the government had actually spent $138 billion on those seven lines.[10] Cicconi's estimates included costs the government had not counted, such as the cost of connecting high-speed lines to the existing rail system and interest on debt.

Under the Maastricht Treaty, and as a condition for joining the European Union, Italy and other European nations had agreed to keep their total debt less than 60 percent of their gross domestic product, and to keep annual deficits no greater than 3 percent of their gross domestic product.[11] Cicconi discovered that Italy avoided these debt limits by hiding high-speed rail debt in the books of private contractors. In a form of public-private partnership known as *availability payments*, the contractors borrowed the necessary money, and the government paid them an annual fee they in turn used to repay their debt. This got around the Maastricht Treaty by keeping the debt off of the government's books even though the government was still legally obligated to repay it.[12]

While the high-speed rail lines cost far more than projected, actual ridership of the lines turned out to be 25 to 35 percent lower than projected.[13] Far from persuading people to abandon their automobiles for trains, the expansion of Italy's high-speed network has been accompanied by a continuing decline in rail's share of travel. In 1990, trains carried 6.9 percent of Italy's surface passenger miles of travel. By 2015, this had declined to 6.2 percent, with automobiles gaining most of the difference.[14]

"The financial results of the implementation of high-speed rail in Italy have been devastating and have imposed enormous obligations on the national budget," say economists David Albalate and Germà Bel. "In terms of socioeconomic benefits, the existing estimates make clear that the level of use of high-speed rail is far below the demand necessary to justify the investment in more general terms."[15]

Despite disappointing results from its early lines, Italy has agreed with France to build a high-speed route from Turin to Lyon that will include a 35-mile-long tunnel. The European Union calls this route a high-priority corridor and has agreed to pay about 40 percent of the cost.[16] The tunnel alone is expected to cost nearly $11 billion, while the entire 170-mile line will cost $33 billion, or nearly $200 million per mile, quite possibly making it the highest cost-per-mile project of any high-speed rail line in the world. Construction was supposed to begin in 2014, but due to opposition from local residents, who say that "every euro spent on the TAV is a euro stolen from something useful for everyone," the start of construction was delayed until 2018.[17]

FRANCE: ONE PROFITABLE TRAIN

The Turin-Lyon route is currently served by French trains operating at conventional speeds. France is often credited with having the first high-speed trains in Europe, but it opened its first *Train à Grande Vitesse* (TGV, meaning very fast train) route between Paris and Lyon in 1981, four years after Italy opened the Florence–Rome route. Since then, France has opened several more routes, and by July 2017 had more than 1,640 miles of high-speed lines, with another 400 miles under construction.

Travelers can now ride the 470 miles between Paris and Marseille in just three hours, for an average speed of 157 miles per hour. While planes can make the same trip in 75 minutes, airfares are considerably higher than rail fares, and Paris' airports are not as conveniently located as the train stations for many residents and workers in France's dense cities. Unlike the *shinkansen*, the TGV operates on the same gauge of tracks as conventional French trains, so passengers from Paris to Turin can go from Paris to Lyon at high speeds and from Lyon to Turin at conventional speeds without a change in trains.

France's high-speed lines carried nearly 50 billion passenger miles in 2015, more than those of any other European nation. Yet the 320-mile *Tōkaidō shinkansen* alone carries as many passenger miles per year as all of the high-speed trains in France. Unlike Italy, whose rail system lost market share of passenger travel despite building high-speed rail, the share of passenger miles by French trains grew from 9.3 percent in 1990 to 9.9 percent in 2015. But all of that growth was at the expense of a decline in bus travel; the automobile's share of travel remained constant at 84.8 percent.[18]

The French government says the original line from Paris to Lyon earned enough operating profits to repay its construction costs by 1992. Later lines did not, however, and by 2013, France's rail programs had accumulated debts of well over $50 billion, most of which was due to construction of TGV lines. In 1991, the government transferred €5.7 billion (nearly $10 billion in today's dollars) worth of debt from Société national des chemins de fer français (SNCF, meaning National Society of French Railways), which operates the trains, to a separate agency. After that debt had increased to €8.0 billion ($8.4 billion), the government absorbed it into the national debt in 2007.

SNCF's debt was still very large, so the government transferred the job of managing the tracks to a separate company, the Réseau Ferré de France (RFF, or the French Rail Network), which also absorbed most of the debt. SNCF continued to operate the trains and paid RFF for use of the tracks. By 2013, RFF's debt was €33.7 billion ($36.4 billion in 2015 dollars), about half of which was from building high-speed rail lines and the other half from the cost of maintaining existing lines that weren't covered by SNCF payments. SNCF had a debt of €7.4 billion ($8.0 billion in 2015 dollars) due to operating losses. Both debts were growing because SNCF failed to earn enough revenues to pay the fees it owed to RFF and RFF failed to collect enough fees from SNCF to pay for infrastructure maintenance. In 2015, France merged the two state-owned companies, claiming the merger could save €1.5 billion per year, but it seems more likely that it is merely rearranging the lounge chairs while the train is derailing.[19]

While France's conventional trains continue to lose money, SNCF claims the TGVs overall earn an operating profit. "All high-speed rail services in France are profitable," asserts Bernard Aubin, head of a railway workers' union.[20] However, according to Marc Fressoz, the author of *Faillite à Grande Vitesse* ("High-Speed Bankruptcy"), more than 30 percent of TGV lines earn less in fares than their operating costs.[21] Moreover, SNCF's calculation of operating profits doesn't include the infrastructure maintenance costs paid by RFF deficits, which are close to a billion dollars a year. "The more we extend the high-speed lines, the less profitable they are," admits SNCF official Barbara Dalibard.[22]

Recently, SNCF's net revenues have declined due to the opening of new, money-losing lines, competition from low-cost airlines and ride-sharing (neither of which existed when the Paris–Lyon line opened), and the 2008 recession. After 2008, SNCF tried to regain customers by reducing fares, but even the lower fares on high-speed lines are "exorbitant" for the average person, complains Fressoz.[23] Although 83 percent of the residents of France have ridden a TGV at least once, only 10 to 15 percent of residents regularly ride the fast trains.

SNCF President Louis Gallois once called the TGV "the train that saved French railways." But it would be more accurate to say that, at best, it was "the train that slowed the decline of French railways." Between 1980 and 2014, passenger miles of rail travel in France grew by 62 percent, but passenger miles of highway travel grew by 84 percent and air travel grew by 225 percent.[24] Thus, rail's share declined even as the country was building more high-speed lines. These numbers aren't precisely comparable because air travel is measured in numbers of passengers, while rail travel is measured in passenger miles. The differences are great enough, however, to show that Europe's 1992 airline deregulation and the subsequent growth of low-cost airlines have done more to change French and European travel markets than high-speed rail.

Despite growing TGV losses, France continues to plan and build more lines. In at least some cases, however, it is doing so more to keep contractors happy and to satisfy other political interests than to provide better transportation. In 2016, French President Francois Hollande ordered new TGV trains that SNCF said it didn't need solely to keep open the factory that makes those trains—20 percent of which is owned by the government.[25] A few days later, he approved the construction of a TGV to Poitiers and Limoges despite the council of state's rejection of the line for not being worthwhile. The line had been opposed by the Fédération Nationale des Associations d'Usagers des Transports (FNAUT, or National Federation of Transport Users Associations) as being "an irrational project."[26] But, Hollande argued, "if you build infrastructure, it is not always to make a financial profit."[27]

SPAIN: POLITICAL TRAINS SERVE THE ELITE

While French high-speed trains carry more passengers than those of any other European country, it doesn't have the most miles of high-speed routes. That title belongs to Spain. Though it did not open its first *Alta Velocidad Española* (AVE, meaning *Spanish high-speed*) until 1992, today it has more than 2,000 miles of such lines. As of 2013, when it had 1,400 miles, it had spent €47 billion build them.[28] Yet its lines carry fewer than one-third as many passenger miles per year as France's smaller system. One of its trains carried so few passengers—an average of just nine per day—that it was terminated after six months, though passengers can still take the same route with a change in trains.[29]

Unlike other countries, Spain makes no pretense that its planned high-speed rail system is economically worthwhile. Instead, it is completely politically driven, based on the goal of linking all of the country's provincial capitals with Madrid by 2020. The government did not even conduct benefit-cost analyses before building any of the lines, but benefit-cost analyses by outside parties found that even the most popular Spanish lines "generated a clearly negative social result."[30] With 44 percent of all government infrastructure spending between 2005 and 2020 dedicated to a high-speed rail system that will carry few people, one critic observed, "the decision to assign enormous amounts of public resources to provide high-quality resources to a minority of Spanish society is a matter of dubious equity."[31]

The Spanish government claims that three of its high-speed routes cover their operating costs. Economists Ofelia Betancor and Gerard Llobet of the Fundación de Estudios de Economía Aplicada (FEDEA, or Applied Economic Studies Foundation) predict, however, that none of the lines will ever earn enough revenues to cover their capital costs. The most popular route between Madrid and Barcelona, they project, will cover only 46 percent of its construction costs, while other routes will cover a far lower share of those costs. Even when environmental and social benefits are counted, those benefits will never cover the construction costs.[32] FEDEA concluded "they should not have been built."[33]

University of Barcelona economist Germà Bel agrees. He notes that, prior to construction, analysts calculated that many of the lines would not generate enough social benefits to justify their high costs.[34] Bel calls the high-speed rail lines "vanity projects" that the government cannot afford and worries that the growing debts are having severe negative effects on the Spanish economy.[35] No doubt the provincial bureaucrats who decided to build them are happy to ride the trains to the nation's capital so they can argue for more subsidies for their regions.

Like France, Spain separated its railroads into two state-owned companies. *Administrador de Infraestructuras Ferroviarias* (ADIF) builds and manages the infrastructure, while *Red Nacional de los Ferrocarriles Españoles* (RENFE) operates the trains. As of 2013, RENFE had a debt of €5 billion, and ADIF was €11 billion in debt.[36] Like Italy, however, much of the debt required to build high-speed rail is probably on the books of private contractors.

Counting both conventional and high-speed lines, Spain loses €2.5 billion a year operating its trains. One reason why conventional trains are losing money is they lost many of their customers to high-speed trains. Whereas France dealt with losses by merging state-owned companies, Spain proposed to split RENFE into separate companies for passenger, freight, and rolling stock maintenance.[37] Despite Europe's growing debt crisis, neither country has seriously considered halting its rail construction program.

As in Italy, Spain's high-speed trains have not maintained their share of passenger travel. In 1990, rails carried 6.9 percent of passenger miles; by 2014, it was 6.7 percent, while the automobile's share grew from 78.1 to 81.4 percent. Buses were the big loser, with their share declining from 14.9 to 11.9 percent. Nor have high-speed trains dented the airlines' share of travel. While passenger miles of rail travel grew by 57 percent, airline travel grew by 145 percent.

GERMANY: SLOWER AND LESS RELIABLE

The other European nation with an extensive high-speed rail network is Germany. Although it opened its first high-speed line in 1991, a year before Spain, it has only about 860 miles of such routes. In contrast to France and Spain, which run their high-speed trains on entirely new tracks, Germany upgraded existing tracks where possible. Although this saved money, it also meant slower average speeds in most corridors.[38] The reliance on existing infrastructure also means the country has a huge maintenance backlog. This has led to an average of nearly 8,000 hours of train delays per day, leading to many disgruntled riders.[39]

Since 1990, Germany has dramatically increased rail's share of surface travel from 5.4 percent in 1990 to 8.4 percent in 2015. But it did so exclusively at the expense of bus travel, which declined from 9.1 to 6.0 percent, while the automobile's share grew from 85.4 to 85.6 percent. While rail passenger miles grew by 49 percent, airline trips grew by 400 percent. Substituting expensive trains for affordable buses is hardly a great accomplishment.

All the European high-speed rail lines have one thing in common: they have not stimulated the growth of the countries that built them. If anything, the debt required to build the lines has slowed economic growth. While cities reached by the lines may grow faster because of them, cities not reached are growing slower, so overall national growth has not increased.

BRITAIN: PRIVATIZATION BOOSTS RIDERSHIP

Rather than build high-speed rail lines, Britain took a different approach to increasing rail ridership. Britain has several trains that reach speeds of 125 miles per hour, which is considered to be less than the minimum for true high-speed trains.[40] Instead of investing in faster trains, Britain privatized its rail operations in 1997, allowing any private operator to bid on rail service in various corridors. In many major corridors, two or more private operators compete with one another. At the time of this writing, intercity trains are run by 18 operating companies owned by 10 parent companies, including companies from China, France, Germany, and the Netherlands, as well as Britain itself.

Britain's privatization program wasn't perfect. It also attempted to privatize rail infrastructure, creating a company called Railtrack that would charge the operating companies fees to use the infrastructure and spend the revenues on maintenance and improvements. Instead, to maximize profits, Railtrack deferred maintenance, leading to many train delays and allegedly contributing to three serious accidents between 1997 and 2000 that killed 42 people.

To solve this problem, the government renationalized Railtrack and now manages the infrastructure through a state-owned company called Network Rail.[41] It seems likely the problem wasn't privatization itself but the separation of the infrastructure company from the operating companies. While intended to promote competition on the same rails, the separation also reduced the incentives to keep the infrastructure in sound condition.

Privatization didn't end government subsidies. In addition to £4.0 billion spent on Network Rail in 2016, Britain subsidizes some of the operating companies to serve routes in sparsely populated areas. Overall, however, the operating companies pay a net of more than £800 million a year to use Network Rail's infrastructure. Thus, not counting new rail construction such as the London Crossrail, net subsidies to British passenger train services totaled about £3.2 billion in 2016.

What privatization did do is increase rail travel. Since privatization began, rail passenger miles have grown faster in Britain than in any other European nation, increasing by 119 percent from 1995 to 2015. By comparison, passenger miles grew by 69 percent in France, 58 percent in Spain, 28 percent in Germany, and just 10 percent in Italy. The growth of rail travel in Britain has come at the expense of automobile travel, as rail's share of passenger miles grew from 4.4 percent in 1995 to 8.5 percent in 2014, while the automobile's share declined from 89.2 to 86.1 percent. Moreover, rail passenger travel is keeping up with airline travel despite low-cost airlines: air travel grew by 120 percent between 1995 and 2015, just 1 percent more than rail travel.

The European Union has ordered its members to allow competition in the rail industry, but many have strongly resisted. France, for example, has prevented any competition and says the earliest it may allow such competition will be 2019.[42] Germany allows competition, but the state-owned Deutsche Bahn has used its economic muscle to maintain a 71-percent share of the business.[43]

The Netherlands spent €7 billion building a high-speed rail line from Amsterdam to Brussels and invited competitive bids to operate the line. "Out of fear that a foreign carrier would soon be providing train service in the Netherlands," the state-owned Dutch Railways bid twice as much as any other competitor. To provide affordable service at that high bid, it ordered equipment from a company that had never before built high-speed trains. Although the tracks were designed to support trains going 300 kilometers per hour, the trains ordered by Dutch Railways could go only 220 kilometers per hour. Delivered two years late, the trains suffered from such serious technical problems that they had to suspend service after little more than a month of operation.[44] Clearly, despite Britain's success, the fear of competition overrides the European Commission's stated desire for such competition.

SWITZERLAND: INCREASING FREQUENCIES

One other European country that has seen rail travel grow at the expense of automobile travel is Switzerland. From 1990 to 2014, rail's share of travel grew from 14.2 to 17.3 percent, while car travel declined from 82.1 to 77.7 percent. At 17.3 percent, Swiss rail's share of travel is higher than any other European country; Austria is a distant second at 12.1 percent. Except in wartime, no other country has managed to attract 5 percent of automobile travelers onto trains as Switzerland has, and it did so without building any high-speed rail lines. Although French high-speed trains enter Switzerland, they do so at conventional speeds.

Switzerland is slightly smaller than New Hampshire and Vermont combined, but with more than four times the population. Its population isn't particularly dense: New Jersey, for example, has far more people per square mile than Switzerland does. What Switzerland has, however, is a high density of rail lines: 196 miles of rail routes per thousand square miles, which is two-and-a-half times that of the European Union and four times that of the United States. Other than city-states such as Hong Kong and Monaco, Switzerland has the highest rail density of any country in the world.

The state-owned Swiss Federal Railways (SBB) owns nearly 2,000 miles of those rail lines, and private companies own another thousand miles or so. The private rail lines are oriented towards tourists, while SBB serves primarily Swiss residents. Instead of building high-speed rail, SBB has concentrated on gaining riders by increasing frequencies and reducing layover times between trains, as well as by increasing the connectivity between trains and buses, whose share of travel also grew, from 3.7 percent in 1990 to 5.1 percent in 2014. The gains in market shares by trains and buses were not free, however, and Swiss Federal Railways relies on about $2.3 billion in government subsidies a year.[45]

CHINA: SWELLING DEBT, NO PROFITS

Although many of the world's largest countries have built high-speed rail lines, the biggest move to high-speed rail has been in China. China in 1997 was where Japan was in 1957: it had a very low rate of automobile ownership and driving, with most intercity travel by trains whose average speed was around 30 miles per hour.[46] Since then, China has built 16,000 miles of high-speed rail lines, more than are found in the rest of the world combined.

With its large high-density cities a few hundred miles apart, rapid industrial growth, and continued low rates of automobile ownership— only one motor vehicle per eight people compared with one for every 1.25 people in the United States—China would seem to be an ideal location for high-speed rail. Yet just one line, the route from Beijing to Shanghai, makes an operating profit, though it hasn't yet earned enough to pay for its $33 billion cost.[47] High fares that keep most people on low-speed trains is one reason why most high-speed trains lose money.

Cost overruns are another reason, as every line built to date has cost far more than the original estimates.[48] One cause of these overruns has been corruption. After a 2011 collision between two high-speed trains that killed 40 people, investigators accused China's Railway Minister, Liu Zhijun, and his deputy, Zhan Shuguan, of accepting hundreds of millions of dollars in bribes from contractors and embezzling billions of dollars of construction funds to personal accounts.[49] Both were convicted and sentenced to death (though their sentences will probably be commuted to life imprisonment). Other deputies have also been convicted of accepting bribes.[50] Further corruption problems were found when a high-speed rail line collapsed in 2012 when it was under construction. Investigators found contractors were using inferior materials, such as soil for rocks; rocks for concrete; and inferior concrete and reinforcement bars rather than those specified by their contracts.[51]

China responded to these problems by dismantling the Railway Ministry and giving most of its functions to the state-owned China Railway Corporation. It also slowed down trains, at least until safety issues were resolved.[52] However, these steps failed to solve another growing problem: debt. As of mid-2016, the China Railway Corporation had a debt of 4.14 trillion yuan ($640 billion), or about 5.8 percent of the country's gross domestic product.[53] Two-thirds of that debt is due to high-speed rail, and the debt is growing by $60 billion a year.[54] Within five years, this debt, relative to gross domestic product, will be larger than Japanese Railway's debt when it was privatized in 1987, and the high debt has already led to calls to break up, though not necessarily privatize, the company.[55]

Despite rapidly growing losses, China is following Japan's example of continuing to build more money-losing high-speed rail lines to stimulate the economy, a policy that won't work in China any better than it did in Japan.[56] "In China we will have a debt crisis: a high-speed rail debt crisis," says Beijing Jiaotong University economist Zhao Jian, who thinks the crisis will have a bigger impact on China's economy than the mortgage crisis had on America's economy.[57]

In short, China has the same problem that Japan, France, and other countries that have built extensive high-speed rail networks have. Although the first line built may have been profitable, these countries were politically driven to extend high-speed rail to many places that were far from profitable. The result has been underutilized trains and inordinate amounts of debt. Even when that debt contributes to economic slowdowns, the political response has always been to build more rail in a doomed effort to stimulate the economy.

THE UNITED STATES: PROFITS, NOT GLAMOUR

The key difference between the United States and these other countries is not that America has some sort of irrational love affair with the automobile but that American railroads are mostly private, while railroads in the high-speed rail countries are mostly or entirely public or state-owned corporations. Although China's railroads were, of course, nationalized by the communists, most European nations other than Britain did not nationalize their railroads because of an ideological belief in socialism. Instead, they did so for nationalistic or military reasons. "Fear of domination by foreign capital, in addition to other political and military reasons, was a powerful factor in the government ownership of railways in many foreign countries," wrote transportation analyst P. Harvey Middleton in 1937.[58]

Although Britain kept its own railroads private until after World War II, for example, it nationalized Indian railroads in the 1850s to help assert military control over that country.[59] Bismarck nationalized Germany's railways after 1870 to help unify the country.[60] The Netherlands nationalized its railroads soon after German unification out of a fear that German companies would end up controlling Dutch railroads, making the Netherlands a tributary of Germany.[61] Similarly, Belgium—which declared its independence from the Netherlands in 1830—nationalized its railways out of fear they would be controlled by the Dutch.[62] Italy, which became independent from Austria in 1870, nationalized its lines out of fear of Austrian control.[63] Switzerland nationalized most of its railways out of fear of German or French domination.[64] The 1902 war between Russia and Japan inspired the latter country to nationalize most of its railroads because of "military necessity."[65] Among the major western European nations, Britain was the last to nationalize its railroads and the only one to do so because of socialist ideology.

Since the beginning of the railroad era, the United States has never had to fear foreign invasion. The only time it seriously considered nationalizing its railroads was during World War I, supposedly for military reasons. That alleged necessity ended in 1920, however, and since then, American railroads have been run to earn financial profits, while most foreign railroads are run to achieve political goals. Politicians crave publicity, so they prefer highly visible government programs over ones that may be essential but are less noticeable. Passenger trains are far more visible to the public than freight trains, so railroads owned by governments tend to emphasize passenger service, while private railroads in the United States and Canada emphasize freight.

As a result, far from being behind the rest of the world, the United States actually has the world's most efficient railway system. Though they are one of the least-subsidized forms of transportation in the country, America's railroads move well over 5,000 ton-miles of freight per person per year.[66] This compares with 500 ton-miles per person in the European Union[67] and less than 170 ton-miles per person in Japan.[68] In order to emphasize passenger service, other countries have given up on profitable rail freight service, allowing most freight to be shipped by truck, while railroads in the United States have given up on unprofitable passenger trains and emphasized freight.

A review of 2006 transportation statistics published by the European Commission found that, despite the emphasis on passenger trains, the automobile was the dominant form of passenger travel in the Europe and Japan as well as the United States (Table 11.1). Intercity rail was important in Japan but only marginally important in Europe.[69] About one quarter of European intercity rail travel, or 1.5 percent of the total, was by high-speed rail.[70]

Table 11.1
Percent of Passenger Travel by Mode

	EU–27	USA	Japan
Auto	74%	85%	56%
Bus	8%	3%	7%
Rail	6%	0%	30%
Tram/metro	1%	0%	★
Water	1%	0%	0%
Air	9%	11%	7%

★ Included in rail.

Source: *Panorama of Transport: 2009 Edition*, Eurostat, Brussels, 2009, p. 100.

The trade-off for attracting a greater share of passenger travel to trains was a huge loss in rail's share of freight movements (Table 11.2). Rail ships more freight than any other mode in the United States, but is rather minor in Europe and Japan, where highways are the dominant form of freight shipments.[71]

Table 11.2
Percent of Freight Shipments, by Mode

	EU-27	USA	Japan
Road	46%	30%	60%
Rail	11%	43%	4%
Pipeline	3%	14%	0%
Water	41%	13%	36%

Source: *Panorama of Transport: 2009 Edition*, Eurostat, Brussels, 2009, p. 57.

The notion that Europe is somehow more environmentally sound than the United States because more people ride trains is a myth. As New York University historian Peter Baldwin notes, "Ecologically speaking, there is no advantage in sending passengers by rail if freight is sent by road."[72] Because the difference in energy consumption between rail and truck freight is far greater than the difference between passenger rail and cars, the United States saves more energy shipping freight by rail rather than truck than Europe saves by moving passengers by rail rather than by car or air.

One argument made for building new high-speed rail lines is that it would "free up" the conventional rail lines for more freight trains. But it hasn't worked out that way in practice: As high-speed rail lines have been built in both Europe and Japan, rail's share of freight has declined at least as fast as rail's share of passengers. Between 1991 and 2014, rail's share of freight in the EU-15 declined from 8.4 percent to 8.1 percent.

The other cost of emphasizing rail is that it sacrifices total personal mobility. In part to promote rail over autos, Europe and Japan heavily tax motor fuel. The result is less driving, but that reduction in mobility is not made up for by an increase in rail and bus travel. As Table 11.3

shows, the average American travels 9,000 more miles per year by car than the average European, while the average European travels only about 400 more miles per year by rail than the average American. Visitors often leave Europe thinking trams (streetcars and light rail) and metros (rapid transit) are highly popular, yet the average European rides them only 124 miles per year, or 62 more miles than the average American.

Table 11.3
Passenger Miles Per Capita

	EU–27	USA	Japan
Auto	5,775	15,090	3,540
Bus	683	559	435
Rail	497	62	1,925
Tram/metro	124	62	0
Water	62	0	0
Air	683	1,987	435
Total	7,825	17,761	6,334

Source: *Panorama of Transport: 2009 Edition,* Eurostat, Brussels, 2009, p. 100.
Note: The 62 miles the average American travels by rail includes both Amtrak and commuter trains. Amtrak's share is about 22 miles, and commuter rail is the other 40.

This means that, overall, the average American travels more than twice as many miles per year as the average European, and close to three times as many miles as the average Japanese. Residents of even the wealthiest countries in Europe do not average more than 10,000 miles per year. This isn't because the United States is such a big country: although data are not available for every country in the world, the second-most mobile people may be Icelanders, who also have one of the highest rates of car ownership in the world.

In short, far from being technologically backward, America's rail system is the envy of the world, carrying more than six times as many ton-miles of freight each year as all of the EU-27 nations combined. Railroads offer advantages for freight that they can't match for passengers. Freight doesn't care about being crammed into tight spaces, delayed a few hours, or being jerkily transferred from ship to rail to truck. Rails will continue to play a dominant role in freight movement, but for passengers, rail travel can't compete with planes that need almost no infrastructure to go faster than any train or soon-to-be-driverless cars that will be able to go anywhere on America's 2.7 million miles of paved roads.

12. RAPIDLY DETERIORATING TRANSIT

I don't know what the fuss is
They can hardly fill the buses
But they want to build a train
They'll lay some rails and trusses
And shut down half the buses
If your city has a train
A billion here a billion there
Why its free federal money who cares.

—Vic Vreeland (sung to the tune of "If I only had a brain")

When I went into a subway station on my first visit to Washington, D.C., in 1977, I felt like I was entering the world of *2001: A Space Odyssey*. Escalators would glide people into vast rooms with arched ceilings that were like a work of art. Trains would burst into the stations in an explosion of displaced air, then smoothly and quietly roll to a stop, always in the same spot. On board, there were plenty of comfortable seats, but the starts and stops were so gentle that those who had to stand didn't have to hold on to a strap or post.

D.C. subways today are more like the world of *Blade Runner*. The escalators may or may not work, and the most common announcement over the public-address system is a list of out-of-service elevators and shuttle buses that disabled people can take to stations whose elevators aren't working. Trains screech into the stations and jerk to a halt, then sometimes have to move again before opening the doors because the driver stopped the train before all the cars were in the station. Not only is it hard to find a seat during rush hour, sometimes there's not even standing room because the transit agency often has only enough cars in service to run six-car trains, even though the platforms have room for eight.

Until Metro finally retired the 1000-series cars (a car whose number began with a "1"), more than a decade after being urged to do so by the National Transportation Safety Board, experienced riders took care to avoid them. These were the first cars delivered in 1976, and they were known to collapse in a collision, killing those inside. Once onboard, passengers must hold onto a pole or overhead strap because the starts and stops are sudden and jerky. And they can't count on the subway to get to a meeting on time: delays due to smoke in the tunnels, broken rails, and other problems are an almost weekly occurrence.

BUILDING NEW RAIL LINES WHILE OLD ONES CRUMBLE

How did such a beautiful system deteriorate into a national embarrassment? The answer is simple. While the federal government paid 90 percent of the $9 billion cost of constructing the original 104-mile system and local governments pay the costs of operating the system, no one budgeted any funds to pay for maintenance. Rail lines require very little maintenance when they are new, but as they age, maintenance requirements grow. By the time they are 30 years old, almost everything—rails, cars, signaling systems, escalators, elevators, power facilities—is worn out and needs to be replaced, and the cost of that replacement is a significant fraction of the original cost of construction.

In 2002, the Washington Metro board of directors adopted, but lacked funds for, a plan to spend $12.2 billion on rehabilitation over the next decade. The system "stands at the precipice of a fiscal and service crisis," the agency warned.[1] Yet local governments that paid most of the costs of Metro's operations ignored the warning, and what money was available was poorly spent. Metro rushed new railcars into production to replace the 1000-series cars at a cost of $383 million. The cars were so poorly built, however, that they broke down almost as often as the old ones. Metro spent another $382 million rehabilitating older cars, but poor oversight resulted in the rehabilitated cars breaking down more often than ones that hadn't been refurbished. Metro spent $93 million rehabilitating escalators, but more than a third of them ended up breaking down more frequently than before they were restored.[2]

In 2007, Metro experienced the first of a series of incidents in which smoke filled the subway tunnels. Each time, trains had to stop so passengers could be evacuated. Officials were "baffled" by the causes of the smoke and suspected terrorism might be the cause.[3] By 2013, such incidents were happening twice a month, and the agency discovered they were caused by water in leaky tunnels short-circuiting fiberglass insulators in the third-rail power system, causing them to catch fire.[4]

In 2009, a Metro train collided with another train that was stopped in a station. Nine people died, most of them in a 1000-series car that had less bracing than newer cars. The National Transportation Safety Board (NTSB) determined that the poorly maintained signaling system had failed, so the computer driving the train didn't stop for the train in front of it.[5] Signal system failures had happened before, but Metro waited until after this disaster before doing anything about it. After the 2009 crash, Metro shut down the computers that had been driving the trains and asked its drivers, whose main job had been to supervise, to actually control acceleration and braking of the trains. Thus, poorly trained drivers are the reason why trains today are so jerky and don't always stop in the right location.

NTSB had already directed Metro to "accelerate retirement" of the 1000-series cars after a 2004 collision. After the 2009 crash, it said that they should be replaced "as soon as possible."[6] It took Metro until the end of 2017 to finally retire the cars.

By 2011, Metro was suffering from an average of nearly one cracked rail and several smoke-related incidents every week.[7] In 2015, smoke in one tunnel was so bad that dozens of passengers required hospitalization and one died.[8] Metro responded by hiring a new general manager who—after another fire in March 2016—shut down the entire system one weekday to inspect every insulator and replace them as needed.[9] In late 2016 and early 2017, Metro interrupted service on most of the system, one line at a time, to do needed maintenance.[10] However, the work that was done only scratched the surface of Metro's maintenance backlog. The "new normal" for Metro, reported National Public Radio, consisted of "explosions and smoke-filled tunnels; turf wars between government agencies; frustrated riders and epic commutes."[11]

Despite all of these problems, the state and local governments funding Metro failed to step up to fix the system. It wasn't as if they lacked the money. Virginia decided that building a new Silver Line to Dulles Airport was more important than rehabilitating the portions of Metro serving Arlington, Vienna, Springfield, and other Virginia communities. Maryland decided that building the Purple Line light rail in the suburbs of Washington was more important than rehabilitating portions of Metro extending to Bethesda, Greenbelt, and other communities. Between the two of them, the cost of these two lines could have funded most of the rehabilitation work needed to return Metro to a state of good repair.

To make matters worse, the Silver Line used the same tunnel under the Potomac River to cross into Washington as the Blue Line, which was already running at capacity, so opening the first segment of the Silver Line to Reston, Virginia, forced a reduction in the number of trains and increased crowding on the other line.[12] Silver Line ridership in its first year was less than 70 percent of expectations.[13] Metro's ridership during that year was 1.3 percent lower than the year before, partly because the number of riders lost due to Blue Line crowding outnumbered riders gained by the opening of the Silver Line.[14]

Washington Metro officials argue that they have to rely on annual appropriations by each local government that supports the system. If they had a specific tax dedicated to their needs, they say, deferred maintenance wouldn't have become a problem. Yet Boston's transit system has a dedicated tax, and its rail system is in as bad a shape as Washington's.

Boston: A Dedicated Fund Won't Save Transit

In 1999, the Massachusetts legislature gave the Massachusetts Bay Transportation Authority (MBTA) a 20 percent share of all state-wide sales tax revenues. At the time, the MBTA had a $3.3 billion debt from building new rail lines, but the state expected sales tax revenues would be sufficient to operate the system and pay down this debt. Instead, a decade later, that debt had grown to more than $8 billion, and the agency had a $2.7 billion maintenance backlog.[15] Part of the problem was that the dedicated sales tax didn't generate as much revenue as expected, but it was primarily that MBTA was operating a huge money-losing system and was politically unable to reduce or stop service on the worst-performing lines.

MBTA estimated it needed to spend $470 million a year just to keep the maintenance backlog from growing. Instead, it spent only about $200 million in 2010. "As a result," said a report commissioned by Massachusetts Governor Deval Patrick, "many projects that would address critical safety or system reliability issues are not funded each year."[16]

By 2016, MBTA's maintenance backlog had grown to $6.7 billion.[17] Annual debt service costs of $452 million were nearly equal to the amount of money the agency needed to keep the backlog from growing further.[18] But instead of funding the maintenance backlog, the MBTA decided to build a new rail line from Cambridge to Medford. In 2005, this 4.3-mile light-rail line was projected to cost $390 million, or about $450 million in today's dollars.[19] By the time construction began, the cost had grown to $2.3 billion—more than $530 million per mile—which would have been enough to cover more than a third of the system's maintenance backlog.[20] Meanwhile, the system was experiencing "near-constant service issues," including nearly one derailment a month, an average of five delayed trains a day, and "below-average" bus service to minority communities relative to non-minority neighborhoods.[21]

Washington Metro and the MBTA weren't the only transit agencies that deferred maintenance. Rail systems in Atlanta, Chicago, New York, Philadelphia, and San Francisco all have multi-billion-dollar maintenance backlogs. The Chicago Transit Authority has a $12.9 billion maintenance backlog, 80 percent of which is for the rail rapid-transit system. The agency estimated it needed to spend $950 million a year to keep the system from deteriorating further, but it was spending less than $500 million a year.[22] Similarly, Metra, Chicago's suburban commuter-rail system, has a $6.6 billion maintenance backlog. It needs to spend $320 million a year to keep it from growing but is spending less than $187 million a year.[23]

New York City's transit system is supported by a variety of dedicated taxes and fees, including the tolls collected on most of the bridges into Manhattan, a sales tax, a petroleum business tax, and a long-lines tax on communications systems.[24] Yet the New York subway system alone has a $10.5 billion maintenance backlog.[25] To dig itself out of a maintenance backlog in the 1980s, the system racked up a debt of $38 billion, which increased by $3.6 billion in 2016 alone.[26]

In 2010, New York's rapid-transit system seemed to be in better shape than those in Boston, Chicago, and Washington, but then the city decided to spend more than $10 billion extending the Long Island Railroad 3.5 miles to Grand Central Terminal—a part of which the *New York Times* called "the most expensive mile of subway on earth"—and $4.9 billion on the first 2.3 miles of an anticipated 8-mile Second Avenue subway, the total cost of which will be $17 billion.[27] These megaprojects led the city to lose sight of maintenance needs, leading to such a dramatic increase in delays, derailments, and other problems that Governor Andrew Cuomo declared a state of emergency.[28] In addition to the agency's maintenance backlog, the Metropolitan Transportation Authority has unfunded health care obligations of $18.2 billion.[29]

Fix It First

Ironically, one of the biggest critics of agencies that build new lines rather than reduce their maintenance backlogs came from within the Obama administration, whose first transportation secretary, Ray LaHood, enthusiastically supported any and all rail projects no matter what the cost. To run the Federal Transit Administration (FTA), President Obama selected Peter Rogoff, who had worked for 14 years as Democratic staff director of the Senate Transportation Committee.

During his first year running the FTA, Rogoff met with numerous transit agency general managers and noticed the meetings "often follow a certain pattern." First, the managers complained about budget shortfalls and "significant chunks of capital reinvestment being deferred." As a result of deferred maintenance, some rapid-transit lines "had deteriorated to the point where trains could operate no faster than 15 miles per hour," or half their designated speed. "It's all very grim," said Rogoff in a speech at a 2010 conference on urban transit in Boston. Yet, in "the second part of the meeting," Rogoff continued, "the consultants start to get excited and the glossy brochures come out" as the agency managers described their new expansion plans.

Concerned about the incongruity, Rogoff asked his staff to assess the transit industry's backlog of deferred maintenance and learned it had reached $78 billion in 2010, nearly $60 billion of which was for rail transit.[30] "If you can't afford to operate the system you have, why does it make sense for us to partner in your expansion?" Rogoff asked. "If you can't afford your current footprint, does expanding that underfunded footprint . . . really advance our economic goals in any sustainable way?"

Transit agencies simply ignored Rogoff and continued to promote new construction rather than maintenance. Rogoff didn't have much choice but to agree to fund new projects because the federal New Starts program provided funding for new projects, most of which went to rail, while offering little funding for maintenance. It made more political sense for transit officials to dedicate local funds to match federal funds, thus doubling their budgets, than to spend those local funds on maintenance and get no federal matching funds.

In 2012, Congress created a new "state of good repair" fund that offered about $2 billion a year for capital maintenance. But this was far less than what is needed for systems nationwide.[31] As a result, by 2015, the industry's maintenance backlog had risen to $90 billion and was growing by $1.6 billion a year. To eliminate the backlog within 20 years, the Department of Transportation calculated, 100 percent of funds now being spent on improvements would have to be shifted to maintenance instead.[32]

"There will never be 'enough money'" to restore the New York City transit system to a state of good repair, lamented David Henley, who was in charge of capital planning and budgeting for the transit system in 2007.[33] Yet there was enough money to build the Second Avenue Subway and the tunnels to provide the Long Island Railroad access to Grand Central Terminal.

It's "unlikely we'll ever have enough money" to restore the BART system, echoed Frank Ruffa, who was in charge of asset management at

BART, in 2012.[34] Yet BART had enough money to spend $484 million on a 3.2-mile rail connection between the BART Coliseum station and Oakland International Airport. The connection, which opened in 2014, had previously been served by a for-profit shuttle bus that charged $3 for a one-way trip. The rail line, originally projected to cost $130 million, charges $6 but operates at a loss, and ridership is dropping thanks to ride-sharing services.[35] BART also had enough money to spend $1.5 billion ($2.0 billion in today's dollars) on an 8.7-mile extension to San Francisco Airport that opened in 2003. The project was originally expected to cost $580 million, but the cost nearly tripled by the time the final engineering was completed. As it turned out, ridership in its opening year was less than 70 percent of projections.

BART also has enough money to build a 10.5-mile, $2.3 billion line into Santa Clara County. Half the funds for this line come from Santa Clara County taxpayers, but the other half comes from federal and state sources that could have been reprogrammed for rehabilitation of the existing BART system.

Rapid-transit systems are not the only ones that wear out. Portland's first light-rail line was two years shy of 30 years old in 2014 when it began experiencing repeated breakdowns.[36] A state audit found that TriMet, Portland's transit agency, had fallen behind on scheduled track and signal maintenance. To make matters worse, TriMet has nearly a billion dollars' worth of unfunded pension and health care liabilities thanks to a generous union contract signed when the agency needed union support for a light-rail grant proposal to the Federal Transit Administration.[37] TriMet's general manager has warned that to keep up with maintenance and its pension and health care obligations, the agency will have to cut all transit service by 70 percent by 2025.[38] Despite these problems, the agency is planning another $2 billion light-rail line.[39]

Virtually every rail transit system in America over 30 years old has a major, often multi-billion-dollar, maintenance backlog. As with the D.C. metro, this is because most of the systems were built with federal or, in the case of very old systems, private dollars; state and local dollars have been used to operate them; and no one has provided adequate funds for maintenance and capital replacement. Agencies planning new rail lines do financial forecasting to insure they will be able to repay the loans needed to build those lines, but those forecasts typically look ahead no further than the duration of the loans—usually 30 years—which means they willfully ignore the huge rehabilitation costs needed after the loans have been repaid.

BUILDING RAIL LINES AS RIDERSHIP DECLINES

Since 1990, transit agencies have spent more than $200 billion on rail transit capital improvements, building dozens of rapid-transit, light-rail, commuter-rail, automated guideway, and streetcar lines in more than 40 urban areas. The number of urban areas with rail transit has grown from 8 in 1974 to 19 at the beginning of 1990 to at least 42 by the end of 2017. The extent of rail transit routes has more than doubled, from under 3,000 miles in 1990 to more than 6,100 miles in 2017. Yet the number of transit rides taken by the average urban resident per year has fallen from 47 in 1990 to 38 in 2017.

Building more rail transit has clearly not enhanced ridership. Given that few if any transit agencies are successfully maintaining their systems in a state of good repair, why do so many still want to expand them? One answer is that public officials are inherently risk takers because they are risking other peoples' money. "The public authorities foresee the potential major benefits of new transport infrastructures," observes University of Lyon economist Yves Crozet. "The entire economic literature indicates that these effects are largely illusory, but all the public decision-makers believe in them in exactly the same way as national lottery players believe in their luck."[40]

The best justification for building new infrastructure—that it will earn a profit—has been deemed irrelevant at least since 1964, when Congress decided to subsidize commuter trains. Every transportation program in the world loses money, the mantra incorrectly states, so therefore no project should be judged on whether or not it is capable of making money. Instead, transit agencies ask politicians and voters to judge their proposals using a variety of other measures, ranging from esoteric criteria such as "sustainability" and "increasing transportation choices" to more quantitative, but sometimes deceptive, criteria such as increased transit ridership and reductions in congestion.

In 1991, Congress directed that federal funding for a rail proposal be "based on the results of an alternatives analysis" and "justified based on a comprehensive review of its mobility improvements, environmental benefits, cost effectiveness, and operating efficiencies."[41] More recent laws have added congestion relief and economic development effects to the list of criteria for selecting projects worthy of federal funding.[42] Transit agencies have done their best—often with the complicity of the Federal Transit Administration—to evade these requirements, either by ignoring them or by fabricating data to make their projects appear worthwhile.

For example, many transit agencies conducted alternatives analyses that considered mostly alternative rail routes and not alternatives to rail. The only nonrail alternatives were "no build," which was invariably rejected as failing to solve any of the made-up problems that supposedly required rail transit, and sometimes minor improvements to bus service collectively known as "transportation system management." Because spending a billion dollars on a new rail line was almost always projected to attract more riders than spending a few million dollars on bus improvements, rail was always the preferred alternative. Yet the bus alternatives invariably cost far less per new rider than the rail alternatives, suggesting that spending a few million dollars more on buses could attract as many new riders as spending a billion new dollars on rail.

STRATEGIC MISREPRESENTATION

A second problem is that transit agencies desiring to obtain funding for a project make overly optimistic estimates about costs and benefits. Almost every rail project built since 1970 has ended up costing far more than projected, and the vast majority have attracted far fewer riders than projected. This problem isn't solved when the agencies contract out their cost and ridership projections to outside consulting firms, for the consultants know that if the project is approved, they are likely to get even more lucrative contracts to help build it.

Since 1990, the Department of Transportation has published at least six reports comparing projected and actual costs and riders of 64 major transit projects. All but two had cost overruns, and one of those two cost less than projections only because it built fewer miles than originally planned. Overruns averaged 43 percent for rail lines and 27 percent for bus lines. All but four projects fell short of ridership projections, with shortfalls averaging 27 percent for rail lines.[43]

Some insight into the planning process that led to such inaccurate estimates was revealed when Transport 2020, an agency formed by the city of Madison, Dane County, and the state of Wisconsin, proposed to build commuter-rail lines in Madison, Wisconsin. The agency hired Parsons Brinckerhoff, the engineering firm that built the first New York City subway in 1904, and that has been involved in perhaps the majority of rail transit projects built since 1970, to analyze the proposed rail lines.

Parsons Brinckerhoff considered three alternatives: no build, spending $40 million to enhance bus service, and spending $222 million on two commuter-rail lines plus bus improvements. The consulting firm's models predicted that the latter two alternatives would each increase ridership over no-build by about 50 percent. To the company's dismay, however, the enhanced bus alternative was predicted to attract more transit riders than the commuter-rail alternative. To "fix" this problem, the consulting firm went back and deleted "unproductive" bus routes, reducing bus ridership to less than the rail alternative—only 1.6 percent less, but less nonetheless. Parsons Brinckerhoff's report then recommended the rail alternative because it produced the highest ridership.[44]

In presenting these results to the public, the agency was even more disingenuous by not even mentioning the possibility of the enhanced bus alternative. The agency's 40-page summary of Parsons Brinckerhoff's 200-page report made it appear that there were only two choices: do nothing or build commuter-rail lines and get a 50 percent boost in transit ridership.[45] Of course, nearly all of that projected increase was actually from the enhanced bus option, which could easily have operated without a commuter-rail line.

Further insight into the world of consultants was revealed when transportation agencies in Oregon and Washington spent several hundred million dollars planning a new Interstate 5 bridge across the Columbia River between Portland and Vancouver. Portland's transit agency, TriMet, desperately wanted to extend its light-rail empire into Vancouver and had already built a line almost to the foot of the existing bridge. A highway-only bridge would have cost less than $1 billion, but including the light-rail line into Vancouver and some other side projects increased the total to $3.5 billion.

As part of the planning process, the Columbia River Crossing consortium paid as much as $78.5 million to a consulting firm called David Evans and Associates to write the environmental impact statement for the bridge.[46] Construction depended on the Oregon and Washington legislatures each appropriating $450 million. During debate, critics discovered that the chief lobbyist for the project in Oregon, Patricia McCaig, had never registered as a lobbyist or revealed her source of income. Instead, she claimed to be a "special advisor" to the governor.

In fact, her employer was David Evans and Associates, which paid her $417,000—a small fraction of the company's contract—to promote the project.[47] A representative of the state Department of Transportation described McCaig as a "subcontractor to David Evans to conduct strategic communications, public information and outreach," suggesting that the transportation agencies were completely complicit with this apparently illegal (because it was unregistered and undisclosed) lobbying effort.[48] Even though Evans had paid her for 800 hours of work, an investigation by the Oregon Ethics Commission finally concluded it could not prove McCaig had spent enough hours lobbying legislators—as opposed to just "conducting public information"—to require registration.[49]

The consistency behind rail transit consultants' large cost underestimates and ridership overestimates has led Danish planning professor Bent Flyvbjerg to call them "strategic misrepresentation."[50] He suggests agencies use "reference class forecasting," meaning that if costs of a particular kind of infrastructure project persistently average 50 percent above the projections, agencies should automatically add 50 percent to the projections for new projects.[51] Of course, since those agencies are just as interested as the consultants in seeing the projects built, they would never follow Flyvbjerg's recommendation.

An alternative proposed by Spanish economist Ginés De Rus is "the creation of an independent agency conducting cost-benefit analysis sheltered from political interference."[52] Yet there is really no such thing as an "independent agency," and even if there were, the legislators making the final decision on megaprojects are most inclined to follow the money no matter what an independent agency may say. The Oregon legislature, for example, ended up voting to build the Columbia River bridge despite revelations about the source of the lobbyist's funds; it was only a very close vote in the Washington legislature that finally killed the project.

Rail advocates hardly blink an eye when the projected costs of projects double or more; instead of seeing the increased cost as a reason to question the project, they argue it is all the more urgent to build it before the cost goes up again. Nor does their support for future projects diminish when the ridership of completed projects repeatedly falls short of expectations.

Rapid-transit lines in Boston, Chicago, New York, and Philadelphia, being the largest and oldest rail transit systems in the country, have the biggest maintenance backlogs. Only six urban areas have built true rapid-transit lines since 1970, and three of those—in Baltimore, Los Angeles, and Miami—were largely considered failures (in spite of that, and after long delays, both Los Angeles and Miami ended up expanding their lines). Two others—Atlanta and the San Francisco Bay Area—may be popular locally, but the people who ride them don't see the huge declines in per capita transit ridership that have taken place due to the diversion of funds from buses to rail. Only Washington, D.C.'s Metro has maintained per capita ridership, although it has recently declined due to poor maintenance. As will be discussed in greater detail in the next three chapters, all the problems surrounding project selection and construction apply to all types of rail transit.

13. LOW-CAPACITY RAIL

*The Los Angeles Long Beach Blue Line light rail service is not the result of
a calculated, let alone reflective, effort to provide for the transportation needs of
Southern California's congested autopolis. It is the creation of a mythology.
A study of the elements composing the myth of rail shows why the idea of
rail systems developed great symbolic appeal in Los Angeles, one little related
to the benefits rail might actually bring. These elements paint bold pictures,
drawing clear-cut answers from out of a web of otherwise intolerable complexity:
they fulfill the human need for simplicity.*

—Jonathan Richmond[1]

In November 2016, Los Angeles voters agreed to raise their taxes so the
county transit agency, the Metropolitan Transportation Authority, could
spend $120 billion on new transit lines. At the same time, Seattle voters
agreed to raise taxes so their regional transit authority, Sound Transit, could
spend $20 billion on 62 miles of new rail lines at a cost of more than
$320 million per mile. The scale and expense of the projects these agencies
proposed to build is breathtaking, especially since most of the money will
go for light rail, a form of transit that shouldn't even exist.

The name *light rail* falsely implies that light railways are lighter
in weight, and by extension lower in cost, than heavy railways (another
name for rapid transit). Indeed, in Britain, the Light Railways Act of
1896 allowed private parties to build light railways with less government

regulation than regular rail lines. These light railways are smaller, lighter, and were less expensive to build than standard railways, and many of them still exist.[2]

Today's light-rail transit is very different, as it is neither small, light, nor less expensive. A typical light-rail car built today weighs about 105,000 pounds, while a typical subway or heavy-rail car weighs 83,000 pounds. The rails they ride on weigh the same as or more than subway rails. So in what sense is light rail light?

Light Rail Means Low-Capacity Transit

The answer can be found in an out-of-print *Glossary of Transit Terminology* published in 1994 by what was then called the American Public Transit Association. The glossary defines *rail, light* as "an electric railway with a 'light volume' traffic capacity compared to heavy rail" and notes it "may use shared or exclusive rights-of-way." The glossary also defines *rail, heavy* as "an electric railway with the capacity for a 'heavy volume' of traffic and characterized by exclusive rights-of-way."[3]

In short, the "light" in light rail stands for "low capacity": light rail is, by definition, *low-capacity rail transit*. That is the big lie of light rail, because most transit agencies that want to build it repeatedly refer to it as "high-capacity transit."

A single light-rail car typically has about 70 seats and room for another 70 to 80 people standing, depending on how willing the passengers are to have their personal space invaded by strangers. Moreover, light-rail cars can be strung together in trains of two, three, or sometimes even four cars. Because light-rail lines usually operate on streets at least part of the time, the length of a train is limited by the length of city blocks: a train cannot be longer than a block or it would obstruct traffic every time it stopped. Portland, whose downtown blocks are unusually small, must limit its light-rail trains to two cars, while Salt Lake City, known for its large city blocks, runs four-car trains. Denver and Seattle also run four-car trains, but in most cities, the limit is three cars.

Even a two-car train can hold 300 passengers, far more than a bus. For safety reasons, however, light-rail lines cannot support more than one train every few minutes. A segment of line on Portland's Steel Bridge across the Willamette River allows 30 trains per hour, but the trains don't stop on the bridge. In general, light-rail stops can support just 20 trains per hour. Capacities are further limited when light-rail lines branch out. The line across the Steel Bridge branches into two lines on the west side of the Willamette River and into four lines on the East Side. Because the bridge can support 30 trains an hour, each of the lines on the west side can carry an average of 15 trains per hour, while on the east side each line can average just 7½ trains per hour.

At 20 trains per hour, Portland's two-car trains can move at most about 6,000 people per hour, while the east side branches can each move an average of only 2,250 people per hour. In cities whose blocks are long enough to support three-car trains, light rail can move 9,000 people per hour. Four-car trains in Denver, Salt Lake City, and Seattle can move 12,000 people per hour, though of course that number declines when the lines split into branches.

These capacities are much lower than heavy-rail lines, whose train lengths are limited only by the length of platforms. Washington, D.C.'s platforms allow for eight-car trains; platforms for some New York City subway lines allow for 11-car trains. Each car can hold about the same number of people as a light-rail car, so a train can hold about 1,200 people in Washington and 1,650 in New York City. Moreover, because they don't have to contend with traffic or wait for stop lights to turn green, the trains can operate more frequently: Washington, D.C., subways can support 28 trains per hour, while the busiest New York City subway lines can support 30 trains per hour.[4] That means the highest-capacity New York City lines can move nearly 50,000 people per hour, though D.C., subways can move only 33,600 people per hour; lines in most other cities have even lower capacities.

TRUE HIGH-CAPACITY TRANSIT: THE BUS

Light-rail capacities are not only lower than those of heavy-rail lines, they are lower than buses. While each bus can hold only a fraction of the number of people on a light-rail train, highways and streets can move far more

ROMANCE OF THE RAILS

buses per hour than light-rail trains. In the 1970s, for example, Portland built a bus mall by dedicating one lane, plus the parking strip, of two parallel downtown streets to buses. For the entire length of those two streets, every block had two bus stops, one at each end. Every bus stopped at every other block, meaning there were stops for four different sets of buses. Buses required less than 90 seconds to stop, discharge and board passengers, and begin moving again, allowing each bus stop to serve 42 buses per hour, or 168 buses per hour for the four stops on every two blocks.

Standard 40-foot transit buses have about 40 seats and room for 25 people to stand. At 168 buses per hour, buses could move nearly 11,000 people per hour in each direction, far more than Portland's two-car light-rail trains. Sixty-foot articulated buses have about 60 seats and room for about 30 people standing. Using these buses, the streets could move more than 15,000 people per hour, more than four-car light-rail trains.

Capacities could be increased further by requiring passengers to pay before they board the bus, as is required for light-rail passengers. This would save time during the boarding process and at least double the number of buses each stop could serve per hour. Articulated buses could thus move more than 30,000 people per hour. A further increase is possible by reducing the number of seats on the buses, as seated passengers take up more room than standing passengers. Note that more than half the people on a full light-rail car must stand while only a third of the people on a full articulated bus stand. Replacing just ten seats with standing room would boost each bus's capacity to more than 100, thus increasing the capacity of the bus mall to close to 40,000 people per hour.

All that capacity is on just ordinary downtown streets that dedicate one lane and a parking strip to bus use. Even greater capacities can be achieved on a dedicated busway parallel to or part of a major highway. Istanbul has a 31-mile busway with stations about every two-thirds of a mile. Buses use these lanes 24 hours a day, with an average of one bus every 28 seconds. During the busiest times of the day, the busway supports one bus every 14 seconds, or 257 buses per hour, and has room for more. The articulated buses used on the route have only 42 seats, allowing standing room for 108 people. The busway can thus move at least 38,500 people per hour in one direction, more than three times as many as any American light-rail line. In actual practice, the entire busway moves about 800,000 people a day, more than four times as many as any light-rail system in the United States.

Istanbul's busway cost less than $12 million per route mile. Costs would probably be greater in the United States, but still far less than for light rail. The Istanbul busway uses about the same amount of land as a light-rail line, so the real estate costs would be the same for each.

Bogotá, Columbia, has 70 miles of busways that, unlike most others, include passing lanes. While this means it requires roughly twice as much land as an ordinary busway or light-rail line, the passing lanes greatly increase the system's capacity and allow for both local and express bus service. The system can move well over 300 buses per hour in each direction, each bus holding up to 270 people, giving it a capacity far greater than any New York City subway line.

Outside of New York City, few if any transit corridors in America can generate enough riders to require a dedicated busway. In fact, most light-rail lines see no more than eight trains per hour, meaning transit planners don't expect even light-rail corridors to attract more than 5,000 people per hour. Buses could move this many people per hour without dedicated busways or even bus lanes on city streets. Unlike trains, buses are *scalable*, meaning that whatever the demand is in a particular corridor, buses can move that many people per hour at roughly the same cost per rider and a far lower cost than light rail.

In short, there is no sweet spot between buses and rapid transit in which light rail makes sense. Buses can handle the loads in low-, medium-, and high-use corridors. Existing subways may still be appropriate for New York City and a few other places that lack the surface space to build busways, but in most American urban areas, buses can adequately substitute for any kind of rail transit. Light rail makes no sense at any level of use or demand. Despite this, many transit agencies insist on building light rail, often claiming it is due to rail's higher capacity.

For example, Los Angeles Metro turned an 18-mile corridor that had once been used by the Pacific Electric interurban system into an exclusive busway called the Orange Line. Opened in 2005 at a cost of about $18 million per mile ($22 million in today's dollars), Metro operates a maximum of 15 buses per hour in each direction.[5] Using Istanbul's standard of one bus every fourteen seconds, that means the busway is used to about 4 percent of its capacity.

Metro built the busway because local residents and so-called "anti-rail zealots" had persuaded the legislature to pass a law in 1991 forbidding the construction of a rail line in the corridor.[6] When that law was repealed in 2014, Metro immediately began planning to replace the busway with a light-rail line. The sole reason given for doing so was to expand the capacity of transit serving the route, even though it would in fact reduce that capacity.[7] Los Angeles' most recently completed light-rail line, phase 2 of the Expo Line, was also built on a former rail right of way and cost $242 million per mile.[8] Reducing the capacity of the Orange Line by converting it to light rail might not cost $242 million per mile, but it would not be worth the cost even if it cost nothing at all.

Buses Cost Less to Operate

Light-rail operating costs per passenger mile do tend to be lower than for buses, but the difference is not large enough to justify the huge amounts of money spent on light-rail construction. In 2016, the average light-rail system spent $0.81 per passenger mile on operations and maintenance, while the average transit bus cost $1.12 per passenger mile. However, this savings is largely an illusion for several reasons. First, the operating costs don't count maintenance. Since most transit systems have failed to adequately fund maintenance, we don't know how much it should really cost, but we do know it is far more for rail than for buses because buses require maintenance only of the vehicles, while rails require maintenance of vehicles, tracks, signals, power facilities, and stations.

Second, cities tend to build rail lines in their busiest corridors, and since operating costs per passenger mile depend heavily on ridership, costs per passenger mile are going to be lower in those corridors no matter what the mode of transportation. In 2016, light-rail cars carried an average of 23 passengers over the course of a day (that is, passenger miles divided by vehicle miles was 23), while the average bus carried just 9.6 passengers. Buses on routes carrying an average of 23 passengers would have far lower operating costs per passenger mile than rail. While transit buses average less than 10 passengers nationwide, many individual routes and some transit systems carry far more. Indeed, Los Angeles Metro's bus system carries an average of nearly 18 passengers per vehicle, and it spends just $0.82 per passenger mile on operations.

Third, light rail doesn't operate in a vacuum, and instead must be supported by an extensive feeder bus network. In many cases, transit agencies replace bus routes that directly link suburbs to downtowns with feeder buses to the light-rail line. Yet instead of taking the feeder buses, many people who once took a direct bus will drive to light-rail park-and-ride stations. This leaves feeder buses with low ridership and thus high operating costs per passenger mile. This high cost is averaged into the cost of buses, but in fact could arguably be charged against light rail.

Trains Don't Boost Transit Ridership

The argument that many people who won't ride buses will be attracted to railcars would be more persuasive if per capita ridership hadn't declined in so many cities after they built light rail. A few regions, such as Salt Lake City, did see significant ridership gains after their first light-rail lines opened. But too many others, including Baltimore, Buffalo, Dallas, Houston, Los Angeles, Norfolk, St. Louis, and Sacramento, saw significant declines in both per capita ridership and transit's share of commuting. As Table 13.1 shows, both trips per capita and transit's share of commuting declined in 10 of the 17 urban areas that have built light rail since 1980; both gained in just three urban areas, and the results for the other four were mixed.

Many of these urban areas have spent extraordinary amounts of money, only to see transit decline. In fact, the decline is often because the region is spending so much money on light rail. Buses in the Los Angeles urban area, for example, carried 584 million transit riders in 1985. Then the region started building rail transit, and cost overruns forced the transit agency to raise bus fares and reduce bus service. Despite (or because of) the opening of two rail transit lines, transit ridership had plummeted to 484 million trips by 1995.

Table 13.1

Change in Trips Per Capita and Transit's Share of Commuting
After Light Rail

	Trips Per Capita	Transit's Share
Baltimore	−35.0%	−33.1%
Buffalo	−23.3%	−73.1%
Charlotte	−13.4%	30.0%
Dallas–Ft Worth	−28.0%	−32.2%
Denver	−0.5%	−3.6%
Houston	−48.4%	−31.6%
Los Angeles	−15.9%	−3.8%
Minneapolis–St. Paul	4.9%	9.6%
Norfolk	−3.7%	−5.7%
Phoenix	−10.9%	−24.3%
Portland	11.9%	−13.4%
Salt Lake City	38.2%	20.4%
San Diego	47.6%	13.0%
San Jose	−9.3%	44.3%
St. Louis	−25.5%	−51.5%
Seattle	−14.5%	17.3%
Sacramento	−13.1%	−32.4%

Sources: Trips per capita are from the *National Transit Database*, with "before" based on a year prior to the opening of the region's first light-rail line and "after" based on 2015. Trips per capita exclude paratransit, which is not really competitive with bus or rail. Transit's shares of commuting are from census data, with "before" based on the decennial census, or, if rail opened after 2005, the American Community Survey prior to opening and "after" based on the 2015 American Community Survey. Although Baltimore's first light-rail line opened in 1992, the region's "before" data are based on years prior to 1984, the year the city's heavy-rail line opened.

The situation was so bad that the National Association for the Advancement of Colored People sued the Los Angeles County transit agency for sacrificing bus service to minority neighborhoods in order to build rail lines to middle-class neighborhoods. This suit resulted in a court order requiring the transit agency to restore bus service for 10 years.

Thanks to this order, ridership was restored to 584 million rides by 2000, and continued to grow to 711 million rides by 2007. After the court order expired, however, the transit agency once again cut bus service and built more expensive rail lines. This cost the system nearly five bus riders for every new light-rail rider, so that by 2016, the region's total transit ridership had fallen to 562 million trips.

Some transit planners can be incredibly smug and callous about their plans to get middle-class people out of their cars at the expense of lower-income riders who may truly need transit. In Minneapolis-St. Paul, the Metropolitan Council—which is both the area's regional planning authority and its transit agency—announced it planned to build a light-rail line to Eden Prairie, one of the wealthiest suburbs in the region, at a cost of $1.5 billion (the projected cost has since grown to $2 billion). To insure "regional transit equity," it planned to also improve transit service to low-income black neighborhoods—by spending $4 million building 75 bus shelters.[9] White, middle-class people get expensive trains; poor blacks get bus shelters.

Many urban areas that have built light-rail lines are entirely unsuited for any form of rail transit. Since the mid-1990s, for example, Dallas has spent well over $6 billion building the nation's longest light-rail system, with more than 100 route-miles, plus another billion dollars on a commuter-rail line between Dallas and Ft. Worth. In 1991, the region's bus systems were carrying 18.9 trips per capita; by 2015, buses, light rail, and commuter-rail combined carried just 13.6 trips per capita, and transit's share of commuting had fallen from 2.7 percent in 1990 to 1.9 percent in 2015.

No urban area where transit carries fewer than 20 trips per capita needs any kind of rail transit. Nothing about Dallas-Ft. Worth matches the characteristics of the urban areas with the nation's most heavily used rail transit systems. Transit in New York, Boston, San Francisco, and Washington, D.C., carried more than 100 trips per capita in 1991, and Chicago and Philadelphia transit carried more than 80 trips per capita. The central cities in all of these regions had 1990 population densities greater than 10,000 people per square mile, with the exception of Washington, which was 9,880. Dallas in 1990 had fewer than 3,000 people per square mile. All of the big rail cities had downtowns with more than 200,000 jobs; downtown Dallas had less than 80,000 jobs.[10]

Having experienced more than 90 percent of its growth in the automobile era after 1950, Dallas–Ft. Worth lacks the job or population density necessary to make rail work. Along with Houston, Phoenix, San Jose, and other postwar urban areas, Dallas–Ft. Worth was totally unsuited for rail transit.

Baltimore, on the other hand, would appear to be more suited for rail transit. The city of Baltimore had more than three times the population density of the city of Dallas in 1990, and downtown Baltimore had nearly 100,000 jobs. In 1982, two years before opening its first rail line, Baltimore transit carried 69 trips per capita, and transit carried 12.3 percent of commuters to work in 1980. Yet by 2015, after having spent at least $4 billion on 44 miles of light- and heavy-rail transit, trips per capita had fallen to 45, and transit's share of commuters had fallen to 8.2 percent.

Paint Is Cheap, Trains Are Expensive

At the same time FTA Administrator Peter Rogoff noted the unsustainability of building new transit lines when agencies couldn't afford to maintain the ones they had, he also observed that many if not most of those rail expansion plans were unnecessary. "Paint is cheap; rail systems are extremely expensive," he pointed out. "You can entice even diehard rail riders onto a bus, if you call it a 'special' bus and just paint it a different color than the rest of the fleet," he continued. With a simple bus rapid-transit program, "you can move a lot of people at very little cost compared to rail." While admitting "there are some corridors with the kind of densities and destinations where only rail makes sense," he pointed out that "bus rapid transit is a fine fit for a lot more communities than are seriously considering it."[11]

Rogoff said officials "need to have the courage to say 'no'" to bad transit proposals. Unfortunately, for the most part, he also lacked the courage (or at least the legal authority) to say no, and during his term of office, he signed agreements for the federal government to help fund dozens of projects collectively costing tens of billions of dollars, most of which were doing things that could have been accomplished with buses for far less money.

As will be discussed more in Chapter 15, Congress had given the Department of Transportation the authority to reject projects that were not cost effective, and the George W. Bush administration decided that any project costing more than $25 per hour of traveler time saved was not cost effective. If the analyses were done correctly, counting the time of both transit riders and auto users, almost all light-rail projects would be rejected because the congestion they create actually wastes more time for auto users than the rail line saves for transit riders. When calculating cost effectiveness, however, most transit agencies counted only the time saved for transit riders, not the time lost for automobile drivers, and Rogoff's agency looked the other way. Eventually, the Obama administration simply replaced the Bush rules with a new rule effectively eliminating the use of "cost effectiveness" as a funding criterion. Although Rogoff clearly said in 2010 that many rail projects were not cost effective compared with buses, it isn't clear what role he played in the decision to eliminate the Bush rules.

In 2016, Rogoff exited the Obama administration to take a job—at a 65 percent increase in salary—with the Central Puget Sound Regional Transit Authority to oversee the expenditure of billions of dollars on new light-rail lines.[12] Perhaps he persuaded himself the Seattle light-rail corridors were among the exceptions "where only rail makes sense." If so, he was wrong.

Like Baltimore, Seattle might appear to be a bit more suitable for rail than Dallas-Ft. Worth or other Sunbelt cities. Its population density in 2000 was more than 6,700 people per square mile, and it had more than 150,000 downtown jobs. Before Rogoff took over, the region had already spent more than $4.7 billion on a phenomenally expensive 20 miles of light rail as well as $2 billion on a commuter-rail line. Yet per capita ridership fell from 55 trips per year in 2008, the year before the first segment of the light-rail line opened, to 47 trips in 2015. While transit's share of commuting grew, three out of four of the new transit commuters after 2008 rode the bus, not some form of rail transit.

Light-rail advocates invariably argue that rail transit is needed to deal with increasing traffic congestion. But programs that reduce per capita transit ridership are not going to reduce congestion. In fact, because light rail often operates in or crosses city streets, it actually increases congestion because delays caused by light-rail cars outweigh the benefit of taking automobiles off the road.

Transportation planners almost always give light-rail cars priority at traffic signals, which disrupts the signals for everyone else. Downtown Portland, for example, once had traffic signals coordinated so that car drivers and fast cyclists could make it from one end of downtown to the other without missing a single green signal. Light rail changed that, so now other vehicles almost always have to stop when reaching those streets with rail lines.

Signal priority can disrupt not only the streets crossed by light rail but also the streets parallel to them. Minneapolis' Hiawatha light rail parallels Hiawatha Avenue, a major route between Minneapolis and Bloomington. When the trains take priority at signals for streets that cross both the rail line and Hiawatha, the signals on Hiawatha change patterns in response to the signals on the cross streets. The result was that peak-hour travel times on parts of Hiawatha more than doubled.[13]

Transportation planners are often honest about their projections of the effect of light rail on traffic, although their findings tend to be buried in technical reports. The environmental impact statement for the Purple light-rail line in suburban Washington, D.C., for example, said the purpose of the line was to "address" the "increasing congestion on the roadway system."[14] As planned, it "addressed" congestion by making it worse. A technical report published as a supplement to the environmental impact statement found that average driving speeds in the region would be reduced by 0.4 percent if it was built.[15] That adds up to more than 10 million hours of time wasted in traffic per year. Since almost no one bothered to read the report, almost no one knew the supposed solution to congestion would actually make it worse.

THE NEXT FAD: HIGH-COST, LOW-CAPACITY TRANSIT

To make matters worse, some cities are proposing or building rail lines that are heavy rail in the sense of being completely separated from auto and pedestrian traffic but light rail in the sense of having lower capacities than true heavy rail. One of the reasons Seattle's light-rail lines have cost more than $230 million a mile is they are almost completely grade separated, either elevated or underground. Yet their platforms are only long enough for four-car trains, meaning they can move only about 12,000 people per hour.

Honolulu is building a 20-mile rail line that is entirely elevated. Although it is called heavy rail, the platforms at each station are only long enough for four-car trains. The cars that will be used on this line are shorter than a light-rail car, but each car will only have about 32 seats, allowing room for as many as 125 standees, so each car can carry about the same number of total riders as a light-rail car. Originally projected to cost under $3 billion, the line is currently projected to cost $8 billion, or $400 million per mile, although the Federal Transit Administration says it may end up costing as much as $540 million per mile.[16]

In choosing to combine grade separation with short train platforms, Honolulu has effectively picked the worst aspects of both technologies: the high cost of heavy rail and the low capacity of light rail. One of the political advantages of a low-capacity system is that politicians can claim rush-hour crowding is proof of the system's success when all it really proves is that they chose the wrong technology.

Buses can not only move more people than light rail, they can do it faster. According to the American Public Transportation Association, the average speed of commuter buses is 31 miles per hour while the average speed of light rail is under 16 miles per hour (Figure 13.1).[17]

Figure 13.1
Average Speed in Miles Per Hour

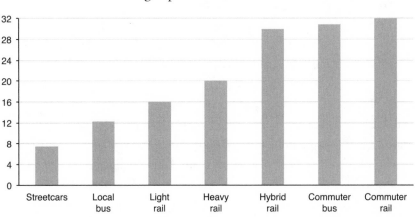

Source: *Public Transit Fact Book 2016,* American Public Transportation Association, tables 29 and 36.

By comparison, average automobile speeds are 30 miles per hour in most cities, and more than 40 miles per hour in cities that have done the most to relieve congestion.[18]

Buses are also safer than rail: Between 2005 and 2014, light-rail accidents killed 12.6 people for every billion passenger miles, while bus accidents killed just 3.2 people.[19] Automobile fatalities in urban areas, by comparison, averaged about 4.3 people per billion passenger miles in 2015.

In short, buses can move more people faster and more safely than light rail at a far lower cost. The only thing light rail can do better than buses is transfer large amounts of money from taxpayers to rail contractors and railcar manufacturers. As noted in Chapter 10, such transfers have grown rapidly since Congressional passage of ISTEA in 1991 gave cities incentives to build expensive rail lines.

In Portland, Oregon, the connection between politicians, rail contractors, and developers is known as the *light-rail mafia*. For years, this mafia's godfather was Neil Goldschmidt, the Portland mayor who made the decision to build the city's first light-rail line, for which he was rewarded by being named Secretary of Transportation. After he left that office, he returned to Oregon, where he was elected governor. Although Oregon's constitution allows two terms as governor, and he had no serious challenger to his re-election, he decided not to run for a second term. He instead started a consulting firm helping transportation builders and developers get contracts and subsidies.

One of his first deals was to give the Bechtel Corporation a no-bid contract to build a light-rail line to the Portland airport. He arranged to have his friend, Tom Walsh, co-owner of Walsh Construction, made general manager of Portland's transit agency, where Walsh could funnel subsidies to developments along the light-rail lines to his family-owned company. Goldschmidt arranged for developers such as Homer Williams to get hundreds of millions of dollars in subsidies for urban-renewal districts that Portland had strategically placed along the light-rail lines. As a member of the board of Oregon Health Sciences University, Goldschmidt persuaded the city to help subsidize an aerial tramway from the university's hospital to an urban-renewal district that had been located on property owned by Goldschmidt's clients that would be redeveloped by Homer Williams.[20]

The public wasn't aware of any of these backroom deals until 2004, when a local reporter uncovered evidence that Goldschmidt once had a long-term sexual relationship with a teenage girl when he was mayor of Portland. The relationship began when she was 13, at which time it would have been considered statutory rape (that by 2004 was past the statute of limitations), and continued until she was 27. The girl had been a straight-A student before the relationship, but ended up dropping out of high school, becoming an alcoholic, and dying at the age of 42.[21] Her request for financial assistance when Goldschmidt was governor was what caused him to not run for re-election.

It was only after this scandal was revealed that local media openly wrote about the light-rail mafia and all the corrupt connections between Goldschmidt, the transit industry, and other politicians and developers.[22] Goldschmidt immediately lost all credibility, of course, but the light-rail mafia survives.

Light rail was supposed to be an efficient way to move moderately large numbers of people around midsized urban areas. But rapidly growing costs have eliminated the efficiencies, and the fact that most urban areas don't need transit systems capable of moving large numbers of people at one time has made such technologies unnecessary. Even in corridors where there is a large demand for transit, the fact that buses can actually move more people at a far lower cost has made light rail completely obsolete.

14. STREETCARS AND THE ECONOMIC DEVELOPMENT HOAX

Streetcars that replace bus lines are not a mobility or access improvement.
If you replace a bus with a streetcar on the same route, and
make no other improvements, nobody will be able to get anywhere any
faster than they could before. Likewise, if you build a streetcar instead
of a good bus line, that money you spend above the cost of the bus line
is not helping anyone get anywhere any faster.

—Jarrett Walker, *Human Transit*[1]

Suppose you are in the market for the latest ultra-high-definition television, and someone offers to sell you a zoopraxiscope, a device for showing moving pictures invented in 1879. Or suppose you are in the market for a laptop computer with word processing software and someone offers to sell you a Remington manual typewriter made in 1895. Not only do the items they offer to sell you work no better today than they did when they were first developed, they cost a lot more than they did then, as well as more than any of the modern alternatives. It seems unlikely that anyone would buy those outdated products, but people who aren't spending their own money are often motivated more by fads than by reality.

This is the situation with streetcars today. Because of their high maintenance costs and inflexibility of operation, there are no good arguments for installing streetcar lines even if their capital costs were no greater than

those for buses, much less at the exorbitant amounts many cities are paying for them. This leads even transit supporters such as Jarrett Walker to
question their usefulness.

Table 14.1 reveals that streetcars in most cities cost far more to operate, earn lower fares, and carry fewer riders than buses. The high costs and
low ridership demonstrate that streetcars are truly an obsolete technology.

The 1994 transit glossary that defined light rail as having a "light
volume traffic capacity" also stated that light rail was "also known as
'streetcar,' 'trolley car' and 'tramway.'" Since then, light rail and streetcars
have come to be distinguished from one another in two major ways. First,
light-rail lines use their own exclusive rights of way for many parts of
their routes, while streetcars are almost always on streets sharing lanes with
other vehicles. Second, light-rail cars can be coupled together to form
trains of two, three, or four cars, while streetcars nearly always operate with
one car and usually have no couplers.

When Frank Sprague perfected the electric streetcar 130 years ago,
other people were developing the first automobiles. Early examples of
both streetcars and automobiles had top speeds of about 15 miles per hour
and average speeds of about 8 miles per hour. Today, automobiles can easily
(and in some states legally) travel at 80 miles per hour, and in some cities,
the average speed of driving is more than 40 miles per hour.[2] Yet the average speed of streetcars is still around 8 miles per hour.[3]

SUPER-LOW-CAPACITY TRANSIT

As in the case of light rail, streetcar advocates have the effrontery to call
streetcars "high-capacity transit." In fact, most of the modern 66-foot
streetcars in service today have only about 30 seats, while a 40-foot bus
has about 40 seats. Like light rail, streetcar lines are limited to about
20 railcars per hour. Counting standing room for about 70 people, that
means a streetcar line can move about 2,000 people per hour, compared
with well over 10,000 people on buses. If anything, streetcars should be
called "super-low-capacity transit."

Streetcars were originally billed as a low-cost alternative to light rail.
Yet most of the cities planning or building streetcar lines today are spending

Table 14.1

2016 Data for Streetcars and Buses in the Same Cities

City	Type	Occupancy	Fare/Trip	Weekday Trips	Op Cost/ VRM	Bus Occupancy	Bus Fare/Trip	Bus Op Cost/VRM
Atlanta	Modern	9.1	0.27	1,956	67.45	10.3	0.99	9.29
Charlotte	Modern	8.2	0	1,755	30.08	8.3	0.95	7.65
Cincinnati	Modern	17.3	0.88	2,206	71.40	9.1	0.99	8.11
Dallas	Modern	2.0	0	155	20.84	5.3	0.87	8.86
Dallas-McKinney	Modern	16.2	0	1,366	20.85	5.3	0.87	8.86
Kenosha	Vintage	3.3	0.49	124	17.34	5.2	0.51	6.76
Little Rock	Vintage	2.1	1.20	153	19.31	5.7	0.72	5.54
New Orleans	Legacy	13.0	0.88	21,641	26.42	7.7	1.02	11.74
Philadelphia	Legacy	18.9	2.70	82,816	21.45	14.8	0.96	15.79
Portland	Modern	12.2	0.20	13,328	40.43	13.4	1.11	12.14
San Francisco	Legacy	21.2	0.78	19,825	28.32	17.1	0.78	23.07
Seattle	Modern	8.1	0.92	4,752	46.93	14.8	1.38	14.43
Tacoma	Modern	10.4	0	3,168	58.06	7.7	1.00	14.06
Tampa	Vintage	7.6	1.98	645	24.10	9.1	0.99	8.11
Tucson	Modern	7.5	0.91	2,913	20.32	8.7	1.84	8.90
Washington, D.C.	Modern	8.0	0	2,582	183.16	10.1	1.10	15.00

Source: 2016 *National Transit Database.*

Notes: Op Cost/VRM is operating cost per vehicle revenue mile. Almost all streetcar ridership and revenues come from three legacy systems existing before 1970. Philadelphia is included here because the FTA classifies its system as streetcars, but in fact it is closer to light rail: cars can be coupled together, and part of its route is on an exclusive right of way.

$50 million to $100 million per route mile. After adjusting for inflation, that's more than the cost of most light-rail lines built before 1995. Light rail has grown even more expensive since then, but foolishly spending $50 million on a super-low-capacity streetcar line makes no more sense than foolishly spending $160 million on a low-capacity light-rail line.

Spending money on streetcars is the result of mission creep within transit agencies. Originally created to transport people who lack automobiles or prefer not to drive, that mission has faded, as nearly everyone today has access to a car. Transit agencies focused next on trying to get people out of what they believed were evil automobiles and onto virtuous transit, but that hasn't worked out very well either. Transit advocates have completely given up their argument that streetcars produce any real transportation benefits. Their high cost is worth it, their advocates now say, because they stimulate economic development.[4]

This is what turned streetcars from merely a foolish idea into a hoax, as there is absolutely no evidence a streetcar line alone will stimulate economic development, and no reason to think a transit line carrying a couple of thousand riders per day, most of whom would be taking some other form of transit if the streetcar weren't there, would lead developers to spend billions on new construction. Yet this argument, along with federal matching funds, has persuaded numerous cities to spend their residents' money on streetcar construction.

The Portland Streetcar Myth

The streetcar hoax, like so many other transit fads, came out of Portland, Oregon, which opened its first streetcar line in 2001. At the time, several cities, including Fort Collins, Kenosha, Memphis, and Tampa had installed vintage streetcar lines using either restored or replica streetcars from the early 20th century. These lines were aimed at attracting tourists and not intended or expected to be heavily used by local residents or to promote local development. But Portland's new streetcar line used streamlined cars with a much more modern appearance and was specifically designed to shunt commuters from dense residential areas just outside of downtown to the city's central business district.

When they were planning the streetcar line, Portland officials already knew light rail would not stimulate economic development. When the region's first light-rail line opened in 1986, the city had zoned all of the land near light-rail stations for high-density, mixed-use development. Such transit-oriented developments would supposedly allow people to give up their cars because they could do their basic shopping in the same development in which they lived and hop on a light-rail train to reach their jobs and other important destinations.

Over the next few years, Portland officials often claimed that light rail had stimulated new development. The public relations department of Portland's transit agency, TriMet, kept a list of all new construction or remodeling that took place near the light-rail line and claimed it was because of the light rail.[5] Because the line went to downtown Portland, this meant almost any new building downtown was supposedly stimulated by the rail line.

The majority of buildings on TriMet's list were government buildings. The ghost of the monocentric city raised its head when then president Bill Clinton and Oregon governor Barbara Roberts each signed executive orders directing all federal and state offices that weren't downtown to relocate to downtown areas.[6] It makes sense for a state attorney's office or a federal reserve bank to locate downtown near courts and commercial banks. But why should a state highway bureau, for example, which maintains roads outside of the city, or the federal Bureau of Land Management, nearly all of whose lands are in rural areas, have to locate their offices downtown? Clinton's and Roberts' executive orders were a boon for downtown property owners, but offices built in response to them had nothing to do with the alleged benefits of light rail.

TriMet took credit for all of the new construction that resulted from these office relocations without mentioning the vacant office space that the agencies left behind. TriMet also took credit when Paul Allen, owner of the Portland Trailblazers basketball team, decided to build a new, larger basketball arena next to the old one, which happened to be near a light-rail line. While it is remotely possible that the rail line influenced the location of the new arena, Allen built it primarily so he could sell more tickets, not because of the light rail.

TriMet based its policies on the *Field of Dreams* slogan: "If you build it, they will come."[7] Yet the reality is that Portland was not getting the economic development it wanted from light rail. In 1996, 10 years after the rail line began operating, Portland city planner Mike Saba sadly testified before the Portland city commission that "We have not seen any of the kind of development of a mid-rise, higher-density, mixed-use, mixed-income type that we would have liked to have seen" along the light-rail line.[8] Several developers testified there was little market for such developments because Portland at the time had plenty of multifamily housing, while it was single-family housing that was in short supply.[9]

"We are in the hottest real estate market in the country," Portland transportation commissioner Charles Hales pointed out, yet city planning maps revealed that "most of those sites [along the light-rail line] are still vacant."[10] Saba, Hales, and the developers all agreed that if the city wanted transit-oriented developments near light-rail stations, it would have to subsidize them. The city commission agreed to use a variety of subsidies, including property tax abatements for residential units, tax-increment financing for other kinds of developments, and grants from the Federal Transit Administration, Department of Housing and Urban Development, and other agencies.

When Hales persuaded the city commission to build a streetcar line a few years later, the city had no intention of simply laying a few rails. Instead, the line was a part of several major urban renewal projects that collectively cost taxpayers hundreds of millions of dollars.

North of downtown Portland was an abandoned rail yard. As of March 31, 2017, the city had borrowed $378 million to tear out the rails, lay down new streets, and provide infrastructure such as water and sewer lines, parks, and parking garages—all things that developers would normally provide on their own.[11] The city then sold the land to developers, often at below-market prices, on the condition that the developers would build high-density, mixed-use projects, meaning projects combining apartments or condominiums in the same structures as stores, restaurants, and offices. This became known as the Pearl District.

South of downtown was an abandoned industrial area on the Willamette River. For this location, the city borrowed $140 million for infrastructure improvements.[12] It also helped build an aerial tramway from the site to a medical center located in the hills above the former industrial area. This became known as the South Waterfront District.

The city then built the streetcar line from the Pearl District, through downtown, to the South Waterfront District. The line through downtown happened to pass through two other urban renewal areas known as the Downtown Waterfront and South Park Blocks districts, for which the city had borrowed $277 million to support new development.[13]

All the money borrowed for these urban renewal programs was to be repaid through tax-increment financing. Under this system, the taxes paid on any increases in property values—whether due to improvements or just inflation—in the urban renewal districts after they were established are used to subsidize the urban renewal. Usually, cities sell bonds and repay the bonds out of the incremental taxes collected for up to 30 years.

Government officials pretend this is free money because, they say, the developments would not have taken place without the subsidies. Yet studies show that the developments would in fact have been built without the tax-increment financing, though not necessarily in the same locations or at the same densities.[14] In fact, at least one study has found that cities that use tax-increment financing grow slower than those that don't.[15] This is because tax-increment financing imposes an extra burden on everyone else in the city, either in the form of higher taxes or a reduced level of urban services, to pay for the schools, fire, police, and other urban services used by the new developments but not funded out of their taxes because those taxes are subsidizing the developments instead.

California invented tax-increment financing in 1952, but it became such a huge burden on the state that the legislature repealed the law in 2010, effectively killing more than 400 urban-renewal agencies.[16] However, every other state except Arizona followed California's 1952 example by allowing cities to use tax-increment financing. None seem to be following California's 2010 example by repealing the authority, and the funding tool is increasingly used to subsidize transit-oriented developments and, in some cases, even the construction of streetcar and light-rail lines.[17]

Tax-increment financing wasn't the only source of subsidies to developments along Portland's streetcar line. Among other things, the city waived at least $12,000 in fees per dwelling unit for thousands of apartments and condominiums built in these urban renewal areas; gave 10 years' worth of property tax exemptions to at least some of those apartments and condominiums; and offered a variety of federal transit and affordable housing grants to developers. In all, subsidies to development in the urban renewal districts traversed by the streetcar totaled around $1 billion.

What happened after the streetcar opened was a classic study in modern political corruption. First, the city published a report adding up the value of all the developments built in the urban-renewal areas—including not only private developments but also buildings constructed by Portland State University, parking garages built by the city with tax-increment finance money, and other government buildings—and credited all of that development to the streetcar. The report never mentioned urban renewal, tax-increment financing, or other subsidies.

One segment of the streetcar line, however, was outside of any of the urban-renewal districts, and the report could find only a few tiny developments in this area, most of which would have happened without the streetcar.[18]

The report claimed the streetcar had other positive effects on development. "Prior to 1997, new projects were built to less than half of the allowable density allowed on a site in the CBD," said the report. "Since the streetcar alignment was chosen in 1997, new development achieved an average of 90% of the" maximum allowable density.[19] But that's not a surprise, because Portland revised its zoning ordinance in 1998 to require that all new development be at least 80 percent of the maximum allowable density. That law would have had the same effect with or without the streetcar lines.

While the report was titled *Development-Oriented Transit*, it didn't specifically claim that all of the developments were due solely to the streetcar. That didn't stop others, however, from saying so. "The $55 million streetcar line has sparked more than $1.5 billion (and growing) in new development," claimed Charles Hales, without mentioning the hundreds of millions of dollars' worth of other subsidies, all of which he voted for.[20]

Proselytizing for Streetcars

Hales resigned his position as city commissioner in the middle of his term to take a job, at much higher pay, with HDR, an engineering consulting firm that wanted to persuade cities to hire it to design streetcar lines for them. Hales would bring city officials and journalists from all parts of the country to Portland and give them a tour of the streetcar route and all of the new developments along it. Hales himself didn't live in one of those developments; instead, to minimize his taxes under his new, higher salary, he moved to the north side of the Columbia River because Washington has no state income tax.

Hales claimed other cities that built streetcars had experiences similar to Portland's. Tampa's streetcar, he asserted, "stimulated over $600 million in public projects and a correspondingly robust $700 million in private projects."[21] In fact, it was similar to the Portland streetcar in that the Tampa streetcar, which began operating in late 2002, traverses three tax-increment finance districts: the Channel District, Downtown, and Ybor City.[22] The $600 million in public projects represents subsidized construction designed to attract private development. Although Tampa has continued to subsidize the districts, a 2015 report stated that the portions of the Channel District served by the streetcar remain "a largely underdeveloped waterfront district."[23]

It isn't credible to think the Tampa streetcar, one of the worst-patronized streetcar lines in the country, could have attracted economic development by itself. Its ridership peaked in 2005, when it carried about 1,000 people a day during weekdays, under 5,000 on Saturdays, and fewer than 1,200 on Sundays.[24] These numbers steadily declined: In 2016, it carried fewer than 650 riders a day on weekdays, 680 on Sundays, and under 1,650 on Saturdays.[25] These numbers aren't nearly high enough to persuade hotels, restaurants, shops, or other attractions to locate along the streetcar line.

Despite the reality that development along the Portland and Tampa streetcar lines received hundreds of millions of dollars in subsidies, HDR prepared reports for several different cities claiming streetcars alone would generate hundreds of millions of dollars in economic development

Table 14.2
Projected Benefits and Costs of New Streetcar Lines (Millions of Dollars)

City	Total Benefits	Econ. Dev. Benefits	Other Benefits	Total Costs
Atlanta	167.8	159.3	8.5	65.5
Cincinnati	240.0	211.3	28.7	169.0
Kansas City	316.7	251.4	65.3	157.0
Salt Lake City	89.1	63.6	25.5	62.2
Tucson	414.3	293.2	121.1	166.3

Sources: "Atlanta Streetcar TIGER II Funding Application Project Narrative," City of Atlanta, 2010, p. 12; "Cincinnati Streetcar TIGER II Application," State of Ohio, 2010, pp. 14–15; "Kansas City Downtown Streetcar TIGER IV Grant Application," City of Kansas City, 2012, p. 21; "Sugar House Streetcar TIGER II Discretionary Grant Program: Economic Analysis Supplementary Documentation," HDR, 2010, pp. 20–21; "Tucson Modern Streetcar Project TIGER Application," City of Tucson, 2009, p. 17.
Note: These projections were made by HDR on behalf of the cities applying for federal stimulus funds.

benefits (Table 14.2). Note that the other benefits alone are much less than the costs of the streetcar lines, so without the claimed economic development, the streetcars make no sense.

In most of these cities, the "other" benefits consist of benefits to streetcar riders. In Tucson, however, $108 million was claimed as "short-term employment benefits." This is apparently the income earned by construction workers and the indirect and induced jobs created when construction workers spent their incomes. However, it is inappropriate to count jobs as a benefit in benefit-cost analyses; after all, any spending will create jobs, but that doesn't mean those jobs are worthwhile. The jobs produced by building streetcars are no more worthwhile than jobs produced by digging holes in the middle of busy streets and then filling them up. The fact that HDR did not claim this as a benefit in any other city shows that even most HDR experts do not consider it to be appropriate.

Some transportation improvements do lead to significant economic benefits, but they do so by stimulating new travel that has an economic value to the travelers or shippers. The Interstate Highway System contributed to economic growth because it produced a net increase in personal travel and shipping that would not have taken place without it. New travel means new economic benefits: employers have access to a larger pool of skilled workers; retailers have access to a larger pool of shoppers; and suppliers of goods and services have access to more raw materials and more customers. In contrast, most of the travel carried by urban rail transit lines would have taken place without it; travelers would simply have used other modes of transit. Unlike highways, rail transit carries virtually no freight, so there is absolutely no benefit there.

To generate new travel, improvements must support transportation that is faster, more convenient, and less expensive than existing modes of transport. It helps if the new transportation is also safer. I call this the *SECS formula*: new transport must be speedy, economical, convenient, and safe to generate new travel that stimulates economic development. Rail transit lines in general, and streetcars in particular, are slow, expensive, inconvenient, and not particularly safe. Thus, they are not going to do anything to help build a region's economic wealth.

ECONOMIC DEVELOPMENT SUBSIDIES ARE A ZERO-SUM GAME

Rapid-transit projects such as the Washington, D.C., Metro and San Francisco's BART carry hundreds of thousands of people a day and do influence property values near stations, but this is a zero-sum game. Rapid-transit lines do not cause a region as a whole to build wealth or develop faster; they merely influence where new development takes place. This means they do not generate new tax revenues that justify the construction of the transit lines. In fact, it is likely that the tax burdens imposed on the regions to pay for the rail lines may actually slow regional growth. Streetcars carrying a few hundred or even a few thousand people a day simply are not going to generate enough business for anyone to undertake significant new development: without other subsidies, they don't even influence where development will take place.

In Cincinnati, at least, streetcar supporters were careful to lower expectations after they succeeded in pushing the city to build a highly controversial streetcar line. Before it was built, advocates were incredulous anyone would oppose it because it was "expected to yield $1.5 billion in new investment in inner-city Cincinnati."[26] After it was completed, advocates admitted that "It isn't reasonable to expect a 3.6-mile loop through Downtown and Over-the-Rhine to single-handedly transform our city."[27]

In 2005, local enthusiasm for the streetcar led Oregon Representative Earl Blumenauer to persuade Congress to carve out a portion of the New Starts fund for *small starts*, projects costing less than $300 million. Blumenauer expected this money would be used to expand Portland's streetcar system and help other cities start their own streetcar lines.

Fortunately for taxpayers, but unfortunately for streetcar advocates, the second Bush administration's cost-effectiveness rules prevented any federal dollars from being spent on streetcar lines while Bush was in office. For streetcar proposals, the rules specifically required grant applicants to show that streetcars were more cost effective than buses. The superiority of buses over existing streetcar lines is plainly visible.

The Federal Transit Administration's 2016 database classifies rail lines in 15 different cities as streetcars. One of these, however, is Philadelphia, even though the railcars there can be coupled together, often operate in their own right-of-way, and are locally called light rail. In the other 14, streetcars cost two to three times as much to operate, per vehicle mile, as buses in these same cities. That would be excusable if the streetcars carried two to three times as many people; instead, most carry fewer passenger miles, per vehicle mile, than local buses. To attract as many riders as they do, most cities charge far less to ride streetcars than they do to ride buses. Portland, for example, collected an average of just 20 cents per streetcar ride, compared with $1.11 per bus ride. Streetcars in Dallas and Tacoma are free, and Atlanta's streetcars were free during their first year.[28]

Because streetcars cost more to build and more to operate yet attract fewer riders than buses, they could never be more cost effective than buses. Rep. Blumenauer complained the Bush administration was biased in favor of buses, but Bush's transportation people responded that their bias was toward moving people, not supporting economic development.[29]

When Obama was elected, he persuaded Congress to include billions of dollars for "shovel-ready" transit projects included in the American

Recovery and Reinvestment Act, which included no rules about cost effectiveness. Using stimulus funds, the Obama administration helped subsidize streetcar construction in all the cities shown in Table 14.2.

THE OREGON STREETCAR FLOP

Portland's first streetcars were built in the Czech Republic at a cost of about $1.9 million each at a time when a 40-seat bus cost about $300,000. Since one of the requirements for federal funding was that streetcars be made in America, Rep. Blumenauer persuaded Congress to provide a $4 million seed fund for an American streetcar factory, and lobbied furiously to have the money be awarded to a Portland-area company called Oregon Iron Works.[30]

Oregon Iron Works had never built a streetcar, but it purchased plans from the Czech company that made Portland's railcars. Its prototype car proved unsatisfactory, however, and another $3 million ($2.4 million of which came from the federal government, the rest from Portland) was needed to make the car work.[31] Thus, taxpayers spent $7 million for a $1.9-million car.

Even before that car was ready for operation, Portland agreed to buy six of them for $20 million.[32] After a series of delays, however, the company announced it would be able to deliver only five cars for that price. "You're not getting less," a company official said in the hope her listeners were innumerate: "I actually think you're getting more." Portland did get more: more problems. Quality control on the streetcars was so poor the city ended up paying another company $2 million to oversee construction.[33] Tucson and Washington, D.C., also purchased streetcars from Oregon Iron Works for about $4 million apiece, but other cities soon learned of the poor quality and bought their streetcars from foreign companies that met the buy-America requirement by opening factories in the United States. As a result, Oregon Iron Works stopped production after making just 18 cars.[34]

To provide even more streetcar funding than was available from stimulus funds, Secretary of Transportation Ray LaHood ordered that the Bush-era cost-effectiveness rule be eliminated. In 2009, the Obama administration had simply ignored this rule when it gave Portland $75 million in nonstimulus transportation funds for expanding its streetcar system. After LaHood repealed the rule, Fort Lauderdale, Los Angeles, Sacramento, Seattle, and other cities lined up to get what they considered to be their share of the funds.

Portland's streetcars were originally free to passengers inside of a downtown free-fare zone; only people getting on outside that zone were expected to pay. At the time, the city collected an average of 4 cents a ride. The free-fare zone ended in 2012, about the same time the city opened a new streetcar line. Ridership grew thanks to the new line and high rates of fare evasion. Fares are paid on an honor system (which is also true of most light-rail lines), with the threat of a $175 fine if someone is caught by a fare inspector without a valid receipt. Although the minimum valid fare is $1 for senior citizens and youths and $2 for everyone else, the city collected an average of only 20 cents a ride in 2016, suggesting fares are not rigorously enforced.[35]

The city officials and planners who subsidized near-downtown housing along Portland's subsidized streetcar line clearly hoped this strategy would boost transit ridership. Instead, it appears to have done the opposite. The Portland Business Alliance conducts an annual census of every downtown business asking, among other things, how employees get to work. It found that the number of downtown jobs grew by 14 percent between 2001, the year the streetcar opened, and 2016. During the same period, the number of downtown workers commuting by car grew by 30 percent, and the number who walk or bicycle to work grew by 83 percent. The number taking transit, however, shrank by 13 percent. Despite more than 12,000 new commuters, there were 5,250 fewer transit commuters but nearly 3,600 more who bicycle or walk to work (Table 14.3).[36]

Table 14.3
Method of Commuting to Downtown Portland

	Auto	Transit	Bike/Walk
2001	42,517	39,914	4,338
2016	55,457	34,661	7,922

Sources: 2001 Downtown Portland Business Census and Survey; 2016 Downtown Portland Business Census and Survey.

A likely explanation for this is that many of the people who moved into near-downtown housing would have taken transit to work from homes if they were further from downtown. Once near downtown, however, they quickly realized that bicycling and even walking is faster than the streetcar—a fact proven by *Oregonian* transportation reporter Joseph Rose—and so stopped commuting by transit.[37]

Portland probably has good reason not to rigorously enforce fares on its streetcars: As shown in Table 14.1, cities such as Tampa that actually charge reasonable fares for their streetcars attract very few riders. The average fare collected in Tampa is $1.98, but the line carries fewer than 650 riders on a typical weekday. Little Rock is even worse, collecting $1.20 a ride but attracting only 153 riders per weekday in 2016. Tacoma's streetcars are free but attract fewer than 3,200 riders per weekday. Atlanta's streetcars were free during their first year; after they began charging, ridership fell by more than 50 percent to fewer than 1,500 trips a day.[38] By comparison, Portland's two streetcar lines carry about 13,300 trips per day, which seems very small for the cost but is far more than any of the other lines built in the last two decades.

Portland's enthusiasm for streetcars has not come without trade-offs. The city's most valuable asset is its 4,800-mile road and street system, which is worth approximately $4.8 billion. Before the city began building streetcars, its Bureau of Transportation rated 62 percent of its streets to be in "good" or "very good" condition.[39] By 2013, the city had completed construction of its second streetcar line, but the street system by then had deteriorated so much that 54 percent of the streets were rated to be in "poor" or "very poor" condition.[40] Portland streetcar planners have identified 138 miles of streets they want to build streetcars on.[41] At the city's average cost of streetcar construction, about $35 million per mile, this would cost $4.8 billion—roughly the cost of repaving all of the city's streets. Every dollar spent on streetcars out of the city's transportation budget is one less dollar to spend repairing those streets.

In the end, streetcars provide an intelligence test. Anyone who thinks it is a good idea to spend hundreds of millions of dollars on a 130-year-old technology that works no better today than it did in 1888 should not be managing a city and its assets.

15. IT WOULD HAVE COST LESS TO BUY ALL
THE RIDERS PRIUSES

*In campaigns to obtain voter support for its proposed rail system, the Dallas
Area Rapid Transit District (DART) overstated the benefits and understated
the costs of the proposed system and attempted, first, to conceal and then to
misrepresent the results of unfavorable travel forecasts.*
*When alternative analyses indicated that the proposed $2.6-billion rail system
would carry only slightly more riders than an unimproved bus system, DART
tried to conceal the information. Subsequently, when a citizen's group obtained
the release of these unfavorable findings, DART attempted to mislead voters
about their significance and released cost-effectiveness analyses based on earlier,
and clearly incorrect, ridership forecasts.*

—John Kain[1]

Most new rail transit lines cost hundreds of millions if not billions of dollars.
But in 2006, Nashville opened the *Music City Star*, a new commuter-rail
corridor, for a mere $41 million. The Regional Transportation Authority of
Nashville bragged it was "the most cost-effective commuter rail start-up in
the nation."[2] However, *cost effective* does not mean what the authority seems
to think it means.

A program is cost effective if, among all the alternatives, it produces
the greatest output per dollar of input or, alternatively, costs the fewest dollars per unit of output. If the desired "output" of rail transit is empty trains,
then the *Music City Star* was cost effective. But the output of transportation

should be the movement of people and goods, not empty rail cars or other vehicles. The *Star* is cost effective only if it costs less than any other alternative, including buses, to move the people it carries. It does not come close to doing so.

The *Music City Star* connects the heart of Nashville with the suburb of Lebanon, about 32 rail miles (but only 30 highway miles) away. The trains, which operate weekdays only, take 50 to 55 minutes to complete a journey that a car can complete in 35 minutes. Four roundtrips per day are offered, plus two more 18-mile roundtrips from Nashville to Mt. Juliet and one extra round trip on Friday nights.[3]

Like almost all rail transit projects, the *Star's* first problem was a cost overrun. In 2000, it was expected to cost $28 million.[4] After adjusting for inflation, the final cost was 25 percent more. Because the federal government ended up paying nearly 80 percent of the costs, the Regional Transportation Authority overlooked that.[5]

After the rail line opened, a much bigger problem was low ridership. The transit agency had predicted the commuter trains would attract an average of 1,900 riders per weekday in the first year. Actual first-year ridership averaged 527 per day. By 2016, the 10th year of operation, this had doubled to 1,055, but that was still less than 56 percent of the number projected for the first year. It should not come as a surprise that few people wanted to take a slow train that didn't go where they wanted to go. Nashville's central business district has only about 6.5 percent of the region's jobs, and most of those jobs aren't within easy walking distance of the train station.[6]

A third problem was that the authority had underestimated annual operating costs. They were supposed to be about $3 million a year, but were instead $3.6 million the first year, growing to $5.2 million by 2016. There is no indication that the authority had bothered to predict annual maintenance costs. These were $2.7 million in the first year, probably because most of the equipment used for the train was used. While maintenance costs went down in the second year, over the first 10 years, it averaged $1.2 million a year in 2016 dollars.

Thus, by 2016, total annual costs, including operating costs, capital costs amortized over 30 years at 3 percent interest, and average maintenance costs were well over $8 million. Fares covered only about 10 percent of that. Higher-than-expected operating costs and lower-than-expected revenues left the agency with such a huge deficit that it briefly considered cancelling the operation. The Federal Transit Administration requires transit agencies to return any federal grants if they cease operations before the expected lifespan of a project, however, so the transportation authority instead resorted to begging the state for supplemental funds to keep the train going.[7]

In 2016, the total subsidy (including average maintenance and amortized capital costs) was more than $28 per ride. Someone who rode the train roundtrip 250 days a year would cost taxpayers more than $14,000. This means it would have cost less to buy every daily roundtrip rider a new Toyota Prius, not just once but every other year for the expected life of the train. Of course, not every rider takes a roundtrip every weekday, but by any measure, the train was extremely expensive, and just about anything else would have cost less.

ORLANDO: FARES DON'T COVER THE COST OF TICKET MACHINES

Another commuter-rail project that is supposedly a success story is in Orlando, Florida. Known as SunRail, this 32-mile line opened in 2014 at a cost of $361 million. SunRail carried just 1,824 daily roundtrip riders in its first full year of operation, and fares paid by those riders covered just 6 percent of operating costs. In 2016, the agency revealed that fare revenues weren't even enough to pay for operating and maintaining the machines used to sell tickets to riders.[8] Orlando could save a considerable amount of money by giving every daily roundtrip rider a new Toyota Prius *every year* (rather than every other year, as in Nashville) instead of running SunRail.

When Congress created the New Starts fund to support rail transit in 1991, one of the criteria it required for selecting projects was whether they were cost effective. A cost-effectiveness analysis is used when not all benefits can be calculated in dollars. If all benefits could be measured in dollars, then an *efficiency analysis*, also known as a benefit-cost analysis, is more appropriate. In requiring a cost-effectiveness analysis, the authors of the New Starts law evidently believed some benefits either could not or should not be expressed in dollars.

Another difference between an efficiency analysis and a cost-effectiveness analysis is that the latter must be done as a comparison between alternatives. While it is helpful to consider alternatives as part of an efficiency analysis, it is not essential. If Ford or Apple makes a profit from a new product, they are not going to go bankrupt if a slightly different product could have made an even higher profit. By contrast, if some of the benefits in a cost-effectiveness analysis aren't measured in dollars, profits can't be calculated, so it is essential that a full range of alternatives be considered to find the one that is most cost effective.

One obvious alternative to rail is bus transit. A plush long-distance bus with more than 50 seats typically costs about $500,000. With only one entrance, the time required for people to get on and off is longer than for a two-door transit bus. However, for $750,000 apiece, Nashville could have purchased two-door double-decker commuter buses with more than 80 comfortable seats, free wi-fi, and easy loading and unloading.[9] While buses have lower capacities than railcars, the *Music City Star* was rarely filled to capacity, averaging only 45 people per train, which may mean 100 or so people at the Nashville end of the route. Six such buses costing about $4.5 million could have operated both faster and more frequently than the three trains needed for the *Music City Star*, with the increased frequencies making up for lower capacities.

Buses also cost less to operate than railcars. Operations and maintenance costs for the *Music City Star* averaged nearly $30 per revenue railcar mile. By comparison, Nashville commuter buses cost around $9 per revenue bus mile. If buses operate twice as frequently as the trains, the operational savings would be $2.5 million a year, and buses would still save money even if they ran three times as frequently. Assuming they can attract the same number of riders, buses are far more cost effective than trains. Since transit riders are highly sensitive to frequencies, and buses could operate more frequently than trains, they would be likely to attract more riders than trains.

Similarly, Orlando could have provided service equal to SunRail with about two dozen buses costing $18 million. Orlando spends $53 per mile operating each SunRail car but just $8 per mile operating its buses, so the buses would have saved money even without counting the capital costs.

FABRICATING COST EFFECTIVENESS

While buses are clearly more cost effective than trains in Nashville and Orlando, the Federal Transit Administration has never required transit agencies to do real cost-effectiveness analyses to show that commuter-rail or light-rail projects make sense. After the 1991 New Starts law was passed, the FTA required agencies to calculate the cost of attracting each new rider to transit. When agencies made this calculation for both buses and rails, buses were always able to attract new riders at a much lower cost, typically around $5 per rider vs. $20 for rail. Rather than make rail appear to be a waste of money, transit agencies sometimes simply failed to consider bus alternatives in their analyses, instead comparing only alternative rail projects.

Later, the FTA reasonably decided that new transit riders weren't the most important output of a transit project; instead, the real output should be the effect of a project on an entire transportation system. The FTA required agencies to measure this effect using transportation models that would calculate how much time the project saved people.[10] If a new rail line was faster than buses and reduced congestion, it would save both transit riders' and automobile users' time. However, if a rail line was faster than buses but actually increased congestion—perhaps because it used lanes previously open to auto traffic, or because it frequently crossed busy streets—then it would save time for transit riders but cost time for car users.

Most commuter-rail, light-rail, and streetcar projects actually create more congestion rather than reduce it. This happens both because the lines are partly built in roads previously open to auto traffic and because the lines frequently disrupt traffic at street crossings. Because there are far more automobile users than transit riders, the net effect is that these projects cost more time for automobile users than they save for transit riders. Such projects can therefore not possibly be considered cost effective. Transit agencies solved this problem by counting only the time saved for transit riders, not the time lost for car drivers. Although the FTA rules explicitly required that both be counted, the agency looked the other way when awarding federal grants to projects that caused more congestion.

As briefly mentioned in Chapter 11, the Bush Administration responded by imposing a limit on how much a transit agency could spend per hour saved. Grant proposals were automatically rejected if a project was estimated to cost more than about $25 per hour (the actual amount was indexed to inflation, so it grew a little each year). Note that this isn't really cost effectiveness because there is no reference to buses or other alternatives. For example, a project could be approved if it cost $24.95 per hour of transit riders' time saved even if bus improvements could produce the same benefit for only $5 per hour. Still, the $25 limit did result in some changes. Charlotte, for example, dropped its grant application for a commuter-rail line that cost far more than $25 per hour limit. On the other hand, local congressional delegations inserted language in appropriations bills exempting projects in Portland, San Francisco, San Jose, and Washington, D.C., from this requirement.

THE PURPLE MONEY EATER INCREASES CONGESTION TOO

The Purple Line, a proposed light-rail line in the Maryland suburbs of Washington, D.C., offers an example of a transit agency—in this case, the state of Maryland—doing everything it can to evade the cost-effectiveness rule. The original estimates for the line predicted that it would carry 47,000 riders per day in 2030.[11] That was optimistic considering that New Jersey's Hudson–Bergen line, which serves an area with nearly four times the population density and far more jobs than the area that would be traversed by the Purple Line, carried only 43,000 riders per day in 2013.

The Maryland Department of Transportation has a long history of overestimating transit ridership. A heavy-rail line built in Baltimore in 1987 was projected to carry 103,000 riders per day; it carried 43,000.[12] A light-rail line built in Baltimore in 1997 was projected to attract 12,230 riders per day; instead, it carried 8,272 riders per day.[13] Improvements to another light-rail line in 2006 were projected to attract 44,000 riders; instead, it gained only 28,541 riders.[14]

Despite this poor track record, the Federal Transit Administration didn't question the 47,000 claim for the Purple Line. But 47,000 riders still weren't enough to bring the cost per hour saved below $25, so then governor Martin O'Malley commissioned the engineering firm Parsons Brinckerhoff to do a new ridership projection that predicted the Purple Line would carry 68,000 riders per day.[15] This was far more than any comparable light-rail line in the country, yet the Federal Transit Administration still did not question the number.

Even at that high number, however, the Purple Line wasn't cost effective at saving people time because it would significantly increase congestion in the corridor, and the time lost due to that congestion swamped the time saved by transit riders using trains instead of buses. The Maryland Department of Transportation, however, certainly did not publicize that fact to anyone unwilling to pore over reams of technical documents.

According to the first page of the Purple Line's draft environmental impact statement, the line was needed because "future roadway congestion in the corridor will have an increasingly detrimental effect on the travel times and reliability of east-west bus transit services in the corridor." Of course, congestion will have detrimental effects on car and truck travel too, but that apparently wasn't considered important. The purpose of the Purple Line, the report continued, was "to improve travel times and reliability by providing more direct services that will operate on dedicated and exclusive lanes and guideways."[16]

Even if the Purple Line improved travel times only for transit riders without affecting travel times for everyone else, there might be some justification for it. A traffic analysis technical report prepared in conjunction with the environmental impact statement, however, predicted that building the Purple Line would reduce average highway speeds in the Washington, D.C., region from 24.5 miles per hour in 2030 without the line to 24.4 miles per hour with it.[17] It is actually pretty impressive that a light-rail line in one corner of the Washington, D.C., metropolitan area could bring down average speeds in the entire region by a tenth of a mile per hour. Average speeds would decline because parts of the light-rail route would use dedicated lanes currently open to auto and truck traffic, while other parts would frequently impede traffic at crossings.

A reduction in automobile speeds from 24.5 to 24.4 miles per hour translates to 36,000 hours of wasted motor vehicle time per day, or about 13 million hours per year. Because motor vehicles average more than one person per vehicle, the amount of personal time wasted would be even greater. Even if the 24.5 and 24.4 miles per hour had been rounded off from, say, 24.46 and 24.44 miles per hour, respectively, the Purple Line would still waste more hours of time for automobile users than it would save for transit riders.

This wasted time played no role in Maryland's cost-effectiveness analysis, however, as it was solely based on the time saved by transit riders and ignored the time lost to road users. Yet even with this evasion of the rules, the environmental impact statement revealed that light rail was not cost effective because bus rapid transit could produce the same benefits at a lower cost. The report considered three bus rapid transit and three light-rail alternatives. The bus alternatives cost between $14.01 and $19.34 per hour of transit riders' time saved, while the rail alternatives cost between $22.82 and $26.51 per hour. By a true interpretation of cost effectiveness, the $14.01 bus alternative was the only cost-effective alternative considered. But under the Bush rules, any alternative costing less than $25 per hour was considered cost effective, so two of the light-rail alternatives passed the test (though they would have failed using the original ridership projections).

After the Purple Line environmental impact statement was completed, the Obama administration simply abandoned the concept of cost effectiveness. Under a new rule issued in 2013, the FTA now requires transit agencies to do no more than estimate the cost of a new project per transit trip.[18] They are not required to compare that cost with any other alternative, which is the whole point of a cost-effectiveness analysis. Nor does it matter what cost the agencies calculate, as there is no threshold cost above which the FTA will reject funding. A proposed rail project could cost a million dollars per rider, and it would be considered cost effective under the Obama rule.

As lax as the old rules had been, this new rule opened the door for many wasteful projects that previously would have been rejected. Naturally, this pleased advocates of expensive rail projects, who care more about whether the projects are built than whether they actually accomplish anything. Yet people who care about transportation in general or transit in particular should agree that it is important to spend our limited funds on projects and programs that will provide the greatest benefit.

In any case, the *Music City Star* and SunRail commuter trains were put into operation without a serious analysis of their cost effectiveness. With ridership well below expectations, Nashville's Regional Transit Authority and SunRail should probably just cancel the trains and replace them with buses. That, however, would require them to return a pro-rated share of the Federal Transit Administration grants to the federal government. Instead, both cities are adopting a far more expensive solution.

Nashville has proposed increasing the frequency of its trains as well as building several new rail lines.[19] Increased frequencies will attract more riders, but there are likely to be diminishing returns: each additional train would carry fewer riders than the train before it. As noted above, buses could operate at greater frequencies but at lower cost than the trains. Despite the failure of the area's first rail line, regional planners want to spend $6 billion building more commuter-rail lines and four light-rail lines.[20]

Orlando has already begun construction on a 17-mile extension of its commuter-rail line at a cost of $187 million. It is also planning two more extensions totaling about 17 miles that will cost well over $200 million.[21] SunRail managers hope the customers of the new extensions will pay enough in fares to cover the cost of the ticket machines.

BUSES VS. TRAINS

Clearly, buses are a better alternative for Nashville and Orlando than commuter trains. Even operated at higher frequencies, they cost less to operate than trains and would be at least as fast if not faster than trains. Transit agencies in about 20 urban areas operate commuter trains. Would buses be better than trains in all of them? If not, where would we draw the line between buses and trains?

Commuter trains on the Long Island Railroad, Metro North, and New Jersey Transit brought an average of 466,000 people into New York City every weekday in 2015. Census data indicate that about 358,000 of them were commuting to work.[22] The region's commuter trains are typically seven to nine cars long, and they carry more passengers per car than Nashville trains, so 15 to 20 buses would be needed to replace a

ROMANCE OF THE RAILS

single train. The Long Island Railroad, Metro North, and New Jersey Transit combined operate well over 1,000 weekday commuter trains in each direction.[23] This means at least 20,000 daily bus trips would be needed to replace them, and there simply isn't room for that many more buses on the streets of Manhattan.

At the other extreme is Austin's 32-mile rail line that gets so little business that it is adequately served by six railcars that run one at a time. Capital Metro, Austin's transit agency, spent $77 per vehicle mile operating these railcars in 2016. By comparison, the agency spent less than $8 a mile operating commuter buses and $10 a mile on its regular bus service. Using 12 double-decker buses in place of the 6 railcars would have saved taxpayers more than $130 million in start-up costs and $20 million per year in operating costs. While Austin's highways are notoriously congested, spending some of that $130 million on congestion relief for everyone would produce far greater benefits than providing for the 1,420 daily roundtrip riders who use the train.

In between New York and Austin, commuter trains fall into three different categories. First are the legacy rail systems—commuter-rail lines that have been around for 100 years or more. In addition to New York, these are found in Chicago, Philadelphia, Boston, and San Francisco. These systems tend to operate longer trains—generally four to nine cars—that carry more people per railcar at a lower operating cost. Their capital costs were paid long ago, but their maintenance costs are high, and transit agencies may not be spending the amount needed to keep them in a state of good repair.

Second are commuter-rail systems less than 40 years old, including lines in Albuquerque, Dallas-Ft. Worth, Los Angeles, Miami-Ft. Lauderdale, Orlando, Minneapolis, Salt Lake City, San Diego, San Jose, Seattle, and Washington, D.C. These systems tend to operate shorter trains—generally two to five cars—attract fewer riders per car and spend more per car mile than the legacy systems.

Third are the hybrid-rail lines: Austin, the Denton County (Dallas) A-train, New Jersey Transit's River Line, Portland's Westside Express, and San Diego's Sprinter. These use diesel-powered railcars, sometimes in pairs or sometimes just singly, and cost even more per car mile than the conventional commuter-rail systems. For each of these systems, three questions to ask are: Were they worth building? Should the transit agencies build more? If they were not worth building, should they be converted to bus lines now or sometime in the future?

The legacy rail lines were all built by private railroads seeking to earn a profit, and most of them did. So it is clear they were worth building. It is also clear that New York cannot survive in its current form without commuter trains, but it isn't clear how they should be paid for, as they collectively cost $2.4 billion per year more than passengers pay in fares. All three New York–area commuter systems—Long Island Railroad, Metro-North, and New Jersey Transit—collect fares equal to more than half their operating costs, and slightly less than half of their operations and maintenance costs. This suggests that it is possible that privatization could make the systems profitable with only modest fare hikes.

One way a private operator could save money would be to hire more full-time employees in order to reduce overtime. Thanks to generous overtime, more than 21,000 New York City transit workers earned more than $100,000 each in 2014. A Metro-North machinist earned $309,000.[24] A Long Island Railroad track foreman earned $332,000 in 2015.[25] Overtime alone cost the three commuter-rail agencies $440 million in 2016.[26] Such overtime is the bane of transit agencies across the nation, which are politically pressured by unions not to hire more workers. Private transit operators tend to pay union wages but are less susceptible to such pressure, thus saving them money.

Despite union pressure, many transit agencies save taxpayers' money by contracting out some of their operations to private companies such as First Transit, Stagecoach, and Veolia. The Colorado legislature passed a law requiring Denver's Regional Transit District to contract out half of its bus services, and the half it contracts out costs only 53 percent as much, per bus mile, as the half it operates itself. The private operators, all of which are unionized, achieved this savings even though they pay property and fuel taxes that the transit agency is exempt from paying on its own bus facilities and fuel. If private operators of New York's commuter-rail lines could achieve similar savings, they could make them profitable with fare increases of 10 percent or less.

Commuter trains are somewhat less important in Chicago, Boston, and Philadelphia than in New York. Chicago commuter trains carried about 132,000 roundtrips per day in 2015, while Boston and Philadelphia trains carried 60,000 to 70,000 roundtrips per day. Commuter trains are even less important in the San Francisco Bay Area, where they carry only 32,000 roundtrips per day, many of which don't even go into San Francisco. Census data indicate nearly all these riders are commuting to work. Census data also say that about 26 percent of commuters in the New York urban area take some form of rail transit to work, compared with 10 percent in the Boston and San Francisco urban areas, 8.5 percent in Chicago, and under 5 percent in Philadelphia. More than half of rail commuters in Philadelphia rely on commuter trains, but it's less than half in Chicago and less than a quarter in Boston, New York, and San Francisco.

Using local bus operating costs for comparison and assuming that two buses would be needed to replace every commuter-rail car, substituting buses for commuter trains would increase operating costs in all of the legacy urban areas. But the amounts depend on what bus operations are used for projecting bus operating costs. In Chicago, for example, operation and maintenance of Chicago Transit Authority buses costs $17.68 per bus mile, but the Pace suburban bus system spends only $9.76 per bus mile. At the former amount, buses cost more than commuter trains, while at the latter amount, they are less expensive.

Assuming buses could save money over trains, do local transportation facilities exist that could handle the necessary increase in bus traffic? As noted above, the answer is almost certainly "no" for New York, but it is almost certainly "yes" for San Francisco, especially because that region is building a network of high-occupancy toll lanes that buses could use, congestion free, along most routes.[27] Specifically, San Mateo County expects to install such lanes on Highway 101, paralleling the existing commuter-rail line, by 2020.[28]

To replace commuter trains, the San Francisco region might need about 250 double-decker buses making about 800 roundtrips per weekday. These buses would cost well under $200 million, which is about two-years' worth of maintenance costs on the rail line. Unfortunately, California is instead spending $1.75 billion electrifying the commuter-rail line—which they call "modernization" even though it is a century-old technology. By increasing acceleration times, this expense is expected to speed commuter trains and increase ridership by about 20 percent, which hardly seems worth the cost.[29]

Replacing commuter trains in Chicago would require about 3,500 new bus roundtrips per day, which could be a problem in downtown traffic. Doing the same in Boston and Philadelphia would require about 1,500 to 1,700 new bus roundtrips per day, which might be more feasible. In all three cases, the best solution would be to privatize operations and let the new private owners decide whether or not to convert to buses.

While the legacy systems made sense when they were built, none of the commuter-train startups in the last 40 years should have been built, as they are not cost effective compared with buses. Now that they are in operation, however, it might cost less to keep a few of them rather than immediately replace them with buses. The most heavily used rail system is in Los Angeles, which carries fewer than 25,000 roundtrips per weekday. Census data indicate that just a quarter of one percent of commuters in the Los Angeles urban area take commuter trains to work. But it would take more than 400 new buses making more than 600 trips per day to replace the trains. The region currently spends $19 per railcar mile operating and maintaining the commuter trains, while the region's main bus operator, the Los Angeles County Metropolitan Transportation Authority, spends $13.75 per bus mile operating its buses. Assuming that two bus trips are needed to replace each railcar trip, substituting buses for trains would actually increase costs unless bus costs could be reduced to less than $9.50 a mile.

The only other urban area where new commuter-rail services carry a significant number of riders is Washington, D.C., where Maryland trains carry about 18,000 daily roundtrips and Virginia trains carry about 9,000. The Maryland trains are much more heavily subsidized than the Los Angeles or legacy trains, collecting enough fares to cover just 30 percent of the operating costs and 17 percent of their operations and maintenance costs. Both states are spending more than $40 per railcar mile on operations and maintenance, so conversion to buses would save well over $100 million per year.

No other recent commuter-rail system carries as many as 10,000 roundtrips per day. While Nashville can brag that it spent "only" $41 million to start a transit service that could have been provided by faster buses for only $6 million, other urban areas have spent truly breathtaking amounts of money for very little return. The most extreme case is Salt Lake City, which opened a commuter-rail line north to Ogden in 2008 and a second 44-mile line south to Provo in 2012. Together, the Ogden, Provo, and Salt Lake urban areas have about two million people. Through 2015, the Utah Transit Authority has spent an unbelievable $2 billion—about $1,000 per resident—on capital improvements and maintenance of rail lines that carried just less than 8,110 roundtrips per weekday in 2016.

Fares collected from those riders cover a mere 18 percent of operating costs, and counting maintenance costs, the system is piling up operating losses of more than $35 million per year. As in Nashville, subsidies to riders are so great that it would cost less to buy every daily roundtrip rider a new Toyota Prius every two years.

One thing that the Utah commuter trains have going for them is low operating costs—almost too low to be credible. Utah Transit spends just over $7 per railcar mile on operations, compared with the national average of nearly $17. The next-lowest agency spends $11 a mile. Including a five-year average of maintenance costs increases Utah's commuter trains to $8 a mile, compared with a national average of $23 per mile and more than $12 per mile for the next-lowest agency, Portland's Tri-Met. Utah Transit's low commuter-rail operating costs mean that the substitution of buses, at a rate of two buses per railcar, would cost more than keeping the trains.

There are several reasons to be suspicious of Utah's low costs, as Utah transit planners and managers have a history of fudging data to make rail transit look good. In 2007, a state audit of Salt Lake City transportation planning found that planners had cooked the books to make rail transit appear more cost effective than it really was. State law required agencies to rank projects by their cost effectiveness, and planners had fabricated data to boost rail projects to the top of the priority list.[30] Also in 2007, an audit revealed that Utah Transit had systematically overcounted light-rail transit riders by at least 20 percent.[31] These overcounts made light rail appear to be more successful and more cost effective, relative to buses, to politicians who were considering expansions of the rail system.

More recent audits have found that Utah Transit has repeatedly overestimated future revenues while underestimating costs, allowed bus service to decline in order to fund rail projects, and built up so much debt that debt service will consume as much as 65 percent of its future revenues, leaving it in a precarious condition during a recession, when tax revenues decline.[32] Most pertinent to rail costs, a 2014 audit estimated Utah Transit is underfunding rail maintenance by $145 million per year.[33] When all costs are counted, buses would save money even if operating costs were a little higher, but it is most likely that long-term operations-and-maintenance costs would be lower for buses than rail.

While replacing commuter trains with buses would lead to too much congestion in New York and possibly Chicago, there is no question that the Utah highway system could handle the increased bus traffic. This is because it rebuilt Interstate 15 from Ogden nearly to Provo, including the addition of high-occupancy/toll (HOT) lanes, at the same time it was building commuter rail. Such HOT lanes charge a toll to low-occupancy vehicles but are free to buses and high-occupancy vehicles. The tolls are set to ensure that HOT lanes never become congested. A fleet of about 60 double-decker buses costing $45 million would be sufficient to carry all the passengers now riding the commuter trains.

All the other regions that have introduced commuter trains over the past four decades would have been better off with commuter buses. In most cases, they would be better off today scrapping their commuter trains and replacing them with buses. The few exceptions would be regions that have such serious congestion that buses would be much slower than trains, which might be the case in Washington, D.C., at least until that region can get its highway system better organized.

On the other hand, Seattle's commuter trains parallel Interstate 5, which is the most congested corridor in the western United States outside of California.[34] The Washington Department of Transportation has installed high-occupancy vehicle lanes for the full length of this corridor, which would allow buses to travel most of the route without congestion.[35] Similarly, Florida either has or is installing high-occupancy vehicle or high-occupancy toll lanes for most of the length of I-95 that runs parallel to the Miami–West Palm Beach Tri-Rail commuter train.[36]

All other recent commuter-rail lines carry too few passengers to justify their cost. The same is true for trains in Austin, Denton County, Texas, Portland, San Diego, and Trenton that the Federal Transit Administration classifies as "hybrid rail" because they are a cross between commuter rail and light rail. The Portland, Austin, and Denton County lines have especially low ridership. While the New Jersey River Line and San Diego Sprinter carry more passengers, they could easily be replaced with buses, saving taxpayers millions of dollars a year.

Most of the new commuter-rail and hybrid-rail projects received federal funding because politicians and Federal Transportation Administration officials willingly ignored the fact that they were less cost effective than buses. In the end, the same is also true for light-rail and streetcar projects. Except for extremely congested areas such as Manhattan, almost no rail project is cost effective compared with buses. If the goal of a project is to reduce congestion, as the FTA's cost-per-hour-of-time-saved measure suggested, then a wide variety of alternatives would be superior to any kind of rail transit.

16. WHY AMTRAK IS BEING REPLACED BY INTERCITY BUSES

The federal government does not run a national airline. It does not run a national bus company. It does not own the interstate highways (the states do), nor does it own toll roads, commercial airports, or bus terminals. From a public policy standpoint, there is no justification for the federal government to own and operate a national railroad passenger system that is essentially irrelevant to the transportation marketplace.

—Joseph Vranich[1]

In 2012, I was honored to be invited to be on John Stossel's Fox Business News show to discuss Amtrak. At the end of the show, Mr. Stossel concluded by telling viewers, "I ride Amtrak to Washington; I thank you for your subsidy." I blurted out, "I take Megabus!" In fact, I happened to be in Washington, D.C., prior to going on the show, so I rode Megabus roundtrip to New York for $17.50. The fare on Amtrak's fastest train, the *Acela*, would have been nearly $300. The *Acela* would have saved me 80 minutes in each direction, but considering I could work on the bus, which offered both electrical outlets and free WiFi, I didn't think the time savings was worth $1.75 per minute.

I am not the only passenger-train lover to be disenchanted with Amtrak. Joseph Vranich, quoted above, is a former Amtrak public affairs spokesman. Anthony Haswell, who is considered the father of Amtrak and who preceded Vranich as director of the National Association of Railroad

Passengers, looked back on his political child 30 years after it began. In that time, "Amtrak has cost the taxpayers a lot more than $20 billion," he wrote, but "they have gotten back a pretty skimpy return." The trains were not only costly, they were slower than trains were 50 to 60 years earlier, and they were often late. As a result, he concluded, "I am personally embarrassed by what I helped to create."[2]

Yet in November 2016, Amtrak issued a press release reporting "exceptionally strong" financial results for fiscal year 2016. The railroad's revenues "covered 94 percent of its operating costs," which the release called "a world-class performance for a passenger railroad." The net operating loss of $227 million was, according to the press release's headline, the "lowest ever," though the text modified that to the "lowest since 1973."[3]

Amtrak's financial claims have been overshadowed by its poor safety record. In 2015, an Amtrak engineer became distracted and failed to reduce speed before reaching a curve in the Northeast Corridor near Philadelphia, resulting in a crash that killed eight people.[4] In December 2017, an engineer making the inaugural run on a new, supposedly high-speed (but really just 79-miles-per-hour) route in Washington state missed a 30-mile-per-hour speed limit sign and crashed the train, killing three.[5] A few weeks later, an Amtrak train carrying several members of Congress hit a truck at a grade crossing, killing the truck driver.[6] A few days after that, the crew of a CSX freight train set a switch incorrectly, diverting an Amtrak train into their train and killing the Amtrak engineer and conductor.[7] Meanwhile, Florida East Coast Railway's Brightline passenger train between Ft. Lauderdale and West Palm Beach managed to kill four people by the end of its first week of revenue service.[8]

These accidents had very different causes, but all point to a questionable railroad safety culture. Though United States airlines carry a hundred times as many passenger miles per year as Amtrak, they have not had a fatal crash since 2009.[9] This means Americans are more likely to be killed by a passenger train, even if they never ride one, than by an airline crash. Though the deadly accidents have led to questions about why Amtrak and other railroads haven't installed positive train control, such safety systems (which Brightline had) wouldn't prevent trains from hitting cars and trucks at grade crossings or pedestrians trespassing on railroad tracks, which together kill about a hundred times as many people per year as crashes that could have been prevented by automatic train controls.[10]

Just as Amtrak's safety is questionable, claims that the company has managed to transform itself from the embarrassment mentioned by Haswell into a world-class financial performer are overblown. In fact, Amtrak's financial results are just as dismal as its safety record. The results reported in Amtrak press releases cover up two accounting tricks—otherwise known as "lies."

First, when it counts "passenger revenues," Amtrak includes hundreds of millions of dollars in annual subsidies to Amtrak provided by 18 states. Amtrak officials reason that such subsidies are the same as if, say, Wal-Mart paid Amtrak to transport some of its 1.3 million employees to work. But there's a difference between a company hiring Amtrak because its services help that company meet its goals vs. state legislators paying Amtrak, often for ideological reasons, out of funds paid by taxpayers, most of whom never ride trains. One is a payment for a worthwhile service consumers actually want, while the other is a political payment intended primarily at placating special interests such as unions and anti-highway groups.

By coincidence, state subsidies to Amtrak in 2016 were $227 million, the same as the losses claimed by the press release (Table 16.1). These subsidies helped double Amtrak's 2016 losses to $454 million.[11]

The second accounting trick was truly magical. In order for Amtrak to claim that its revenues covered 94 percent of operating costs, it had to make one of the largest items on its income statement disappear: depreciation. This amounted to $826 million in 2016, nearly four times as much as the $227 million in claimed losses.[12] Although Amtrak financial reports list depreciation as one of its largest expenses, the press release simply pretended it didn't exist.

Depreciation accounting is supposed to be a way for corporations to signal to investors that they are responsibly earning enough money to replace worn-out capital improvements. In the case of railroads, this includes the cost of rails, roadbeds, signals, power supplies, and rolling stock. Until 1983, the railroads were not required to report depreciation of fixed assets, and many railroads claimed to be profitable when in fact they were deferring maintenance and becoming increasingly decrepit.[13]

Table 16.1

Summary of Amtrak's 2016 Consolidated Income Sheet (millions of dollars)

Income	
Ticket Revenue	$2,136
Food and Beverage	132
State Support	227
Total Passenger Revenue	$2,496
Other Revenue	677
Total Revenue	$3,173

Expenses	
Salaries, Wages, and Benefits	$2,057
Operations, Fuel, and Materials	692
Facilities and Office	175
Advertising and Sales	105
Casualty and Claims	67
Depreciation	826
Other Expenses	532
Amortization and Capitalization	−155
Total Expenses	$4,299
Net Income	−$1,128

Source: *Monthly Performance Report for September 2016, Amtrak,* p. A-4.1.

Notes: Amtrak counts state subsidies as "passenger revenue," and when it reports its year-end results to the media, it pretends its second-largest expense, depreciation, doesn't exist.

For example, the Rock Island Railroad had been profitable until 1960, when Union Pacific offered to merge with it, giving Union Pacific its own entry into Chicago. Federal consideration of the merger dragged on for 14 years, during which Rock Island attempted to maintain profitability by deferring maintenance. By 1974, when the federal government finally approved the merger, the railroad was in such poor shape that Union Pacific backed out.

Rock Island was one of the railroads that refused to join Amtrak in 1971, and in 1975, it hired Anthony Haswell—the founder of the National Association of Railroad Passengers—to run its passenger operations. If Haswell wanted to show passenger trains could make money, he couldn't have picked a worse example of a railroad to prove it.

In many places, the dilapidated condition of the tracks forced the railroad to reduce passenger train speeds to 10 miles per hour, and trips that once took 2½ hours were lengthened to 4½. Although the railroad petitioned to eliminate the intercity trains in 1976, the Illinois Commerce Commission and ICC—either of which could have approved the discontinuances—both dragged their feet.

Instead, the state agreed to subsidize operations, which Haswell thought was "a profligate waste of public funds" because no one would invest the money needed to restore speeds to be competitive with cars or buses. Average ridership on the railroad's train between Chicago and Peoria dropped from 91 passengers per day in 1974 to 13 in 1977, while ridership on the train between Chicago and Rock Island fell from 143 per day to 26. Despite this, the railroad was forced to keep operating the trains until 1979.[14] Problems with deferred maintenance on the Rock Island and other railroads led the ICC in 1983 to order railroads to depreciate track and other structures in their accounting.

Requiring railroads to account for depreciation may have eliminated an incentive for marginally profitable railroads to defer maintenance, but it did nothing for money-losing operations such as Amtrak. Supported by congressional appropriations rather than private investors, Amtrak replaced or rehabilitated its capital assets when Congress provided the funds and deferred work when funds were short. After decades of ignoring $800 million or so per year in depreciation, Amtrak built up a huge maintenance backlog. As of 2013, Amtrak estimated its backlog for the portion of the Northeast Corridor that it owns had reached $5.8 billion ($6.2 billion in current dollars).[15] The real backlog for the corridor is much larger, and no estimates seem to be available at all for deferred maintenance on Amtrak's other assets. Since Amtrak doesn't collect enough revenues to cover even its basic operating expenses, there was no possibility of it banking surplus revenues in good years to spend on maintenance.

Table 16.1 shows that, after wages, depreciation is the second-largest cost on Amtrak's balance sheet. Yet when Amtrak brags that revenues cover a high percentage of operating costs, it deftly excludes depreciation as one of its costs. After deducting state subsidies from revenues and adding depreciation to costs, Amtrak's net losses in 2016 were more than $1.1 billion, roughly five times greater than Amtrak claimed in its press release. Passenger revenues covered only about 53 percent, not 94 percent, of these costs.[16]

Not only does Amtrak ignore depreciation in its press releases, it doesn't allocate depreciation to individual trains, so estimates of the profitability of those trains are exaggerated. As early as 2001, the Congressional Research Service criticized Amtrak for not counting maintenance among its operating costs, which it said it should do under generally accepted accounting principles.[17]

Since 2005, the Government Accountability Office has criticized Amtrak's reporting as "incomplete because it does not allocate its depreciation costs by line of business." The failure to allocate depreciation to individual routes puts Amtrak "at risk of misstating financial information used for decision making," said the agency, "which could result in misallocation of internal and federal resources." Amtrak claims to have developed a way of allocating depreciation to individual trains in 2010 but doesn't use it because officials "do not have confidence" in it.[18]

Amtrak knows the decision of where to run trains is a political one, not a financial one, so the fact that one train may cost $10 a rider and another $200 a rider is irrelevant. Ever since it was created, its political strategy has been to run trains through as many states as possible, thus generating support for passenger trains from as many senators and representatives as possible. Similarly, Amtrak has a sound political reason for pretending that it is close to making a profit, as the claim that profitability is just around the corner provides political cover for members of Congress representing fiscally conservative parts of the country.

After adjusting for inflation, total federal and state subsidies to Amtrak from 1971 through 2017 were close to $75 billion. That $75 billion hasn't bought very much. While Amtrak ridership has grown since 1971, most

Figure 16.1
Per Capita Amtrak Travel

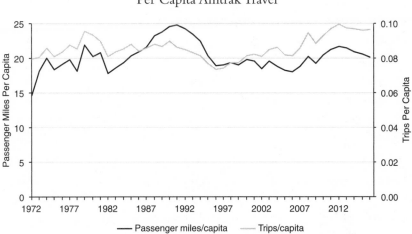

Source: Calculated from Amtrak annual reports and census population estimates.
Note: Amtrak travel has fluctuated, but per capita travel hasn't significantly grown since the company's first full year of operation in 1972.

of that growth reflects population growth. As shown in Figure 16.1, the average American rides Amtrak less than once every 10 years, which is only a slight improvement over once every 12½ years in 1972. The average American travels close to 2,000 miles a year by plane and 15,000 miles a year by car, but just 20 miles a year on Amtrak.

Amtrak has divided itself into three divisions: the Northeast Corridor between Boston and Washington; state-subsidized day trains; and the overnight long-distance trains. Each of these are supposed to have differing levels of viability, with the Northeast Corridor supposedly earning a profit, the state-supported trains doing well as long as states continue to fund them, and the long-distance trains providing critical services to communities that would otherwise be without transportation. In fact, a close examination reveals none of these are viable.

THE NORTHEAST CORRIDOR

Amtrak likes to brag that it carries more passenger miles in the Northeast Corridor than the airlines. But Amtrak really isn't competitive with the airlines between Washington and Boston and is barely competitive between New York and Boston. Only its service to intermediate points such as Providence, New Haven, Philadelphia, and Baltimore allows Amtrak to rack up more passenger miles than the airlines—but when those cities are included, Amtrak loses out to buses.

The Northeast Corridor, which carries about 30 percent of Amtrak's passenger miles, is really two separate corridors: 231 miles from Boston to New York City and 226 miles from New York City to Washington. While a few trains go all the way from Boston to Washington, they simply aren't competitive with the airlines. For fares that, as of this writing, start above $180, Amtrak's Acela requires more than six hours, for an average speed of less than 70 miles per hour, to go between Boston and Washington, while conventional trains cost $80 or more and take eight hours, for average speeds under 60 miles per hour. By comparison, airfares start at less than $50 for trips that take around 90 minutes.[19]

Amtrak is more competitive in the shorter corridors that terminate in New York City. Between Washington, D.C., and New York, conventional train fares start at around $50 for a 3½-hour trip, with an average speed of 65 miles per hour, while Acela fares start at around $165 for a nearly three-hour trip, with an average speed of 80 miles per hour (Figure 16.2). JetBlue has flights for $52 and other airlines for $64 for trips of about 90 minutes. Amtrak fares are about the same from Boston to New York, with conventional fares starting around $50 and Acela fares as low as $117, compared with airfares under $60. But rail speeds in this corridor are slower: more than 4 hours on Amtrak's conventional trains and 3½ hours on the Acela, for average speeds of 56 to 66 miles per hour, respectively, while air travel times are under 90 minutes.

Although planes are faster, rail advocates argue that downtown-to-downtown times for the train are often shorter because of the time required to get from the airport. This is a valid argument for downtown Manhattan, which has more than 20 percent of the jobs in the New York urban area and is also close to large numbers of residents. The down-town-to-downtown claim is less relevant in most other urban areas, how-ever, where downtowns average only about 7 percent of regional jobs

Figure 16.2

Average Passenger Train Speeds in Miles Per Hour

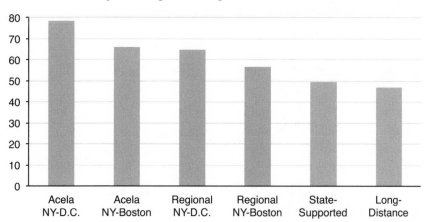

Source: Amtrak December 2016 timetable.

Notes: Speeds for state-supported trains are based on an average of 25 trains. Speeds for long-distance trains are based on all trains using the largest terminus cities when trains split to reach two termini.

and less than 1 percent of residents. Many major urban areas are served by multiple airports, and the number of people living and working close to these airports can easily outnumber those living or working close to their downtowns.

The Bus Alternative

Amtrak's real competitor in much of the Northeast Corridor is not the airlines but buses. Intercity buses became a serious threat to Amtrak after the emergence of the Megabus model of operation. This model consists of:

- Few bus stations—most buses instead load and unload at designated curbsides;
- Few ticket sellers—most tickets are sold on the internet;
- No baggage handlers—passengers help drivers to load and unload baggage;

- Few to no intermediate stops—rather than stop at Philadelphia, Wilmington, and Baltimore on their way to Washington, D.C., the Megabus model has separate buses from New York to each of the other cities;
- Yield-management fares—the first two seats on most Megabus routes go for $1.50 (they advertise $1 but add a 50-cent reservation fee), while the rest are increasingly expensive but still far less than Amtrak or conventional bus service;
- Free Wifi and power ports at each seat;
- Extra-comfortable seats.

Before the Megabus model—sometimes called the *city-to-city* model because of its nonstop services—conventional bus ridership through companies such as Greyhound and Trailways had declined in the United States from about 140 million passengers per year in 1960 to 40 million in 1990, leading Greyhound to declare bankruptcy in 1991.[20] The revival of bus service can be traced to 1997, when an immigrant Chinese entrepreneur named Pei Lin Liang started a bus route between Chinatown in New York and Chinatown in Boston. Called Fung Wah, which was short for Fenghua Jieyun Gongsi, or Elegant Rapid Transit Company, the buses went nonstop from curbside to curbside and offered low, fixed-rate fares and minimal customer service. Fung Wah soon had many imitators, collectively known as Chinatown buses, on routes from New York City to Boston, Washington, D.C., Philadelphia, and other cities.

Meanwhile, bus ridership in Britain surged after it deregulated its intercity bus system in 1986, leading to the rise of two major companies: Stagecoach and FirstGroup. The competition between these and other companies led to many innovations. Several of those innovations were brought together in 2003, when Stagecoach introduced the Megabus brand using a yield-management fare system and selling tickets by phone or on the internet. Unlike America's Chinatown buses, Megabuses in Britain used bus stations rather than curbside stops.

In 2006, Stagecoach's American subsidiary, Coach USA, introduced the Megabus brand to the United States with routes from Chicago to other

Midwestern cities and from Atlanta to other Southern cities. The service was so popular that in 2007, Megabus purchased double-decker buses for most of its routes. These buses have 81 seats instead of the 55 in conventional motor coaches yet take no more roadway space. Megabus started operating out of New York City in 2008, and today it serves 31 states, the District of Columbia, and Ontario.

In 2007, FirstGroup purchased Laidlaw, a Canadian company that owned what remained of Greyhound. Greyhound joined with Peter Pan buses in 2008 to start Bolt Bus, a Megabus-like service that competes in the Northeast Corridor and on the West Coast. A variety of other companies also began operating in the Northeast Corridor, some using the curbside model to offer transportation between suburbs such as Bethesda, Maryland, or Arlington, Virginia, to New York and other destinations. This gave travelers a choice of routes instead of forcing everyone to go to a central bus terminal.

Joining the competition were several premium bus services, including LimoLiner between New York and Boston and Vamoose Gold between New York and Washington, D.C. These luxury buses have about half as many seats as a regular bus, offering far more leg room, wider seats with three-across seating instead of four-across, on-board food service, and large-screen televisions. Fares are comparable to Amtrak's conventional trains, meaning they are higher than Megabus but lower than the *Acela*.

The Chinatown buses ran into problems in the early 2010s when the federal government shut down several for safety violations. Another problem was that Boston didn't like the curbside model and insisted that all buses use South Station, which tended to limit competition. After spending hundreds of thousands of dollars improving bus safety to meet federal requirements, for example, Fung Wah was forced to permanently shut down in 2015 because, its owner said, Boston had given the spaces it had used at South Station to Megabus.[21]

Despite the federal safety crackdown, at least nine companies continue to operate between New York and Washington, with several more between New York and Boston. Exact ridership numbers are not available, but the American Bus Association reports that its member companies (including Megabus and Bolt Bus) fill about 60 percent of their seats in intercity service, while Chinatown bus companies (most of which are not members of the association) tend to fill an even higher share of seats.[22] Based on published bus schedules, the various companies provide about 4 billion seat-miles of service in the Northeast Corridor each year. If 60 percent of their seats are filled, this translates to about 2.4 billion passenger miles. By comparison, Amtrak offered about 3.6 billion seat-miles in the corridor in 2016 and filled about 55 percent of them, for slightly less than 2.0 billion passenger miles.[23] Even if the bus companies fill only half their seats, they equal or exceed Amtrak's ridership in the corridor.

Nationally, intercity buses carry about twice as many passengers each year as Amtrak: 62 million on the bus vs. 31 million by train in 2015. Passenger mile data are harder to obtain, but intercity buses carried about 22 billion seat-miles in 2015 vs. 12.9 billion on Amtrak.[24] Amtrak fills slightly more than half of its seat-miles and intercity buses probably do about the same or better.

Planes, trains, and buses may each serve slightly different markets, but the subsidies each receive are very different. Although the federal government once helped cities build airports, today airline subsidies are negligible, as most airport and air traffic control costs are paid out of ticket fees. The main federal airport subsidies go to little-used airports that Congress has deemed provide "essential air service," but none of these are in the Northeast Corridor.[25] For buses, a 2013 analysis of bus subsidies estimated that road construction and maintenance costs not paid out of fuel taxes and other highway user fees average 0.13 cents—about an eighth of a penny—per bus passenger mile.[26]

By comparison, Amtrak subsidies are so great they call into question the real need for passenger trains in the corridor. Unfortunately, it is impossible to precisely calculate these subsidies because Amtrak doesn't report its actual maintenance expenses; it commingles costs of its Northeast Corridor trains with costs of other trains, and—despite years of promises—it has failed to allocate depreciation of capital improvements to individual corridors or routes.

Amtrak reports its high-speed *Acela* earned $293 million in operating profits in 2016, mainly by charging fares averaging 93 cents a passenger mile. Other Northeast Corridor trains netted another $186 million from fares averaging 49 cents a passenger mile, for a total of $479 million.[27] These numbers have persuaded some Republican members of Congress that the corridor no longer needs to be subsidized, so they have proposed to privatize it.[28] In fact, considering the cost of depreciation and the corridor's multibillion-dollar maintenance backlog, it seems unlikely that a private party would be willing to take over the Northeast Corridor, much less invest the billions necessary to make trains in the corridor go even faster.

When all costs are counted, says transportation journalist and Amtrak supporter Don Phillips, the Acela "hemorrhages money." Phillips agrees that it's "impossible to tell" exactly how much "because of Amtrak's odd methods of accounting." For example, "when some long-distance trains enter Northeast Corridor territory, their 'costs' triple," reports Phillips. "That helps make Corridor trains look better."[29]

Amtrak admits it *should* be spending $370 million a year in 2010 dollars (more than $400 million in 2016 dollars) on maintenance in the Northeast Corridor to keep it from deteriorating further.[30] It also says that the capital value of its fixed assets and rolling stock is about $20 billion, around half of which is attributable to the Northeast Corridor.[31] Given a 30-year depreciation period, the annual depreciation on the Northeast Corridor's share of that $20 billion is at least $333 million a year. Adding this $333 million to the $400 million in maintenance and subtracting it from the operating profit results in an annual loss of $250 million, or an average subsidy of 11 cents per passenger mile. This is nearly one hundred times the subsidies to buses. If Phillips is correct that Amtrak attributes some Northeast Corridor costs to long-distance trains, then the actual subsidy is even greater.

Amtrak may claim a maintenance backlog of around $6 billion, but this doesn't count several important pieces of infrastructure that it says also need replacement. According to a five-year capital investment plan, the $6 billion represents the backlog for "basic infrastructure" such as tracks, power supplies, and rolling stock. But on top of that are "major backlog projects," including aging bridges and tunnels. Replacing bridges over the Connecticut, Hackensack, Susquehanna, Bush, and Gunpowder rivers, all of which are more than 100 years old, is estimated to cost more than

$3.6 billion. Replacing several other bridges on a segment of the corridor owned by Metro North would cost $3.1 billion. The biggest projects of all are tunnels under the Hudson River and in Baltimore whose replacement costs are estimated at more than $24 billion.[32]

Not all the costs of this infrastructure are attributable to Amtrak, as the Northeast Corridor actually sees more commuter trains than Amtrak trains. But these trains also all lose money, so they can't make up for losses on Amtrak trains. As Congress and state officials debate such expensive projects as new Hudson River tunnels, they need to seriously ask whether it is truly worthwhile to keep Amtrak going in the Northeast Corridor. With buses providing the best short-distance service and planes the best long-distance service, is it really necessary for taxpayers to shell out tens of billions of dollars on replacement infrastructure so Amtrak can continue to fill some imaginary sweet-spot between these two?

As an alternative to privatization, transportation expert Robert Serlin has proposed Amtrak be split into two, similar to what has been done in several European countries, with one part managing the infrastructure and the other operating the trains. Under a proposal called American Intercity Rail Network for the 21st Century (AIRNet-21), the infrastructure manager could get private investment and federal loans to rebuild the Northeast Corridor. This would relieve Amtrak of this cost, which Serlin says "accounts for the majority of Amtrak's financial losses and poses a major threat to the sustainability of a national rail passenger network."[33]

The problem remains that someone would have to repay the loans, which means Amtrak and the various commuter railroads that use the Northeast Corridor—including New Jersey Transit and Maryland Transit—would have to pay the infrastructure manager enough to repay those loans. Serlin suggests the federal government loan $30 billion out of the Railroad Rehabilitation and Improvement Financing program to the infrastructure manager, yet that program loans out less than a billion dollars a year and has authority to loan only $35 billion, nearly all of which is meant to help regional freight railroads improve their infrastructure.[34] Whether Amtrak is one company or two, the problem remains that it loses so much money that private investors are not going to risk their funds.

Any federal loans would likely become federal grants because they would likely never be repaid.

With financial support from 18 states, Amtrak runs about 90 daily trains in each direction over 29 sometimes overlapping routes. These trains earned less than $500 million in ticket revenues but cost well over $900 million to operate in 2016, though food-service revenues made up a small part of the difference.[35] They carried about 30 percent of Amtrak's passenger miles for an operating loss of 15 cents per passenger mile (plus depreciation and maintenance). State taxpayers contributed about $227.5 million in 2016, or about 12 cents per passenger mile, leaving federal taxpayers to pick up the rest, including all the depreciation and maintenance.

The 363 route-miles Amtrak owns in the Northeast Corridor are not Amtrak's only tracks. It also owns 260 miles elsewhere, including lines between New Haven and Springfield, Philadelphia and Harrisburg, and part of the route between Chicago and Detroit. These routes are used mainly by state-supported trains. Because state-supported trains carry far fewer passengers than those in the Northeast Corridor, the depreciation cost per passenger mile is much greater, probably at least 25 cents. This means federal taxpayers are really paying nearly 30 cents per passenger mile on top of the 12 cents paid by state taxpayers. Of course, not all state-supported trains use tracks owned by Amtrak, but all of them lose a considerable amount of money after accounting for depreciation.

When measured per passenger, federal subsidies averaged $30, and on half the routes, they were more than $45. On one route, the Chicago–Detroit *Wolverines*, the 2016 subsidy was more than $160 per passenger. As with other Amtrak costs, these do not include depreciation or maintenance, so the actual federal subsidies are much larger, especially since the *Wolverines* use tracks owned by Amtrak for part of their journey.

Most of these trains cover routes less than 250 miles long; only three of the 90 daily trains venture over routes longer than 500 miles. On at least three-quarters of these routes, Amtrak competes directly against

Table 16.2
Amtrak and Megabus/Bolt Bus Frequencies, Times,
and Costs on Selected Routes

Route	-------- Amtrak --------			-------- Bus --------		
	Frequency	Time	Cost	Frequency	Time	Cost
Chicago–Indianapolis	1	5:05	$31	6	3:30	$19.50
Chicago–Milwaukee	7	1:30	$25	4	1:45	$10.50
Chicago–St. Louis	4	5:20	$27	2	6:00	$25.50
Chicago–Detroit	2	5:18	$37	4	5:10	$29.50
New York–Pittsburgh	1	9:15	$59	4	8:00	$49.50
Washington, D.C.–Richmond	2	2:40	$27	5	2:15	$30.50
New York–Toronto	1	12:00	$123	3	11:30	$55.50
New York–Albany	11	2:30	$34	4	3:00	$13.50
New York–Charlotte	1	12:00	$118	1	16:50	$94.50
Charlotte–Durham	3	2:45	$26	2	3:30	$14.50
Portland–Seattle	4	3:40	$26	8	3:45	$19.50
Portland–Eugene	3	2:35	$21	4	2:20	$15.50

city-to-city buses that nearly always charge lower fares and are often faster.[36] For a number of these routes, Table 16.2 shows that the *lowest* cost someone might pay with an advance purchase on Amtrak is typically about 50 percent greater than the *highest* cost someone might pay by purchasing a last-minute ticket on Bolt Bus (in the Northwest) or Megabus (everywhere else). While the lowest-cost tickets on Megabus are generally $1.50, the highest coach fares on Amtrak are typically three-and-a-half times greater than the lowest rail costs shown in the table.

The table also shows that buses are often more frequent than Amtrak trains. Bus frequencies in the table show only Megabus and Bolt Bus, so when other bus companies are added, buses may be more frequent in even more corridors. For example, Greyhound has 11 daily buses from New York to Albany. Finally, the table shows buses are faster than trains in half the corridors and only a few minutes slower in many of the rest. Overall, buses are highly competitive with trains in every corridor with the possible exception of New York to Charlotte. In that 700-mile corridor, however, airfares for nonstop flights of about 90 minutes start at under

$50 for Spirit Airlines and $82 for American Airlines, so Amtrak again is at a disadvantage.

On average, only about 42 percent of the seats on state-supported trains are filled with passengers. The few trains that fill more than 60 percent of their seats are mainly those that spend at least part of their time in the Northeast Corridor, which means Northeast Corridor riders are boosting the ridership of what are supposed to be other corridors' trains. This includes trains from Lynchburg, Newport News, and Charlotte to Washington, and from Pittsburgh to Philadelphia, all of which continue to New York City. In 2016, some of the emptiest trains were those in California—Sacramento–San Jose, Sacramento/Oakland–Bakersfield, and San Luis Obispo–San Diego—which filled less than a third of their seats, as did the Portland–Boston *Downeaster* and Chicago–Indianapolis *Hoosier State*.

In 2015, the state officials in Indiana were disappointed in Amtrak's operation of the *Hoosier State*, so they contracted with another railroad, Iowa Pacific, to provide train service between Chicago and Indianapolis. Amtrak continued to handle ticket sales and provide engineers and conductors, while Iowa Pacific provided railcars, locomotives, and on-board food service. Iowa Pacific restored a number of pre-Amtrak passenger cars and used a dome car and three coaches painted in former Illinois Central colors. In its first year of operation by Iowa Pacific, ridership grew by 6 percent and revenues by 33 percent. However, Iowa Pacific discovered a quirk in the contract that resulted in a much smaller payment than it expected: when the state refused to renegotiate the contract, it withdrew from the operation after two years.[37]

Despite the contract mix up, the *Hoosier State* experiment might offer hope that private operators could do better than Amtrak by providing superior service. Yet there is a limited number of non-Amtrak passenger cars in suitable running condition, and because new cars cost several million dollars each, private operators are not likely to order such cars without taxpayer support for 100 percent of the capital costs and at least part of the operating costs.

In 2009, the Obama administration gave hundreds of millions of dollars to the states of Illinois, Michigan, and Washington to speed up trains between Chicago–St. Louis, Chicago–Detroit, and Seattle–Portland. This money was supposed to go to "shovel-ready" projects. As will be described in the next chapter, however, as of the end of 2017, the trains in these corridors were no faster than they were in 2009 and remain uncompetitive with buses.

Long-Distance Trains

The *California Zephyr* through the Colorado Rockies to the San Francisco Bay Area. The *City of New Orleans, Crescent*, and *Sunset Limited* to the Big Easy. The *Empire Builder* to Glacier Park and the Pacific Northwest. The *Silver Meteor* and *Silver Star* to Florida. Amtrak's long-distance trains have the historic names, romantic destinations, and scenic views that make them icons for Amtrak.

They also lose a lot of money. In 2016, the 14 daily and two tri-weekly trains cost taxpayers more than half a billion dollars (again, not including depreciation or maintenance), which is significantly more than the 90 daily state-supported trains. Of course, the long-distance trains cover longer distances than the day-trains, so they carried about 40 percent of Amtrak's passenger miles in 2016 compared with 30 percent by the state-supported trains and 30 percent in the Northeast Corridor. Even so, Amtrak reported operating losses averaging nearly 19 cents per passenger mile, and more than $100 per passenger, in 2016, which as usual does not include depreciation or maintenance. Most of Amtrak's long-distance trains do not run on Amtrak-owned tracks, so the depreciation is mainly due to locomotives and cars and probably adds 2 to 5 cents per passenger mile to federal subsidies.

Some of the trains do far worse than others. The worst is the tri-weekly Los Angeles–New Orleans *Sunset Limited*, which Amtrak says lost 44 cents per passenger mile and $349 per passenger in 2016. The best is the Auto Train, which carries families and their cars nonstop from Lorton, Virginia, to Sanford, Florida, and lost only about a penny per passenger mile in 2016. In between, the Chicago–New York *Cardinal*, the New York–New Orleans *Crescent*, and Chicago–Los Angeles *Southwest Limited* each cost taxpayers more than $150 per rider, while the Chicago–Seattle *Empire Builder*, Chicago–Oakland *California Zephyr*, Chicago–San Antonio

Texas Eagle, and Seattle–Los Angeles *Coast Starlight* each cost more than $100 per passenger.

These trains may be romantic, but they also provide an important political function for Amtrak. In addition to the District of Columbia, the Northeast Corridor serves just eight states, albeit heavily populated ones. State-supported trains reach 15 more, but that's still less than half the states, which—because each state has two senators—is problematic from a political perspective. The long-distance trains bring 23 more states into the picture: with them, Amtrak reaches every state except Alaska (which has its own government-supported passenger trains), Hawaii, South Dakota, and Wyoming.

Despite serving all those states, Amtrak's share of the intercity travel market is miniscule. Automobiles moved more than two-thirds of intercity passenger miles in 2015, while airlines carried about 30 percent. Buses carried about two-thirds of a percent, and Amtrak was less than a third of a percent.[38] In other words, intercity buses carry about twice as many passenger miles as Amtrak, while airlines carry a hundred times as many.

Though passing through 46 states, Amtrak trains don't necessarily reach the largest cities in those states. The nearest stop to Phoenix, the nation's sixth-largest city, is 34 miles away. The train serving Houston, the nation's fourth-largest city, operates just three days a week. Las Vegas, Columbus, Nashville, Louisville, and Billings lack any service at all. The only city in Idaho reached by Amtrak is a town of about 7,500 people that is hundreds of miles from the state's population centers. Amtrak serves just four small towns in Kentucky whose collective populations are less than 35,000 people. Even when reaching major cities, the choice of destinations is limited. For example, Amtrak trains go east or west from Denver, but not north or south.

Rail advocates see these gaps in Amtrak's map as reason for expanding the company's routes. But Las Vegas, Nashville, and many other cities are thriving without Amtrak. Amtrak does serve Reno, and in 2016, a few more than 70,000 people got on or off the train in Reno. Considering a tourist would get both off and on, that's considerably less than 1 percent of the 4.6 million people who visit Reno each year. If Amtrak restored service to Las Vegas, it might slightly reduce the profitability of airlines or bus companies, but it would add nothing to the local economy.[39]

Some of Amtrak's most popular long-distance trains are the ones to Florida. In 2016, about 138,000 people got on or off the train in Orlando, meaning 69,000 roundtrips. That's barely more than one-tenth of a percent of the 60 million people who visited Orlando that year.[40]

At the other extreme from major tourist destinations such as Reno and Orlando are small cities and towns to which Amtrak carries very few travelers. Out of the 500 or so cities served by Amtrak are dozens in which fewer than five passengers a day get on or off each train stopping in that city. More than a third have fewer than 15 passengers getting on or off each train. Despite these small numbers, rail advocates are quick to claim Amtrak is somehow vital to the survival of these cities.

For example, a resident of Havre, Montana, claims the loss of Amtrak service "would be devastating" to that city of around 10,000 people, which has no bus service.[41] Yet it is hard to believe the eight people who get off and eight who get on each Amtrak train that stops in the city are somehow preventing the devastation of that city. Of course, one reason why Havre doesn't have bus service is that buses would have to compete against heavily subsidized trains.

The American Intercity Bus Riders Association has identified well over 100 communities with more than 25,000 people each that have no rail or bus service.[42] There are thousands of smaller communities that also lack service. Due to an accident of history, a few communities get heavily subsidized rail service while others get none.

If the train disappeared from Havre and no bus service sprang up in its place, it would be far less expensive for taxpayers to subsidize buses rather than trains, assuming taxpayers really believed such services were both vital to the communities and that each community's survival was somehow a vital national issue. Similarly, if subsidizing transportation to unserved communities were really in the national interest, it would be far more effective to use buses, both because they cost less and because buses can travel over any of the 2.7 million miles of paved roads in the country rather than be confined to the 148,000 miles of rail lines.

Yet there is no reason why it is in the national interest to subsidize transportation to potentially underserved communities. Most Americans are highly mobile, and they base their decisions on whether to live in big cities, small towns, suburbs, or rural areas on many factors, including the cost of transportation and other services in those areas. No one should have the right to decide to live in a place with higher transportation costs and then expect taxpayers to subsidize them.

QUESTIONABLE SOCIAL BENEFITS

The other arguments often used to justify subsidies to Amtrak are that passenger trains relieve congestion and save energy.[43] Amtrak does use a little less energy per passenger mile than flying. According to the Department of Energy, the average car uses about 3,100 British thermal units (BTUs) per passenger mile, while the average commercial plane uses about 2,500 and Amtrak about 2,200. In making this calculation, the department assumed the average car contained 1.55 passengers, which is the correct number for urban travel (1.67 is the average for cars and light trucks together). However, cars in intercity travel tend to have higher occupancies: An independent analysis for the California High-Speed Rail Authority found that intercity cars average 2.4 people.[44] At that occupancy rate, cars beat Amtrak by using only about 2,000 BTUs per passenger mile.

Even if the lower occupancy rate for automobiles is correct, passenger trains are not an effective way of saving energy. Amtrak carried about 6.5 billion passenger miles in 2016.[45] In the same period, domestic airlines carried 650 billion passenger miles, 100 times as much as Amtrak.[46] Cars and light trucks traveled more than 2 trillion miles, of which about 800 billion was rural (which serves as a proxy for intercity travel).[47] If intercity automobile occupancies range between 1.67 and 2.4, Amtrak carries just one-quarter to one-third of a percent of intercity travel, which isn't enough to relieve congestion or make a dent in energy consumption anywhere.

Economist Charles Lave once stated what he called the Law of Large Proportions: "the biggest components matter most."[48] If automobiles carry two-thirds of intercity travel and airplanes carry nearly a third, then making either automobiles or airplanes 1 percent more energy efficient will save more energy—and probably cost far less money—than trying to double the ridership of trains that are only slightly more energy efficient than flying or driving and currently carry under one-third of one percent of intercity travel.

Similarly, there are far better remedies to traffic congestion than intercity trains. Airline congestion can be relieved with an improved air traffic control system. Increasing demand for air travel can be met with larger airplanes. Coordinating traffic signals is inexpensive and will do more to relieve congestion than getting half a percent of people out of their cars. Most intercity highway congestion is due to slow human reflexes, and the increasing use of adaptive cruise control and, eventually, self-driving cars, will fix or at least greatly reduce that problem.

Rewriting History

Could passenger trains have been saved if the government had deregulated the railroads in 1950 instead of 1980, including not imposing unnecessary costs on high-speed trains or allowing labor unions to impose high labor costs on management? No one will know for sure, but there are several reasons to doubt it.

First, railroad deregulation in 1980 led to a major resurgence of the volume of freight shipped by rail, yet it is unlikely that passenger service, if it had still been private, could have made a similar recovery. The growth in rail freight was primarily from large volumes going from point A to point B: coal from mines to power plants; petroleum from oil fields to refineries; grain from elevators to ports; and containers from ports to distribution centers. The railroads left smaller shipments to trucks, which were also deregulated. Between 1980 and 2006, the ton-miles of freight shipped in the United States grew by 37 percent, but both deregulated railroads and deregulated trucks doubled their ton-miles. The Railway Express Agency, a company that once handled small shipments for the railroads, went out of business in 1975.

The experience with freight could not be replicated with passengers because large numbers of passengers rarely want to go from point A to point B. Airlines deal with this by using hub-and-spoke systems that allow passengers to get from point G to point Q with one or two changes of planes. Amtrak deals with it by making many stops between major terminuses. Even in the New York–Washington, D.C., corridor, Amtrak's busiest, Amtrak runs no nonstop trains. Americans who have tens of thousands of possible origins and destinations each day are simply not going to fit into a unit-train mold.

Second, airlines were deregulated at about the same time as the railroads. In 1960, rail fares per passenger mile had been less than half as much as airfares. In 1970, when Amtrak was created, airfares were still 50 percent more than rail fares. Thanks to airline deregulation, however, airfares dropped below rail fares by 1990. By 2012, the most recent year for which complete data are available, Amtrak fares were double the average airfare, as shown in Table 16.3.[49] When subsidies—including depreciation—are added, Amtrak costs per passenger mile were more than three-and-a-half times the costs of air travel. Part of the high cost of Amtrak fares may be

Table 16.3
2012 Costs and Subsidies per Passenger Mile, in Cents

	Fares	Subsidy	Total
Amtrak	28.9	30.8	59.7
Driving	24.2	1.3	25.5
Airlines	13.8	2.5	16.3
Buses	13.8	0.1	13.9

Sources: Amtrak fares (including food & beverage revenue) and subsidies from Monthly Performance Report for September 2012, Amtrak, pp. A-2.2 and A-4.1; driving expenses, including vehicle purchases, operations, and insurance from National Income and Product Accounts, table 2.5.5, Bureau of Economic Analysis; passenger miles calculated by multiplying vehicle miles in cars and light trucks from *Highway Statistics 2012,* table VM1, by average occupancies of 1.67; highway subsidies from National Transportation Statistics, tables 3-32 and 3-35; airline fares and subsidies from National Transportation Statistics, tables 1-40, 3-20, 3-32, and 3-35; bus fares estimated from Joseph Schwieterman, Justin Kohls, Marisa Schulz, and Kate Witherspoon, *The Traveler's Tradeoff: Comparing Intercity Bus, Plane, & Train Fares across the United States,* Chaddick Institute for Metropolitan Development, p. 6; bus subsidies from Robert Damuth, "Federal Subsidies for Passenger Transportation, 1960–2009: Focus on 2002–2009," Nathan Associates, 2011, p. 24.

due to government inefficiency, but much of it is because railroads require far more dedicated infrastructure than airlines.

Third, subsidies to airports and highways exist, but they are a lot smaller today than many rail advocates believe. The numbers vary slightly from year to year, but in general, subsidies to air travel and driving average 1 to 3 cents per passenger mile, whereas subsidies to Amtrak are close to 30 cents per passenger mile. We should end highway and airline subsidies, but doing so wouldn't push large numbers of people into intercity trains.

Fourth, Morgan's idea that there is a "sweet spot" of trips long enough for passenger trains to compete with cars and buses while short enough to compete with airlines may have seemed realistic in 1959, but not today. This idea is still promoted by the Federal Railroad Administration, which says rail has a "comparative advantage" in the 100- to 600-mile travel market.[50] In fact, while there may be some trips for which Amtrak is less expensive than flying, there is no length of trip where Amtrak is the least expensive among air, bus, driving, and rail.

Finally, the growth of the city-to-city bus model pioneered by Megabus has taken over whatever claims Amtrak had to short- and medium-haul markets. While Amtrak provided 12.8 billion seat-miles of service in 2015 and filled about half those seats, buses provided 22.0 billion and filled about 60 percent of the seats.[51] That represents a 40 percent growth in bus service since 2008 vs. an 8 percent growth in Amtrak service over the same period.

In terms of speed and convenience, the automobile's ability to go door to door on the traveler's own schedule gives it a huge advantage over any mode of travel that requires people to go from somewhere they aren't to somewhere they don't want to go on someone else's timetable. By the time trips become long enough for this advantage to disappear, they are also long enough for air travel's speed and cost advantages to overwhelm the comforts of rail, including high-speed rail. People who don't have cars or don't want to drive can find lower-cost bus or air alternatives to rail in almost every market (Table 16.4).

For the most part, the passenger equipment running when Amtrak took over the railroads was at the end of its service life. No railroads were still earning an operating profit on passenger trains in 1970, but even if

Table 16.4

2017 Advance-Purchase Fares over Various Long-Distance Routes

Route	Airline	Amtrak	Greyhound
Atlanta–New Orleans	52	59	16
Atlanta–Washington, D.C.	67	92	40
Boston–Washington, D.C.	75	76	41
Chicago–Denver	44	91	89
Chicago–Detroit	124	37	16
Chicago–Los Angeles	59	132	98
Chicago–Memphis	112	80	35
Chicago–Minneapolis	56	52	18
Chicago–New Orleans	65	100	84
Chicago–Oakland	79	128	119
Chicago–Seattle	114	136	119
Chicago–St. Louis	127	27	20
Cincinnati–Washington, D.C.	40	58	53
Denver–Oakland	72	107	99
Denver–Salt Lake City	49	62	62
Houston–San Antonio	103	29	7
New York–Chicago	59	81	43
New York–Orlando	51	115	73
New York–Seattle	148	309	139
Oakland–Portland	69	68	72
Oakland–Seattle	97	82	84
Oklahoma City–San Antonio	143	66	59
Portland–Seattle	85	26	16

some were, they couldn't have afforded to replace worn-out equipment. As a result, it is unlikely rail passenger service could have survived, except in the form of tourist trains, until 1980.

American passenger trains are a classic example of technology replacement arrested by government fiat. They have been kept alive by a combination of special interest groups, nostalgia, unrealistic expectations, and exaggerated claims regarding their social benefits. The best solution for the American traveler is to end subsidies to all forms of transportation and let the chips fall where they may. Sadly, for lovers of passenger trains, that will probably mean the end of scheduled intercity rail service.

17. THE FALSE PROMISE OF HIGH-SPEED RAIL

The need for a bullet train exists only in the minds of its ardent backers. While California has many local transportation problems, traveling between the state's northern and southern regions isn't one of them.

—Dan Walters, *Sacramento Bee*[1]

In February 2009, President Obama asked Congress to include $8 billion for high-speed trains in the American Recovery and Reinvestment Act. High-speed rail, he said, would be his "signature issue" in the stimulus program.[2] Later that month, Obama's 2010 budget proposed to spend an additional $1 billion per year for five years on high-speed rail.[3]

In April, Obama presented his national high-speed rail vision to the public. Under the plan, about 8,500 route-miles of high-speed trains would connect key cities in 33 states along the eastern and Gulf Coast seaboards, in the Midwest, Texas-Oklahoma-Arkansas, California, and the Pacific Northwest.[4] In June, the Federal Railroad Administration published its guidelines for state applications for a share of the stimulus funds for local rail projects.[5]

The White House claimed the high-speed rail plan "mirrors that of President Eisenhower, the father of the Interstate Highway System, which revolutionized the way Americans traveled."[6] Just as Eisenhower borrowed his 40,000-mile interstate highway plan from an existing proposal developed years before by the Bureau of Public Roads, Obama's 8,500-mile high-speed rail network was identical to one proposed by the Federal Railroad Administration (FRA) in 2001.[7] Former FRA administrator Gilbert Carmichael called the program "Interstate 2.0."[8]

WHY HIGH-SPEED RAIL IS NOT INTERSTATE 2.0

There were three crucial differences, however, between interstate highways and high-speed rail. First, the Bureau of Public Roads gave President Eisenhower a reasonable estimate of how much the interstates would cost (the estimate turned out to be low, mostly due to inflation). But the FRA did not offer anyone an estimate of how much its high-speed rail network would cost. It wasn't until more than a year after Congress had agreed to spend several billion dollars on high-speed rail that Secretary of Transportation Ray LaHood casually estimated that the proposed network would cost "about $500 billion," or more than 50 times as much as Congress had appropriated.[9] Other experts thought it would be even more expensive. "Make no mistake about it," BNSF CEO Matt Rose testified to Congress. "This is a trillion-dollar funding proposition."[10] Either way, Obama's proposal to spend $8 billion in 2009 plus $1 billion a year for five years wouldn't even make a decent down payment.

Second, the Bureau of Public Roads had a plan for paying for interstate highways: gas taxes and other highway user fees. In fact, the entire system was built on a pay-as-you-go basis out of such user fees; not a single dollar of general taxpayer money was spent on the roads, nor was any money borrowed to build them. In contrast, the FRA has no financial plan for high-speed rail, no source of funds, and no expectation that passenger fares will cover all of the operating costs, much less any of the capital costs.

The third key difference is that the interstates truly did revolutionize American travel, while high-speed rail would never be more than a tiny but very expensive part of the American transportation network. The average American travels on the interstates some 4,000 miles a year—more than 20 percent of all passenger travel—while 2,000 ton-miles of freight per person are also shipped annually on the interstates.[11] Because interstate highways serve all major cities in all 50 states (even Alaska and Hawaii), most Americans use an interstate at least once if not several times a week. In contrast, high-speed trains would reach only a few major cities and be used mainly by a relatively wealthy elite.

One optimistic analysis projected that if the FRA high-speed rail network were completely built by 2025, the average American would ride this system 58 miles per year.[12] That's three times as much as people ride Amtrak today, but only about one-seventieth as much as people use the Interstate Highway System. High-speed trains would carry virtually no freight, nor would they enhance the capacity of existing railroads to haul freight. Moreover, considering the premium fares to ride high-speed trains and the fact that trains would mainly serve downtown areas, most passenger use would be by bankers, lawyers, government workers, and other downtown employees whose employers pay the fare, while all other taxpayers would share the cost of the subsidies.

LaHood's $500 billion estimate was about the same as the inflation-adjusted cost of the Interstate Highway System. For that cost, the rail network would have less than one-fifth as many route-miles reaching just 34 states. Calling it a "network" is a bit misleading, because it would actually consist of six unconnected clusters of rail routes: California, the East Coast, Florida, the Midwest, the Pacific Northwest, and South Central. Under this plan, no state in the interior West would be served by a high-speed train, nor would Alaska, Hawaii, Tennessee, or West Virginia.

To remedy the political defect of a plan that would reach only 34 states, the Obama Administration released a revised map in 2010 that added several routes. These included trains from Los Angeles to Las Vegas, Phoenix to Tucson, Cheyenne to El Paso, Kansas City to Oklahoma City via Wichita, Chicago to Omaha, and Atlanta to Nashville, thus bringing seven more states into the system. The political nature of the new plan was revealed by a proposed line from Minneapolis to Duluth. Duluth isn't exactly a major urban center, but it was in the district of Representative James Oberstar, who was then chair of the House Transportation Committee. The revised map still left out West Virginia, although it probably would have been added if Senator Richard Byrd, the king of pork who died in 2010, had remained at the peak of his political power.

No Build: The Environmentally Preferred Alternative

The premise of the 2009 stimulus bill was that it would get the economy going again. For that to work, infrastructure projects had to be "shovel-ready," which meant that all environmental documents had to be completed. At the time, this included just two true high-speed rail projects, one in Florida and one in California. The Florida plan was to build an 85-mile line from Tampa to Orlando that would eventually be extended from Orlando to Miami. Because the initial line was much shorter than the proposed California line between Los Angeles and San Francisco, it had the prospect of being completed during Obama's term of office, thus giving the president the glory of christening the new train.

A difficulty with the Florida project was that the environmental analysis prepared for the authority had concluded that "the environmentally preferred alternative is the No-Build Alternative" because it "would result in less direct and indirect impact to the environment."[13] The analysis considered gas-turbine trains and electric trains and found that the former would consume six times as much energy, while electric trains would consume three-and-a-half times as much energy as would be saved by the automobiles they took off the road.[14] Pollution from the trains would also be greater than from cars.[15]

The document did not assess the impact on greenhouse gas emissions, but because emissions are directly proportional to fuel consumption in petroleum-powered vehicles, such emissions would be roughly six times greater for gas-turbine trains than for automobiles. Florida gets 80 percent of its electricity from fossil fuels, and three British thermal units (BTUs) of fossil fuels must be burned to deliver one BTU to electricity users. The electric-powered trains would therefore also generate far more greenhouse gases than the automobiles they would take off the road.

Nor would the trains do much to relieve congestion. While planners predicted the train would capture 11 percent of travelers between Orlando and Tampa, most people driving between the two cities on the existing highway, Interstate 4, began at other origins or were driving to other destinations, so the train would capture no more than 2 percent of total freeway traffic. Traffic on Interstate 4 is growing by more than 2 percent per year, so the rail line would provide, at most, about one year's worth of traffic relief. As the environmental document noted, the traffic "reduction would not be sufficient to significantly improve the LOS [levels of service, a measure of congestion] on I-4, as many segments of the roadway would still be over capacity."[16]

For a time, Florida vacillated between the turbo trains, which were less expensive, and the electric trains, which had a much higher top speed but in practice would get from Orlando to Tampa only five minutes faster than the turbo trains. But in 2004, based on the project's high fiscal and environmental costs, Governor Jeb Bush persuaded state voters to cancel the project. In 2009, however, the new governor, Charles Crist, entered office, and—despite the environmental cost—he was happy to accept the federal government's offer to pay well over half the dollar cost of the rail project. Fortunately, voters replaced Crist with Rick Scott in 2010, and Scott once again cancelled the project. This greatly slowed the momentum behind high-speed rail in the United States.

California: Massive Cost Overruns, But Build It Anyway

California created its state high-speed rail authority in 1996 with the goal of planning and building a line connecting Sacramento, San Francisco, San Jose, Los Angeles, and San Diego. That year, an engineer named David Levinson from the University of California at Berkeley estimated that the portion of the line from Los Angeles to San Francisco would cost just under $10 billion (about $15 billion in today's dollars), and at that price, he calculated it would cost much more to transport someone between the two cities by train than by air, and slightly more by train than by car.[17]

But Levinson greatly underestimated the cost. In 2000, the rail authority issued its own cost estimate, saying the entire system would cost about $25 billion in 1999 dollars (about $36 billion today), while the Los Angeles-to-San Francisco portion alone would cost $13.7 billion (about $20 billion today). Operations and maintenance of the trains were expected to cost $550 million per year. The authority wasn't bothered by these high costs; it figured it could make up the cost by the volume of passengers it would carry, predicting the line would attract 32 million riders per year.[18]

Since Amtrak's Acela and its conventional trains combined carry less than 12 million riders per year between Boston and Washington in a corridor that has more people than the Los Angeles–San Francisco corridor, the authority's ridership number was exceedingly unrealistic. While the California trains would be faster than the Northeast Corridor trains, most Northeast Corridor trips are anchored by New York City, which is in the middle of the corridor. The California corridor had no such anchor: the Fresno urban area has well under a million people, while the Bay Area has more than 5 million and Los Angeles 13 million. That means most trips would be between Los Angeles and the Bay Area. This would greatly reduce the attractiveness of the train compared with flying.

In 2008, the authority asked California voters to allow it to sell $9 billion worth of construction bonds, which were conditional on receiving matching funds from other sources. By this time, the authority had increased its estimate of the Los Angeles-to-San Francisco line alone to $31 billion in 2008 dollars (plus $2 billion more for Los Angeles-to-Anaheim), or nearly double the 2000 estimate after adjusting for inflation. Projected operating costs had also grown to more than $1.1 billion even though the new estimate was only for Anaheim to San Francisco, while the $550 million in the previous estimate included extensions to San Diego and Sacramento.[19] In exchange for all this money, the authority promised voters that trains from San Francisco would reach Los Angeles in under 2½ hours.

Despite these growing costs, the authority claimed that profits from train operations would be so great that private investors would gladly put up their own money to run the trains. The authority's 2008 business plan called for a "design-build-operate" contract under which a private company would build the rail line and operate the trains, keeping all the operating profits for itself. The trains were supposed to be so lucrative that private investors were expected to contribute between $6.5 billion and $7.5 billion to the construction fund.[20]

The plan didn't specify how the $9 billion in bonds would be repaid, and since it called for no new taxes, voters approved it. The Obama administration gave California $1.8 billion of stimulus funds for the high-speed rail project, which triggered a like amount in state bonds. The resulting $3 billion or so was still no more than a down payment on the entire project.

In 2010, several House Democrats were facing close election campaigns, so two weeks before the election, the administration handed out another $2.5 billion. Instead of letting the Federal Railroad Administration announce the grants, which was the usual procedure, Secretary of Transportation Ray LaHood telephoned members of Congress and invited them to make the announcements to bolster their campaigns. California's share of this money was $902 million, and it was conditioned on being spent in California's Central Valley, whose Democratic representatives were facing the closest races.[21] As it turned out, Representative Jim Costa won re-election by just 3,000 votes, so the announcement may have made a difference in the election.

The 2010 election also put two anti-high-speed-rail candidates in the governor's offices in Ohio and Wisconsin. Before they even took office and had a chance to change their minds, the Obama administration withdrew the $1.2 billion in grants it had given to those states and gave them to other states, with California getting half. This gave California a total of about $3.3 billion in federal grants. With matching funds from the state bonds, it now appeared to have about 20 percent of the money needed to build the line, or so it thought. But in 2012, the authority greatly increased its cost estimates, and the new estimate for the Anaheim-to-San Francisco route was between $61.4 billion and $70.5 billion in 2010 dollars.[22] After adjusting for inflation, this was about double the 2008 cost estimate and four times the 2000 estimate. Because the project would not be completed before 2021, however, the actual amount that Congress or other legislators would have to appropriate would be closer to $100 billion in inflated, or "year of expenditure," dollars.

Because the authority didn't have anything approaching $61.4 billion (or, in inflated dollars, $100 billion), it proposed to build the rail line in stages. The first stage would build high-speed rail only in certain segments,

while trains would use existing rails at conventional speeds in other segments. The authority projected that by 2029, it would have built high-
speed rail from San Jose to Los Angeles at a cost of $53 to $62 billion in
2011 dollars, but it would still not have high-speed trains to San Francisco
or Anaheim, meaning trains would take longer than the promised 2½ hours
to get from San Francisco to Los Angeles.[23] Due partly to high real estate
costs, another $10 billion or so would be needed to complete the line and
meet that schedule.

By this time, the rail authority had lost any hope of finding private
investors who would put up several billion dollars of their own money in
advance. Instead, it expected that after train operations began with high-
speed service on only about 300 miles of the 510-mile route, private investors would see how profitable the trains could be and put up $10 billion
to finish the system. Even with this optimistic assumption, however, the
authority's plan still depended on getting at least $28 billion in additional
federal funds.[24] Moreover, with the initial trains taking much longer than
2½ hours, ridership would be a lot lower than the initial projections, with
the authority estimating a range of between 6 million and 10 million trips
per year.[25]

The authority claims the trains are worth the cost because they will
relieve congestion, save energy, and reduce greenhouse gas emissions
and other pollution. The alternative to building high-speed rail, says the
authority, is much more expensive: building several whole new airports
and adding lanes to the entire length of freeway between Los Angeles and
the Bay Area. But there are much better ways of dealing with congestion.
For example, airlines can meet increased travel demand without building
new airports simply by using bigger planes.

As for highway congestion, the authority's environmental impact
statement predicted that high-speed trains would reduce highway traffic
between the Bay Area and the Central Valley by just 6.6 percent. In most
other segments, the reduction would be less than 3.5 percent.[26] Between
1996 and 2006, travel on California's rural freeways grew by 2.7 percent
per year. This means California could spend $70 billion and 15 years build-
ing high-speed rail, and just 17 months later, all the congestion relief it
would provide would have been absorbed by new traffic growth.

To make the claim that the trains would save energy, the authority made the mistake of assuming that automobiles and airplanes in 2030 would be no more energy efficient than they are today.[27] In fact, the fuel economy of both cars and airplanes is growing by an average of about 2 percent per year. After correcting for this assumption, train operations are still projected to save energy, though far less. But building the rail line would use large amounts of energy and emit similar amounts of greenhouse gases and other pollutants. Mikail Chester and Arpad Horvath, engineers at the University of California, Berkeley, calculate that using the authority's midlevel ridership projection, it will take 30 years to pay back the energy cost of construction and 70 years to pay back the greenhouse gases emitted during construction. Based on the authority's low ridership projection, neither would ever be repaid.[28] At the end of 30 years, of course, the rail line would need extensive reconstruction and rehabilitation, which will require more energy and generate even more greenhouse gas emissions.

The high-speed rail authority had already proven itself guilty of optimism bias when it originally projected construction costs that were only a quarter of the agency's current projection. Even that projection was optimistic, as the Federal Railroad Administration estimates that the actual cost of the first segment, which is now under construction, will be about 50 percent more than the projected amount.[29] If its ridership estimates are only half as optimistic as its cost estimates, the trains will have virtually no impact on congestion, energy consumption, and pollution.

MODERATE-SPEED RAIL FOR OTHER STATES

In addition to Florida and California, the Obama administration made high-speed rail grants to several other states, including Illinois, Michigan, New York, Ohio, Washington, and Wisconsin. It would be more appropriate to call these projects *moderate-speed rail*, because they propose to increase top speeds to no more than 110 miles per hour, and in many cases to no more than 79 miles per hour. In some cases, they also planned to increase the frequencies of trains, and rail advocates are counting on those increased frequencies, rather than increased speeds, to improve ridership.

Unlike the California and Florida plans, these projects would mix passenger and freight trains on the same tracks. BNSF and CSX, two of the nation's largest freight railroads, have stated they don't believe it would be safe to run passenger trains faster than 90 miles per hour on tracks shared with freight. Norfolk Southern has gone further by limiting passenger trains to 79 miles per hour, though all three railroads are willing to allow the government to build new tracks within their rights of way for trains that could travel up to 110 miles per hour.[30] Union Pacific seems willing to accept trains that would travel up to 110 miles per hour, but that may be because Illinois' Chicago–St. Louis high-speed rail project is also doubling Union Pacific's capacity to run freight trains in the corridor.

Illinois is spending $1.6 billion, $1.4 billion of which came from the federal government, on the Chicago–St. Louis route.[31] Although the state brags that the top speed on this route has been increased to 110 miles per hour, the truth is that trains reach this speed only on one 15-mile segment of the 284-mile route. Trains began operating at 110 miles per hour on that segment in 2012, yet as of early 2018, overall trip times remain the same that they were in 2009.[32]

The goal was to reduce travel times by about 40 minutes, increasing average train speeds from 51.6 miles per hour to 56.8 miles per hour.[33] These changes were supposed to take effect in 2014 but have been delayed to sometime in 2018 at the earliest. Even when the project is completely finished, however, the fastest train on the route will still be slower than driving.

The number of trains per day are also supposed to double, from four to eight in each direction. Despite the small speed improvement, Illinois planners predicted the additional trains would attract about 177,000 people a year out of planes and 800,000 people a year out of their cars. Amtrak trains currently have just 1 percent of the travel market in the corridor, and this project will not increase that by more than a fraction of a percent.

The state of Washington received $800 million in high-speed rail funds, and added $70 million of its own dollars, to improve the line between Seattle and Portland.[34] This project is supposed to reduce trip times by 10 minutes, from 3 hours and 40 minutes to 3 hours and 30 minutes. Over the 187-mile trip, train speeds will increase from an average of 53.4 to 56.1 miles per hour. Top speeds will be no more than 79 miles per hour anywhere in the corridor. The project is also supposed to increase frequencies from five daily roundtrips to seven. Although work began in 2010, speeds and frequencies remain unchanged as of 2017.

In this corridor, Amtrak has to compete against airlines, which offer 25 flights a day at prices starting around three times Amtrak's lowest fare; automobiles, which—if there is no traffic—take 30 fewer minutes than the fastest trains after the project is completed; and Bolt Bus, which offers six trips per day that take only 3 hours and 15 minutes and fares that are a bit more than half of Amtrak's. While increased frequencies may attract a few riders from Bolt's relatively unsubsidized buses to Amtrak's heavily subsidized trains, the 2.7-mile-per-hour speed increase is not going to change anyone's travel habits.

The Washington state Department of Transportation says the main purpose of the rail project is to deal with traffic congestion.[35] While Interstate 5 is heavily congested, especially near Portland and Seattle, a few trains per day are not going to do much to relieve that congestion even if every seat is filled with people who would otherwise drive.[36] Interstate 5 south of Seattle typically carries well over 100,000 vehicles a day each way, a number growing by more than half a percent per year. Amtrak's Seattle–Portland trains carry about 250 passengers, so two additional trains per day won't take more than 500 cars off the road, or less than half a percent of existing traffic.[37] Because only about half the seats on these trains are typically filled, the actual reduction will be much less. Considering traffic growth, any congestion relief will be negated in a few months.

Despite relying on existing tracks rather than building entirely new routes, both the Illinois and Washington projects cost more than $300 million for each one-mile-per-hour increase in average travel speeds. Moderate-speed rail projects in Michigan, New York, Pennsylvania, and other states produced similar results: high costs and trivial benefits.

AMTRAK'S $158 BILLION PROJECT

President Obama's initial round of high-speed rail grants specifically excluded Amtrak's Northeast Corridor from funding, as that route already has the fastest trains in America. Amtrak was a little upset about that, possibly because many people claim that Amtrak's Acelas aren't truly high-speed rail because they reach top speeds of only 130 miles per hour between New York and Washington, D.C., and 150 miles per hour, briefly, between New York and Boston. In order that it not be forgotten in the future, Amtrak prepared its own plan for turning the Northeast Corridor into a true, 220-mile-per-hour high-speed rail line. To make sure its plan would be shovel-ready the next time Congress was willing to shovel out high-speed rail funds, it wrote an environmental impact statement for the proposal.

In 2010, Amtrak published a brief paper estimating such a line would cost $117 billion (about $128 billion in today's dollars).[38] In 2012, it published an updated paper estimating the cost would be $150.5 billion in 2011 dollars (more than $160 billion today).[39] But the 2015 environmental impact statement contained the most in-depth analysis.

That report estimated that merely bringing the existing Northeast Corridor up to a state of good repair would cost $65 billion and increase ridership by 75 percent, from 19.3 million to 33.7 million riders per year. Building a completely new, 220-mile-per-hour line would cost between $272 billion and $302 billion, depending on the route, and at best would attract just 39.8 million riders per year. In other words, spending four times as much money would increase ridership by just 18 percent. The environmental benefits of such an increase would, of course, be trivial. Whereas the state-of-good-repair alternative was projected to reduce auto traffic in the corridor by 1.4 percent, the full high-speed rail alternative would reduce it by just 0.6 percent more.[40] Thus, the real question is not whether Congress should fund a new truly high-speed rail line in the corridor—it obviously shouldn't—but whether it should fund even the $65 billion to return the corridor to a state of good repair.

THE HYPERLOOP HYPE

As an alternative to high-speed rail, Tesla founder Elon Musk proposed in 2013 what he called a hyperloop, which would be small capsules or pods traveling between major cities at near supersonic speeds through tubes powered by linear-induction motors. He estimated it would be possible to build a pair of tubes—one for each direction of travel—between Los Angeles and San Francisco for $7.5 billion, roughly 10 percent of the cost of high-speed rail, and each tube could move capsules containing 28 people every two minutes, for a total of about 6 million trips per year.[41]

If it sounds too good to be true, it probably is. A company called Hyperloop One raised $160 million to try to implement Musk's idea, and soon thereafter, it calculated a cost-per-mile up to 10 times greater than Musk's original estimate.[42] Like the California high-speed rail, the actual costs would probably go much higher. Worse than that, any particular hyperloop can have only one origin and one destination (according to Musk), whereas trains can serve several destinations and automobiles millions. While it might be possible to design high-speed switches so hyperloop capsules could go to multiple destinations, they would complicate the system and increase costs even more.

Another alternative, a magnetically levitated train (maglev), has the same problem. At a cost of at least $36 billion, or more than $200 million per mile, Japan is planning to build a maglev line to supplement the high-speed trains between Tokyo and Nagoya, with an eventual extension to Osaka. To be completed no sooner than 2027, the line will have a top speed of more than 300 miles per hour and an average speed of more than 260 miles per hour.[43] As with the original *shinkansen*, this line could be successful because most of the travel in the corridor is by lower-speed trains.

Maglev will be less successful in the United States because people are already using automobiles for much of their travel. At a cost of about $200 million per mile, China built a 19-mile maglev line between Pudong airport and downtown Shanghai that reaches a top speed of 267 miles per hour. It fills only about 20 percent of its seats and loses up to $100 million a year, however, because it doesn't go where most people want to go. Interviews by *New York Times* reporter Howard French found most people preferred to take a taxi from the airport straight to their destination rather than take the maglev to downtown, only to have to take a taxi from there.[44]

The real problem with maglev, the hyperloop, and similar seemingly futuristic technologies is that they are infrastructure-heavy, point-to-point systems that cannot possibly compete with personal vehicles that can go just about anywhere or with an airline system that requires very little infrastructure and can serve far more destinations. The United States has 2.7 million miles of paved roads, 1.3 million miles of unpaved roads, and 15,000 airports. Any new transportation technology that can use this infrastructure at faster speeds or a lower cost than existing systems has a strong likelihood of success. New technologies that need new infrastructure will have to be significantly faster, more convenient, and less expensive than road- or airport-based technologies, or it simply won't be cost effective to build new infrastructure systems paralleling the existing ones.

Airplanes are successful because they don't require a lot of infrastructure. Unlike cars, they can't take people from door to door, but they can compete with driving because of their high speed and because they use so little infrastructure that the cost of flying is less than driving distances longer than a few hundred miles. High-speed rail, magnetically levitated trains, the hyperloop, and other fixed systems can't make that claim, and the cost of their infrastructure makes them prohibitively expensive relative to both flying and driving.

Echoing David P. Morgan's sweet-spot argument, the Federal Railroad Administration argues that high-speed rail is competitive with automobiles and airlines over distances of 100 to 600 miles.[45] The high speed overcomes the convenience of the automobile, while the potentially higher speed of airlines is hampered by airport security systems, boarding and taxi times, and time getting to and from airports that are typically on urban peripheries as opposed to centrally located rail stations.

In fact, high-speed trains fail to compete with the convenience of the automobile on routes up to several hundred miles. As previously noted, Amtrak brags that its Northeast Corridor trains carry more people than the airlines but admits that 89 percent of travel in the corridor is by car or bus.[46] This includes trips of 75 miles or longer, and most of those trips are no more than 230 miles (the distance from New York to Boston and New York to Washington). The automobile's convenience advantage rapidly declines on trips longer than 230 miles.

American airlines average 430 miles per hour from take-off to landing, but only 358 miles per hour from ramp to ramp.[47] This is still much faster than the fastest high-speed trains. Because shorter flights spend a higher percentage of their time taxiing, however, their average speeds are even lower, which helps to make high-speed rail more competitive.

Still, there are several ways of speeding air travel that cost far less than building high-speed rail. One is to complete the installation of modern, "nextgen" air traffic control systems. These systems promise to reduce airline delays, increase airport capacities, and boost average speeds by reducing the time waiting to land and reaching the gates.[48]

Another air travel improvement would be to speed airport security. To date, American rail travelers have been immune from lengthy security lines for the same reason Apple Macintosh computers were once immune from viruses: there simply aren't enough of them to attract attacks. Since the bombing of a high-speed train in Spain, however, security for European high-speed trains has become more stringent, as I learned when I arrived with seemingly plenty of time to spare at London's St. Pancras station to take a Eurostar train to Paris, only to find a lengthy security line complete with baggage x-ray machines that caused me to almost miss my train.

As for air travel, security lines have been nearly eliminated for air travelers who take the trouble to obtain "trusted traveler" status from the Transportation Security Administration (TSA). This requires a brief interview and an $85 fee every five years. The TSA says 99 percent of trusted travelers make it through security lines in less than five minutes. As of mid-2017, five million people have signed up for this program.[49]

The responsibility for air travel security should be transferred from the Transportation Security Administration to the airports themselves, with the TSA in a monitoring and regulatory role. Currently, the TSA regulates itself—never a formula for high quality control. In most European countries, the screening is done by the airports themselves or by government-certified security companies. Airport and private screeners tend to work faster but with higher quality control (meaning they find more proscribed items than TSA does).[50]

Security issues aside, it is possible that high-speed trains could compete with airline speeds on routes of 400 miles or less. However, they could not compete with airline costs. Airline fares average around 15 cents per passenger mile, whereas Amtrak collected fares averaging 90 cents per passenger mile for its Acela trains.[51] Projects such as the California high-speed train and high-speed trains elsewhere can compete with airline fares only with heavy taxpayer subsidies. With those subsidies, being able to outcompete airlines is not a victory but "an additional social cost of this investment," say Spanish economists Daniel Albalate and Germà Bel. They add that even where high-speed trains manage to emit less greenhouse gases and other pollutants than aircraft, "it turns out to be an extremely expensive way of achieving only modest reductions of emissions."[52]

Japan proved high-speed rail can work in extremely dense corridors in a country with very low rates of auto ownership and large numbers of riders on low-speed trains. On the other hand, Europe proved that heavily subsidized high-speed trains in countries with high rates of auto owner-ship fail to significantly increase rail's share of overall travel. There is no reason to think it would be any different in the United States and every reason—including the actual predictions of rail proponents—to think high-speed rail here would cost a lot and produce insignificant benefits.

18. PASSENGER RAIL IN AMERICA'S TRANSPORTATION FUTURE

It would be simpler if the train were just a means of moving people. But the train is also photogenic and nostalgic and fun, a source of employment and taxes, the pride of every Chamber of Commerce, and something on which you hang mail and express cars at one end and a business car at the other. And because trains stir up so much emotion, they are susceptible to the magnificent myth, if not the lie.

—David P. Morgan

Americans love passenger trains; at least many of them do. They may not ride Amtrak or rail transit, but they flock to the roughly 200 tourist railroads and 100 or more railroad museums scattered around the country. Steamtown National Historic Site in Scranton, the Strasburg Railroad, the Railroad Museum of Pennsylvania near Lancaster, and other rail attractions may be the biggest sources of tourist dollars in Pennsylvania. Fans have formed historical societies for every major railroad and many of the minor ones, and most of these organizations publish quarterly journals that dig down into the most intricate details of rail operations. In 2010, someone estimated there are at least 900 groups around the United States dedicated to railroads and rail history, not counting model railroad groups.[1] Though they study all trains, a disproportionate amount of their efforts focus on passenger trains and the locomotives that pull them.

Model railroading is a billion-dollar industry, with dozens of manufacturers vying to produce the most precise replicas, down to the last rivet, of locomotives, passenger, and freight cars. Again, passenger trains receive a disproportionate share of attention, with several manufacturers issuing replicas of entire trains such as the *California Zephyr, Empire Builder,* and Southern Pacific *Daylight.* Online modeler forums see endless debates about the best way to imitate the look of stainless steel in plastic or brass, the exact shade of green Pullman used to paint its passenger cars, and whether the dimensions of each particular manufacturer's models are correct to the nearest scale inch.

Those who don't have the time or budget to model but still like to look at trains can use Microsoft Train Simulator, which comes with a number of landscapes, including Amtrak's Northeast Corridor and the Great Northern Railway's main line across the Rocky Mountains along the southern boundary of Glacier National Park. Using Simulator, you can pretend you are in the cab of a locomotive, a domecar, or a helicopter watching the train wind its way through the mountains and prairies. Various other companies have issued add-ons to Simulator, including different landscapes and trains such as photo-perfect versions of Great Northern's *Empire Builder,* that allow train enthusiasts to ride across the Rockies or any other landscape.

In 1983, I rode the final run of the domecar–laden *Rio Grande Zephyr,* the last Silver-Age train in America, and wrote about it for *Passenger Train Journal.* Afterward, depressed about Amtrak's relatively mediocre train service, I joined the thousands of people who collect railroad memorabilia, including sleeping car blankets, dining car china and tablecloths, and especially booklets, brochures, and other paper advertisements issued by the railroads to entice people to take their trains to Yellowstone Park, California, or various other destinations. I've digitized most of my collection of paper items and posted some 20 gigabytes of PDF versions on line at streamlinermemories.info.

All these things—modeling, collecting, simulating, restoring, and operating steam locomotives and passenger cars—are ultimately futile attempts to recreate our nostalgic view of what life was like when people traveled by train rather than by airplane or automobile. In a very real sense, Amtrak and urban rail transit projects are just more attempts to do the same.

The last piece of research I did for this book was to ride three Amtrak long-distance trains on a 3,770 trip across the United States: the *Coast Starlight* from Portland to Sacramento, the *California Zephyr* from Sacramento to Chicago, and the *Capital Limited* from Chicago to Washington, D.C. The trains I rode were clean and comfortable; Amtrak personnel were friendly and helpful; the food was more expensive than Denny's but not as good; and the large windows in the sightseer lounge cars offered thrilling views of outstanding scenery, even if not as good as those from the domecars of the 1950s and 1960s.

Although Amtrak has successfully resisted Transportation Security Administration screening programs similar to those in airports, I learned on this trip that it hasn't been able to prevent Drug Enforcement Administration personnel from boarding trains in the middle of the night, waking passengers to paw through their luggage in search of drugs or, even better, cash they can confiscate under asset forfeiture programs.[2] I'd rather have the TSA.

Along the way, I chatted with many of my fellow passengers and realized these long-distance trains serve two different markets. The cost of a coast-to-coast trip across the country by coach starts at about $232, but a room in a sleeping car adds anywhere from $1,000 to $1,750. Although the sleeping room can be shared by two people and the price includes meals in the dining car, that's still a hefty premium that makes planes less expensive for most long-distance travel. Amtrak doesn't separate its costs between coach and sleeping cars, so it is hard to tell if subsidies to sleeping car passengers are the same, more, or less than those to coach passengers.

The people in the sleeping cars tend to be well-to-do and often retired; people for whom time isn't an issue and who don't like the cramped seating on board planes. They wanted a cruise-train experience where they could walk around, watch scenery in the lounge, eat in the dining car, enjoy a shower, and fall asleep to the rocking train. The most common comment I heard from these people was that the trains were "pleasant," and they were probably willing to pay even higher fares if the federal government ended subsidies to the trains.

The people in the coaches tended to be lower income and young, people for whom the main issue was cost. They chose the train over the plane because planes were either more expensive or not available on the particular route they were taking. Most of them would choose to fly if it were less expensive on the route they were taking, but they agreed trains were more pleasant than buses and would be willing to pay a little more for the train than a bus. When I told them the subsidy for each of the trains we were riding on was more than $100 per passenger, they admitted that, if fares were raised that much, they would probably end up flying or taking a bus.

Although Amtrak trains may be more pleasant than planes or buses, they manage to carry only about one-quarter to one-third of a percent of intercity travelers in the United States. Thus, for the vast majority, that pleasant experience is not enough to offset the higher costs, slower speeds, unreliability, and inconvenience of train travel. Even that tiny percent that rides the rails could make air travel almost as pleasant as Amtrak by obtaining a Known Traveler Number from the Transportation Security Administration, which would allow them to bypass most security lines, while purchasing first-class or premium coach tickets would provide them more legroom and other amenities.

THE TRANSIT APOCALYPSE

As I was writing this book, the nation's transit industry was undergoing a traumatic and possibly irreversible decline. Nationally, ridership has fallen every year since 2015. Forty-eight of the nation's 50 largest urban areas saw fewer transit riders in 2017 than 2016.[3]

In many cases, the declines are catastrophic for transit agencies that depend on fare revenues for a significant portion of their operating budgets. Since 2009, Memphis has lost 41 percent of its transit riders; Sacramento lost 36 percent; Detroit 34 percent; Milwaukee 26 percent; and Cincinnati 17 percent. Similarly, since 2012, Virginia Beach-Norfolk lost 24 percent; San Antonio lost 22 percent; Riverside-San Bernardino 21 percent; and Austin 19 percent of their riders. Of the nation's 10 largest urban areas, seven have seen double-digit losses in the last few years.[4]

Rail transit has not immunized transit agencies and regions from ridership declines. In many cases, it accelerates it as agencies cannibalize their bus services to pay for rail construction and maintenance. An August 2017 article in the *Washington Post* lauded Los Angeles for "find[ing] a way to get people out of their cars": new light-rail lines.[5] What the article failed to note, however, was that light-rail construction was accompanied by severe cuts in bus service, resulting in the loss of nearly five bus riders for every new rail rider.[6]

Only two major urban areas have so far avoided the post-2010 decline in transit: Seattle and Houston. Seattle gained new riders by opening two extremely expensive light-rail lines—one cost $200 million per mile and the other more than $600 million per mile—without, so far at least, cutting bus service. Houston followed the more typical pattern of opening a light-rail line in 2004, cutting bus service, and then losing more bus riders than it gained rail riders. However, in 2015, Houston took the brave step of completely redesigning its bus system on a grid pattern rather than a hub-and-spoke pattern centered on downtown.[7] This shortened the ride for many passengers who weren't going downtown. Since then, ridership has been growing, but it has not yet recovered to its prerecession levels.

A major cause of the national decline in transit ridership appears to be ride-sharing services such as Uber and Lyft. A recent survey found that one-third of Uber and Lyft patrons said that were it not for ride-sharing, they would have taken transit.[8] Ridesharing is growing about twice as fast as transit ridership is falling, so roughly two-thirds of the decline may be due to the growth of ridesharing.

Since 1970, the transit industry has been able to count on periodic spikes in oil prices, usually due to Mideast troubles, to help recover ridership, not to mention provide justification for further subsidies to rail. Thanks to hydraulic fracturing, however, the United States has become, if not energy independent, at least more in control of its energy prices. Thus, neither low gas prices nor ridesharing are going away anytime soon.

Freefalling transit ridership has so far failed to discourage cities and transit agencies from planning expensive new rail lines. The mayor of San Antonio, where transit ridership dropped by 22 percent between 2012 and 2016, nevertheless wants to bring rail transit back to the first major city in America to replace its streetcars with buses.[9] The mayor of Nashville proposed a $5.2 billion transit plan, including 29 miles of light rail, a plan that voters rejected in May 2018.[10] Tampa's transit agency wants to build a light-rail line to St. Petersburg.[11] Durham has proposed a $2.4 billion light-rail line that would take an extremely circuitous route to Chapel Hill.[12] All of these plans are based on an outmoded view of cities and transportation that fails to account for new transportation technologies and urban land-use patterns.

TECHNOLOGY REPLACEMENTS

The history of passenger transportation is really a story of successive technology replacements. Omnibuses replaced walking, horsecars replaced omnibuses, cable cars replaced some horsecars, and then electric streetcars replaced both horsecars and cable cars. Railroads replaced steamboats; coal-powered, steel passenger trains replaced wood-powered, wooden passenger trains; and they in turn were replaced by diesel streamliners. While streamliners temporarily boosted rail travel, the long-run trend was for automobiles and buses to replace urban and short-distance intercity trains and for airplanes to replace long-distance trains.

One of the most abrupt technology replacements in history was when the railroads replaced steam locomotives with diesels in the 1950s, much to the distress of those who loved the sounds and sights of expanding water vapor pushing pistons turning wheels and sending clouds of steam and smoke high into the sky. "The end is in sight for much that is picturesque and stirring to the imagination in the railroad scene," mourned popular writer Lucius Beebe in 1938. "Electrification, diesel power and the frequently fatuous devices of streamlining do not quicken the heart. Romance and glory are implicit in outside motion, in side rods, crossheads, eccentrics and the implacable rhythm of counter-balanced driving wheels reeling off the miles."[13]

"As for diesels, I respect what they will do," said photographer O. Winston Link in 1957, "but a world without steam engines would appear almost as bad as a world without women, Beethoven, autumn foliage, or peppermint stick ice cream."[14] Lovers of steam locomotives pleaded with the railroads to preserve some examples of the more than 100,000 steam locomotives that had been built in America, and some 1,400 were placed in museums or allowed to rust in city parks. Eventually, about 350 were restored to operation, mostly by volunteers. But no one ever suggested the federal government should spend a billion dollars a year to subsidize steam locomotives so that people could have the pleasant experience of hearing a steam locomotive and getting cinders in their eyes from burning coal. Likewise, horses are no longer used for serious travel, but America has the largest horse population in the world thanks to people who love horses, not federal subsidies.[15]

WHY DO WE SUPPORT TRAINS WE DON'T RIDE?

Given that Americans have accepted other technology replacements without demanding that the federal government try to turn back the clock, what makes passenger rail different? Why are we spending more than $20 billion a year building, operating, and poorly maintaining rail transit lines? Why are we spending a billion and a half dollars a year subsidizing Amtrak and contemplating spending hundreds of billions, if not trillions, more building high-speed trains?

Other than the fact that politically powerful contractors make a lot of money from rail engineering, design, and construction, the most important answer is that too many people have misconceptions about transportation and cities. Many still think in terms of monocentric cities. Others fantasize that everyone else will ride trains so they can drive on uncongested roads. Few realize trains were always about serving the elite, not the common people.

"Imagine it's 1881," rail proponent James Howard Kunstler suggested to the Florida chapter of the American Institute of Architects in 1998. "You leave the office on Wabash in the heart of vibrant Chicago, hop on a train in a handsome, dignified station full of well-behaved people, and in thirty minutes you're whisked away to a magnificent house surrounded by deep, cool porches, nestled in a lovely, tranquil, rural setting with not a single trace of industrial hubbub—no crowds, no machines, no stinking gutters, no noise, and, course, no highways, no strip malls, no muffler shops, no parking lots. Just the flowers and the trees." "This must have been a glorious way to live," he continued, both "heavenly" and "idyllic."[16] What he didn't say was that it was also expensive, and that only a tiny number of Americans, probably around 1 percent, were able to live that way.

For a time, streetcars and trains may have been the only mechanized forms of travel that allowed travelers to get to many places, but they were never the ubiquitous form of travel people misremember. At the 1920 peak of rail travel, the average American traveled 400 miles a year on intercity trains, and the average urban American took fewer than 300 urban transit trips per year, which probably equaled about 1,200 miles per year. But most Americans weren't average: for one thing, only about half in 1920 lived in urban areas, and rural Americans rarely if ever rode a streetcar or rapid-transit train. Even among urbanites, most unskilled workers couldn't afford to take transit to work, at least until assembly-line production led to pay increases that enabled those workers to buy cars. Even then, they still didn't ride transit. Before World War I, it is likely that a majority of Americans had never been on a streetcar or train, or, if they had, only once or twice in their lifetimes. After World War I, the car quickly replaced transit.

The mobility offered by trains and streetcars in 1920 pales in comparison to the mobility Americans enjoy today. The average American travels well over four times as many miles per year by commercial aircraft as Americans ever rode on intercity passenger trains, and today they travel at least 15 times as many miles per year by automobile as Americans ever rode on urban rail transit. While higher-income Americans do travel more than those with lower incomes, the difference is not as stark as it was in 1920: 92 percent of Americans live in households with at least one car, and almost all of them regularly travel by car. While the most expensive Bentley and cheapest Yugo have the same access to the road, trains were always an elitist form of travel.

Air travel is not quite as egalitarian as automobiles, but it is more so than trains. Polls show that about half of all Americans fly in any given year, and 90 percent have flown at least once in their lives.[17] Americans are more mobile today than they were a hundred years ago, partly because travel is less expensive than it was and partly because mobility has made us wealthier. We can't go back to exclusive reliance on more expensive forms of travel without also suffering a decline in incomes and an increase in inequality.

Passenger trains and urban transit grew simultaneously with American cities because of an unprecedented confluence of technologies that promoted both mass transit and centralized cities. Steam powered the early trains and centralized factories. Bessemer steel provided the rails for trains to roll on and the frames to hold up skyscrapers. Electricity powered the streetcars and rapid-transit trains as well as the elevators to access the upper floors of those skyscrapers, some of which contained electric-powered factories and offices. The telegraph and other electric communications allowed railroads to put more trains on the same tracks and helped financiers trade stocks and commodities. The result was the monocentric city with financial firms, factories, and shops at the center surrounded by residential areas with streetcars, rapid transit, and commuter trains giving those who could afford to ride them access to the downtowns.

Such monocentric cities had never been seen before in history and lasted less than a century before new technologies reversed the trends toward centralization. The first was the moving assembly line, which shifted factories to the suburbs, where land was cheap. The second was the automobile, produced in some of those factories, which made it affordable for ordinary workers to move to the suburbs previously reserved for the upper and middle classes. The third was the electrical and telecommunications grid that enabled people in the suburbs to enjoy the same comforts originally found only in city centers.

The most important result of these changes was that monocentric cities became polycentric cities. In 1920, nearly 40 percent of American workers (which means well over half of urban workers) worked in factories, so the movement of those factories from city centers to the suburbs represented a huge change in transportation patterns.

These decentralizing forces had an impact on intercity rail travel. The automobile gave people a more flexible, convenient, and lower-cost alternative to trains. Autos also allowed working class families to find low-cost land and build homes in urban peripheries, thus achieving what became known as the American dream but which was really more of an immigrant or working-class dream.[18] The resulting lower density development made getting to and from train stations less convenient than when most urbanites lived within walking distance of either city centers or a rail transit line going to the center. For a time, trains remained the mode of choice for long-distance travel, but autos and buses displaced them for trips of 100 miles or less.

THE DOWNTOWN COUNTERREVOLUTION

Downtown property owners and central city officials attempted a counterrevolution that aimed to restore the monocentric city to its former glory. Cincinnati's failed attempt to build a subway, San Francisco's later construction of the Bay Area Rapid Transit system, and Atlanta's construction of its rapid-transit system were all examples of this counterrevolution. BART was only a partial success: downtown San Francisco has more jobs than all but three other downtowns in the country (New York, Chicago, and Washington), but still has less than 15 percent of jobs in the San Francisco-Oakland area (and barely 10 percent if San Jose is included). Because Atlanta, unlike San Francisco, had never been a monocentric city, its rapid-transit system was a complete failure, as only 7 percent of the region's jobs are located in the city center today.[19]

It took many urban planners more than 50 years to finally accept the fact that the polycentric city had replaced the monocentric city. It wasn't until the 1990s that planners began actively planning for polycentric urban areas in the name of *new urbanism* and *smart growth*. Yet they were too late: by that time, the polycentric city had been replaced by the nanocentric city, as service jobs replaced manufacturing jobs in importance. New urbanism would fail as a counterrevolution against nanocentrism just like the construction of rapid-transit lines in San Francisco and Atlanta failed as a counterrevolution against polycentrism. Even in the polycentric era, the planners' notion of connecting job centers with rapid transit or light rail, as Denver and Dallas are trying to do, did not work as well as using buses, because buses are far less expensive and can quickly and easily change routes as new job centers open and others close.

Government programs to promote monocentric cities by building rapid transit and promote polycentric urban areas by building light rail have almost invariably suffered cost overruns averaging close to 40 percent and, in most cases, ridership shortfalls also averaging 40 percent. To pay for the cost overruns, transit agencies cut bus service, raised fares, and put themselves deeply in debt, which reduced their ability to respond to changes in the economy. If a recession reduces the tax revenues that support an agency by 10 percent, but the agency has dedicated half of those revenues to debt service, then it may have to cut transit service by 20 percent, a simple equation that devastated transit service in San Jose after the dot-com crash.

High-speed rail programs outside the United States have produced similar results: cost overruns, ridership shortfalls, and huge debts that threaten the economic future of entire nations. A large part of Japan's and Spain's economic doldrums can be traced directly to politically driven programs of providing high-speed train service to every corner of those countries. If California were a country, its economy would be larger than France's, yet it apparently cannot afford to build a Los Angeles–San Francisco high-speed rail line. Attempts to do so will create similar problems for that state's economy for decades.

After Buffalo opened a light-rail line in 1989 that cost 50 percent more and attracted 50 percent fewer riders than projected, the city was wise enough to build no more. But such wisdom has been rare, especially with the federal government offering billions of dollars a year for rail construction and contractors lobbying local governments to build anything at all that could earn them profits. Given the high costs and high risks from building rail transit or intercity rail lines, it is hard to imagine just what, aside from the political benefits, their advocates consider to be a success, and how expensive a project would have to be before they are willing to say it doesn't make sense.

Certainly, potential profitability is absolutely *not* a criterion they consider valid. Based on the untrue claim that all transportation is subsidized, they don't want anyone to judge their projects according to the subsidies they require. Once potential profitability as a criterion is jettisoned, it is a few short steps to go from spending $20 million a mile on San Diego's original light-rail line to spending $626 million a mile on Seattle's latest light-rail line. Nor do proponents lose their enthusiasm for a high-speed rail line that an economic analysis shows will cost more to use than flying or driving even after the projected cost quadruples or more.

Once the projects are completed, it is easy for reporters to find passengers who think they are great. Who wouldn't be thrilled to pay less than $3 to ride a train that costs taxpayers another $55 per ride? Because that cost is distributed among thousands of taxpayers, it is hard to find ones who are even aware they are paying it much less ones who are disgruntled about it. If you subsidize something enough, people will use it—but that doesn't make it a success.

One of the criteria proponents frequently bring up is the need to have "balanced" transportation systems. No one ever suggests that the federal government should create balance by subsidizing dirigibles, sailing ships, or Conestoga wagons. Instead, "balanced" apparently means trains, and some advocates argue that the federal government should spend as much on Amtrak, high-speed rail, and urban rail transit as it spends on highways, even though highways carry 85 percent of all passenger travel and 30 percent of freight, while passenger trains and rail transit together carry less than 1 percent of passenger travel and virtually no freight. Moreover, since 1956, nearly all the money the federal government has spent on highways, and most of the money spent by states, has come from highway users, whereas almost none of the money they spend on trains comes from train riders.

Rail is the high-cost solution to any problem involving passenger transport. Need to get from New York from Washington, D.C.? Amtrak's *Acela* charges 90 cents a passenger mile, while airfares start at 25 to 35 cents a mile and the most expensive tickets sold by Megabus and Bolt Bus are less than 20 cents a mile. Need a transit line from Denver to Boulder? A rail project for this corridor is projected to cost $1.4 billion, while a bus rapid-transit line cost $511 million, including construction of new highway lanes open to other vehicles that will relieve congestion for everyone.[20] Need a downtown circulator to help shoppers and tourists reach stores and landmarks? A streetcar line can cost upwards of $200 million, while a few trolley-style buses might cost less than $2 million.

To many politicians, of course, the cost *is* the benefit—especially when the federal government is paying a large share of it—because it means more money to hand out to contractors and suppliers. To everyone else, it is an increased tax burden that can last for decades.

Instead of building transit that fits American cities, transit agencies and urban planners want to build rail transit suitable only for very high-density cities and then become land-use czars to force massive lifestyle changes so that people will be more likely to ride their trains and cities will look more like the monocentric or polycentric regions that urban planners dream of.

In short, political support for Amtrak and rail transit comes from a variety of interest groups. Some expect to profit from rail construction. City officials see rail as a way of controlling where people live, thus herding tax revenues into their own treasuries rather than those of the suburbs. Transit agencies and urban planners want to turn back the clock to the days when working class families were stuffed into high-density housing while middle- and upper-class families could enjoy the peaceful suburbs. Senators and representatives realize that the small minority of citizens that gain from funding passenger rail are much louder than the majority who share the costs. The commercial interests are happy to gain the support of nostalgia buffs and environmentalists who pretend that rail is green transportation.

Bucking these interest groups, the Trump administration has proposed to end federal support for Amtrak's long-distance trains and transit capital grants under the New Starts and TIGER programs.[21] Whether Congress will go along with this remains to be seen, but it is a good first step toward ending policies designed to maintain and expand obsolete forms of transportation. A better step, in Amtrak's case, would be for the federal government to simply offer to pay Amtrak 10 cents for every passenger mile it carries and then let Amtrak decide which routes to keep and which to shut down. Then the debate could focus on how much the subsidy should be rather than whose trains get subsidized.

THE REAL FUTURE OF TRANSPORTATION

As urban leaders plan for the future by trying to recreate the past, a new replacement technology that is just around the corner doesn't fit into any of those plans: autonomous, or self-driving, cars. Ford, GM, Google (under the name of Waymo), Nissan, Tesla, Uber, and Volkswagen are among the many companies racing to put such cars on the market by 2020 or soon thereafter.

"Ford is going to be mass-producing vehicles with full autonomy in five years," Ford's president Mark Fields promised in 2016. "That means there's going to be no steering wheel, there's not going to be a gas pedal, there's not going to be a brake pedal, and of course, a driver is not going to be required."[22] Initially, Fields predicted, these cars will be in an Uber-like ride-sharing service in major American cities, but eventually they will be for sale to those who prefer to own rather than share cars. Not to be outdone, General Motors has promised to have fleets of autonomous cars, with no steering wheel or pedals, in driverless taxi service by 2019.[23] Waymo has already begun such service on a limited scale in the Phoenix area.[24]

Autonomous ride-sharing will give potential travelers who don't want to own their own cars a choice between having an autonomous car pick them up at their door and take them straight to their destination or walking to a transit stop, waiting for a bus or train, taking that transit vehicle as it makes several intermediate stops, possibly transferring to another transit vehicle, then walking from their stop to their destination. Autonomous ride-sharing is expected to cost much less than Uber and Lyft cost today because there will be no need to pay drivers. Obviously, most people will prefer the ride-sharing service, and even if it costs a little more than transit fares, it will cost less than transit's total costs, including subsidies.

Some transit agencies admit that human-operated ride-sharing services are responsible for low transit ridership numbers.[25] Despite declining ridership, some people continue to support construction of new rail transit lines. Most of that support comes from contractors expecting to profit from construction and environmentalists who irrationally hate automobiles even though it is far easier to build a green auto than it is to persuade people to stop driving and start riding transit.

Once driverless ridesharing is available, there will be little justification to continue subsidizing transit, and most rail transit lines outside of New York City will turn into streaks of rust. At most, state or local governments may want to give transportation vouchers to low-income people that they can use for any ride-sharing service or other common carrier, a step that would cost much less than subsidizing transit for people of all incomes. In the end, the argument for subsidies to any form of transportation is weak. The main beneficiaries of transportation are the people who use it, and all that subsidies do is create demand for more subsidies. Ideally, the federal, state, and local governments will end all subsidies to transportation.

We have the technology to collect road user fees based on the number of miles people drive without invading their privacy. My home state of Oregon was the first to impose a gas tax to pay for roads in 1919, and now is the first to experiment with a mileage-based user fee. I was one of the first volunteers in this experiment, and one of the things the experiment taught me is how little I actually pay to use the roads I drive on. Nearly all gas taxes go to the states, which share only a small portion with local governments, forcing those local governments to spend tens of billions of dollars in general funds on city streets and county roads. This means state highways are relatively unsubsidized while local roads are subsidized. Mileage-based user fees will mean the fees people pay will go to the actual owners of the roads they are driving on, allowing cities and counties to end these local subsidies.

American airports today are funded mostly out of ticket fees collected by the airports and federal government. The federal fees, however, are distributed mainly to small airports. Sixty large airports accounting for 88 percent of air travel receive only 27 percent of the funds, while small airports that account for just 12 percent of air travel receive 73 percent of the funds. The nation would be better off privatizing airports, as has been done elsewhere. In Europe, for example, nearly three-quarters of air traffic uses airports that have been partially or wholly privatized.[26]

Once subsidies to highways and air travel completely end, one of the last arguments justifying subsidies to Amtrak and rail transit will fade away as well. New rail transit construction will grind to a halt the day the federal government stops dangling billions of dollars in subsidies in front of state and local governments. Existing rail lines should be replaced with buses as they wear out. If autonomous cars really do replace most transit in the cities, as I expect, Congress should permit cities that want to stop running empty railcars to do so, in spite of the federal grants that were used to build those rail lines.

Subsidies to Amtrak are only a small fraction of those to rail transit, but they are no easier to justify. Ending the subsidies would almost certainly mean an end to intercity passenger trains. Though the Northeast Corridor supposedly earns an operating profit, no private company would be willing to take it over so long as it has a $6 billion maintenance backlog, not to mention another $44 billion or so worth of ancient bridges and tunnels that need to be replaced. Even if the federal government were to replace all of that infrastructure and bring the rail lines up to a state of good repair before giving the line away, a private operator would only be able to keep running the trains until they and the tracks they roll on wore out again.

State-supported trains make even less sense than the Northeast Corridor, especially over routes where Amtrak owns and maintains the infrastructure or where states have been putting money into so-called high-speed trains such as between Chicago and St. Louis or New York City and Albany. Even discounting the infrastructure cost, an end to federal subsidies would mean states would have to increase their support by an average of at least 25 percent to keep the trains running. Many states may not be willing to pick up this additional cost, especially as innovative bus lines like Megabus and Bolt Bus expand and ride-sharing becomes more common.

The Florida East Coast Railway is attempting to start a moderately high-speed—up to 125 miles per hour—passenger service that will take cruise ship passengers docking in Miami to theme parks in Orlando. Known as Brightline, it has so far opened a line on existing tracks between Miami and West Palm Beach but has yet to raise the money needed to build 38 miles of new tracks between Cocoa and Orlando. If successful, it could be a model for private operation of day trains—but there are few other places in the country that have attractions such as cruise ships and Disneyworld located 200 miles apart.

Some long-distance trains might have a better chance of survival if reformulated as cruise trains catering to the wealthy who are willing to pay the full cost of running such trains. Attempts to create such trains in the past, such as the American Orient Express, have failed, but that failure was arguably because they had to compete with Amtrak. Most railroads that now host Amtrak would be willing to accept trains whose owners could pay for the variable costs of adding one more train to the rail line, while freight trains would pay most of the costs of maintenance and depreciation of that line.

When Via, Canada's version of Amtrak, ceased operating its trains over the beautiful mountain passes between Vancouver and Calgary through Banff, a private company named the Rocky Mountaineer started a successful cruise train on that route. Instead of providing sleeping accommodations, all passengers ride in coaches with large windows, and the trains operate only during daylight, stopping in cities so passengers can spend the nights in hotels. Without competition from Amtrak, such cruise trains might be successful on such scenic routes as San Francisco to Denver, Los Angeles to the Grand Canyon, Seattle to Glacier and/or Yellowstone parks, Seattle to Los Angeles, and New York to Florida. But long-distance cruise trains probably could not succeed in the Great Plains and Midwest, where the scenery is much less exciting, which would mean there would probably be no national system that people could ride coast to coast.

All this is, of course, speculation. As much as I love intercity passenger trains, I am pessimistic that any could or should survive except for tourist trains and a few cruise trains.

If I am uncertain that many intercity passenger trains could survive without subsidies, I am absolutely positive that no rail transit lines outside of New York and, possibly, Chicago and San Francisco could or should survive. If it is true, as suggested by Denver's experience with private bus operations, that a private operator could reduce costs by 50 percent, then only those lines that are covering close to half their operating costs out of fares have any chance of survival. That's pretty much limited to lines in the Big Six transit regions of Boston, Chicago, New York, Philadelphia, San Francisco, and Washington, D.C.

Of those regions, there would be no need to keep rails in Boston and Philadelphia, and possibly Chicago, where buses can almost certainly handle all the traffic now carried by rail for less money. The BART system offers relief for the Bay Bridge choke point between Oakland and San Francisco, but the advent of autonomous cars may provide equal relief, allowing the Bay Area to retire its expensive rapid-transit system. Only in Manhattan is the density of traffic too great for buses or autonomous cars to handle. In any case, the decision about whether to keep or shut down these lines should be made locally by the people who will have to pay for them.

On an Amtrak train at night, after most people have gone to sleep in their coach seats or sleeping car rooms, I like to stay in the sightseeing car, watching the lights of farms and towns go by and listening to the faint horn of the diesel locomotives signaling that we are about to cross a road or street. On the last night of my trip from Oregon to Washington, D.C., I thought about an article I had read asking, "Why can't America have great trains?"[27] I hope this book has made it clear that there are at least three answers to that question.

First, when we had great trains, they were used mainly by the elite, and that remains true of great trains in other countries today. Before 1910, it is likely that a majority of Americans had never traveled more than 50 miles from home, and most had never been on a train, while many others had taken only one or two train trips in their life. As James Hill observed, "the so-called 'travelling public' forms in reality but a small, and the more fortunate class of the community." If he was prejudiced against passenger trains, as some claim, it may have been for altruistic reasons, as the people who relied on freight trains "direct and indirect, include all. Hence, justice requires that railway systems . . . should be cautious not to favor passenger traffic at the necessary expense of freight payers."[28] It is neither sensible nor fair for the government to subsidize transportation catering mainly to the wealthy.

Second, new transportation technologies have replaced trains and streetcars. Planes are faster and less expensive for long distances; cars and buses are more convenient and less expensive for short distances; and there is no midrange distance at which passenger rail has an advantage over both cars and planes.

Third, and just as important, other new technologies, including the moving assembly line, telecommunications, and the electrical grid, have reshaped our cities so the urban patterns that once made rail convenient to large numbers (though never a majority) of people have been replaced by patterns in which rail makes no sense for passenger travel.

Although we might want great trains in our fantasy of what the world should be like, the reality is we don't need trains. Most Americans don't ride the trains we have, nor would they ride them even if they met some arbitrary definition of "great." We love passenger trains, and we will remember them in museums and tourist lines. But if the government stays involved in transportation at all, it should be to prepare for the next revolution in transportation, not to try to reverse the previous ones.

NOTES

Introduction

1. Robert Le Massena, "The Big Engines," *Trains*, June 1968, p. 43.
2. Ibid., p. 41.
3. Thomas G. Marx, "Technological Change and the Theory of the Firm: The American Locomotive Industry, 1920–1955," *Business History Review* 50, no. 1 (Spring 1976): 17.
4. David P. Morgan, "The Diesel That Did It: The Story of the 83,764-Mile Test That Doomed Steam," *Trains*, February 1960, pp. 22, 24; David P. Morgan, "Farewell to the FT: It's the End of the Line for the Original Diesel Freighters," *Trains*, March 1962, p. 42.
5. Ibid., p. 20.
6. Albert Churella, "Corporate Response to Technological Change: Dieselization and the American Railway Locomotive Industry During the Twentieth Century," *Business and Economic History* 25, no. 1 (Fall 1996): 28.

Chapter 1: The Transcontinental Railroads

1. Interview with WTMJ, Milwaukee, February 16, 2011, tinyurl.com/jfqezuh; Andrew Malcolm, "New Gaffe: Obama Hails America's Historic Building of 'the Intercontinental Railroad,'" *Los Angeles Times*, September 23, 2011, tinyurl .com/3c4p6sd.
2. George Rogers Taylor, *The Transportation Revolution: 1815-1860* (Armonk, NY: M. E. Sharpe, 1951), pp. 132–133.

3. Daniel Klein, "America's Toll Road Heritage," *in* Gabriel Roth (ed.), *Street Smart: Competition, Entrepreneurship, and the Future of Roads* (Oakland, CA: Independent Institute, 2006), pp. 280–281.

4. Ibid., pp. 290–291.

5. Taylor, *The Transportation Revolution*, pp. 33–34.

6. Ibid., pp. 44–45.

7. Ibid., pp. 49–50.

8. Ibid., pp. 36, 79.

9. Ibid., pp. 58–59, 63.

10. Ibid., p. 75.

11. Ibid., pp. 90–95.

12. Ibid., p. 96.

13. Ibid.

14. Richard White, *Railroaded: The Transcontinentals and the Making of America* (New York: Norton, 2011), pp. 17, 20.

15. Harry J. Carman and Charles H. Mueller, "The Contract and Finance Company and the Central Pacific Railroad," *The Mississippi Valley Historical Review* 14, no. 3 (December 1927): 336–337.

16. Ibid., p. 338.

17. White, *Railroaded*, pp. 29, 35.

18. Ibid., p. 23.

19. H. R. Meyer, "The Settlement with the Pacific Railways," *The Quarterly Journal of Economics* 13, no. 4 (July 1899): 433–444.

20. Albro Martin, *James J. Hill and the Opening of the Northwest* (St. Paul: Minnesota Historical Society, 1991), p. 277.

21. Ibid., p. 146.

22. Ibid., p. 348.

23. Ibid., p. 414.

24. Richard White, "Fast Train to Nowhere," *New York Times*, April 23, 2011, tinyurl.com/nxjfa2a.

25. White, *Railroaded*, p. 517.

CHAPTER 2: The Growth of Urban Transit

1. Robert M. Fogelson, *Downtown: Its Rise and Fall, 1880–1950* (New Haven, CT: Yale University Press, 2001), p. 11.

2. Andrea J. Sutcliffe, *Steam: The Untold Story of America's First Great Invention* (New York: Palgrave Macmillan, 2004), p. 209.

3. *Gibbons v. Ogden*, 22 U.S. 1 (1824).

4. Charles H. Winfield, *Hopoghan Hackingh: Hoboken, A Pleasure Resort for Old New York* (New York: Caxton Press, 1895), p. 53.

5. John Stevens, *Documents Tending to Prove the Superior Advantages of Rail-Ways and Steam Carriages over Canal Navigation* (New York: T&J Swords, 1812), p. x.

6. "The Stevens Family: First Family of American Railroading," Hoboken Museum, tinyurl.com/zspb3gm.

7. Ezra M. Stratton, *A World on Wheels, or Carriages, with their Historical Associations from the Earliest to the Present Time* (New York: Stratton, 1878), pp. 431–432.

8. Josette Desrues, *En Coach, En Tram, En bus: Le Paris-Saint-Germain* (Paris: Les Presses Franciliennes, 2005), pp. 34–36.

9. "A Word for All," World Wide Words, 1999, tinyurl.com/yaovw4vj.

10. Ezra M. Stratton, *A World on Wheels, or Carriages, with their Historical Associations from the Earliest to the Present Time* (New York: Stratton, 1878), pp. 432, 437–438.

11. *Facts and Figures 1979* (New York: New York City Transit Authority, 1979), p. 3.

12. Kenneth Jackson, *Crabgrass Frontier: The Suburbanization of America* (New York: Oxford University Press, 1985), p. 34.

13. Charles J. Kennedy, "Commuter Services in the Boston Area, 1835–1860," *The Business History Review* 36, no. 2 (Summer 1962): 155, 157–158, 161.

14. E. B. Grant, *Boston Railways: Their Condition and Prospects* (Boston: Little, Brown, 1856), p. 98.

15. *Historical Statistics of the United States Millennial Edition: Volume 1, Population* (New York: Cambridge University Press, 2006), table As14783, Boston Urbanized Area Population, 1800–1990.

16. Carl Abbott, "'Necessary Adjuncts to Its Growth': The Railroad Suburbs of Chicago, 1854–1875," *Journal of the Illinois State Historical Society* (1908–1984) 73, no. 2 (Summer 1980): 117–118, 121–122. Price of working-class homes from Donald L. Miller, *City of the Century: The Epic of Chicago and the Making of America* (New York: Simon & Schuster, 1996), p. 279.

17. Martina D'Amato, "Furnishings and Factory Life in the Modern Metropolis," *Visualizing Nineteenth-Century New York*, tinyurl.com/19CNYFurniture; Allan Pred, "Manufacturing in the American Mercantile City: 1800–1840," *Annals of the Association of American Geographers* 56, no. 2 (June 1966): 317, 324.

18. Stanley Lebergott, "Wage Trends, 1800-1900," *in* Conference on Research in Income and Wealth, *Trends in the American Economy in the Nineteenth Century* (Princeton: Princeton University, 1960), p. 457.

19. Pro Bono Publius, "Broadway Railway: Reply to the Omnibus Association's Objections," *New York Times*, August 3, 1852, p. 4.

20. Frank R. Ford, "Traffic Conditions of New York City," *Street Railway Journal* 18, no. 4 (October 1901): 226.

21. George W. Hilton, "Transport Technology and the Urban Pattern," *Journal of Contemporary History* 4, no. 3, Urbanism (July 1969): 123; "Street Railways During the Last Decade," *Street Railway Journal* 24, no. 15 (October 8, 1904): 598.

22. John A. Brill, "Twenty Years of Car Building," *Street Railway Journal* 24, no. 15 (October 8, 1904): 562.

23. Linda Cameron, "Before the Twin Cities Had Streetcars, There Were Horsecars," *MinnPost*, February 9, 2016, tinyurl.com/htaet4k.

24. "The Bentley-Knight Electric Railway System," *The Manufacturer and Builder* 21, no. 1 (January 1889): 8.

25. John R. Stilgoe, *Borderland: Origins of the American Suburb, 1820-1939* (New Haven, CT: Yale University Press, 1988), p. 131.

26. Ibid., p. 132.

27. Clay McShane and Joel Tarr, *Horse in the City: Living Machines in the Nineteenth Century* (Baltimore: Johns Hopkins University Press, 2001), pp. 64–65.

28. Roger D. Simon, *The City-Building Process: Housing and Services in New Milwaukee Neighborhoods, 1880–1910* (Philadelphia: American Philosophical Society, 1978), p. 15.

29. Hardin H. Littell, "History of the American Street Railway Association," *Street Railway Journal* 24, no. 15 (October 8, 1904): 517.

30. George W. Hilton, *The Cable Car in America: Revised Edition* (San Diego: Howell-North, 1982), p. 15.

31. John H. White, "War of the Wires: A Curious Chapter in Street Railway History," *Technology and Culture* 46, no. 2 (April 2005): 374.

32. Gerald Best, "Early Steam Suburban Railroads in Los Angeles," *The Railway and Locomotive Historical Society Bulletin*, No. 99 (October 1958): 10.

33. Ibid., pp. 23–26.

34. Hilton, "Transport Technology," p. 125.

35. John Anderson Miller, *Fares Please! From Horse-Cars to Streamliners* (New York: D. Appleton-Century, 1941), p. 43.

36. Hilton, "Transport Technology," p. 31.

37. William D. Middleton and William D. Middleton III, *Frank Julian Sprague: Electrical Inventor and Engineer* (Bloomington: Indiana University Press, 2009), pp. 82–84.

38. Charles W. Cheape, *Moving the Masses: Urban Mass Transit in New York* (Cambridge, MA: Harvard University Press, 1980), p. 7.

39. Hilton, "Transport Technology," p. 126.

40. Hugo R. Meyer, "Municipal Ownership in Great Britain," *Journal of Political Economy* 13, no. 4 (September 1905): 481.

41. Robert Peschkes, *World Gazetteer of Tram, Trolleybus, and Rapid Transit Systems—Part Four: North America* (London: Rapid Transit Publications, 1998), pp. 148–149.

42. Sean Craft, "The History of Speculative Real Estate Development and Streetcars in Northside (1880-1949)," *Brookland Park Post*, October 19, 2015, tinyurl.com/hyltbrh.

43. James Duane Bolin, "From Mules to Motors: The Street Railway System in Lexington, Kentucky, 1882-1938," *The Register of the Kentucky Historical Society* 87, no. 2 (Spring 1989): 128.

44. "Trolley Parks and Real Estate Development," Chevy Chase Historical Society, 2013, tinyurl.com/CCRkCkRy.

45. Jim Dubelko, "The Shaker Lakes Trolley," *Cleveland Historical*, tinyurl.com /ShakerTrolley.

46. "Rediscovering San Francisco's Parkside Neighborhood," *California History* 88, no. 2 (2011): 56.

47. William Friedricks, "Henry E. Huntington and Real Estate Development in Southern California, 1898-1917," *Southern California Quarterly* 71, no. 4 (Winter 1989): 339.

48. William Fulton, "'Those Were Her Best Days': The Streetcar and the Development of Hollywood Before 1910," *Southern California Quarterly* 66, no. 3 (Fall 1984): 238.

49. Greg Borzo, *Chicago Cable Cars* (Charleston, SC: History Press, 2012), p. 109.

50. George W. Hilton and John F. Due, *The Electric Interurban Railways in America* (Stanford: Stanford University Press, 1960), pp. 255, 394.

51. Ibid., pp. 395–396.

52. *Public Transportation Fact Book: 56th Edition* (Washington: American Public Transportation Association, 2005), p. 7.

53. Middleton, *Frank Julian Sprague*, p. 120.

54. Ibid., pp. 177–178.

55. Andrew Martin, *Underground, Overground: A Passenger's History of the Tube* (London: Profile Books, 2012), pp. 42–44.

56. "History of the Elevator," Mitsubishi Electric, tinyurl.com/ElevatorHist.

57. Middleton, *Frank Julian Sprague*, pp. 94–104.

CHAPTER 3: The Golden Age of Passenger Trains

1. Christiane Diehl-Taylor, "Passengers, Profits, and Prestige: The Glacier Park Hotel Company, 1914–1929," *Montana: The Magazine of Western History* 47, no. 2 (Summer 1997): 28.

2. *Historical Statistics of the United States: Colonial Times to 1970* (Washington: Census Bureau, 1975), volume II, series Q315, p. 730.

3. Martin, *Railroads Triumphant*, p. 121.

4. Emory M. Stevens, *A Manuscript History of the Stevens Family*, unpublished work, 1933, pp. 4, 9, 12.

5. Ralph Budd, Speech given at Glacier National Park, 1925, on file at Minnesota History Center, St. Paul, Great Northern Railway archives, advertising records, 133.H.4.4F, box 1, file 861.

6. Georgia Ray and Grace Flandrau, *Voice Interrupted* (Roseville, MN: Edinborough Press, 2007), pp. 81, 87.

7. Ibid., pp. 94, 103.

8. Letter from R. C. Craige, et al., to Great Northern Railway, February 1, 1925, on file at Minnesota History Center, St. Paul, Great Northern Railway archives, advertising records, 133.H.4.5B, box 2, file 861-7.

9. Lisa Blee, "The Fort Union Indian Congress: Divergent Narratives, One Event," *American Indian Quarterly* 31, no. 4 (Fall 2007): 585.

10. Agnes Laut, *The Blazed Trail of the Old Frontier: Being the Log of the Upper Missouri Historical Expedition* (New York: Robert McBride, 1926), p. 265.

11. Michael Kammen, "Business Leadership and the American Heritage," *Cornell Enterprise*, Fall 1986, p. 18.

12. Douglas V. Shaw, "The Great Northern Railroad and the Promotion of Tourism," *Journal of Cultural Economics* 13, no. 1 (June 1989): 70.

13. Diehl-Taylor, "Passengers, Profits, and Prestige," p. 33.

14. Ralph Budd, "The Relation of Highway Transportation to the Railway," Speech before the American Society of Civil Engineers, Kansas City, April 14, 1926, p. 8.

15. Ibid., p. 6.

16. "The Early Years: Expansion Continues," Greyhoundhistory.com.

17. Douglas V. Shaw, "Ralph Budd, the Great Northern Railway, and the Advent of the Motor Bus," *Railroad History* 166 (Spring 1992): 68, 73.

18. Ibid., pp. 74–75.

19. Martin, *James J. Hill*, p. 600.

CHAPTER 4: The Golden Age of Rail Transit

1. 2016 *Public Transportation Fact Book* (Washington: American Public Transportation Association, 2016), appendix A, table 1. This table shows numbers for 1890, 1902, 1907, 1912, 1917, and annually thereafter. Data for 1905 interpolated. Per capita urban trips were calculated using *Historical Statistics of the United States Millennial Edition: Volume 1, Population* (New York: Cambridge University Press, 2006), series Aa30.

2. Thomas Curtis Clarke, "Rapid Transit in Cities," *Scribner's Magazine*, May–June 1892, p. 567.

3. Clifton Hood, *722 Miles: The Building of the Subways and How They Transformed New York City* (Baltimore: Johns Hopkins University Press, 1993), p. 123.

4. Lawrence H. Officer and Samuel H. Williamson, "Annual Wages in the United States, 1774–Present," *Measuring Worth*, 2016, measuringworth.com/USwages/.

5. Hood, *722 Miles*, pp. 155–158.

6. Ibid., pp. 194–195.

7. Zachary M. Schrag, "'The Bus Is Young and Honest': Transportation Politics, Technical Choice, and the Motorization of Manhattan Surface Transit, 1919-1936," *Technology and Culture* 41, no. 1 (January 2000): 58.

8. Frederic C. Howe, "Municipal Ownership—The Testimony of Foreign Experience," *The Annals of the American Academy of Political and Social Science* 57, *Proceedings of the Conference of American Mayors on Public Policies as to Municipal Utilities* (January 1915): 194.

9. Robert H. Bremner, "The Civic Revival in Ohio: The Street Railway Controversy in Cleveland," *The American Journal of Economics and Sociology* 10, no. 2 (January 1951): 185–206.

10. Howe, "Municipal Ownership," p. 196.

11. Meyer, "Municipal Ownership in Great Britain," pp. 481–483.

12. Walt Crowley, "Street Railways in Seattle," *HistoryLink.org*, 2000, tinyurl.com /SeattleStRy.

13. Ibid., pp. 231–234.

14. Ibid.

15. "Monroe," *American Street Railway Investments: Edition of 1909* (New York: McGraw, 1909), p. 109.

16. *Report of the Street Railway Investigation Commission on the Problems Relating to the Street Railways of the Commonwealth* (Boston: State of Massachusetts, 1918), appendix E.

17. Jacob Riss, *How the Other Half Lives* (New York: Scribner's, 1890).

18. Edward M. Bassett, "Discussion of Transportation, Port and Terminal Facilities," *Proceedings of the Academy of Political Science in the City of New York* 5, no. 3, The Government of the City of New York (April 1915): 258.

19. John Francis Hylan, *John Francis Hylan, Mayor of New York: An Autobiography* (New York: Rotary Press, 1922), pp. 24–25.

20. Hood, *722 Miles*, pp. 203–205.

21. Ross D. Eckert and George W. Hilton, "The Jitneys," *Journal of Law & Economics* 15, no. 2 (October 1972): 293–294.

22. O. A. Mather, "Rise of Insull Power Empire Epic of Times," *Chicago Tribune*, April 16, 1932, p. 1, http://archives.chicagotribune.com/1932/04/16/page/27 /article/rise-of-insull-power-empire-epic-of-times.

23. Ibid., p. 170.

24. John F. Wasik, *The Merchant of Power: Samuel Insull, Thomas Edison, and the Creation of the Modern Metropolis* (New York: Palgrave McMillan, 2006), pp. 79, 179.
25. David Nye, *Electrifying America: Social Meaning of a New Technology* (Cambridge, MA: MIT Press, 1990), p. 277.
26. "Fifth Ave. Coach, Part 1," *Coachbuilt.com*, 2012, tinyurl.com/5thAveCoach.
27. Ibid.

CHAPTER 5: The Silver Age of Passenger Trains

1. John White, *The American Railroad Passenger Car* (Baltimore: John Hopkins University Press, 1978), p. 161.
2. Claudia Roth Pierpont, "The Silver Spire: How Two Men's Dreams Changed the Skyline of New York," *The New Yorker*, November 18, 2002, tinyurl.com/zfw7jf5.
3. Richard C. Overton, "Ralph Budd, Railroad Entrepreneur," *The Palimpsest*, November 1955, p. 457.
4. Mark Reutter, "Building a Better Iron Horse," *Railroad History*, Millennium Special (2000), p. 44.
5. Franklin M. Reck, *The Dilworth Story: The Biography of Richard Dilworth, Pioneer Developer of the Diesel Locomotive* (New York: McGraw-Hill, 1954), pp. 6, 10, 104.
6. Richard C. Overton, *Burlington Route: A History of the Burlington Lines* (New York: Knopf, 1965), pp. 394–395.
7. Reck, *The Dilworth Story*, p. 55.
8. Philip Hampson, "Chicago to Get One of World's Fastest Trains," *Chicago Tribune*, January 17, 1940, p. 1.
9. "Report on Streamline, Light-Weight, High-Speed Passenger Trains," Coverdale & Colpitts, New York, 1938, p. 6.
10. "83rd Annual Report of the Chicago, Burlington & Quincy Railroad Company," Chicago, Illinois, 1937, p. 9, tinyurl.com/TZFastest.
11. Richard C. Overton, "Ralph Budd—1879–1962," *The Railway and Locomotive Historical Society Bulletin*, No. 106 (April 1962), p. 84.

CHAPTER 6: The Decline of Urban Rail Transit

1. Eckert & Hilton, "The Jitneys," pp. 294–295.
2. Mitch Taylor, "Ford Model T Original Prices," *FordModelT.net*, 2011, www.fordmodelt.net/model-t-ford-prices.htm.

3. Carlos A. Schwantes, "The West Adapts the Automobile: Technology, Unemployment, and the Jitney Phenomenon of 1914-1917," *Western Historical Quarterly* 16, no. 3 (July 1985): 308.

4. Ibid., p. 314.

5. Eckert & Hilton, "The Jitneys," pp. 307–316.

6. Ibid., p. 322.

7. Albion W. Small, "The Ford Motor Company Incident," *American Journal of Sociology* 19, no. 5 (March 1914): 656.

8. Daniel Gross, "Henry Ford Understood That Raising Wages Would Bring Him More Profit," *The Daily Beast*, January 6, 2014, tinyurl.com/AffordtheProduct.

9. Tim Worstall, "The Story of Henry Ford's $5 a Day Wages: It's Not What You Think," *Forbes*, March 4, 2012, tinyurl.com/gwl7mwp.

10. *Highway Statistics Summary to 1995* (Washington: Federal Highway Administration, 1997), table MV-200; *Historical Statistics of the United States, Millennial Edition*, table Ae1–28, series Ae2.

11. Schrag, "The Bus Is Young and Honest," p. 58.

12. William S. Worley, *J. C. Nichols and the Shaping of Kansas City: Innovation in Planned Residential Communities* (Columbia, MO: University of Missouri Press, 1990), pp. 103–4.

13. Cynthia Mines, "Nichols' Folly," *Retail Traffic*, May 1, 1999, tinyurl.com/3.l9cyyu.

14. Fred Leeson, *My-T-Fine Merchant: Fred Meyer's Retail Revolution* (Portland, OR: Irvington Press, 2014), pp, 196–197.

15. Fogelson, *Downtown*, p. 229.

16. Ibid., pp. 240, 241.

17. William A. Luke, *Fageol & Twin Coach Buses: 1922–1956 Photo Archive* (Hudson, WI: Enthusiast Books, 2002), p. 8.

18. Fogelson, *Downtown*, pp. 60–61.

19. Walter Jackson, "The Past, Present and Future of the Motor-Omnibus," *Journal of the Society of Automotive Engineers* X, no. 3 (March 1922): 200–203.

20. Luke, *Fageol & Twin Coach Buses*, p. 5.

21. Henry R. Porter, "The Eastern and American Trackless Trolley Companies," *Trackless Trolley Gazette*, no. 504 (2015), pp. 1–3.

22. Henry R. Porter, "Laurel Canyon Utilities Company: America's First Trackless Trolley," *Trackless Trolley Gazette*, no. 505 (2015), pp. 1–3.

23. Felix E. Reifschneider and Henry R. Porter, "Staten Island Trolleybuses, 1921–1927," *Trackless Trolley Gazette*, no. 509 (2015), pp. 1–2, 10.

24. "Tom's North American Trolley Bus Pictures," trolleybuses.net, website accessed November 11, 2016.

25. Walter Jackson, "The Past, Present, and Future of the Motor Omni-Bus," *Electric Railway Journal* 59, no. 2 (January 14, 1922): 62.

26. Casey Piket, "History of the Trolley in Miami," Miami-History.com, February 6, 2012, tinyurl.com/MiamiTrolley.

27. Schrag, "The Bus Is Young and Honest," p. 58.

28. Hilton & Due, *Electric Interurban Railways*, pp. 186–187.

29. Ibid., p. 3.

30. Waskik, *The Merchant of Power*, p. 231.

31. Van Wilkins, "The Conspiracy Revisited," *The New Electric Railway Journal*, Summer 1995, p. 20.

32. William S. Lind and Glen D. Bottoms, "Expanding Public–Private Partnerships in Electric Railways: A Zero-Cost Conservative Proposal," Center for Public Transportation, 2016, pp. 4–5.

33. Bradford Snell, "The Streetcar Conspiracy: How General Motors Deliberately Destroyed Public Transit," originally published in *The New Electric Railway Journal*, reprinted in *Lovearth Network*, tinyurl.com/2ezr3r.

34. W. H. Lines, "Present Developments in Portland's Traction Problem," presentation to the Portland City Club, May 3, 1935.

35. Dan Haneckow, "Off Line Too Soon: Portland's Electric Buses," *Café Unknown*, October 9, 2006, tinyurl.com/PDXElectricBuses.

36. James J. Flink, *The Automobile Age* (Cambridge, MA: MIT Press, 1990), p. 365.

37. Gerry O'Regan, "The PCC Car—Not So Standard," *NYCSubway.org*, 1995, tinyurl.com/PCCNotStd.

38. Bradford Snell, Testimony before the Senate Subcommittee on Antitrust and Monopoly, *The Industrial Reorganization Act: Hearings before the Subcommittee on Antitrust and Monopoly on S. 1167, Part 4A*, 93rd Congress, 2d sess., 1974, p. 1839.

39. Bradford C. Snell, *American Ground Transport: A Proposal for Restructuring the Automobile, Truck, Bus, and Rail Industries* (Washington: U.S. Senate, 1973), p. 28.

40. Ibid., p. 3.

41. George Hilton, Testimony before the Senate Subcommittee on Antitrust and Monopoly, *The Industrial Reorganization Act: Hearings before the Subcommittee on Antitrust and Monopoly on S. 1167, Part 4A*, 93rd Congress, 2d sess., 1974, p. 2204.

42. Ibid., p. 2230.

43. Ibid., p. 2205.

44. Wilkins, "The Conspiracy Revisited," pp. 19, 21.

45. David M. Jones, *Urban Transit Policy: An Economic and Political History* (Englewood Cliffs, NJ: Prentice Hall, 1985), p. 62.

46. Snell, "American Ground Transport," p. 32.

47. Quoted in James A. Dunn, Jr., *Driving Forces: The Automobile, Its Enemies, and the Politics of Mobility* (Washington: Brookings Institution, 1998), p. 10. See also Sy Adler, "The Transformation of the Pacific Electric Railway: Bradford Snell, Roger Rabbit, and the Politics of Transportation in Los Angeles," *Urban Affairs Quarterly* 27 (September 1991): 51–86.

48. Scott L. Bottles, *Los Angeles and the Automobile: The Making of the Modern City* (Berkeley: University of California Press, 1987), p. 255.

49. John W. Diers and Aaron Isaacs, *Twin Cities by Trolley: The Streetcar Era in Minneapolis and St. Paul* (Minneapolis: University of Minnesota, 2007), p. 293.

50. Stephen B. Goddard, *Getting There: The Epic Struggle Between Road and Rail in the American Century* (Chicago: University of Chicago Press, 1994), pp. 125–135.

51. Jane Holtz Kay, *Asphalt Nation: How the Automobile Took over America and How We Can Take It Back* (New York: Crown Publishers, 1997), p. 171.

52. Martha J. Bianco, "Kennedy, 60 Minutes, and Roger Rabbit: Understanding Conspiracy-Theory Explanations of the Decline of Urban Mass Transit," presented at the 78th Annual Conference of the Transportation Review Board, Washington, D.C., January 1999, p. 19, tinyurl.com/BiancoConspiracy.

53. Harry Reasoner, "Clang! Clang! Clang! Went the Trolley," *60 Minutes*, December 6, 1987, tinyurl.com/zfu2erh.

54. Bianco, "Kennedy, 60 Minutes, and Roger Rabbit," p. 20.

55. Cliff Slater, "General Motors and the Demise of Streetcars," *Transportation Quarterly* 51, no. 3 (Summer 1997): 50–53, tinyurl.com/yuth5m.

56. Quoted in *Divided Highways: The Interstates and the Transformation of American Life*, Florentine Films, 1997, tinyurl.com/DividedHwys.

CHAPTER 7: The Decline of Intercity Passenger Trains

1. Chuck Spinner, *The Tragedy at Loomis Street Crossing* (Bloomington, IN: Author-House, 2012), p. 17.

2. William Patterson, "Investigation No. 2988: Accident at Naperville, Ill," Interstate Commerce Commission, Washington, D.C., July 30, 1946, pp. 7–8.

3. Ibid., p. 10.

4. Spinner, *The Tragedy at Loomis Street Crossing*, p. 85.

5. Patterson, "Investigation No. 2988," p. 12.

6. Ibid., p. 13.

7. Ibid., p. 2. Some reports say that 47 people were killed, but Spinner could document the names of only 45 people, the number in the ICC's report.

8. Spinner, *The Tragedy at Loomis Street Crossing*, p. 83.

9. Ibid., p. 84.

10. Patterson, "Investigation No. 2988," p. 2.

ROMANCE OF THE RAILS

11. Ibid., p. 12.

12. Middleton, *Frank Julian Sprague*, pp. 202–203, 217.

13. "Signaling Ordered on High Speed Lines," *Trains*, August 1947, p. 4.

14. Wallace W. Abbey, "Millions for Signals," *Trains*, November 1950, p. 45.

15. Theodore Brand, "ICC Is Charged with Slowing of Fast Trains," *Chicago Tribune*, October 19, 1947, p. 42.

16. "News of the Month," *Railway Signaling and Communications* 32, no. 9 (September 1939): 513.

17. Abbey, "Millions for Signals," p. 49.

18. *Report on Streamline, Light-Weight, High-Speed Passenger Trains* (New York: Coverdale & Colpitts, 1950), p. 11.

19. Ibid., p. 13.

20. Ibid., pp. 30, 40, 53, 64–65.

21. Ralph W. Hidy, Muriel E. Hidy, Roy V. Scott, and Don L. Hofsommer, *The Great Northern Railway: A History* (Cambridge, MA: Harvard Business School Press, 1988), p. 272.

22. John F. Strauss, Jr., *Great Northern Pictorial, Volume 3* (La Mirada, CA: Four Ways West, 1993), pp. 113–116.

23. Wesley S. Griswold, "Riding the Santa Fe's Split-Level Train," *Popular Science*, January 1957, pp. 138–139.

CHAPTER 8: The Municipalization of Urban Transit

1. John Pucher, Anders Markstedt, and Ira Hirschman, "Impacts of Subsidies on the Costs of Urban Public Transport," *Journal of Transport Economics and Policy*, Vol. 17, No. 2 (May 1983), p. 155.

2. "Ralph Budd," *Chicago Tribune*, February 6, 1962, p. 18.

3. "The CTA Takes Over: Resurrection by Modernization (1947–1970)," Chicago-L.org, 2000, chicago-l.org/history/CTA2.html.

4. Glenn Yago, *The Decline of Transit: Urban Transportation in German and U.S. Cities, 1900–1970* (New York: Cambridge University Press, 2006), pp. 171–172.

5. *Sixth Annual Report of the Chicago Transit Board for the Fiscal Year Ended December 31, 1950* (Chicago: Chicago Transit Authority, 1951), p. 9.

6. John Keats, *The Crack in the Picture Window* (New York: Houghton, 1956), p. xii.

7. Fogelson, *Downtown*, p. 11.

8. *Statistical Abstract of the United States: 1999* (Washington: Census Bureau, 1999), table 1432.

9. Edward M. Bassett, "The Freeway-A New Kind of Thoroughfare," *The American City*, February 1930, p. 95.

10. A complete list of municipalizations through 1975 can be found in the American Public Transportation Association's *2016 Public Transit Fact Book*, appendix A, table 130. In the text, "large cities" refers to the 100 largest cities at a given date.

11. Charles Lave, "It Wasn't Supposed to Turn Out Like This: Federal Subsidies and Declining Transit Productivity," *Access*, no. 5 (Fall 1994): 21–22.

12. American Public Transportation Association, *2016 Public Transportation Fact Book*, appendix A, tables 68 and 92. Dollars adjusted for inflation using gross national product deflator.

13. Ibid.

14. Ibid., table 20.

15. Ibid., tables 68 and 92.

16. Charles S. McCaleb, *Tracks, Tires and Trolleys: Public Transportation in California's Santa Clara Valley* (Glendale, CA: Interurban Press, 1981), pp. 124–125.

17. Ibid., pp. 125–127.

18. Bill Hale, "Passengers in Last Ride on Red Cars," *Los Angeles Times*, April 10, 1961, p. B1; "Streetcars Go for Last Ride," *Los Angeles Times*, March 31, 1963, p. N5.

19. Tim O'Neil, "Hodiamont Line Streetcar Closed Out 107 Years of Service," *St. Louis Post-Dispatch*, May 23, 2010, tinyurl.com/LastStLStreetcar.

20. John R. Schmidt, "The Last Years of Chicago Streetcars," WBEZ.org, October 5, 2012, tinyurl.com/LastChiStreetcar.

21. John Pucher, et al., "Impacts of Subsidies on the Costs of Urban Public Transport," p. 173.

CHAPTER 9: The Nationalization of Intercity Passenger Trains

1. Albro Martin, *Railroads Triumphant: The Growth, Rejection, and Rebirth of a Vital American Force* (New York: Oxford University Press, 1992), p. 127.

2. William Cameron Johnston, *Bathroom's Down the Hall: Or Roomers I Have Known* (New York: Exposition Press, 1951), p. 174.

3. Peter Lyon, *To Hell in a Day Coach: An Exasperated Look at American Railroads* (New York: Lippincott, 1968), p. 223.

4. Robert W. Harbeson, "The Transportation Act of 1958," *Land Economics* 35, no. 2 (May 1959): 168.

5. Morgan, "Who Shot the Passenger Train?" pp. 21–22

6. Gus Welty, "The Strange Case of NP's 'Mainstreeter': The Train the ICC Won't Let Die," *Railway Age*, December 15, 1969.

7. "Federal Supervision of Railroad Passenger Service: The Sunset Case, Dawn of a New Era or Monument to the Old?" *Duke Law Journal* 19, no. 3 (June 1970): 530.

8. Robert Downing, "Introduction," *in* John F. Strauss, Jr., *Rocky's Robe of Many Colors* (La Mirada, CA: Four Ways West, 1998), p. 6.

9. Fred Frailey, *Twilight of the Great Trains* (Milwaukee: Kalmbach Books, 1998), pp. 40–41.

10. Ibid., pp. 11, 18.

11. *Historical Statistics of the United States, Millennial Edition*, p. 4–785.

12. Howard Hosmer, *Railroad Passenger Train Deficit* (Washington: Interstate Commerce Commission, 1958), p. 69.

13. Stanley Berge, "Why Kill the Passenger Train?" *Journal of Marketing* 28, no. 1 (January 1964): 1.

14. Hosmer, *Railroad Passenger Train Deficit*, pp. 3–6.

15. Ibid., p. 16.

16. Ibid., p. 39.

17. Ibid., p. 43.

18. *Staff Report on Federal Aid to Airports* (Washington: Commission on Intergovernmental Relations, 1955), p. 26.

19. *The Commission on Intergovernmental Relations: A Report to the President for Transmittal to the Congress* (Washington: Commission on Intergovernmental Relations, 1955), pp. 170–171.

20. Hosmer, *Railroad Passenger Train Deficit*, p. 44.

21. Ibid., p. 39.

22. Hidy et al., *The Great Northern Railway: A History*, p. 251.

23. Hosmer, *Railroad Passenger Train Deficit*, p. 71.

24. Ibid., p. 28.

25. Ibid., pp. 29–30.

26. Ibid., p. 24.

27. Ibid., p. 69.

28. George W. Hilton, *Amtrak: The National Railroad Passenger Corporation* (Washington: American Enterprise Institute, 1980), p. 10.

29. David P. Morgan, "Who Shot the Passenger Train?" *Trains*, April 1959, pp. 16–17.

30. Ibid., pp. 21–25.

31. Ibid., pp. 45, 48.

32. Hosmer, *National Passenger Train Deficit*, pp. 59–60.

33. Morgan, "Who Shot the Passenger Train?" p. 29.

34. Ibid., pp. 36–39.

35. Ibid., p. 51.

36. James J. Hill, "The Country's Need of Greater Railway Facilities and Terminals," Speech before the annual dinner of the Railway Business Association, New York, December 19, 1912, p. 10.

37. Joseph B. Eastman, "The Advantages of National Operation," *The Annals of the American Academy of Political and Social Science,* vol. 86 (November 1919): 80–82.

38. James C. Nelson, "Regulation of Transport Agencies," *Southern Economic Journal* 5, no. 1 (July 1938): 8.

39. Ralph Budd, "Review of *The Politics of Railroad Coordination*," *The Journal of Economic History* 21, no. 1 (March 1961): 115–116.

40. Earnest W. Williams, Jr., "Looking Back: 50 Years of American Railroading," *The Railway and Locomotive Historical Society Bulletin*, no. 125 (October 1971), p. 26.

41. Mark Reutter, "The Lost Promise of American Railroads," *The Wilson Quarterly* 18, no. 1 (Winter 1994): 17–19.

42. Reutter, "The Lost Promise of American Railroads," p. 21.

43. Earl Latham, *The Politics of Railroad Coordination, 1933–1936* (Cambridge, MA: Harvard University Press, 1959), p. 268.

44. Charles L. Dearing and Wilfred Owen, *National Transportation Policy* (Washington: Brookings Institute, 1949), p. 153.

45. Budd, "Review of *The Politics of Railroad Coordination*," p. 116.

46. Jean Gottmann, *Megalopolis: The Urbanized Northeastern Seaboard of the United States* (Cambridge, MA: MIT Press, 1962), pp. 7, 12.

47. Jane Jacobs, *The Death and Life of Great American Cities* (New York: Random House, 1961), p. 410.

48. Geoffrey Freeman Allen, *The Worlds' Fastest Trains: From the Age of Steam to the TGV* (Sparkford, UK: Haynes, 1992), p. 142.

49. "The Metroliners," StreamlinerSchedules.com, tinyurl.com/MetrolinerSched.

50. "About the Author," *Trains*, March 1983, p. 45.

51. *Passenger Train Service Legislation*, Hearings before the Subcommittee on Surface Transportation of the Senate Committee on Commerce 91st Cong., 1st sess., September 23–25, 1969.

52. Stephen Salsbury, *No Way to Run a Railroad: The Untold Story of the Penn Central Crisis* (New York: McGraw-Hill, 1982), p. 179.

53. "Corporation Created to Operate Rail Passenger System," *CQ Almanac 1970*, Congressional Quarterly, 1971, tinyurl.com/y72t4shx.

54. Robert Lindsey, "For Generations, Railroad Gauged the Nation's Growth," *New York Times*, May 1, 1971, p. 34.

55. "Senators Assail Railpax System," *New York Times*, April 6, 1971, p. 85.

56. Tom Murray, *Southern Railway* (St. Paul, MN: Voyager Press, 2007), p. 131.

57. George W. Hilton, *Amtrak: The National Railroad Passenger Corporation* (Washington: American Enterprise Institute, 1980), p. 1.

58. Ibid., p. 13.

59. Lindsey, "For Generations."

60. Rush Loving, Jr., "*Trains*' Formula for Fixing Amtrak," *Trains*, March 2009, p. 28.

61. Anthony Haswell, Testimony before the Transportation and Aeronautics Sub-committee of the House Committee on Interstate and Foreign Commerce, June 17, 1974.

62. George Hilton, "Railfanning without Railroads," *Trains*, September 1984, p. 74.

63. Thomas J. Lueck, "Amtrak Unveils Its Bullet to Boston," *New York Times*, March 10, 1999, tinyurl.com/BullettoBoston.

64. "Turboservice Timetable," Penn Central, 1969, tinyurl.com/TurboTT.

CHAPTER 10: American Cities Rediscover Rail Transit

1. *An Assessment of Community Planning for Mass Transit—Volume 8: San Francisco Case Study* (Washington: Office of Technology Assessment, 1978), p. 29.

2. Joseph A. Rodriguez, "Planning and Urban Rivalry in the San Francisco Bay Area in the 1930s," *Journal of Planning Education and Research* 20, no. 1 (September 2000): 66.

3. *An Assessment of Community Planning for Mass Transit—Volume 8: San Francisco*, p. 29.

4. Melvin M. Webber, *The BART Experience—What Have We Learned?* (Berkeley: Institute of Transportation Studies, 1976), monograph no. 26, pp. 25–26.

5. Ibid.

6. Ibid., p. 19.

7. Ibid., p. 28.

8. Belinda Griswold, "Tunnel Vision," *San Francisco Bay Guardian*, November 5, 1997.

9. Webber, *The BART Experience*, p. 45.

10. *An Assessment of Community Planning for Mass Transit—Volume 9: Seattle Case Study* (Washington: Office of Technology Assessment, 1978), pp. 19–23.

11. Don H. Pickrell, *Urban Rail Transit Projects: Forecast Versus Actual Ridership and Costs* (Washington: Urban Mass Transit Administration, 1990), p. xi.

12. Ibid.; *The Predicted and Actual Impacts of New Starts Projects—2007: Capital Cost and Ridership* (Washington: Federal Transit Administration, 2008), p. 23.

13. Zachary M. Schrag, *The Great Society Subway: A History of the Washington Metro* (Baltimore: Johns Hopkins University Press, 2014).

14. Ibid., p. 184.

15. National Capital Transportation Act of 1969 (Public Law 91-143).

16. Pickrell, *Urban Rail Transit Projects*, p. xi; American Community Survey, "Journey to Work," table B08301, for Washington urbanized area.

17. Schrag, *The Great Society Subway*, p. 172.

18. Bent Flyvbjerg, Mette Skamris Holm, and Søren Buhl, "Underestimating Costs in Public Works Projects: Error or Lie?" *Journal of the American Planning Association* 68, no. 3 (Summer 2002): 279.

19. Ibid., p. 281.

20. Ethan N. Elkind, *Railtown: The Fight for the Los Angeles Metro Rail and the Future of the City* (Berkeley: University of California Press, 2014), p. 52.

21. Ibid.

22. Tom Fudge, "San Diego Trolley Turns 30 Amid Praise and Higher Expectations," KPBS, September 2, 2011, tinyurl.com/SDTrolleyat30.

23. Kevin Recter, "After 50 Years, I-95 Still East Coast's Common Thread and Economic Backbone," *Baltimore Sun*, November 9, 2013, tinyurl.com/I95Backbone.

24. Pickrell, *Urban Rail Transit Projects*, p. xi.

25. Neil Schickner, "Audit of the Champlain Flyer Commuter Rail Service," Joint Fiscal Office, Vermont Legislature, 2003, pp. 3, 15–16, attachment D, pp. 6, 8.

26. Peter Calthorpe, Andres Duany, et al., "The Ahwahnee Principles for Resource Efficient Communities," 1991, pp. 2–3, tinyurl.com/AhwahneePrinciples.

27. "New Urbanism Basics," Congress for the New Urbanism, Chicago, 2000.

28. "Charter of the New Urbanism," Congress for the New Urbanism, Chicago, 1998.

29. Dee J. Hall, "The Choice: High Density or Urban Sprawl," *Wisconsin State Journal*, July 23, 1995.

30. Joel Garreau, *Edge City: Life on the New Frontier* (New York: Doubleday, 1991), pp. 465–466.

31. Hillel Italie, "Author Jacobs Sets City Standard," *Wilmington Morning Star*, November 24, 2000, p. 20, tinyurl.com/hoovnks.

32. *FasTracks Plan* (Denver: Regional Transit District, 2004), p. ES-11.

33. "Memo from Mike Burton to JPACT re: South/North LRT Proposal," Metro (Portland, Oregon), December 11, 1996.

34. "University Link LRT Extension," Federal Transit Administration, 2013, pp. 1–3; Laura J. Nelson, "Metro to Unveil Mass Transit Blueprint That Includes Tunnel Through the Sepulveda Pass," *Los Angeles Times*, March 11, 2016, tinyurl.com/zol6ogw.

35. *2016 Public Transportation Fact Book*, tables 68, 80, and 92.

36. Kerri Sullivan, "Transportation & Work: Exploring Car Usage and Employment Outcomes in the LSAL Data," National Center for the Study of Adult Learning and Literacy, 2003, p. 27; Katherine M. O'Regan and John M. Quigley, "Cars for the Poor," *Access*, Spring 1998, p. 24.

37. Randal O'Toole, *Does Rail Transit Save Energy or Reduce Greenhouse Gas Emissions?* Cato Institute Policy Analysis no. 615, April 14, 2008, p. 14.

38. Thomas A. Rubin and Fatma Mansour, *Transit Utilization and Traffic Congestion: Is There a Connection?* (Los Angeles: Reason Foundation, 2013), p. 3.

CHAPTER 11: Keeping Up With the Joneses

1. Simon Van Zuylen-Wood, "Why Can't America Have Great Trains?" *National Journal*, April 17, 2015, tinyurl.com/l7rea4r.

2. Mitsuhide Imashiro, "Dawn of Japanese National Railways," *Japanese Railway and Transport Review*, January 1997, p. 48.

3. Ryohei Kakumoto, "Sensible Politics and Transportation Theories—Japanese National Railways in the 20th Century," *Japanese Railway and Transport Review*, December 1999, pp. 26–27.

4. Yoshitaka Fukui, "Twenty Years After," *Japanese Railway and Transport Review*, March 2008, p. 6. Japan's 1987 GDP was ¥349 trillion; Thayer Watkins, "Japan: Economic Statistics," San Jose State University, 1996, tinyurl.com/JPEconStats.

5. Mitsuhide Imashiro, "Changes in Japan's Transport Market and JNR Privatization," *Japanese Railway and Transport Review*, September 1997, p. 52.

6. *Japan Statistical Yearbook 2017* (Tokyo: Statistics Japan, 2016), table 13-2.

7. Christopher P. Hood, "The Shinkansen's Local Impact," *Social Science Japan Journal* 13, no. 2 (Winter 2010): 219.

8. Eiji Shiomi, "Do Faster Trains Challenge Air Carriers?" *Japan Railway and Transport Review*, March 1999, pp. 4–5.

9. Ibid., p. 133.

10. Ibid., p. 136.

11. "Stability and Growth Pact," European Commission, 2016, /index_en.htm.

12. Ivan Cicconi, "The Project Financing Scam," *Beppe Grillo's Blog*, March 13, 2012, http://www.beppegrillo.it/en/2012/03/passaparola_the_project_financ_1.html.

13. Daniel Albalate and Germà Bel, *The Economics and Politics of High-Speed Rail: Lessons from Experiences Abroad* (New York: Lexington Books, 2014), p. 132.

14. "Modal Split of Passenger Transport," European Commission, 2017, tinyurl.com/y9m4jmpz.

15. Ibid., p. 137.

16. "Turin-Lyon High-Speed Rail Project: Controversy at the Heart of Europe," *Railway Technology*, May 23, 2016, http://www.railway-technology.com/features/featureturin-lyon-high-speed-rail-project-controversy-at-the-heart-of-europe-4896951/.

17. "#NoTAV: Thousands of Italians protest high-speed railway construction in Turin," RT.com, February 22, 2015, https://www.rt.com/news/234511-italy-no-tav-protest/.

18. "Modal Split of Passenger Transport," European Commission, 2017, tinyurl.com/y9m4jmpz.

19. Julie de la Brossa, "SNCF: Les Cinq Signaux d'Alarme du Rail Français," *l'Express*, October 6, 2014, http://lexpansion.lexpress.fr/entreprises/sncf-les-cinq-signaux-d-alarme-du-rail-francais_1548090.html.

20. John Litchfield, "Francois Hollande's TGV Vanity Project Is on a High-Speed Railway to Nowhere," *The Independent*, December 26, 2014, http://www.independent.co.uk/news/world/europe/francois-hollandes-tgv-vanity-project-is-on-a-high-speed-railway-to-nowhere-9945932.html.

21. "TGV: 'Revenir à la raison' (Marc Fressoz)," *France Soir*, September 24, 2011, http://archive.francesoir.fr/pratique/transport/tgv-revenir-raison-marc-fressoz-140618.html&usg=ALkJrhgsMdbmcLGx191BN9qAj7jNJLLeSQ.

22. Litchfield, "Francois Hollande's TGV Vanity Project."

23. de la Brossa, "SNCF."

24. "Air Transport, Passengers Carried," World Bank, 2016, tinyurl.com/WBAirTravel.

25. Anne-Sylvaine Chassany, "France to Buy Unneeded Trains to Save Belfort Factory," *Financial Times*, October 4, 2016, https://www.ft.com/content/9e7deeee-8a07-11e6-8aa5-f79f5696c731.

26. "Poitiers-Limoges DUP Overturned," *Railway Gazette*, April 19, 2016, http://www.railwaygazette.com/news/single-view/view/poitiers-limoges-dup-overturned.html.

27. "François Hollande Relance le Projet de TGV Poitiers-Limoges, Jugé Trop Cher par le Conseil d'Etat En Savoir Plus Sur," *le Monde*, October 8, 2016, http://www.lemonde.fr/politique/article/2016/10/08/francois-hollande-relance-le-projet-de-tgv-poitiers-limoges-juge-trop-cher-par-le-conseil-d-etat_5010540_823448.html#xEWFByjPkGWp04mH.99.

28. Elena G. Sevillano, "One in Four AVE Stations Used by Fewer Than 100 Passengers a Day," *El Pais*, May 24, 2016, tinyurl.com/zspejz9.

29. Fiona Govan, "Spain Cuts High Speed 'Ghost Train,'" *Telegraph*, June 28, 2011, tinyurl.com/5w22n6r.

30. Albalate and Bel, *The Economics and Politics of High-Speed Rail*, p. 104.

31. Ibid., pp. 96, 110.

32. Ofelia Betancor and Gerard Llobet, *Contabilidad Financiera y Social de la Alta Velocidad en España* (Madrid: FEDEA, 2015), p. 1, tinyurl.com/zu34m2o.

33. "Las Infraestructuras en España: AVE y Aeropuertos," FEDEA, March 26, 2015, tinyurl.com/ndmyd95.

34. Daniel Albalate and Germà Bel, "High-Speed Rail: Lessons for Policy Makers from Experiences Abroad," Research Institute of Applied Economics, 2010, p. 17.

35. Phillip Inman, "Spain Must Halt Rail Expansion, Expert Says," *The Guardian*, May 3, 2012, tinyurl.com/zom42cl.

36. Julien Toyer, "Spain's Obsession with High-Speed Trains Runs into Budget Reality," Reuters, June 17, 2013, tinyurl.com/z86z4uj.

37. "Rail Reform Tackles Spanish Debt Crisis," *Railway Gazette*, July 25, 2012, tinyurl.com/z76nuxj.

38. Eric Eidlen, "High Speed Rail in France and Germany: Speed Versus Connectivity," German Marshall Fund, October 19, 2013, tinyurl.com/hzlfqzk.

39. Kate Conolly, "Why German Trains Don't Run on Time Any More," *The Guardian*, June 11, 2016, tinyurl.com/hdlo63f.

40. "General Definitions of High Speed," International Union of Railways, 2006, tinyurl.com/HSRDef.

41. Brendan Martin, "The High Public Price of Britain's Private Railway," Public World, November 2010, pp. 2–3, 7, tinyurl.com/9t4g7dn.

42. Keith Barrow, "France Moves Towards Regional Rail Competition," *International Railway Journal*, March 19, 2015, tinyurl.com/n9x3xjw.

43. Sebastian Storch, "Competition in Regional Rail Transport (Germany)," Presentation before the Danish Rail Conference, Copenhagen, Denmark, 2016, tinyurl.com/hfwynlq.

44. Ronald Woudstra, "Fyra: The Dutch High-Speed Rail Debacle," *DutchReview*, July 10, 2013, tinyurl.com/DutchHSR.

45. *2015 Financial Report*, Swiss Federal Rail, Bern, Switzerland, 2016, p. 76, tinyurl.com/gtkhh22.

46. Yang Jing, "High-Speed Rail Era," China National Geographic Network, May 7, 2010, tinyurl.com/z8am238.

47. Rose Yu, "China's Busiest High-Speed Rail Line Makes a Fast Buck," *Wall Street Journal*, July 20, 2016, tinyurl.com/ChinaHSRProfit.

48. Keith B. Richberg, "Are China's High-Speed Trains Heading off the Rails?" *Washington Post*, April 23, 2011, tinyurl.com/h8v7e9h.

49. "Off the Rails?" *The Economist*, March 31, 2011, tinyurl.com/hxfgl8q; Malcolm Moore, "Chinese Rail Crash Scandal: 'Official Steals $2.8 Billion,'" *Telegraph*, August 1, 2011, tinyurl.com/6rcwn3t.

50. "China Rail Official Given Death Sentence for Corruption," BBC, October 17, 2014, tinyurl.com/zdp3dgf.

51. Elaine Kurtenbach, "Report of China Rail Section Collapse Jolts Shares," *Deseret News*, March 12, 2012, tinyurl.com/7z6g3q6.

52. Steven Jiang, "China Recalls Bullet Trains, Slows Down High-Speed Rail," CNN, August 12, 2011, tinyurl.com/z7ysuwj.

53. Keith Barrow, "China Railway Debt Reaches $US 640bn," *International Railway Journal*, May 6, 2016, tinyurl.com/hk67sd8.

54. Adam Minter, "Just Say No to High-Speed Rail," Bloomberg, July 6, 2016, tinyurl.com/NotoHSR.

55. Zhong Nan and Lyu Chang, "Debts Spark Calls to Split Up China Railway Corp," *China Daily*, May 7, 2016, tinyurl.com/BreakUpCRC.

56. "China's Li Spends on Fast Rail Like It's 2010 to Cushion Economy," Bloomberg, September 29, 2015, tinyurl.com/CHHSRStimulus.

57. Richberg, "Are China's High-Speed Trains Heading off the Rails?"

58. P. Harvey Middleton, *Railways of Thirty Nations: Government versus Private Ownership* (New York: Prentice-Hall, 1937), p. 305.

59. Ibid., pp. 119–120.

60. Ibid., pp. 130–131.

61. Ibid., p. 156.

62. Ibid., p. 159.

63. Ibid., p. 204.

64. Ibid., p. 163.

65. Ibid., p. 242.

66. *National Transportation Statistics*, table 1-50.

67. *EU Transport in Figures* (Brussels: European Union, 2016), tables 1.5 and 2.2.5.

68. *Railway Statistics: 2015 Synopsis* (Paris: International Railway Union, 2016), table 2.

69. *Panorama of Transport: 2009 Edition* (Brussels: European Commission, 2009), p. 100, tinyurl.com/ykks2bu.

70. Ibid., p. 106.

71. Ibid., p. 57.

72. Peter Baldwin, *The Narcissism of Minor Differences: How America and Europe Are Alike* (New York: Oxford University Press, 2009), p. 127.

CHAPTER 12: Rapidly Deteriorating Transit

1. "America's Transit System Stands at the Precipice of a Fiscal and Service Crisis," Washington Metro, 2002, p. 1.

2. Lyndsey Layton and Jo Becker, "Efforts to Repair Aging System Compound Metro's Problems," *Washington Post*, June 5, 2005, tinyurl.com/hyeafff.

3. Lena H. Sun and Martin Weil, "More Metro Stations Shut Down by Smoke," *Washington Post*, August 28, 2007, tinyurl.com/jjy8gyn.

4. "What Is Arcing?" Washington Post, January 13, 2015, tinyurl.com/h68vybd.

5. "Collision of Two Washington Metropolitan Area Transit Authority Metrorail Trains Near Fort Totten Station Washington, D.C., June 22, 2009," National Transportation Safety Board, 2010, p. 127.

6. "Collision Between Two Washington Metropolitan Area Transit Authority Trains at the Woodley Park-Zoo/Adams Morgan Station in Washington, D.C., November 3, 2004," National Transportation Safety Board, 2005, p. 51.

7. Dana Hedgpeth, "Cracked Rails Vex Metro," *Washington Post*, February 8, 2012, tinyurl.com/gnrt95a.

8. Matthew Stabley, Jackie Bensen, Adam Tuss, Derrick Ward, and Darcy Spencer, "One Dead, Dozens Hospitalized After Heavy Smoke at D.C. Metro Tunnel," NBC Washington, January 13, 2015, tinyurl.com/ml5gc7j.

9. Robert McCartney and Lori Aratani, "Questions on Cables' Safety Demand 24-Hour Metro Shutdown, Wiedefeld Says," *Washington Post*, March 15, 2016.

10. "SafeTrack," Washington Metro, tinyurl.com/hjf5ljn.

11. "Metropocalypse," NPR, May 25, 2016, tinyurl.com/zapmg9j.

12. Martin Di Caro, "Among Metro's 'Hard Truths' Are Silver Line Problems with No Easy Fix," WAMU, March 7, 2016, tinyurl.com/zzbj5gw.

13. Fredrick Kunkle, "Instead of Building the Silver Line, Metro Should Have Fixed the System It Had," *Washington Post*, June 8, 2016, tinyurl.com/h997vrj.

14. "Transit Ridership Report, Second Quarter 2015," American Public Transportation Association, Washington D.C., p. 2.

15. Brian Kane, *Born Broke: How the MBTA Found Itself With Too Much Debt, the Corrosive Effects of this Debt, and a Comparison Of the T's Deficit to Its Peers* (Boston: MBTA Advisory Board, 2009), p. 5.

16. David F. D'Alessandro, Paul D. Romary, Lisa J. Scannell, and Bryan Woliner, *MBTA Review* (Boston: Commonwealth of Massachusetts, 2009), p. 22, mbtareview.com.

17. *Capital Investment Program: FY2016* (Boston: MBTA, 2016), p. 10.

18. "MBTA Fiscal Year 2016 Preliminary Budget Update," Presentation before the Massachusetts Department of Transportation Board of Directors, March 11, 2015, p. 3, tinyurl.com/jbkr99o.

19. *Beyond Lechmore Northeast Corridor Study* (Boston: MBTA, 2005), pp. 5–55.

20. "Green Line Extension—Cambridge to Medford, Massachusetts," Federal Transit Administration, December 2015, p. 2.

21. "Transit System Plagued by Near-Constant Service Issues," *Boston Herald*, February 26, 2018, tinyurl.com/ycqbym87.

22. *CTA: Investing in Chicago—President's 2015 Budget Recommendations* (Chicago: Chicago Transit Authority, 2015), pp. 91–92.

23. *Program & Budget Book: 2015* (Chicago: Metra, 2015), pp. 3–4.

24. Christopher MacKechnie, "New York State Public Transit Funding," ThoughtCo.com, April 7, 2016, tinyurl.com/lvk6cxl.

25. John Petro, "Without Action from Cuomo, Subways Doomed to Endless State of Disrepair," StreetsblogNYC, March 14, 2014, tinyurl.com/n7cl4ft.

26. "Metropolitan Transportation Authority: Consolidated Interim Financial Statements as of and for the Nine-Month Period Ending September 30, 2016," Metropolitan Transportation Authority, 2016, p. 22, tinyurl.com/msdoeaw.

27. Brian M. Rosenthal, "The Most Expensive Mile of Subway Track on Earth," *New York Times*, December 28, 2017, tinyurl.com/y76twxgt.

28. Emma G. Fitzsimmons, "Cuomo Declares a State of Emergency for New York City Subways," *New York Times*, June 29, 2017, tinyurl.com/y9lz6j5h.

29. "Metropolitan Transportation Authority: Consolidated Interim Financial Statements as of and for the Nine-Month Period Ending September 30, 2016," p. 84.

30. *National State of Good Repair Assessment: 2010* (Washington: Federal Transit Administration, 2010), p. 3.

31. "Fact Sheet: State of Good Repair Grants," Federal Transit Administration, 2016, p. 1, tinyurl.com/SOGRFS.

32. *2015 Status of the Nation's Highways, Bridges, and Transit: Conditions and Performance* (Washington: Department of Transportation, 2017), p. L (Roman numeral 50).

33. Dave Henley, presentation before the 2009 State of Good Repair Roundtable, Washington, D.C., July, 2009, p. 15.

34. Frank Ruffa, "Asset Management at BART," Presentation before the 2012 State of Good Repair Roundtable, Philadelphia, Pennsylvania, July 2012, p. 5.

35. Erin Baldassari, "BART's Oakland Airport Connector Losing Money; Uber, Lyft to Blame?" *East Bay Times*, November 27, 2016, tinyurl.com/jxppqg8.

36. Joseph Rose, "TriMet's MAX Trains Knocked Off Track by Expensive, Deferred Maintenance, Records Show," *The Oregonian*, August 12, 2014, tinyurl.com/mfwma8t.

37. "TriMet: General Management Review and Issues Deserving Additional Attention," Secretary of State Audit Report, Salem, Oregon, 2014, pp. 1, 41.

38. Joseph Rose, "TriMet General Manager Warns of 70 Percent Service Cuts by 2025 If Union Doesn't Budge on Health Benefits," *The Oregonian*, February 13, 2013, tinyurl.com/goba5d8.

39. "Staff Memo Recommends Light Rail for Portland-to-Bridgeport Village Rapid Transit," Metro, Portland, Oregon, April 4, 2016, tinyurl.com/jr4lwgx.

40. Yves Crozet, "High-Speed Rail and PPPs: Between Optimization and Opportunism," *in* Daniel Albalate and Germà Bel, eds., *Evaluating High-Speed Rail: Interdisciplinary Perspectives* (New York: Routledge, 2017), p. 183.

41. Intermodal Surface Transportation Efficiency Act of 1991, section 3010(i)(1)(B).

42. 49 USC §5309(e)(2)(A)(iv).

43. D. H. Pickrell, *Urban Rail Transit Projects: Forecast versus Actual Ridership and Cost* (Washington: Department of Transportation, 1990), p. xi; *Predicted and Actual Impacts of New Starts Projects—2003* (Washington: Federal Transit Administration, 2003), table 2; *The Predicted and Actual Impacts of New Starts Projects—2007* (Washington: Federal Transit Administration, 2008), p. 11; *Before and After Studies of New Starts Projects: Report to Congress* (Washington: Federal Transit Administration, 2011); *Before and After Studies of New Starts Projects: Report to Congress* (Washington: Federal Transit Administration, 2013); *Before and After Studies of New Starts Projects: Report to Congress* (Washington: Federal Transit Administration, 2016).

44. "Transportation Alternatives Analysis for the Dane County/Greater Madison Metropolitan Area Final Report," Parsons Brinkerhoff, 2002, pp. 7-6, 10-2, and 10-22.

45. "Transport 2020 Oversight Advisory Committee Summary Report," Transport 2020, Madison, Wisconsin, 2003, pp. 32–33.

46. Tiffany Couch, "CRC Project Forensic Accounting Update," Acuity Group, 2013, p. 26.

47. Andrea Damewood, "The Woman Behind the Bridge: The Force Behind Oregon's Massive Freeway Project Works for the Governor—And a Private Company That Wants It Built," *Willamette Week*, February 26, 2013, tinyurl.com/go2ove8.

48. Nigel Jaquiss, "Serving Two Masters: Kitzhaber's Columbia River Crossing Adviser Also Works for the Project's Biggest Contractor," *Willamette Week*, March 2, 2011, tinyurl.com/juatl37.

49. Hillary Borrud, "Ethics Watchdog Wants Tighter Lobbyist Registration Rules," *The Oregonian*, July 1, 2016, tinyurl.com/gwrzdkl.

50. Bent Flyvbjerg, Mette Skamris Holm, and Søren Buhl, "Underestimating Costs in Public Works Projects: Error or Lie?" *Journal of the American Planning Association* 68, no. 3 (2002): 285.

51. Bent Flyvbjerg, "Curbing Optimism Bias and Strategic Misrepresentation in Planning: Reference Class Forecasting in Practice," *European Planning Studies* 16, no. 1 (January 2008): 3.

52. Ginés De Rus, "The Economic Evaluation of Major Infrastructure Projects," in Daniel Albalate and Germà Bel, eds., *Evaluating High-Speed Rail: Interdisciplinary Perspectives* (New York: Routledge, 2017), p. 18.

CHAPTER 13: Low-Capacity Rail

1. Jonathan E. D. Richmond, "The Mythical Conception of Rail Transit in Los Angeles," *Journal of Architectural and Planning Research*, vol. 15, no. 4 (Winter 1998), p. 315.

2. Anthony Burton and John Scott-Morgan, *Light Railways of Britain and Ireland* (Barnsley, England: Pen & Sword, 2015), p. 7.

3. *Glossary of Transit Terminology* (Washington: American Public Transit Association, 1994), p. 23, tinyurl.com/y8nvuq4t.

4. John Petro, "Quit Whining Brooklyn—Your Subways Aren't That Crowded," New York YIMBY, October 15, 2014, tinyurl.com/j8xh96s.

5. "Metro Orange Line Timetable," Los Angeles Metro, effective December 11, 2016, tinyurl.com/LAOrangeTT.

6. Neal Broverman, "State Could Be About to Repeal Ban on Light Rail in the Valley," *Curbed Los Angeles*, February 4, 2014, tinyurl.com/hugwe3n.

7. Dana Bartholomew, "Officials Support Turning Orange Line Busway into Light-Rail System," *Los Angeles Daily News*, July 25, 2014, tinyurl.com/h9noh3a.

8. Jason Islas and Joe Linton, "Expo Line Phase 2 Opening Announced for May 20," *Streetsblog LA*, February 25, 2016, tinyurl.com/hfg7jgd.

9. "Council Announces Regional Transit Equity Plan," Metropolitan Council, St. Paul, Minnesota, 2014, tinyurl.com/h8vya57.

10. Wendell Cox, *United States Central Business Districts (Downtowns): 50 Largest Urban Areas 2000 Data on Employment & Transit Work Trips* (Belleville, IL: Demographia.com, 2006), p. 9.

11. Peter Rogoff, Speech before the Boston Federal Reserve Bank, "National Summit on the Future of Transit," May 18, 2010.

12. Mike Lindbloom, "New Sound Transit CEO Expected to Work Nonstop for $300,000," *Seattle Times*, January 10, 2016, tinyurl.com/jjcxg3w.

13. Laurie Blake, "Light Rail Always Will Slow the Flow," *Minneapolis Star-Tribune*, December 12, 2004, tinyurl.com/cdkb3gc.

14. Maryland Department of Transportation, *Purple Line Alternatives Analysis, Draft Environmental Impact Statement* (Baltimore: Maryland Department of Transportation, 2008), p. 1-1.

15. Maryland Department of Transportation, *Purple Line: Traffic Analysis Technical Report* (Baltimore: Maryland Department of Transportation, 2008), pp. 4-1–4-2.

16. Adam Nagourney, "Hawaii Struggles to Keep Rail Project from Becoming a Boondoggle," *New York Times*, March 20, 2016, tinyurl.com/jecz8xg; Mileka Lincoln, "New 'Worst-Case Scenario' Report Reveals Full 20-Mile Rail Route Could Cost $10.79B," *Hawaii News Now,* June 23, 2016, tinyurl.com/hfvvu6l.

172015. *Public Transportation Fact Book* (Washington: American Public Transportation Association, 2015), pp. 35, 40.

18. "How Fast Is Your City?" Infinite Monkey Corps, 2009, tinyurl.com/j8y6jlb.

19. *National Transportation Statistics* (Washington: Bureau of Transportation Statistics, 2016), tables 1–40, 2–33, and 2–35.

20. Jim Redden, "Neil's Network," *Portland Tribune,* May 21, 2004.

21. Margie Boulé, "Neil Goldschmidt's Sex-Abuse Victim Tells of the Relationship That Damaged Her Life," *The Oregonian*, January 31, 2011, tinyurl.com/4epqeyk.
22. Redden, "Neil's Network."

CHAPTER 14: Streetcars and the Economic Development Hoax

1. Jarrett Walker, "Streetcars: An Inconvenient Truth," *Human Transit*, July 3, 2009, tinyurl.com/ybe3we3a.
2. "How Fast Is Your City?" Infinite Monkey Corps, October 8, 2009, tinyurl.com/CitySpeeds.
3. *2015 Public Transportation Fact Book*, p. 40.
4. Aaron Weiner, "Why Streetcars Aren't About Transit: The Economic Development Argument for Trams," *Next City*, January 12, 2014, tinyurl.com/h3353wo.
5. G. B. Arrington, *At Work in the Field of Dreams: Light Rail and Smart Growth in Portland* (Portland, OR: TriMet, 1998), tinyurl.com/394bsd.
6. William J. Clinton, Executive Order no. 12988, Civil Justice Reform, February 5, 1996, and Executive Order no. 13006, Locating Federal Facilities on Historic Properties in Our Nation's Central Cities, May 21, 1996; Barbara Roberts, Executive Order no. 94-07, Siting State Offices in Oregon's Community Centers, June 7, 1994.
7. Arrington, *At Work in the Field of Dreams*, p. 1.
8. Mike Saba, Testimony before the Portland City Council, October 23, 1996, tinyurl.com/6mfxtl9.
9. Wayne Remboldt, Testimony before the Portland City Council, October 23, 1996, tinyurl.com/86sbgu3; Dan Steffey, Testimony before the Portland City Council, October 23, 1996, tinyurl.com/7xx3wbh.
10. Charlie Hales, Comments before the Portland City Council, October 23, 1996, tinyurl.com/ 88qpspe.
11. *Adopted Budget: FY 17–18* (Portland: Prosper Portland, 2017), p. 15.
12. Ibid.
13. Ibid.
14. David Swenson and Liesl Eathington, "Do Tax Increment Finance Districts in Iowa Spur Regional Economic and Demographic Growth?" working paper, Iowa State University, 2002, p. 1, tinyurl.com/3463tow.
15. Richard Dye and David Merriman, "The Effects of Tax Increment Financing on Economic Development," *Journal of Urban Economics* 47, no. 2 (March 2000): 306.
16. Roger Showley, "Court Ruling Kills State's Redevelopment Agencies," *San Diego Union-Tribune*, December 29, 2011, tinyurl.com/hd45pad.

17. *Tax-Increment Finance State-by-State Report* (Columbus, OH: Council of Development Finance Agencies, 2015), p. 3; *2008 State-by-State TIF Report* (Columbus, OH: Council of Development Finance Agencies, 2008), inside front cover.

18. "Portland Streetcar: Development Oriented Transit," City of Portland Office of Transportation, April 2008, p. 2.

19. Ibid., p. 3.

20. Charles Hales and Robert Cone, "Streetcars Bringing People, Businesses Back to the City," HDR Transit Line, 2006, p. 2, tinyurl.com/2nx6x5.

21. Ibid.

22. *Recommended Tax Increment Financing Budgets for the Fiscal Year Ending September 30, 2016* (Tampa: Community Redevelopment Agency, 2015), p. vii.

23. Luis Enrique Ramos-Santiago, Jeffrey Brown, and Hilary Nixon, "A Cautionary Tale of Two Streetcars: Little Rock's River Rail and Tampa's TECO Line," *Journal of Public Transportation* 18, no. 1 (2015): 5.

24. *2005 National Transit Database* (Washington: Federal Transit Administration, 2006), service spreadsheet.

25. Ibid.

26. Angie Schmitt, "Ohio Gov. John Kasich vs. the Cincinnati Streetcar," Rustwire, March 10, 2011, tinyurl.com/j3yywdz.

27. "What Streetcar Success Will Look Like," *Cincinnati Enquirer*, September 2, 2016, tinyurl.com/hdbuqse.

282015. *National Transit Database* (Washington: Federal Transit Administration, 2016), fares, operating costs, and service spreadsheets.

29. Dylan Rivera, "Streetcar Bumps into Federal Bias for Buses," *The Oregonian*, September 25, 2007, tinyurl.com/br3v75z.

30. Ryan Frank and Brent Hunsberger, "A Streetcar Named Acquire," *The Oregonian*, June 25, 2007, p. 1.

31. "Feds Give TriMet $2.4M for Streetcar," *Portland Business Journal*, April 16, 2010, tinyurl.com/y3gvh92.

32. Dylan Rivera, "Portland Inks $20 Million Deal for Locally Made Streetcars," *The Oregonian*, August 14, 2009, tinyurl.com/o6g9ft.

33. Brad Schmidt, "Portland's $148.3 Million Eastside Streetcar Project Delayed Five Months, Includes Five Streetcars Instead of Six," *The Oregonian*, July 19, 2011, tinyurl.com/3ty3zu5.

34. Brad Schmidt, "Before Shutdown, How Many Jobs Did United Streetcar Deliver?" *The Oregonian*, March 18, 2015, tinyurl.com/opvjm3q.

35. "Fare Info," Portland Streetcar, 2017, tinyurl.com/zzbgpt2.

36. "2006 Downtown Portland Business Census and Survey," Portland Business Alliance, 2007, pp. 3, 11; "2015 Downtown Portland Business Census and Survey," Portland Business Alliance, 2016, pp. 3, 9.

37. Joseph Rose, "Joseph Rose vs. the Portland Streetcar: Walking Wins in Showdown of City's Poky Commuting Modes," *The Oregonian*, February 8, 2013, tinyurl.com/RosevsSC.

38. Catherine Beck and Julie Wolfe, "Atlanta Streetcar: Desire or Disaster?" 11live.com, November 7, 2016, tinyurl.com/guczhka.

39. Gary Blackmer, "Street Paving: More Proactive Maintenance Could Preserve Additional City Streets Within Existing Funding," Portland City Auditor, 2006, p. 1.

40. *Asset Status and Condition Report 2013* (Portland, OR: Bureau of Transportation, 2013), p. 33.

41. *Portland Streetcar System Concept Plan* (Portland, OR: City of Portland, 2009), p. 32.

CHAPTER 15: It Would Have Cost Less to Buy All the Riders Priuses

1. John F. Kain, "Deception in Dallas: Strategic Misrepresentation in Rail Transit Promotion and Evaluation," *Journal of the American Planning Association*, vol. 56, no. 2 (Spring 1990), p. 184.

2. "Rail on a Budget: Nashville's Music City Star," *Metro Jacksonville*, September 18, 2007, tinyurl.com/nwk296.

3. "*Music City Star* East Corridor Regional Rail Ride Guide," Regional Transportation Authority of Middle Tennessee, March 2016, p. 2, tinyurl.com/jf3f26r.

4. "Nashville Regional Commuter Rail East Corridor Study," STV, Douglasville, Pennsylvania, 2000, p. 1, tinyurl.com/gnxkyfc.

5. *Annual Report on New Starts: Proposed Allocations of Funds for Fiscal Year 2007* (Washington: Federal Transit Administration, 2006), p. A-126.

6. Cox, *United States Central Business Districts*, p. 4.

7. "Music City Star Falls Well Shy of Projected Ridership Targets," *Trains*, June 26, 2008, tinyurl.com/gmfgqh7; "TDOT Could Bail Out Music City Star Commuter Train," WVLT-TV, July 17, 2008, tinyurl.com/zyupevx.

8. Kevin Spear, "SunRail Ticket Revenue Is Less Than Ticketing Expense," *Orlando Sentinel*, February 24, 2017, tinyurl.com/z358oun.

9. "Megabus.com Invests $10.5m in New Double-Decker Coaches as Part of North America Expansion Plans," Stagecoach Group, January 22, 2014, tinyurl.com/j7en9c3.

10. 49 CFR 611, appendix A, (d)(1), adopted December 7, 2000.

11. Katherine Shaver, "How Many People Will Ride the Purple Line?" *Washington Post*, September 26, 2015, tinyurl.com/osf833o.

12. D. H. Pickrell, *Urban Rail Transit Projects: Forecast versus Actual Ridership and Cost* (Washington: U.S. Department of Transportation, 1990), p. xi.

13. *Predicted and Actual Impacts of New Starts Projects–2003* (Washington: Federal Transit Administration, 2003), table 2, tinyurl.com/mx4ea7d.

14. *The Predicted and Actual Impacts of New Starts Projects–2007* (Washington: Federal Transit Administration, 2008), p. 11, tinyurl.com/8kpnyr.

15. Shaver, "How Many People Will Ride the Purple Line?"

16. *Purple Line Alternatives Analysis and Draft Environmental Impact Statement* (Baltimore: Maryland Department of Transportation, 2008), p. ES-1.

17. *Purple Line Traffic Analysis Technical Report* (Baltimore: Maryland Department of Transportation, 2008), p. 4-1.

1849. CFR 611, appendix A, (e)(1), adopted January 9, 2013.

19. Tony Gonzolez, "Nashville Struggles to Fill Commuter Train, But Says Offering More Trips Will Help," Nashville Public Radio, August 19, 2016, tinyurl .com/j7llqwt.

20. Joey Garrison, "Metro Recommends $6 Billion Transit Plan for Nashville Region," *Tennessean*, August 17, 2016, tinyurl.com/gvlh55c.

21. *Annual Report on Funding Recommendations: Fiscal Year 2017 Capital Investment Grant Program* (Washington: Federal Transit Administration, 2016), project profiles for SunRail, phase II south, SunRail phase II north, and SunRail connector to Orlando International Airport.

22. *2015 American Community Survey*, Census Bureau, 2016, table B08301, "Means of Transportation to Work" for urbanized areas.

23. "Long Island Railroad—General Information," Metropolitan Transportation Authority, 2016, tinyurl.com/hlcr9dk; "NJ Transit Facts at a Glance," New Jersey Transit, 2015, tinyurl.com/j38e3x8.

24. Erin Durkin, "1 in 4 MTA workers Made Six-Figure Incomes Last Year, Up from 2013," *New York Daily News*, July 17, 2015, tinyurl.com/z9q2ad9.

25. Dan Rivoli, "MTA Paid $876M in Overtime to Workers Last Year, With Top Earners Tripling Their Salary Thanks to Bonus Hours," *New York Daily News*, March 9, 2016, tinyurl.com/h8w84lj.

26. Ibid.; Larry Higgs, "NJ Transit's Biggest Overtime Earners," NJ.com, December 28, 2016, tinyurl.com/hmnwzl2.

27. "HOT Toll Lanes Commute to Bay Area," *Daily Journal*, February 27, 2009, tinyurl.com/zraaaqz.

28. "101 Corridor Managed Lanes," San Mateo County Transportation Authority, 2016, p. 7, tinyurl.com/jqdo87m.

29. *Peninsula Corridor Electrification Project Final Environmental Impact Report, Volume 1: Revised Draft EIS*, Peninsula Corridor Joint Powers Board, 2015, p. ES-11.

30. "A Review of the Transportation Prioritization Process," Legislative Auditor General, Salt Lake City, 2007, pp. 5–6, tinyurl.com/35uw36.

31. Brandon Loomis, "New TRAX Passenger Tracking System Shows Ridership Lower Than Thought," *Salt Lake Tribune*, December 20, 2007.

32. "A Performance Audit of the Utah Transit Authority," Legislative Auditor General, Salt Lake City, 2012, pp. 14, 15; "A Performance Audit of the Utah Transit Authority," Legislative Auditor General, Salt Lake City, 2014, p. iv.

33. "A Performance Audit," 2014, p. iii.

34. *Unclogging America's Arteries 2015: Prescriptions for Healthier Highways* (Washington: American Highway Users Alliance, 2015), p. vii.

35. "HOV System Map," Washington State Department of Transportation, 2016, tinyurl.com/hehmol4.

36. "Using 95 Express in Broward," Florida Department of Transportation, 2016, 95express.com; "Florida's High-Occupancy Vehicle Lanes," Florida Department of Transportation, 2017, tinyurl.com/hnjr2t2.

CHAPTER 16: Why Amtrak Is Being Replaced by Intercity Buses

1. Joseph Vranich, *End of the Line: The Failure of Amtrak Reform and the Future of America's Passenger Trains* (Washington: American Enterprise Institute, 2004), p. 8.

2. Anthony Haswell, "Amtrak: The Reality Tarnishes the Crusade," *Journal of Commerce*, January 7, 2000, tinyurl.com/9u9z8k7.

3. "Amtrak Delivers Strong FY 2016 Financial Results: New Ridership Record and Lowest Operating Loss Ever," Amtrak, November 17, 2016, tinyurl .com/h5uduow.

4. "Train Engineer's Loss of Situational Awareness Led to Amtrak Derailment," National Transportation Safety Board, May 17, 2016, tinyurl.com/ycelr7nf.

5. Scott Bronstein, Drew Griffin, and Collette Richards, "Workers Say They Warned Amtrak Before Deadly Crash," CNN, January 29, 2018, tinyurl.com/yaqzymhp.

6. Chad Pergram and Judson Berger, "Train Carrying GOP Lawmakers to Retreat Hits Truck on Tracks, 1 Killed," FoxNews, January 31, 2018, tinyurl.com/y7drkwb9.

7. "South Carolina Train Crash: Amtrak 'on the Wrong Track,'" BBC, February 4, 2018, tinyurl.com/yaxduj96.

8. Tariq Tahir, "Brightline Outlines New Safety Campaign After Four Deaths on the Tracks Spark Calls for the High-Speed Train Service to Be Shut Down," *Daily Mail*, January 18, 2018, tinyurl.com/yatmxzfp.

9. Dan Reed, "In a Dangerous World, U.S. Commercial Aviation Is on a Remarkable Safety Streak," *Forbes*, December 28, 2016, tinyurl.com/ybgqfvjy.

10. *National Transportation Statistics* (Washington: Bureau of Transportation Statistics, 2017), table 2-1. Of the rail fatalities shown on the table, only those in the line titled "train accidents"—about 1 percent of the total since 2007—could be reduced by positive train control."

11. *Monthly Performance Report for September 2016* (Washington: Amtrak, 2016), p. A-4.1.

12. Ibid.

13. Jan R. Heier and A. Lee Gurley, "The End of Betterment Accounting: A Study of the Economic, Professional, and Regulatory Factors That Fostered Standards Convergence in the U.S. Railroad Industry, 1955–1983," *The Accounting Historians Journal* 34, no. 1 (June 2007): 42–46.

14. Anthony Haswell, "My Ride on the Rocket," *Trains*, March 1983, pp. 39–45.

15. *Fiscal Years 2013–2017 Five Year Plan* (Washington: Amtrak, 2013), p. 12.

16. *Monthly Performance Report for September 2016* (Washington: Amtrak, 2016), p. A-4.1.

17. David Randall Peterman, "Amtrak: Overview and Options," Congressional Research Service report RL30659, January 25, 2001, p. 5, tinyurl. com/8jvqf2w.

18. "Better Reporting, Planning, and Improved Financial Information Could Enhance Decision Making," Government Accountability Office report GAO-16-67, 2016, pp. 26–27.

19. Based on rail schedules and fares from Amtrak.com and airfares and schedules from kayak.com.

20. Joseph P. Schwieterman, Lauren Fischer, Sara Smith, and Christine Towles, "The Return of the Intercity Bus: The Decline and Recovery of Scheduled Service to American Cities, 1960–2007," Chaddick Institute for Metropolitan Development, Chicago, Illinois, p. 5.

21. Chris Fuchs, "Fung Wah Bus Company Shuts Down for Good," NBCNews, July 17, 2015, tinyurl.com/jy2gnqx.

22. Robin Phillips, American Bus Association, interview with author, June 18, 2009.

23. *Monthly Performance Report for September 2016* (Washington: Amtrak, 2016), p. C1.

24. Joseph P. Schwieterman, Brian Antolin, Alexander Levin, Matthew Michel, and Heather Spray, *The Remaking of the Motor Coach: 2015 Year in Review of Intercity Bus Service in the United States* (Chicago: Chaddick Institute, 2016), pp. 14, 17; *Monthly Performance Report for September 2015* (Washington: Amtrak, 2015), p. A-2.2.

25. "Eligible EAS Communities as of October 2016," U.S. Department of Transportation, 2016, tinyurl.com/zkfh2vg.

26. Dana Lowell and David Seamonds, "Supporting Passenger Mobility and Choice by Breaking Modal Stovepipes," M. J. Bradley & Associates, Manchester, New Hampshire, 2013; subsidies per passenger mile calculated by dividing subsidies for various trips in table 4 by miles for those trips in table 2.

27. Ibid.

28. Ashley Halsey III, "House GOP Proposal Would Privatize High-Speed Rail along Amtrak's Northeast Corridor," *Washington Post*, May 26, 2011, tinyurl.com /jqyd3z7.

29. Don Phillips, "Acela, Apples, Watermelons—and Profit?" *Trains*, June 2013, pp. 10–11.

30. *Northeast Corridor State of Good Repair Spend Plan* (Washington: Amtrak, 2009), p. 16.

31. *Consolidated Financial Statements: National Railroad Passenger Corporation and Subsidiaries (Amtrak), Year Ended September 30, 2016* (Washington: Amtrak, 2017), p. 3.

32. *Northeast Corridor Capital Investment Plan: Fiscal Years 2017–2021* (Washington: Northeast Corridor Commission, 2016), pp. 12–13.

33. Frank N. Wilner, "Is Robert Serlin Amtrak's Merlin?" *Railway Age*, February 22, 2016, tinyurl.com/hp8jdet.

34. "Railroad Rehabilitation & Improvement Financing (RRIF)," Federal Railroad Administration, 2016, tinyurl.com/zjegfch.

35. *Monthly Performance Report for September 2016* (Washington: Amtrak, 2016), pp. A-3.4, C-1.

36. Brian Antolin and Joseph P. Schwieterman, *Running Express: 2017 Outlook for the Intercity Bus Industry in the United States* (Chicago: Chaddick Institute, 2017), p. 11.

37. Stan Jastrzebski, "Financial Missteps Lead Iowa Pacific to Give Up on Hoosier State Line," WBAA, January 31, 2017, tinyurl.com/hxhgq56.

38. Auto travel data from *Highway Statistics 2015*, table VM-1, using rural travel as a proxy for intercity travel; airlines and Amtrak data from *National Transportation Statistics*, table 1-40; bus data estimated from Joseph P. Schwieterman, Brian Antolin, Alexander Levin, Matthew Michel, and Heather Spray, *The Remaking of the Motor Coach: 2015 Year in Review of Intercity Bus Service in the United States* (Chicago: Chaddick Institute, 2016), p. 17.

39. Doresa Banning, "Nevada's Tourist Industry," *Nevada Business*, June 1, 2015, tinyurl.com/zbrqk5c.

40. "Orlando Becomes First Destination to Surpass 60 Million Visitors, Sets New Record for U.S. Tourism," VisitOrlando, April 9, 2015, tinyurl.com/jmuvjeg.

41. Michael Jamison, "Critics: Amtrak Funding Too Low," *The Missoulian*, February 11, 2008, tinyurl.com/hnxeh6a.

42. "Unserved Counties, Parishes, and Independent Cities with 25,000+ Population Greater than 25 Miles from Nearest Bus or Train Station," American Intercity Bus Riders Association, 2017, tinyurl.com/Unserved.

43. Kevin DeGood, "Understanding Amtrak and the Importance of Passenger Rail in the United States," Center for American Progress, June 4, tinyurl.com /h6x9mwy.

44. *California High-Speed Rail Final Program EIR/EIS* (Sacramento, CA: California High-Speed Rail Authority, 2005), appendix 2-F, p. 2-F-1.

45. *Monthly Performance Report for September 2016*, p. A-2.2.

46. "U.S Air Carrier Traffic Statistics," U.S. Bureau of Transportation Statistics, tinyurl.com/h5budbw.

47. Vehicle miles of travel from *Highway Statistics* (Washington: Federal Highway Administration, 2017), table VM-1, multiplied by average occupancy rates from *Summary of Travel Trends: 2009 National Household Travel Survey* (Washington: Federal Highway Administration, 2011), table 16.

48. Charles Lave, "The Mass Transit Panacea and Other Fallacies About Energy," *The Atlantic*, October 1979, tinyurl.com/6c58os.

49. *National Transportation Statistics* (Washington: Bureau of Transportation Statistics, 2016), table 3-20 compares airfares with Amtrak fares, but Amtrak fares are overstated because they include state subsidies to Amtrak.

50. *Vision for High-Speed Rail in America* (Washington: Federal Railroad Administration, 2009), p. 1.

51. Joseph P. Schwieterman, Brian Antolin, Alexander Levin, Matthew Michel, and Heather Spray, *The Remaking of the Motor Coach: 2015 Year in Review of Intercity Bus Service in the United States* (Chicago: Chaddick Institute, 2016), p. 17.

CHAPTER 17: The False Promise of High-Speed Rail

1. Dan Walters, "Is California High-Speed Rail an Ego Trip for Gov. Jerry Brown?" *Sacramento Bee*, June 3, 2012.

2. David Rogers, "Obama Plots Huge Railroad Expansion," *Politico*, February 17, 2009, tinyurl.com/d2kylj.

3. *A New Era of Responsibility: Renewing America's Promise* (Washington: Office of Management and Budget, 2009), p. 91, tinyurl.com/dyk3l2.

4. *Vision for High-Speed Rail in America* (Washington: Federal Railroad Administration, 2009), p. 6, tinyurl.com/pe4ud2.

5. "Implementing the American Recovery and Reinvestment Act of 2009," Federal Railroad Administration, Washington, D.C., March 2009, tinyurl.com/lbvjvb.

6. "President Obama, Vice President Biden, Secretary LaHood Call for U.S. High-Speed Passenger Trains," White House, Washington, D.C., April 16, 2009, tinyurl.com/d4whzy.

7. "High-Speed Rail Corridor Descriptions," Federal Railroad Administration, 2005, tinyurl.com/6s94zd.

8. John D. Boyd, "Former FRA Chief Urges High-Speed Push for Rail Plan," Journal of Commerce Online, June 5, 2009, tinyurl.com/m8sp5q.

9. Paul Nussbaum, "LaHood Sees Bright Future for High-Speed Trains in U.S.," *Philadelphia Inquirer*, August 11, 2010, tinyurl.com/humuuht.

10. Matthew Rose, Testimony before the Subcommittee on Transportation, Housing and Urban Development of the House Appropriations Committee, "The Future of High-Speed Rail, Intercity Passenger Rail, and Amtrak," April 1, 2009, p. 2.

11. *Highway Statistics 2007* (Washington: Federal Highway Administration, 2008), table VM-1; *National Transportation Statistics* (Washington: Bureau of Transportation Statistics, 2009), table 1-46a.

12. "High Speed Rail and Greenhouse Gas Emissions in the U.S." Center for Clean Air Policy and Center for Neighborhood Technology, Washington, D.C., 2006, p. 1, tinyurl.com/m4a5fs; "National Population Projections," Census Bureau, 2008, tinyurl.com/car7xw.

13. Federal Railroad Administration, *Final Environmental Impact Statement: Florida High Speed Rail—Tampa to Orlando* (Washington: Federal Railroad Administration, 2005), pp. 2–38.

14. Ibid., pp. 4–111.

15. Ibid., pp. 4–48.

16. Ibid., pp. 4–119.

17. David Levinson, "The Full Cost of High-Speed Rail: An Engineering Approach,"

18. *California High-Speed Rail Business Plan* (Sacramento: California High-Speed Rail Authority, 2000), pp. 16, 18, 22, tinyurl.com/gn7ys4x.

19. *California High-Speed Train Business Plan*, pp. 17, 19, tinyurl.com/guqzcw9.

20. Ibid., p. 21.

21. Matthew Roth, "California High Speed Rail Central Valley Corridor Gets Federal Grant," *Streetsblog SF*, October 28, 2010, tinyurl.com/hlflzul.

22. *Cost Changes from 2009 Report to 2012 Business Plan Capital Cost Estimates* (Sacramento: California High-Speed Rail Authority, 2012), p. 2, tinyurl.com/hn3h5c2.

23. *California High-Speed Train Program Revised 2012 Business Plan*, (Sacramento: California High-Speed Rail Authority, 2012), pp. 3–11, tinyurl.com/jqenhpj.

24. Ibid., pp. 7–20.

25. Ibid., p. ES-17.

26. *Final Program Environmental Impact Report/Environmental Impact Statement for the Proposed California High-Speed Train System: Volume 1* (Sacramento: California High-Speed Rail Authority, 2005), pp. 3.1–12.

27. *Environmental Impact Report/Environmental Impact Statement Energy Technical Report, Appendix A* (Sacramento: California High-Speed Rail Authority, 2005), p. 7.

28. Mikhail Chester and Arpad Horvath, "Life-Cycle Environmental Assessment of California High Speed Rail," *Access*, Fall 2010, p. 30.

29. Ralph Vartabedian, "California's Bullet Train Is Hurtling Toward a Multibillion-Dollar Overrun, a Confidential Federal Report Warns," *Los Angeles Times*, January 13, 2017, tinyurl.com/js4jqy6.

30. Angela Cotey, "States Are Delving Deeper into High-Speed Rail Planning, But Are the Host Railroads Onboard?" *Progressive Railroading*, June 2010, tinyurl.com/lpzh3sv.

31. "Midwest Regional Fact Sheet," Federal Railroad Administration, 2016, p. 2, tinyurl.com/zsll9fv.

32. Julie Sneider, "High-Speed Rail Makes Incremental Progress on Chicago-St. Louis Route," *Progressive Railroading*, August 2013, tinyurl.com/h6tfsgx.

33. "Application HSR2010000239, High-Speed Intercity Passenger Rail," Illinois Department of Transportation, 2009, page 59.

34. "Northwest Regional Fact Sheet," Federal Railroad Administration, 2016, tinyurl.com/zp39b85.

35. *Pacific Northwest Rail Corridor, Washington State Segment—Columbia River to the Canadian Border, Program Environmental Assessment* (Olympia: Washington Department of Transportation, 2009), p. 2-1.

36. 2015. *Annual Traffic Report* (Olympia: Washington Department of Transportation, 2016), p. 24.

37. "Amtrak Cascades Train Equipment," Washington Department of Transportation, 2017, tinyurl.com/zzal2se.

38. *A Vision for High-Speed Rail in the Northeast Corridor* (Washington: Amtrak, 2010), p. 20.

39. *The Amtrak Vision for the Northeast Corridor: 2012 Update* (Washington: Amtrak, 2012), p. 24.

40. *A Rail Investment Plan for the Northeast Corridor: Tier 1 Draft Environmental Impact Statement* (Washington: Amtrak, 2015), pp. 4–79, 5–20.

41. Elon Musk, "Hyperloop Alpha," Tesla Motors, 2013, tinyurl.com/gogncnt.

42. Benjamin Wallace, "A Kink in the Hyperloop," *New York Magazine*, October 18, 2016, tinyurl.com/hymswxn.

43. Yoshihiko Sato, "JR Central's Chuo Maglev Project Approved," *International Railway Journal*, October 31, 2014, tinyurl.com/pzryzv2.

44. Howard W. French, "Shanghai Journal; All Aboard! But Don't Relax. Your Trip Is Already Over," *New York Times*, April 22, 2004, tinyurl.com/glhp5bg.

45. *A Vision for High-Speed Rail in America* (Washington: Federal Railroad Administration, 2009), p. 1.

46. *A Vision for High-Speed Rail in the Northeast Corridor* (Washington: Amtrak, 2010), pp. 4, 5.

47. Calculated from Transtats, "U.S. Air Carrier Traffic and Capacity Summary by Service Class," U.S. Bureau of Transportation Statistics, table T1.

48. *The Business Case for the Next Generation Air Transportation System* (Washington: Federal Aviation Administration, 2014), p. 9.

49. "TSA Pre✓® reaches milestone with more than 5 million travelers enrolled," Transportation Security Administration, July 5, 2017, tinyurl.com/yb3utbdz.

50. Shirley Ybarra, "Overhauling U.S. Airport Security Screening," Reason Foundation, 2013, pp. 2–5.

51. Airline fares from *National Transportation Statistics*, table 3-20; Amtrak Acela fares calculated from *Monthly Performance Report September 2016*, Amtrak, page C1.

52. Albalate and Bel, *The Economics and Politics of High-Speed Rail*, pp. 27, 110.

CHAPTER 18: Passenger Rail in America's Transportation Future

1. H. Roger Grant, *Railroads and the American People* (Bloomington, IN: Indiana University Press, 2012), p. 261.

2. Conor Friedersdorf, "How the DEA Harasses Amtrak Passengers," *The Atlantic*, May 19, 2015, tinyurl.com/lhvwzvp.

3. Calculated from *National Transit Database*, "December 2017 Adjusted Database" spreadsheet (tinyurl.com/ y7ohoxb4).

4. Ibid.

5. Steven Hill, "L.A.—the City of Traffic Jams—Finds a Way to Get People Out of Their Cars," *Washington Post*, August 8, 2017, tinyurl.com/yc3e4lst.

6. Yonah Freemark, "Los Angeles Bus Service Declined as Rail Expanded," *Streetsblog*, August 23, 2017, tinyurl.com/y7mqyysq.

7. Chris Peak, "This City Fixed Its Public Transit System Without Spending a Dime," *Nationswell*, March 3, 2015, tinyurl.com/yarms8ow.

8. Susan Shaheen, Nelson Chan, and Lisa Rayle, "Ridesourcing's Impact and Role in Urban Transportation," *Access* 51 (Spring 2017), tinyurl.com/y9y97dkk.

9. Bruce Selcraig, "'Transformational' Transit Changes Will Take Money, Panel Told," *San Antonio Express-News*, October 10, 2017, tinyurl.com/ycqxd73z.

10. Joey Garrison, "Mayor Barry Unveils Sweeping $5.2 Billion Transit Proposal for Nashville with Light Rail, Massive Tunnel," *Tennessean*, October 17, 2017, tinyurl.com/yb6q3vzg.

11. Caitlin Johnston, "Imagine: Light Rail Along I-275 from Wesley Chapel to Tampa to St. Pete," *Tampa Bay Times*, September 29, 2017, tinyurl.com /ycdo7afu.

12. Sarah Willets, "Sticker Shock: Why Does the Durham-Orange Light Rail Transit Project Suddenly Cost $3.3 Billion?" *Indy Week*, April 12, 2017, tinyurl .com/yc6fky2n.

13. Lucius Beebe, *High Iron: A Book of Trains* (Modesto, CA: Bonanza Books, 1938), p. 1.

14. "The Man Behind the Camera: O. Winston Link," *Trains*, March 1957, p. 44.

15. "World Horse Population Estimated at 58 Million," *Horsetalk*, September 12, 2007, tinyurl.com/ya3lvlqv.

16. James Howard Kunstler, "Remarks to the Florida AIA," Orlando, Florida, 1998, tinyurl.com/j5pga3y.

17. "Airlines," Gallup, 2006, tinyurl.com/mn3ekj3; "Post-ABC Poll: Terrorist Attacks," *Washington Post*, September 13, 2001, tinyurl.com/grcr29z.

18. Randal O'Toole, *American Nightmare: How Government Undermines the Dream of Homeownership* (Washington: Cato Institute, 2012), p. 38.

19. Cox, *United States Central Business Districts (Downtowns)*, p. 4.

20. Karen Antonacci, "Citizens for Finishing FasTracks Demands RTD Bring Rail to Longmont," *Longmont Times-Call*, June 29, 2015, tinyurl.com/htzuvsm; "U.S. 36 Managed Lanes/BRT Project, Denver, CO," U.S. Department of Transportation, 2014, tinyurl.com/hcg3dhy.

21. *America First: A Budget Blueprint to Make America Great Again* (Washington: Office of Management and Budget, 2017), p. 35.

22. Speech by Mark Fields, Ford Motor Company Research Center, Palo Alto, California, August 16, 2016, tinyurl.com/hrcvmek.

23. Harry Pettit, "GM Will Roll Out Its Driverless Taxi Service in 2019, Two Years Ahead of Its Rival Ford," *Daily Mail*, November 30, 2017, tinyurl.com /ybhvax8a.

24. Ryan Randazzo, "Waymo Self-Driving Cars in Arizona Now Truly Driverless," AZCentral, November 7, 2017, tinyurl.com/y9pryvo2.

25. Erin Baldassari, "BART's Oakland Airport Connector Losing Money; Uber, Lyft to Blame?" *Oakland East Bay Times*, November 27, 2016, tinyurl.com /jxppqg8.

26. Michael Sargent, "End of the Runway: Rethinking the Airport Improvement Program and the Federal Role in Airport Funding," Heritage Foundation, 2016, pp. 9, 12.

27. Simon Van Zuylen-Wood, "Why Can't America Have Great Trains?" *National Journal*, April 17, 2015, tinyurl.com/l7rea4r.

28. Michael P. Malone, *Empire Builder of the Northwest* (Norman, OK: University of Oklahoma Press, 1996), p. 199.

INDEX

ABOUT THE AUTHOR

Randal O'Toole is a senior fellow at the Cato Institute who has written five previous books and numerous papers on transportation, urban growth, and public land issues, including his most recent books, *American Nightmare: How Government Undermines the Dream of Homeownership*, *The Best-Laid Plans: How Government Planning Harms Your Quality of Life, Your Pocketbook, and Your Future* and *Gridlock: Why We're Stuck in Traffic and What to Do about It*. Described by *U.S. News and World Report* as a researcher who "has earned a reputation for dogged legwork and sophisticated number crunching," he has been a leader in innovative thinking on environmentalism, natural resources, and urban land use. From 1975 through 1995, O'Toole helped the nation's leading environmental groups eliminate government subsidies that were harmful to the environment. In 1998, Yale University named O'Toole its McCluskey Conservation Fellow. He was the Scaife Visiting Scholar at UC Berkeley in 1999 and 2001 and the Merrill Visiting Professor at Utah State University in 2000. In 2003, he helped form the American Dream Coalition, which is a grassroots group that promotes free-market solutions to urban problems. An Oregon native, O'Toole currently resides in Camp Sherman, Oregon.

ABOUT THE CATO INSTITUTE

Founded in 1977, the Cato Institute is a public policy research foundation dedicated to broadening the parameters of policy debate to allow consideration of more options that are consistent with the principles of limited government, individual liberty, and peace. To that end, the Institute strives to achieve greater involvement of the intelligent, concerned lay public in questions of policy and the proper role of government.

The Institute is named for *Cato's Letters*, libertarian pamphlets that were widely read in the American Colonies in the early 18th century and played a major role in laying the philosophical foundation for the American Revolution.

Despite the achievement of the nation's Founders, today virtually no aspect of life is free from government encroachment. A pervasive intolerance for individual rights is shown by government's arbitrary intrusions into private economic transactions and its disregard for civil liberties. And while freedom around the globe has notably increased in the past several decades, many countries have moved in the opposite direction, and most governments still do not respect or safeguard the wide range of civil and economic liberties.

To address those issues, the Cato Institute undertakes an extensive publications program on the complete spectrum of policy issues. Books, monographs, and shorter studies are commissioned to examine the federal budget, Social Security, regulation, military spending, international trade, and myriad other issues. Major policy conferences are held throughout the year, from which papers are published thrice yearly in the *Cato Journal*. The Institute also publishes the quarterly magazine *Regulation*.

In order to maintain its independence, the Cato Institute accepts no government funding. Contributions are received from foundations, corporations, and individuals, and other revenue is generated from the sale of publications. The Institute is a nonprofit, tax-exempt, educational foundation under Section 501(c)3 of the Internal Revenue Code.

CATO INSTITUTE
1000 Massachusetts Ave., N.W.
Washington, D.C. 20001
www.cato.org